Historiography and Writing Postcolonial India

This book is a critical examination of postcolonial Indian history writing.

In the years preceding formal Independence from British colonial rule, Indians found themselves responding to the panorama of sin and suffering that constituted the modern present in a variety of imaginative ways. This book is a critical analysis of the uses made of India's often millennial past by nationalist ideologues who sought a specific solution to India's predicament on its way to becoming a postcolonial state. From Independence to the present, it considers the competing visions of India's liberation from her apocalyptical present to be found in the thinking of Gandhi, V. D. Savarkar, Nehru and B. R. Ambedkar as well as V. S. Naipaul and Salman Rushdie. It examines some of the archetypal elements in historical consciousness that find their echo in often brutal unhistorical ways in everyday life.

This book is a valuable resource for researchers interested in South Asian History, Historiography or Theory of History, Cultural Studies, English Literature, Postcolonial Writing and Literary Criticism.

Naheem Jabbar is Honorary Research Fellow in the School of Social Sciences at the University of Birmingham, UK. His current research interest explores the vital 'pre-political' role that religious consciousness plays as a mode of resistance for subordinated groups.

Routledge Studies in South Asian History

1 **The Social History of Health and Medicine in Colonial India**
   Edited by Biswamoy Pati and Mark Harrison

2 **Decolonization in South Asia**
   Meanings of freedom in post-independence West Bengal, 1947–52
   Sekhar Bandyopadhyay

3 **Historiography and Writing Postcolonial India**
   Naheem Jabbar

Historiography and Writing Postcolonial India

Naheem Jabbar

LONDON AND NEW YORK

First published 2009 by Routledge
2 Park Square, Milton Park, Abingdon, Oxon, OX14 4RN

Simultaneously published in the USA and Canada by Routledge
711 Third Avenue, New York, NY 10017

Routledge is an imprint of the Taylor & Francis Group, an informa business

First issued in paperback 2011

© 2009 Naheem Jabbar

Typeset in Times New Roman by Pindar NZ, Auckland, New Zealand

All rights reserved. No part of this book may be reprinted or reproduced or utilised in any form or by any electronic, mechanical, or other means, now known or hereafter invented, including photocopying and recording, or in any information storage or retrieval system, without permission in writing from the publishers.

British Library Cataloguing in Publication Data
A catalogue record for this book is available from the British Library

Library of Congress Cataloging in Publication Data
Jabbar, Naheem.
Historiography and writing postcolonial India / Naheem Jabbar.
  p. cm.
  Includes bibliographical references and index.
  1. India—Historiography. 2. Nationalism—India—History. 3. English literature—South Asian authors—History and criticism. I. Title.
  DS435.J33 2009
  954.04072—dc22   2008050958

ISBN 10: 0-415-48847-8 (hbk)
ISBN 10: 0-415-67226-0 (pbk)
ISBN 10: 0-203-87668-7 (ebk)

ISBN 13: 978-0-415-48847-1 (hbk)
ISBN 13: 978-0-415-67226-9 (pbk)
ISBN 13: 978-0-203-87668-8 (ebk)

For Samera
Who has been her brother's keeper

Contents

Preface ix
Acknowledgments xi

PART 1
Re-thinking Indian histories 1

1 **Historiography and narrative** 3
   Introduction 3
   *Interpretive modes: modern and
      postmodern 19*

2 **The historical sense** 49
   Introduction 49
   History and the myth of science 50
   History as knowledge and sense 64

3 ***Hindutva* and writing postcolonial India** 84
   Introduction 84
   Interpretive modes 106
   A nation is born 115
   The concept of Hindutva *as the primitive
      sublime 122*
   The concept of Hindutva *and history 125*

4 **B. R. Ambedkar and the Hindu past** 133
   Introduction 133
   Improving the apocalyptic present 139
   Dissolving the Hindu past 144

PART 2
Re-imagining Indian pasts   157

5 V. S. Naipaul's 'India': history and the myth of antiquity   159
Introduction 159
Figuring a history of the present 162
India as multitude 165
History and the myth of purity in antiquity 173

6 Salman Rushdie and the *agon* of the past   180
Introduction 180
The tragic form and its discontents 184
History as the tragic form 196

Conclusion   201

Notes   207
References   230
Index   241

Preface

> The lamp of history illuminates the 'whole mansion of the womb of Nature'.
> Vyasa[1]

This book is an investigation into Romila Thapar's understated conclusion that Indian nationalist histories are the articulation of interests singly in terms of monolithic religious identities following the 'success of anti-colonial nationalism'.[2] This is a characteristic understatement for an historian who deals in epochal terms with the 'pre-historical' past. More importantly, in the following chapters we will examine *how* the 'intellectual foundations of historical discourse' are threatened by this communal ordering of the past.[3] Is it enough to state alongside the eminent historian that the intellectual foundations of historical discourse are subverted by tendencies or 'ideologies' because the appeal of these ideologies is based on emotion and faith? How successful are historians in excising their practice of emotion and faith? Is the relationship between nationalism and historiography determined by emotion and faith for one and a disinterested appeal to Reason for the other? My conclusion is that periodicity becomes a more arbitrary affair when perceptions of the past are informed by a nationalist historiography rather than a more realistic view of historical change. We can see how the religious affiliation of rulers, instead of being one among a number of factors, becomes 'the pre-eminent motivating factor of change'.[4]

I have in the end decided to divide the concerns of this book into two parts. Like many decisions in history, we begin with arbitrary distinctions. In Romila Thapar's terms, the concerns debated in the first part under the heading 'Re-thinking Indian Histories' ought to be austerely arranged, the minutiae given forensic labels and placed in the tray (or chronological table) according to the dictates of Reason. The idea is to pursue questions according to the incremental appearance of 'evidence' so that, if nothing else, at least the verifying norms of scientific investigation are satisfied. However, where questions about the past are raised in the context of fulfilling and filling the political category 'nation' with historical content, we quickly discover that thinking about Indian pasts cannot be isolated from our feeling about the virtual or ethical possibilities. This is gainsaying the crudely reductive emotional appeals of partisan history made by priests and politicians – in Thapar's sceptical terms – that might help us to limit or expand the geography of our own imaginations. Borrowing Ranajit Guha's metaphor (itself borrowed second-hand from Freud's interpreter, Lacan) to describe the 'overdetermined' nature of history in 'our political culture of the colonial period', he describes the following outcome:

> Whatever is indigenous in that culture is all borrowed from the past, whatever is foreign is contemporary. The element of the past, though dead, is not defunct. The contemporary element, so vigorous in its native metropolitan soil, finds it difficult to strike roots as a graft and remains shallow and restricted in its penetration of the new site. *The originality of our politics of the period lies in such paradoxes* which pervade the entire spectrum of power relations.[5]

The somewhat lengthy treatment of the subject in the first two chapters does not merely reflect the axiomatic complexity of defining history as an attempt to bring the dead past into the vigorous element of the present; it serves as a prologue to the generic distinction (as Thapar implies) between Reason and Imagination in historiography that are each examined in Parts One and Two of the book. Neither is the first part intended to provide the entire spectrum of power relations so that the originality of the literary vision might be tested against it. Before investigating the 'imaginative' response of writers to the intrusion of colonialism as the definitive historical paradox, we ought to begin by examining the sterile site Guha mentions above for the fragile root of the past that at least attempts to take hold.

Acknowledgements

The smaller a circle of helpmates, the more intense perhaps one's sense of gratitude ought to be. I begin with François de Blois at the School of Oriental and African Studies, University of London, whose idea it was to collect these concerns within the pages of a single book. I thank Dorothea Schaefter, the Asian Studies editor, for commandeering and the rest of the team at Routledge, including Diane Carlyle, the copy-editor, for realising the project for publication. If I could, I would cite the anonymous readers whose careful engagement with earlier drafts helped me to focus the argument. A shorter version of Chapter 5 has appeared in *Textual Practice* (20: 1, 2006) and I thank the editor for allowing this material to be published here. The document supply team at Birmingham University's main library deserve a mention for their patience in dealing with sundry requests. To Malika Mehdid, I owe my warmest regards for being a stalwart voice of encouragement during good times and bad. Mavish Sikander has been a mainstay these past few years. Kirk Houston knows why I include him here. And to Samera, what words of love can suffice for one without whom not a single word in this book could have been written?

Part 1
Re-thinking Indian histories

1 Historiography and narrative

> The historical event which we witness, or learn from the testimony of those who witnessed it, runs much more variously, contradictorily, and confusedly; not until it has produced results in a definite domain are we able, with their help, to classify it to a certain extent; and how often the order to which we think we have attained becomes doubtful again, how often we ask ourselves if the data before us has not led us to a far too simple classification of the original events!
>
> Erich Auerbach[1]

Introduction

This book is concerned with the *writing* of history, and more specifically, with the historiography of India. The practice of historiography now occupies a position where its 'ideological' implications are quite easily susceptible to examination. This is in no small part due to that 'incredulity towards metanarratives' that define our peculiar age and I will be analysing the nature of this assertion in some detail below.[2] The subject of the first two chapters is the fragile consensus about the political uses of history that *has* emerged in the twentieth century: historian and layperson alike can question the chronicling of historical reality, firm in the conviction that even the finite details of past events will never find themselves fitting adequately into our greater consciousness of the past. There is no point criticising the ideological appropriation of the past without first questioning the received wisdom that historiography is *sui generis* ideological. I will have occasion to break with this consensus at specific points when dealing with Indian historiography, but for now we must proceed by taking seriously the terms of the confrontation between history and 'the paradox of how to represent the unrepresentable other'.[3]

To be sure, there are a whole series of concerns that prevent the absolute denotation of the past from taking place: the precise nature of the event confronts us in its idiographic and phenomenal rarity. What is the cause of this incomprehension but the fragility with which the 'Chaos of Being' is subsumed by the historical process? Carlyle in the nineteenth century differentiated between this 'existential' phenomenon and History as it is written, concluding that the actual process of historical becoming 'is an ever-living, ever-working Chaos of Being, wherein shape after shape bodies itself forth from innumerable elements'.[4] We will examine this principle of active anarchism in historiography when considering the fictive responses to the past in the second part of this book. For now, it is sufficient to note how the questioning of the event as a type – by using the social and the political as analogies to make it resemble other types of historical occurrence – helps us to remove a little of our uneasiness about its 'novelty' or its specialness that qualifies its place in the historian's consciousness. This metaphorical understanding of past reality where an event is regarded as typical of the social process does not prevent the sociological and the political having an oblique relationship to the matter dealt with by historians. In other words, the effort of attaining 'objectivity' by modern historians is not about conforming to the procedural rules of sociological, economic or political science. Why not? Talking about the documentary evidence hastily collected to indict war criminals at the Nuremberg trials, A. J. P. Taylor discriminates between the use of material to establish guilt and, in contrast, the effort to establish a wider context for singular events implicating those sitting in judgment. 'The lawyer aims to make a case', Taylor writes, 'the historian wishes to understand a situation.' He goes on:

> The evidence which convinces lawyers often fails to satisfy us; our methods seem singularly imprecise to them. But even lawyers must now have qualms about the evidence at Nuremberg. The documents were chosen not only to demonstrate the war-guilt of the men on trial, but to conceal that of the prosecuting Powers. If any of the four Powers who set up the Nuremberg tribunal had been running the affair alone, it would have thrown the mud more widely.[5]

Even if this certainty about the content of history is achieved at the cost of sacrificing our spirit of adventure about the otherness of the past, the result of our scepticism concerning human societies in the past by a 'new post-structuralist' practice is often, ironically, exemplified by a profound faith in our ability to grasp the human record with all the attendant perversities that such a record might imply. Whatever its disputed character among historians, even when historians behave like lawyers, this is largely why history as an account about the human condition remains a tenable form of knowledge. What explains the clamour on behalf of history if it is 'a verbal imitation of a human productive power which in itself does not speak?'[6] When the productive power realises itself as an instrument of destruction – when it applies itself to human material to systematically expel all that is squalid and foreign on the road to instituting the golden age – the historian's task is *as if* he or she still belongs to the suffocating partiality of a nineteenth-century cosmology. The contemporary historian will do almost anything to prove their modernity in distancing themselves from habits of the *ancien régime*, including cling to science as the last consoling myth: 'The writing of history is an art, but no one doubts that scientific principles are involved in the historian's treatment of evidence, and that the presence of this scientific element is what distinguishes history from legend.'[7] When science itself proved fallible, the narrative impulse that informs historiography also had to forgo this 'element'. However, in this atmosphere of extreme scepticism we might still demur with some justification from the conclusion that the attempt to write history as a 'non-totalising discourse' is commensurate with the ethical ambitions that the proponents of a new post-structuralist history like to think they have inaugurated.[8] Is not ethics an attempt to make just such 'totalising' possibilities emerge in an epistemological climate that is hostile to the idea of an integrated subjectivity? The idea of a subject in the historical milieu, no matter how diffuse the latter might be, is a vital tenet of historical practice, thus the hostility of historians who do not count themselves 'post-structuralist' for theoretical innovations in their discipline that might doubt the presence of such a subject. After all, the tools of history are supposed to enable us to chart the influence of this subjectivity, whether it is personal or institutional, in order to explain the human dimensions of any historical event. Taylor's scepticism about the material limits of prosecuting individuals is an old-fashioned concern. There is a profounder doubt about the procedural attempt to establish temporal continuity by analysing discourse. This approach inevitably means behaving as if factors larger than the individual of the kind Taylor wanted to include in his example were ultimately responsible for how the analysis of texts is to be carried out; an approach that instead turns out to be about 'the internal transformation of an individual consciousness'. What were the Nuremburg trials but an attempt to erect 'a great collective consciousness as the scene of events'?[9] Foucault continues:

> The individual is not to be conceived as a sort of elementary nucleus, a primitive atom, a multiple and inert material on which power comes to fasten or against which it happens to strike, and in so doing subdues or crushes individuals. In fact, it is already one of the prime effects of power that certain bodies, certain gestures, certain discourses, certain desires, come to be identified and constituted as individuals. The individual, that is, is not the *vis-à-vis* of power; it is, I believe, one of its prime effects. The individual is an effect of power, and at the same time, or precisely to the extent to which it is that effect, it is the element of its articulation. The individual which power has constituted is at the same time its vehicle.[10]

Eichmann would have found a home by pleading along these lines if the Vichy Republic had lasted. Why do historians feel compelled to complicate their straightforward task of documenting the past by alluding to processes of a psychological nature? Despite the novelty of the new historiography, this philosophical question is over a century-and-a-half old. Old truths are repeated in new guises. Hegel characterised the aesthetic and ethical questions arising from the historical field as a 'panorama of sin and suffering' superimposed on another arena in which the competition of individual wills almost reigns supreme, 'that such needs, passions, and interest are the sole springs of action – the efficient agents in this scene of activity'.[11] Before Carlyle's observations about the anarchic character pertaining to History that reflects our modern conception of the multifarious conditions of *written* history, the Hegelian consciousness of the historical process was able to give a specific shape to the metamorphoses that the Victorian critic marvelled at (the bodying forth of innumerable elements). Historians would recognise the importance of this assertion later in the nineteenth century and the whole intellectual climate of Europe would derive its emancipatory character from this summation, albeit culminating with different conclusions reached in Nietzsche's and Marx's writing. There is no space here to consider the shortcomings of the Hegelian dialectic. This said, a post-structuralist historiography is the latest desire in the historian's attempt to inhabit the difference between these two fields: 'Hegel's fundamental rule is that "objective" excess – the direct reign of abstract universality which imposes its law mechanically and with utter disregard for the concerned subject caught in its web – is always supplemented by "subjective" excess – the irregular, arbitrary exercise of whims.'[12] Moral reflection is complicated by our reaction to the corruption latent in the 'simply truthful combination of the miseries that have overwhelmed the noblest of nations and polities and the finest exemplars of human virtue'. What is the good human to do? When faced with history as this arena of aggression to infinity, the Beautiful Soul of the *Phenomenology of Spirit* retreats 'into the more agreeable environment of our individual life, the present formed by our private aims and interests'.[13] The characteristic mark of this realisation by the consciousness is unhappiness, 'since the entire contents of its natural consciousness have not been jeopardized, determinate being still *in principle* attaches to it; having a "mind of one's own" is self-will, a freedom which is still enmeshed in servitude'.[14] Tagore's poetic image of India's heroic past comes to mind, of thrones passing over the heads of her people, 'like clouds, now tinged with purple gorgeousness, now black with the threat of thunder. Often they brought devastations in their wake, but they were like catastrophes of nature whose traces are soon forgotten.'[15] Here is the expression of Foucauldian scepticism about the possibilities of giving shape to historical process in terms of a subject beyond the exercise of power in embryo: self-consciousness is being aware that one's freedom is *already* an illusion of Power. In other words, the exceptional state of being for Power in modern society (the way, for example, welfare for the State typifies the ancient function of *patria potestas*) is in actuality the normal or normative state of affairs.[16] That this determinate being might be historical and the attempt to attain individuality to accord with it, delineated with such tedious care by Hegel in his famous metaphor of Lordship and Bondage is a *bourgeois* consciousness has failed to exercise some very sophisticated literal readings.[17]

By dividing our comprehension from the field of historical action and foregrounding our ethical responsibility to the catalogue of events – Hegel's idea of a 'picture of such a horrifying aspect' – post-structuralist historiography is prompting the identical question that Hegel posed: 'to what principle, to what final aim these enormous sacrifices have been offered'; the only difference being that contemporary reflections are proceeding as if Marx hadn't attempted to provide an answer.[18] Then there is the dream of encountering an event that actualises itself in such a way that we *cannot* find analogies for it. Hayden White described this tendency of an essential perversity in things that eludes the mimetic function of discourse as 'tropological'.[19] We need to explore the organic elements of historiography and how they function together before examining some of the explanations used to promote this timid confidence over the actions, mentalities of peoples and civilisations past. How effective are the measures adopted to avoid the occasional failure of this historical sense by schematising the murmur of suspicion as an essential component of historical practice in the way signalled above? This desire for objectivity, of course, already presupposes an Archimedean point outside the maelstrom of processes concerning the nature and uses of History. As Taylor's research shows, the court oughtn't to be the theatre of History, if only because judgements about the past can never entirely free themselves of the excess of subjectivity. The violent play of events in which individuals have participated will turn out to be the kind of problem of 'excess' that Hannah Arendt explored.[20] The guiding principles of the observations in this book are expressed by Althusser without being, I hastily add, Althusserian: 'Any body of thought qualifying as knowledge thinks in terms of *forms*, that is, relationships which combine determinate elements.'[21] These first two chapters then are an introduction to more systematic considerations of the political uses made of Indian historiography. Ideas about India and its relationship to history will feature but the primary focus remains on some of the 'formal' methods used to secure the value of historiography as a veridical practice (the combination of determinate elements) whose object of analysis is the past.

Let us begin our account of the 'crisis' in historiography with that idiosyncratic measure of truth, history-wise, namely Walter Benjamin's 'Theses on the Philosophy of History'.[22] What form does self-determination take if it is about annulling the difference established by history? In the highly ironic mode of voice that – according to White – is the universal mode of modern historiography, Benjamin comments on the good tidings expected from the historian by an age in which any image of the past that seems alien to it is threatened with irretrievable disappearance.[23] The differences established by history – whether tribal, racial, ethnic, cultic and so on – belie the desire for sameness, similarity, contiguity that any individual needs in order to survive the bewildering array of experience that such differences bring about. The idea of nationalism is a potent consoling myth in this context. An image of the past nevertheless forces its appearance *by history* at a dangerous moment. For Hegel, the dangerous moment in actual history that presented a horrifying aspect was the Terror in revolutionary France. Foucault's use of power as a concept to describe the fertile possibilities for subjectivity (the negation of a negation, in Hegelian terms) also arrives as an incongruent image after the repressive uses whose effects have become apparent to us in the gulag and concentration camp. The casual symbolism of these cryptic assertions shouldn't fool us: for Benjamin, the primary impulse behind an historical sense in modern times is an optic sense. To witness with one's eyes is perhaps to free oneself from the imbroglio of Irony. Society only relegates to the past those segments of history in which it fails to discover a narcissistic reflection of itself. In this sense, the amnesiac tendency of the present age (more of which below) resembles the condition suffered by the neurotic patient whose life is a catalogue of unconscious compromise formations. In dealing with the past for whole societies, the sagacious historian resembles the routine authority adopted by the analyst who is leading the patient in search of a cure through the labyrinth of suppressed truths. There will similarly be few glad tidings to report in articulating some of the concerns about the Indian past in this book; as Benjamin concludes 'The danger affects both the content of the tradition and its receivers'.[24] The Messiah in Benjamin's *Theses* is no crude figure supplied by the sects to the *yishuv*. It is the Species Being whom the Young Hegelians celebrated, to Marx's consternation; the individual consciousness *in whom* history has concentrated itself so strongly that the two fields of history Hegel imagined, one as the staple of the speculative intellect and the other as the instance of individuated horrific experience that escapes the moral function of human cognisance, are realised as a totality. For such a consciousness, history as the panorama of sin and suffering is no longer an opportunity for ironic reflection but the occasion of a Gethsemane. Though history forces unflattering realities on the present, the ideologues of nationalism – on the floor of parliaments, in schools, on the street, in secret societies – still pursue their ceaseless quest through the long stream of time in order to discover genial images of the past that conform to their vision of the desirable order of things to be brought about by the naked implementation of state power. Let us not be mistaken, this hunger for the precise image from the past that fits the utopian ideal does not satisfy itself on niceties of judgements – 'epistemological revolutions' – as Edward Said once rather oddly put it in the context of Frantz Fanon's revolutionary spirit.[25] In drawing attention to the misremembered histories that are said to be the root cause of conflicts in the wake of nationalist movements across the world, Said's objective in his last book was to deploy the historical sense, with the authority of the therapist, it has to be said, to remedy the 'post-colonial predicament'. As we will see, the poet T. S. Eliot's recommendation of the historical sense as an essential for the modernist aesthetic that Said is adapting for his own rhetorical purposes was a defensive, 'formal' or Hegelian response to the efflorescence of nationalisms after the victory of the allied Powers in Europe. Having said this, it seems that the kind of textual irony ordinarily grouped under the rubric of postmodernity has not touched the thinking of some of the protagonists Said has in mind. Hayden White, of course, would not characterise his endeavour of emphasising the definitive role the narrative component or the 'emplotment' of historiography plays in these terms.

What does a project concerning the functioning of elements in historiography entail? Basically, my explanation about the relationship between history and narrative will bear on three major aspects: the *reduction* of historical reality to interpretive modes; the *elevation* of historical reality into an historical sense; and the narrative or literally *mythical* means through which a generic sense of the past is mobilised for ideological purposes. More straightforwardly, one can say that the mythical conception of cultural longevity figures as an invention of the past. Achieving the last objective, in other words, often implies the second preoccupation and hampering it, the first. For convenience, the first aspect may be defined essentially as a theory of history perspective, the second as a political debate about the meaning of history and the third as an anthropological interest in the modality of history. These aspects, then, form the focus of the first two chapters.

The historical enterprise in White's account remains in a state of infancy of the kind the physical sciences were in during the sixteenth century, because historiography, unlike the nomological-deductive status of the scientific paradigm, is based on a more complicated idea of consensus between its practitioners. Instead of eventually subordinating data to a single empiricist standard, historical inquiry into any particular event operates at three levels of generic explanation, each of which may function independently of each other: the mimetic or descriptive; the diegetic or the narrative; and the diatactic, tropological or discursive function.[26] Part of the disconcerting reaction in White's reading of Hegel has to be how 'Metonymical reduction and Irony are to be avoided by bracketing data (the panorama of sin and suffering) within the concept adequate to their apprehension as a means to some end'.[27] Hegel had already surmised the impossibility of a utilitarian solution to the problem of history. We are entitled to question White's priorities, rather than Hegel's, where the human substance of history parenthesised as 'data' involves a purely narrative hazard. This is the ethical problem that both White and Foucault might be said to share, but White refuses to make use of the rhetorical strategies implicit in the 'idea' of discourse for his own tropological understanding of historiography; indeed, he relegates it to the unedifying realm of error:

> [Foucault's] discourse stands as an abuse of everything for which 'normal' or 'proper' discourse stands. It looks like history, like philosophy, like criticism, but it stands over against these discourses as ironic antithesis. It even assumes a position superior to that of Foucault's own heroes, for Foucault's 'discourse about discourses' seeks to effect the dissolution of Discourse itself. That is why I call it catachretic.[28]

I will return to the problem in White's own discursive use of 'narrative' below. There is, however, nothing sequential to the ordering of the three aspects identified by White that constitute historiography. One might say, with Foucault, that White is concerned with describing the elements of articulation that enable the individual to be a vehicle of power.

Let us take the first and last aspects as an example, the mimetic and the mythical enumerated above. The ritual function of rendering the memory of past events in primitive societies has not been superseded completely by a technical reporting of social reality. The temptation of looking at historiography in these progressive terms is symptomatic of our modernity; our capacity to represent reality with all its vagrant minutiae has advanced far beyond the technologies of societies past. This confidence in the documentary aspect of research into the past might even have successfully infected our attitude to the contents of the past, but this does not mean that we live in a society emptied of mythical consciousness. We instead yearn to invent the past in a more *visibly* material way. This is the predominant myth of our 'postmodernity'. Retrieving the past philologically is insufficient: we need to *see* the glorious parade of Pharaoh's retinue beneath the hieroglyphs that have long since been reduced to silence by the passing of time. Events in the past, then, are as susceptible to the mythologising impulse as they ever were. However, the archaeological passion of bringing these events in more intimate proximity to our own times is not regarded in these terms. The curatorial task meticulously ignores the danger the ancients revered (perhaps that is its precondition); it is as if the historian who 'seizes hold of a memory as it flashes up at a moment of danger' willingly adopts the magical role of reinvesting the past with an enchantment that periodically fades from view.[29] The 'Theses on the Philosophy of History' rest on this crux between the 'scientific' anatomising of the present to reveal the latent laws or rules that govern the past that ultimately lead to the conjuncture of the Present and a desire to return to a moment before this conjuncture ripened into Apocalypse. That is to say, Benjamin's text from 1940 is a poetic solution to the encounter between the Mechanistic or Marxist interpretation of historical process and the Organicist or Hegelian conception of history that is ultimately conceived as the dramatic 'Procession' of the gnostic Idea of freedom. The classicism of the latter conclusion is filtered through Jewish mysticism: 'For every second of time was the strait gate through which the Messiah might enter.'[30] Benjamin's association with Zionist movements in his youth and his friendship with Gershom Scholem leaves its compelling, idiosyncratic mark on the direction in which the 'scientific' comprehension of the past in Marx's historical materialism sought to take it.[31] In short, narrative and history are in tension here. The theorist of the 'postmodern' Present, Jean Baudrillard offers us an explanation (in Benjamin's aphoristic style) for the mimetic and mythical components of historical understanding. 'The West is seized with panic', writes Baudrillard, 'at the thought of not being able to save what the symbolic order had been able to conserve for forty centuries, but out of sight and far from the light of day.' He continues:

> Ramses does not signify anything for us, only the mummy is of an inestimable worth because it is what guarantees that accumulation has meaning. Our entire linear and accumulative culture collapses if we cannot stockpile the past in plain view. To this end the pharaohs must be brought out of their tomb and mummies out of their silence. To this end they must be exhumed and given military honours. They are prey to both science and worms. Only absolute secrecy assured them this millennial power – the mastery over putrefaction that signified the mastery of the complete cycle of exchanges with death. *We only know how to place our science in service of repairing the mummy, that is to say restoring a visible order, whereas embalming was a mythical effort that strove to immortalise a hidden dimension.*[32]

The plurality of interpretive modes, a unifying historical sense and the mythological function of history may, then, each serve independent aims. In Baudrillard's critique, these are necessarily divided aims and this state of affairs reflects 'the violence of a civilisation without secrecy'; in other words, our historical attitude to the past unconsciously reflects the dystopia of Science. Bringing life itself into the bright foreground is consistent with the project of Enlightenment, even if all that is essentially recovered in this immediacy is the fleeting dross of decay. This melancholy at being unable to give mythical form to the hidden dimension of past human experience is lyrically expressed by Yeats in 1928: 'gather me into the artifice of eternity'. It is only by inhabiting the eternal form 'Once out of nature' that the prophetic substance of historical consciousness properly receives its power to *sing* 'Of what is past, or passing, or to come'.³³ Individual lives habitually concern themselves with these aspects in singular isolation from each other. Whether it is aware of it or not, the mind has to divide its critical awareness of the sociological nature of myth from its ritual function in order to achieve a 'mastery of the complete cycle of exchanges with death'. In this critical awareness, no dimension of historical experience may be allowed to remain opaque unless it is consciously placing the past before the corrosive judgement of science to make the life-world of practices visible in 'linear and accumulative' terms. What I am talking about is our inability to transform the agonistic processes of historical existence, especially with the mandarin injunction *never to forget*, into the sensuous interplay of images that Nietzsche thought was the hallmark of Tragic art before the Platonic dialogue got a hold of it. His early essay *The Birth of Tragedy* is a recommendation to the age in which dialectical or moralistic conceptions (Socratism and Christianity) have displaced the human capacity to heal culture by frolicking in images: 'And here stands man, stripped of myth, eternally starving, in the midst of all the past ages, digging and scrambling for roots, even if he must dig for them in the most remote antiquities.' Nietzsche goes on to conclude the following about the poverty of the Ironic comprehension that lies behind the ecumenicism of contemporary history:

> What is indicated by the great historical need of unsatisfied modern culture, clutching about for countless other cultures, with its consuming desire for knowledge, if not the loss of myth, the loss of the mythical home, the mythical womb?³⁴

This is the spurious or cold Augustan solemnity described by Baudrillard through which we fail to rediscover the mystery of human experience in the warm and protective womb of Nature. Walter Benjamin tried but failed to perceive the ecumenical possibilities of history for modern culture in the near future when the technology of representation would provide the audience (the new collective personality whose ritual character was discerned as *spectatorship* by Burke, Kant and Hegel in the classical age) with a 'tremendous shattering of tradition'.³⁵ There is no exit from the debilitating conditions of history in the orgiastic excess of memory. In the *Theses*, this eudemonic view – the desire to produce moments from the historical catalogue of events that are not simply a panorama of futility – is frustrated and all that results from reflecting on the past is the obverse of the rich condition that Nietzsche thought necessary, a sterile narcissism. In other words, pity and terror notwithstanding, we have realised our bad fortune in having lived life not as individuals but as part of the life-force whose procreative lust has all but brought society to near extinction.³⁶ This is death pretending at life. Yet many of us do not feel the need to stockpile the past in order to give authentic life to our rituals. How might this point be illustrated?

Let us consider more closely the mythological function of time. This function in different calendrical traditions reflects the unconscious processes of 'simulacra and simulation' that have made up a national history. The Mughal emperor Akbar's decision in the sixteenth century to establish a new calendar, the *Tarikh-ilahi*, silently influences the sacred time of the Bengali *San*. Who would have thought that the Muslim calendar, *Hijri*, also determines the auspicious movement of Hindu life? Amartya Sen strikes a note of moderation for India by commenting on his own regional tradition: 'When a Bengali Hindu does religious ceremonies according to the local calendar, he or she may not be aware that the dates that are invoked in the calendrical accompaniment of the Hindu practices are attuned to commemorating Muhammad's journey from Mecca to Medina, albeit in a mixed lunar–solar representation.'[37] This division of time is a more esoteric legacy of the Nawabs of Bengal than the division of geography that the British inherited. With *Hindutva* (Indian nationalism – defined more fully in Chapter 3) comes the deliberative break in which the 'cardinal fact' of Indian history, a 'process of coexistence and reabsorption', becomes ever more obsolete, a desire to see the new forms supplant preceding forms grows ever more irrepressible, so that the 'stratified stockpiling' of the past becomes an embarrassing and promiscuous pile of folkloric lore.[38]

The transcendent quality of the historical sense is not always a conservative reaction to the forces which threaten the integrity of the narrative or mythical form of knowledge, a form whose rhythm is described as a 'synthesis of a meter beating time in regular periods and of accent modifying the length and amplitude of certain of those periods'.[39] The subjection of historical texts to the rigour of scientific investigation is not necessarily a radical enterprise in which historians are complicit in domesticating the hazardous reality of historical events into clinical epistemological issues. The scientific explanation also pursues its objectives of modifying the longevity and depth of historical eras not only according to the needs of the age in which it emerges, but even as it does so, in the hope of legitimating itself beyond the debate of its efficacy as method: thus, allusions to the 'legitimation crisis' in Lyotard's highly influential account of the status of knowledge in our societies. What then is the reason for the durability of narrative or mythical explanation? Instead of discovering some innate human essence that requires a mythological comprehension of an otherwise chaotic reality, narrative knowledge entertains a kind of indulgence towards the rational explanation for the order of things; with the wisdom of the village elder, no doubt, it regards this discourse as 'a variant in the family of narrative cultures'. In contrast, the 'scientist', by which Lyotard means the positivist approach *tout court*, 'classifies [narrative knowledge/mythological beliefs] as belonging to a different mentality: savage, primitive, underdeveloped, backward, alienated, composed of opinions, customs, authority, prejudice, ignorance, ideology'. He goes on:

> Narratives are fables, myths, legends, fit only for women and children. At best, attempts are made to throw some rays of light into this obscurantism, to civilize, educate, develop ... This unequal relationship is an intrinsic effect of the rules specific to each game. We all know its symptoms. It is the entire history of cultural imperialism from the dawn of Western civilization. It is important to recognize its special tenor, which sets it apart from all other forms of imperialism: it is governed by the demand for legitimation.[40]

The piecemeal disenchantment of the world remains the technocrat's means of conquering the reality of other peoples, including the modest reality shared by its most historically negligible actors, women and children, up to their life-world or indigenous outlook for domestic consumption. The rigour in which *some* sense of history manifests itself as a perception of totality is prone to a variety of political objectives; indeed, opposing political traditions may make use of it. Calling this endeavour totalitarian or 'totalising' is far too simple. For example, Frederic Jameson recommends the historical sense to combat the regressive qualities of postmodernism. After the Second World War, where internationalism began to be conceived as a political reality and the responsibility for governance by *every* nation by 'legitimate' means as a realisable goal for the first time in the world's history, T. S. Eliot responded by recommending, often esoterically, the historical sense and the preservation of distinctive national traditions to combat what he instead saw as the encroachment of a dangerous tendency towards cultural homogeneity. Eliot does not *say* this though, and arguably both Jameson and Eliot share an acute sense of the anthropological uses to which the modality of high Modernism may be put. It is Lyotard's critical manifesto about the function of narrative in postmodernity that signals a discontinuity from this project. The bold endeavour of fanning a spark of hope in the past doubtless involves the conviction 'that *even the dead* will not be safe from the enemy if the historian wins', but the generic elements of historiography, its modality, its epochal character or its communitarian possibilities preclude neat distinctions where we might describe these ideological uses as essentially conservative or radical.[41] Let me be plain. This does not mean that the invocation of the historical sense is essentially arbitrary – one which dissipates as a coherent explanation for the order of things once it is subjected to scientific scrutiny. All that is being said is that the implications of the historical mode for understanding social reality – that is, the artificial, collective act of recovering the past – can at one instance function as an argument for conserving institutions, adapting them to the changing needs of the present, or it can be a call to annihilate time-honoured factors that are seen to inhibit the growth of human potential (including in *our* modern society). This tenet of Whig history is an important consideration in the context of postcolonial societies and this ambiguity will emerge as we look below at a variety of points of view about the Indian past. Before looking at the issue of historiography as an interpretive mode, I want to preface my analyses by saying what this book is not about.

The great question of the relationship between our present and the past has been posed by historians to define the nature of their discipline – a question that has intrigued other sage individuals since at least the inception of the historical *attitude* in human consciousness, perhaps in some remote primal past, if not with the actual discipline of history itself. The answers to this question posed in ever new, bewildering forms reflect the spectrum of cogent beliefs represented in society at any one particular time. In this sense, history is a barometer of the kinds of society possible. This book is not an attempt to answer a more fundamental question (though fundamental questions will arise) that, for example, Alex Callinicos admirably tackles, about the permutations of 'discourse' upon which history is written and made.[42]

I am going to take for granted the consequences of the unequal relationship between the modalities of historical and mythical explanations that Lyotard described above with such persuasive brevity. Any brief survey of nationalist writing in the early twentieth century, as well as the pronouncements about the value of native culture during British colonialism in India during the last quarter of the nineteenth century, will show that history and historiography are not free of 'structures of feeling' that in the end define what species of historicity are possible. This partly reflects the anxiety of 'historicism' expressed in such stylish terms by Baudrillard and an anxiety with which Yeats worked his own poetic solution to the problems of the past encumbering the present, in June 1922, with De Valera's refusal to accept the terms under which Ireland was to achieve her independence from Crown rule.[43] For Raymond Williams, historicity or the description and analysis of culture and society 'in an habitual past tense' also lends a spurious distinction between the 'always moving substance of the past' and the ever receding particularity, in an Eliot-like phrase, of 'living presence'.[44] The form that Williams gives to this idea of living presence, its importance beyond the reductive tendencies of *post hoc* systematic thought, is 'practical consciousness'. This practical consciousness was the hidden object of Lyotard's attack on positivism in the human sciences and the conclusion, elliptically arrived at, that science does not tell stories. Although the evidence I will be presenting will often seem to be to the contrary, a kind of analysis that examines the peculiar nature of a hiatus, or 'subjective excess', when it comes to the influence of nationalism on Indian historicity, it is worth remembering that we are also engaging with 'characteristic elements of impulse, restraint, and tone'. For Williams, this subtle process is symptomatic of, but irreducible to, more crudely mechanistic uses of 'world-view' or 'ideology'. Structures of feeling are 'specifically affective elements of consciousness and relationships'. They are, he continues

> not feeling against thought, but thought as felt and feeling as thought: practical consciousness of a present kind, in a living and interrelating continuity. We are then defining these elements as a 'structure': as a set, with specific internal relations, at once interlocking and in tension. Yet we are also defining a social experience which is still *in process*, often indeed not yet recognised as social but taken to be private, idiosyncratic, and even isolating, but which in analysis (though rarely otherwise) has its emergent, connecting, and dominant characteristics, indeed its specific hierarchies. These are often more recognizable at a later stage, when they have been (as so often happens) formalized, classified, and in many cases built into institutions and formations. By that time the case is different; a new structure of feeling will usually already have begun to form, in the true social present.[45]

This distinction between the ontological experience and the epistemological value of the historical sense is a lucid simplification of the complex engagements with history (though by no means simple in itself) that commentators like Callinicos have made about the true social present, the seemingly independent entities that determine history, which, 'of necessity', remain unknown to persons except as purely mental processes. For us, in the end, these diffuse structures of feeling (if one can describe them like that) about the past are themselves reducible to a single frame of reference. Questioning the nature of the discourse that history is about is an important consideration. This book takes for granted the a priori nature of the discourse informing views of the Indian past in the way Williams described above. I am concerned with the impact of nationalism on historiography – often in the common sense form of a structure of feeling about *our* community; that is, the discourse whose influence is analysed in this book. Take Bernard Cohn's distinction, among Indian villagers, of traditional and historic pasts that orders the daily lives of different communities, both occupational castes and religious groups; in the end, it is a synthetic product of the anthropologist's imagination but it does not stop there: 'I would speculate that a society is modern when it does have a past, when the past is shared by the vast majority of the society, and when it can be used on a national basis to determine and validate behaviour.'[46] The validation of behaviour according to historicity is more nuanced than Cohn suggests. History is here supposed to supply the ideal conditions for an instrumental end: the formation of the modern nation-state. The problem with Cohn's attitude of objective detachment from these uses of history in a northern Indian village on a national level is that the contradictions he notes as arising locally, *between* traditional or epic and historical pasts, are given communalist significance for what constitutes 'valid' behaviour. Cohn does remark on the deficiencies of Indian society where an appeal made on behalf of the 'central government', presumably for psephological advantage, leads 'to antagonistic reactions of major parts of the population'. Indian society in this view fails the test of modernity. But the idea that modernity arrives when the vast majority shares a past and that this common reinvention of the past then defines 'valid' behaviour places great faith in a corporatist view of all things historical. Cohn's recommendation reflects the spirit of the times in which he was writing; his conception is a rather simplified version of the Nehruvian ideology of secular nationalism that was seen to be the ideal model for India's plural social realities. We will return below to Nehru's idea of the world historical role of Indian civilisation. The legend of Thakur heroes who combated the Ghurid invasions in northern India on the behalf of a Hindu king, Prithviraj, from the eleventh and twelfth centuries, inspires the pride of the Hindu community. There is a reluctant version of Muslim hegemony in the village's past over the ancient *zamindari* (landowning) antecedents who were eventually replaced by the Thakurs' specifically Hindu culture. Cohn is right in drawing our attention to this microcosm: these versions of the past are a reflection and a result of conflicts over the past *throughout* Indian society. However, there is, in my view, an untenable voluntarism in Cohn's conception of history where individuals ought only to appropriate a past that is most useful for the larger polity of the nation. Do people will their discrepant pasts into a finite order? This marshalling of often inchoate expressions of historicity – a conscious reproduction of a unifying past in the sense Williams intended, in his celebrated phrase about the culture of peoples, or the kind Yeats represented symbolically in his poetry – is the legitimising task that ideologues of nationalism feel compelled to take on themselves. V. S. Naipaul's documentary writing on India and Muslim countries relinquishes the kind of control that the rational intelligence is supposed to be able to exert over irredentist nationalism. Whether this burdensome use of the past is typical of Indian history is a more interesting question, which Cohn does not address at this point. What is certain is that these conflicts over the past are played out less quaintly than the satire of an Englishman as one of Sita's suitors in the Hindu villagers' *Ram Lila* that Cohn remarks on. I will examine the idea of history as a didactic resource in the rest of this chapter.

What about writing a history of Indian nationalism as discourse? We quickly discern that this objective is prone to the same technical vulnerability or *aporia* as the one concerning the discursive nature of historiography that Foucault, White, Baudrillard, Lyotard, Williams, Callinicos and countless others have engaged with in their researches. The generic problem latent in all diachrony has been expressed in the following debatable formula: *ideology has no history*. Thinking about the lives of people in the past in ideological terms is also to concede the observation that 'Ideology represents the imaginary relationship of individuals to their real conditions of existence'. This problem is at the heart of the metaphysical dilemmas posed by Raymond Williams about historical analyses of formative and organic culture. Althusser continues:

> We commonly call religious ideology, ethical ideology, legal ideology, political ideology, etc., so many 'world outlooks'. Of course, assuming that we do not live one of these ideologies as the truth (e.g. 'believe' in God, Duty, justice, etc ...), we admit that the ideology we are discussing from a critical point of view, examining it as the ethnologist examines the myths of a 'primitive society', that these 'world outlooks' are largely imaginary, i.e. do not 'correspond to reality.'[47]

I will return to Naipaul's attempt to represent an imaginary relationship as if it were a product of authentically lived experience. At first sight, the Asiatic mode in Indian feudal life resembles the promiscuous combination of categories in Borges' famous Chinese encyclopaedia.[48] The panegyrist Abu al-Fazl's chronicle, the *Akbar-Nama*, is a fair reflection of the kinds of pressure of having to live ideology in the way described above – that is, with the necessity of having to take seriously the consistency of a version of the truth propagated at court, in ritual and word, that seeks to inspire the laity with the belief that the emperor is the shadow of Divinity on earth. But is the sixteenth-century chronicle dedicated to the Enlightened Timurid despot of Indian history useless and no more than a compendium of lies designed to glorify the dominion of Akbar, Abu al-Fazl's patron? Nothing escapes this imaginary relationship between individuals and their real conditions of existence, and with the Mongolian origins of the Mughal dynasty even one of Christianity's most potent elements finds itself domesticated to the requirements of temporal power. The design of the *Akbar-Nama* is to challenge the set of imaginary relationships that obtained in the more distant Puranic version of events in the Hindu past. In the conflict to establish Akbar's dispensation over the allied forces of the Afghani claimants to Sher Shah Sur's throne, this distant past served a vital political function to re-establish Hindu power in Delhi. The pseudo-Christian myth of Alanquwa, a childless widow of king Zubun Biyan, ruler of Mughalistan, who conceives the Mughal dynasty by *nur* or divine light entering her throat, recounted by Abu al-Fazl, is no counterweight to the less miraculous but equally implausible terrestrial claims of the sovereign title Vikramaditya, after a king in ancient Bharat, made by Hemu, a Hindu minister serving in the waning Sur Afghan regime.[49] The immaculate conception of the Virgin, Fazl informs us, happened in an identical way and he leaves his reader with no doubt about the auspicious nature of Akbar's descent: 'That day [of the Alanquwa miracle] was the beginning of the manifestation of his Majesty, the king of kings, who after passing through diverse stages was revealed to the world from the holy womb of her Majesty Miryam-makani for the accomplishment of things visible and invisible.'[50] Alanquwa must have had an intimation of this event because she places vigilant watchmen around her tent to act as witnesses to it, so that their minds may be illuminated by the Divine mystery. The idea of the divine germ evolving through the ages before it is revealed as an avatar is also un-Islamic. The glory of the classical age of the Gupta dynasty in the fifth century CE is no more an appropriate sport of the martial imagination than the Christian myth for the matriarchal indolence of the Mughal's court.

Are these details the embarrassing residues of Oriental despotisms? We are entitled to doubt how the most active intelligences at the Mughal court would receive this fabulous genealogy. Let us turn to contemporary developments in the courts of Europe. The scientists of the great age in Europe also welcomed the marriage of the Elector Palatine with the daughter of James I with all the ingenuity of esoteric wisdom. When the couple accepted the crown of Bohemia from the Czechs, the millennial hopes of a new golden age were not expressed in the rationalised sovereignty of Divine Right adumbrated by Hobbes. For men like Francis Bacon, Isaac Newton and the scientists who founded the Royal Society, the King and Queen of Bohemia in their short reign were the mystical embodiment of Reason in an age still riven with religious conflict. As the secret Palatinate publisher's output shows, this belief in Reason was expressed in supernatural terms. Fazl's chronicle also begins by describing Man's perfect duty to his ruler, both divine and temporal, by at least attempting to let speech venture into God's store-houses (*makhzunat*) and the Sultan's privy chamber. That the Rosicrucian Enlightenment failed to realise its dream of perfect harmony between Man and Nature because of the king's lack of support made little difference for the esoteric publications in which allegories for the 'chemical wedding' were compiled.[51] This new monarchy in Europe to the magi of scientific knowledge represented the perfect symbol of the libertarian state. The King and Queen of Bohemia were to recreate the earthly paradise at Heidelberg and in the gardens of their palace free thought would roam unfettered by Church and State. Over sixty years earlier, the *Akbar-Nama* also reflects the somewhat confused order of things temporal and divine characterising the European early modern. As the catalogue of Rosicrucian exotica shows, this *does* presuppose a fantastic degree of voluntarism in the choices the protagonists

18 *Re-thinking Indian histories*

made in identifying with the past. It seems that they failed singularly to tame the wildness of their imaginations. However, when we examine a document from the past, even if the text concerns itself with the arcane specificity of religious ideology, or legal ideology, the problem of recovering the world outlook of that society means being able to conceive historiography in terms of imaginary relationships that individuals had in *their own time*. To choose not to conclude this is to promote a fictitious representation of the past as the historical truth. White puts it succinctly: 'The consciousness of an age is always more or less than what pure perception, were it not clouded by inherited preconceptions about what reality *must be*, would reveal to be the actual social reality of that age.'[52] How then ought we to treat Indian historiography that presents the Sanskriti worldview as if it were a more authentic realisation of the lives of Indians among foreign Muslim elements? In this sense, history is untraditional to the degree it determines the social relations between communities of individuals inhabiting a delimited space.

Let us turn to arguably the most celebrated figure of anti-colonial resistance to British power, to explore these concerns. For M. K. Gandhi, Indic civilisation is not pyramidal, in the way the preceding reflections imply, but concentric. This is a traditional metaphoric image; it dominates the minds of the Congress technicians of the postcolonial constitutional arrangement after the departure of the colonial power, and by signifying the native social order of India as the *charkha* or wheel represents a kind of sociological advance in its simplicity over the crude redactions of India's feudal past:

> In this structure composed of innumerable villages, there will be ever-widening, never-ascending circles. Life will not be a pyramid with the apex sustained by the bottom. But it will be an oceanic circle whose centre will be the individual always ready to perish for the village, the latter ready to perish for the circle of villages, till at last the whole becomes one life composed of individuals, never aggressive in their arrogance but ever humble, sharing the majesty of the oceanic circle of which they are integral units.[53]

In this vision, the individual is at the heart of the majestic span of the nation, a span which is majestic because it never ascends above the individual. The individual here is conceived as the *satyagrahi* or freedom fighter, who is engaged in pacifist resistance to colonial domination. What can we say about this vision? First, it is worthy of Herder's anthropological account of the peaceable Hindu and I will return to this Romantic trope in historiography below. For now, we note that this organic conception of *politēs* or citizenship is profoundly ahistorical: no peoples in history ever conceived social order in these terms. For Gandhi, of course, this is not an objection to but an argument *for Hind Swaraj*. Arguably, the expression of Indian communities past and present was always conceived in terms of *Homo hierarchicus*. One can go further. Perhaps the impulse behind historicity itself in terms of rediscovering the harmonious social order according to the Great Chain of Being rather than the perfect Circle of Equity, the desire to submit to a force that arranges the atoms of society in a perfectly functioning *hierarchy*, is natural

Historiography and narrative 19

to the human condition because the circle is itself a claustrophobic social reality? After all, who would not dream of a glorious past in which martial splendour occasionally invigorates the eternal slowness of life as an antidote to the sheer tedium of always meeting at the village corner the same member of one's own *gotra* or *biraderi*? I will be looking at the ideology informing the Thakurs' 'traditional' reinvention of their local past in more classical terms in Chapter 3. Having said all this, Partha Chatterjee's account of the modern evolution of Indian nationalism, where Gandhi's conception of social order is promoted as a subversion of 'civil society', is derived from a perspective similar to the kind developed by Callinicos. This discursive reconstruction of history will be examined in the fourth chapter of this book. B. R. Ambedkar's strategic interpretations of the Hindu past will help to explain how Gandhi's critique of colonial modernity has some inherent limitations that have nothing to do with the formation of civil society. Here one *can* talk of an instrumental use of tradition as 'official consciousness' and, *contra* Williams, 'a matter of relative freedom and control'.[54] In the section below, I want to look at historiography in terms of the desire to attain a 'few degrees of freedom from the master narrative' after a 'situation [where] we now find ourselves in is that the master narrative of modernity has been thrown into question and subjected to critical scrutiny with an intensity that seems to surpass any previous attacks'.[55] For every offensive manoeuvre in the epistemological domain, as on the field of battle, there is a defensive response.

Interpretive modes: modern and postmodern

The magi at Ephesus when the temple of Artemis was burned down – the same day, Plutarch reports, as Alexander's birth – thought it a portent of the day 'a great scourge and calamity for Asia'.[56] Over three-and-a-half centuries later, the Pauline letter to the Ephesians, though not by the Roman convert's own hand, symbolically places Christ as the cornerstone in the metaphoric temple of Jerusalem. Messianic eternity comprehends the sum and substance of history. There is no other way that the aspirations of the early Christian community could be expressed. Francis Fukuyama and the other technocrats divine for Hegel in a more optimistic spirit than the Ephesians. The millennial hopes of a world history, sharing in but amplifying to a secular and global degree the sense of persecution that must have been felt by the early Christians – with their Hebraic sentiment of endurance of struggles 'throughout all ages, world without end' – are now to be realised when technology is to be raised 'far above all rule and authority, power and dominion, and every title that can be given, not only in the present age, but also in the one to come'.[57] The inheritors of the soothsayer's task have substituted the whim of the gods for a human pantheon. Unfortunately, in Fukuyama's table of nations who have successfully surmounted the gory elements of actual history to become one of the comities of 'Liberal Democracies Worldwide', India in 1975 is registered as a democracy.[58] Perhaps we should overlook this error as an excess of faith. In contrast to the ideologue of the free market, including some less sanguine sages predicting the Republic's waning influence over the eventual shape of the world, there is Frederic

Jameson who, like Raymond Williams, wants to discover his master Marx's will in the aesthetic.[59] I will return below to Jameson's aesthetic view of historicity to contrast with Hayden White's conclusions about narrative as the functional element of historiography, but a careful reading of Theodor Adorno, one of Marx's former disciples from Europe, will show that Jameson is also wasting his time. In the *mauvaise foi* engendered as much by the procedures of the melancholy science as the illusion of reality it is supposed to interrogate, Jameson is nevertheless inclined to go along for *just* long enough with Adorno's view of the work of art as 'the last refuge of individual subjectivity from the historical forces that threaten to crush it'. An antidote to the universe of dead objects that litter our reality is to be discovered in 'the humanized substance of the work of art'.[60] This humanisation revealed itself in the objects fashioned by Surrealism. I say *had* revealed because it, along with the symbolic object, has 'gone without trace' in post-industrial capitalism and the plastic of products in our milieu 'is totally incapable of serving as a conductor of psychic energy ... All libidinal investment in such objects is precluded from the outset.'[61] I am not sure what a fetishist would think of Jameson's austere pronouncement. Callinicos challenges Jameson's conclusion that the absence of sensuous particularity in social reality necessarily entails 'a historical break of an unexpectedly absolute kind'.[62] Admittedly, this is not where Jameson's strength as a *marxisant* critic of the present lies. Jameson had attempted to provide an 'in-house' debate about the generic qualities of realism among the protagonists in the great Left tradition with a contemporary value where he states, 'in different historical circumstances the idea of nature was once a subversive concept with a genuinely revolutionary function, and only the analysis of the concrete historical and cultural conjuncture can tell us whether, in the post-natural world of late capitalism, the categories of nature may not have acquired such a critical charge again'.[63] Beyond the European experience, there is plenty of room for doubt as to the efficacy of Nature as an analogy in the Romantic tradition for the kind of revolutionary conjunction that Jameson is drawing attention to.[64] I will be coming to the subversive possibilities of Nature as a metaphor for the social order soon enough. Jameson's acuity of vision lies in providing specific instances in this conjunction. The spirit of realism is perfectly consistent with an historicism ('a transitional and special combination of historical circumstances') where the methods of Nazism are retained even as parliamentary democracy – as the ideology of capitalism – formally distinguishes itself from fascism. For example, Jameson successfully predicts routine torture and the institutionalisation of counter-insurgency techniques as the staples of the *société de consommation*.[65]

From the insular recommendation of Art as a place to rediscover one's authenticity in troubled times, when it comes to the development of nations, some have preferred to emphasise 'the acquisition of the bundle of skills which enable men to perform well in the general conditions of an industrial division of labour'. And in these general conditions for the transition from agrarian to industrial society, 'Capital, like capitalism, seems an overrated category'.[66] To see nationalism as the story of class conflicts is to opt for 'a somewhat empty and quasi-metaphysical claim'.[67] The alien terror of past events can *always* be domesticated because, in comparison to the vale of tears through which humanity has passed in history, the use of myth is an antidote to the Hegelian interpretation of the contents of history; it is 'simply a way of controlling, of ordering, of giving shape and a significance to the immense panorama of futility and anarchy that is contemporary history'.[68] Eliot's precepts are derived from Nietzsche here. If the Third World novel fails to offer the Western reader the same satisfactions as the European modernist canon, this is not a moralising conclusion but an historicist one, a conclusion 'which challenges our imprisonment within the present of postmodernism and calls for a reinvention of the radical difference *of our own* cultural past and its now seemingly old-fashioned situations and novelties'.[69] This sounds like a crucial development. Jameson goes on to detail how an affluent mode of living needn't necessarily find a kind of parochial hindrance in the impossibility of engaging with Third World realities, urban or otherwise. The object of this difficulty, however, is far from parochial; it is a ghostly Other, envisaged as a reader for whom the naive realism of novels about Third World realities is seriously intended. For Jameson

> [t]he fear and the resistance I'm evoking has to do, then, with the sense of our own non-coincidence with that Other reader, so different from ourselves; our sense that to coincide in any adequate way with that Other 'ideal reader' – that is to say, to read this text adequately – we would have to give up a great deal that is individually precious to us and acknowledge an existence and a situation unfamiliar and therefore frightening – one that we do not know and prefer *not* to know.[70]

History never lacked so much confidence in articulating its concerns on humanity's behalf. If only Jameson had been able to associate his just condemnation of the present with the otherness or alterity of the Third World in less existential–psychologistic terms. I am not certain whether Marx would have endorsed this view of the empirical limits of literature in a capitalist world, even if we take seriously his invention of an 'Asiatic Mode of Production'. In fact, as we will see, Marx and Engels shared a contrary view of the cosmopolitan benefits of an instrumental capitalism. Confronting our own fear and resistance *in fiction* enables the realisation that the fragmentation of the self which we have all had to grow accustomed to in our postmodern brand of reality – a reality brought about by the symbolic poverty of mass consumerist culture – is a phenomenon that has not yet reached the Other in the Third World. The shallow pathos of this Left-doxology is represented thus: with 'spectacular triumphs in art and thought', contrary to the effete boredom with which the 'national allegory' in Third World writing is received by Western audiences, the last stage of capitalist development and, with it, 'the developing [always immature] world culture of modernism', public culture loses its organic totality. '[I]t shatters into a multitude of fragments, speaking incommensurable private languages ... [resulting in an] incapacity to organize and give meaning to people's lives.' This intellectual response to the postcolonial predicament concludes: 'As a result of all this, we find ourselves today in the midst of a modern age that has lost touch with the roots of its own modernity.'[71] Again, this conclusion is properly historicist rather than aesthetic in orientation. Perhaps Eliot's fears were well-founded, after all. History as yet has not obviously intruded in these magisterial evocations of difference which, in the end, are essentially about *similarity*:

> One important distinction would seem to impose itself at the outset, namely that none of these cultures can be conceived as anthropologically independent or autonomous, rather, they are all in various distinct ways locked in a life-and-death struggle with first-world cultural imperialism – a cultural struggle that is itself a reflexion of the economic situation of such areas in their penetration by various stages of capital, or as it is sometimes euphemistically termed, of modernization. This, then, is some first sense in which a study of third-world culture necessarily entails a new view of ourselves, from the outside, insofar as we ourselves are (perhaps without fully knowing it) constitutive forces powerfully at work on the remains of older cultures in our general world capitalist system.[72]

The situation of emergency before the outbreak of the First World War for the empires still obtains. The formative structures composed of the internal tensions that Williams described – the kind that ossify too late to be recognised as the distillation of social experiences into a *single* hegemonic instant, 'the true social present' – are now to be conceived in *marxisant* rather than Marxist terms. I will look closely at the *fin-de-siècle* anxieties that Jameson is reworking here in Ernest Gellner's case of the Ottoman past, but we note how moments of beauty and truth, the purpose of the aesthetic, are now rare if not entirely absent as possibilities in the benighted rigour of daily life. Peoples in the Third World may struggle against all odds to maintain a semblance of normality, but this illusion of civil society is an epiphenomenon of the huckster capitalism of the nationalist elites. Enter the rhetorical conflation of culture and nature, a vision of extended human sensorial experiences and the 'post-structuralist' referents of difference, ambivalence, third space, third politics, and so on: 'the regulation and negotiation of those spaces that are continually, *contingently*, "opening out", remaking the boundaries, exposing the limits of any claim to a singular or autonomous sign of difference – be it class, gender or race'. The postcolonial theorist continues to assert the novel value of the form that this immanence ought to take as a solution to social problems that have all too often grown intractable since the liberation from the colonial past:

> Such assignations of social differences – where difference is neither One nor the Other but *something else besides, in-between* – find their agency in a form of the 'future' where the past is not originary, where the present is not simply transitory. It is, if I may stretch a point, an interstitial future, that emerges *in-between* the claims of the past and the needs of the present.[73]

There is a fatal density in describing the aspirations of millions in terms of a spurious quest for an originary past. Perhaps Homi Bhabha's aestheticism of the colonial past *qua* postcolonial present means that he has succeeded in arriving at

Yeats' fabulous city? The implausibility of discovering visions of the future in some metaphysical twilight realm between the actual forces of history needn't occupy us too long. Let us return to the more solid if naive dialectical foundations of experience whose co-ordinates Jameson is using to assert the 'contingency' of cultural value, the encounter between capitalist and non-capitalist (Asiatic and tribal) modes. Despite the ingenious renderings of experience where no foundation of reality, for either a class, racial or sexed subject exists – to adopt the nomenclature of this new phenomenological science – the new colonial encounter has left a residue in the consciousness of those who seek to represent non-Western realities. He concludes:

> Third-world texts, even those which are seemingly private and invested with a properly libidinal dynamic necessarily project a political dimension in the form of national allegory: the story of the private individual destiny is always an allegory of the embattled situation of the public third-world culture and society. Need I add that it is precisely this very different ratio of the political to the personal which makes such texts alien to us at first approach, and consequently, resistant to our conventional western habits of reading?[74]

I do not want to continue drawing attention to the problematic distribution of aesthetic categories (what exactly is an *improper* libidinal dynamic?) with the structural modes that define non-Western realities. They are self-evident enough. Perhaps it is the inability to identify the transition of societies to modernity in recognisably class terms that makes us conclude that something as instrumental as nationalism is essentially about the identification, as Gellner states, of a 'population' with 'high culture'? What are the positive terms of the 'congruence' that Gellner cites, contrasting with the esoteric *incongruence* that Jameson's epigones draw our attention to, between the political and the national in his definition of 'nationalism'? For Gellner, nationalism

> is about entry to, participation in, identification with, a literate high culture which is co-extensive with an entire political unit and its total population, and which must be of this kind if it is to be compatible with the kind of division of labour, the type or mode of production, on which society is based.[75]

Conflict in societies past culminating in nationalism as the decisive form of anti-colonial resistance is to be conceived in terms that are strictly functionalist and cultural. This reworking of the Marxist explanation reflects how all that matters for a postmodern historiography of nation-states is that any incompatibility between the infrastructural mode and ideological elements to which the nationalist leaders bring a general (and not to say often violent) awareness in the name of the People is now essentially a matter of identification by a people with cultural symbols. The implicit idea here is that if this identification fails to meet the requirements of a new division of labour or a new type or mode of production, the cultural symbols no longer reflecting but dictating the new order will have to be fashioned anew. If they are not, a conflict soon arises between rulers and ruled but this latent antagonism between these groups – what does one call them in the absence of the term 'classes'? – can be resolved in the same shadowy realm of the superstructural (to use the old vocabulary). Although he will have the obverse to say about the Ottoman version of the Circle of Equity elsewhere, Gellner states: 'The ethnic distinctiveness, territorial discontinuity and religious stigma of the most effective producers made it hard for them to co-operate with the rulers in the intimate, production-oriented manner required by modernization-from-above.'[76] Nature is not so much a spur here but an obstacle to 'revolutionary' activity in history. Braudel in his classic account albeit too briefly cites the formidable obstacle posed by territorial discontinuity, in the form of the mountain ranges encircling the basin of the Mediterranean, to the writ of the Ottoman caliphate in the sixteenth century. If Turkish despotism was indeed a poor despotism, ceasing at the Balkan highlands, the Albanian hills or the mountains of Crete, the quiet confidence of the Berbers in the Atlas mountains, where 'No one raises his voice and [where] it is impossible from watching them to discover which is their president', is symptomatic of the fundamental democracy that flourishes in the absence of the kinds of modern 'cultural symbols' Gellner thinks typical of nationalism. He may be right to a degree. The rough insularity of mountain folk was a species of independence looked on jealously by the Spanish Inquisition within the borders of the Iberian peninsula.[77] One Pedraça in his *Historia eclesiastica de Granada* (1637) has the following remarks on the Christian inhabitants of the Alpujarras, the high range in the Kingdom of Granada:

> [T]hey are subjects of a Catholic king; and yet, for lack of instruction and following the oppression to which they are subjected, they are also ignorant of what they should know to obtain eternal salvation that they have retained only a few vestiges of the Christian religion. Can anyone believe that if the Infidel were to become master of their land tomorrow (which God forbid) these people would remain long without abandoning their religion and embracing the beliefs of their conquerors?[78]

The mountain fastnesses have traditionally been the home of vestigial resistance to civilising missions. For Gellner, irredentist nationalism is more violent in the means it uses to achieve its objectives than the empires of the past:

> [I]deologically uninfected authorities ... such as the Ottoman Turks ... had kept the peace and extracted taxes, but otherwise tolerated, and been indeed profoundly indifferent to, the diversity of faiths and cultures which they governed. By contrast, their gunmen successors seem incapable of resting in peace till they have imposed the nationalist principle of *cuius region, eius lingua*. They do not want merely a fiscal surplus and obedience. They thirst after cultural and linguistic souls of their subjects.[79]

Let us examine this proposition more closely. It will bring us no closer to explaining the tragic fate of individual Greeks and Turks with Mustapha Cemal's founding of the Turkish state and the razing of villages and lives in the western demesne of the broken Ottoman Empire that culminated in the great conflagration of Smyrna in 1923. The primary motivation in history by the Ottoman for extending *Dar-e-salaam*, the Realm of Peace, is mercantilist. Gellner described it as an equation: 'fiscal surplus' plus obedience. The modern ideology of nationalism is by definition atavistic. How plausible is this specific detail in Braudel's conception of transhumance in the Mediterranean? Is there any slight possibility that Turkish nationalism relies on ancient glories in seeking to capture the souls of the various ethnicities who were once the indifferent subjects of the Sultan in Istanbul as well as being nostalgic about ever new domains (including to the east, with the establishment of a Turkic sultanate in Delhi) to exploit in order to add to the grandeur of the empire's wealth? Perhaps cultural symbols are always specific to the age in which they are used? Gellner's remark about gunmen successors is an allusion to the activities of the leaders of the ruling bloc in the Ottoman government, the Committee of Union and Progress (CUP) or Ittihad ve Terraki Cemyeti, formed out of the loose opposition groups collectively known as the Young Turks who were responsible for formulating the ideological policy of displacement of insurgent elements (read genocide) as well as the coup against the last important sultan, Abdülhamid II, in 1908. The CUP's attitude in exile from Paris, while its leader Ahmed Riza in the late nineteenth century was intolerant of non-Muslims not being Ottomanised through conversion to Islam, Donald Bloxham records, nevertheless saw the inhumanity from 1912 of the Ottoman Senate's forced deportation of Armenians.[80] Gellner's description of the Young Turks above is used to conclude the following: 'Culturally plural societies often worked well in the past: so well, in fact, that cultural plurality was sometimes invented where it was previously lacking.'[81] Why then did Ataturk feel the need to establish the Turkish state by enforcing cultural homogeneity? The use of deconstructive theory by Homi Bhabha to invent cultural plurality anew fails to be a serious attempt in halting the cynical appropriation of the emancipatory narrative of nationalist movements in the past. Nkrumah's symptomatic account, especially the coincidental processes of world and African revolutions, where the peoples of Asia, Africa and Latin America come together to defeat the elites both internal and external to Africa and in their own neocolonised societies, seems a relic of an age in which optimism in the Marxist revolutionary narrative and more importantly, in the agency of the State at times of *coups d'état*, had many adherents.[82] The perennial hold of religion on national consciousness seems to us an anomaly where social egalitarianism, in the Ottoman case, is better delivered by a more 'scientific' understanding of the social formation. To this end, Abdülhamid II invited German military expertise to modernise the Ottoman military establishment (the single most important institution of the polity) in the figure of Major von der Goltz in 1883. It is to the Goltz generation of officers that Cemalist modernisation in the early twentieth century owes its impetus.[83] What this patient delineation of the militarised polity fails to mention is its own failure to look after the Christian Armenians in eastern Anatolia at the hands of migrants into the empire from seceding Balkan provinces. So, when revolutionary elements tried more radical measures rather than ineffectual appeals to the Porte, the

Ottoman authority charged by France and Britain to reform Abdülhamid's regime, to combat repressive taxation and periodic depravations against their women in Kurdish-run Sasun province, 80,000–100,000 Armenian Christians were massacred from 1894 to 1896.

Part of the jaded nature of scepticism about the value of *grands récits* is an historical condition in which appeals to the long-distant past led to the mass killing of ordinary people. Religion is the first *grand récit*. In the absence of this faith in the great narratives, however, will 'post-structuralist' remedies for the recurrent condition described as follows reflect any more than the ambivalences (Lacanian or otherwise), for example, customarily exaggerated by Homi Bhabha into theoretical concepts in Fanon's existential observations about race in *Black Skins, White Masks?*[84] 'By the 1970s, nationalism had become a matter of ethnic politics, the reason why people in the Third World killed each other – sometimes in wars between regular armies, sometimes, more distressingly, in cruel and often protracted civil wars, and increasingly, it seemed, by technologically sophisticated and virtually unstoppable acts of terrorism.'[85] These are late reflections of Europe's own history in the earlier twentieth century. With the idea of 'ideologically uninfected authority', Gellner's remarks are nostalgic for a more elegant cultural process from the dynastic past. He is alluding to the Ottoman practice established with Murad I (1362–1389). The Janissaries of the Sultan's standing army 'were recruited by the *devşirme* (collection) system whereby Christian males between fifteen and twenty were periodically rounded up and Ottomanized'.[86] It is hard for us to believe that the Young Turks could still avail themselves of this early medieval system in the early twentieth century as a native solution to the Armenian question. In turn, the 'enlightened' nature of the Sultan's policy ought to be placed in the context of the forced conversion of Muslims in Spain after Ferdinand and Isabella betrayed the Castillian agreement of 1492 to 'allow King Abi Abdilehi [Boabdil] and his [officials], military leaders, and good men and all the common people, great and small, to live in their own religion [*su ley*] …'[87] By 1499, a court historian will record the intemperate policy pursued by Jiménez de Cisneros, Isabella's confessor, if, after 'kind words' of persuasion and the bestowing of gratifications, the Moors of Granada refused.

> [T]hose who refused, he had put in prison, and kept locked up until they were converted … When he heard that many Muslim leaders were attacking his methods as being contrary to the agreements … [he] imprisoned the dissidents in chains, and though it ran counter to his temperament, he allowed them to be dealt with by methods that were not correct.[88]

In contrast to the wars of religion in Europe, the 'enlightened despotism' of Ottoman and Mughal regimes may seem perfect exemplars of a pluralistic vision of cultural diversity in the past. However, the point about describing imperial sovereignty in a pre-colonial (pre-European hegemonic) context as 'ideologically uninfected authority' is worth exploring in a little more detail. This is not gainsaying some parodic impulse in Enlightenment thinking about Oriental despotism that might be used to reveal the spurious nature of political ideals in European societies.[89] Armenians as an 'economically brilliant group' might have surrendered their right of defence in order to service the Ottoman Turkish economy but, along with the other linguistically different group in Anatolia, the Kurds, they present the same problems for the project of nationalist unification, albeit within a smaller statist territorial unit, imagined explicitly on secular lines, as the infidels did to Othman I as the founder of the Turkish dynasty in the thirteenth century. In the late nineteenth and early twentieth centuries, as we have seen in the Empire's eastern provinces, the perpetrators of crimes against their Armenian subjects by local Kurdish notables were carried out in part by *muhajir* or those expelled from their territories with the dissolution of the empire under Abdülhamid II. The genocide begun by the Ottoman government in 1915, leaving dead an estimated million of the Armenian peoples by 1918, testifies to the fact, even if nobody was cashiered for this crime by any international tribunal – because of the complicity of the great Powers emerging from the devastating failure of their own ambitions, as well as their hopes of monopolising the resources of the Middle East. If Ottoman successors tolerated the cultural diversity of their subjects, there will always be a clerisy to remind them that their policy is a deviation of the perfect and in comparison extremely humble model of community (the *Umma*) established by the Prophet of Islam. Part of the most intractable problem with 'originary' myths (*pace* Bhabha) is that they are cast in millenarian terms. Virtually all the architects of Ottoman reform and celebrators of Turkish identity at the cost of so many Armenian lives were secularists informed by the most virulent strains of social Darwinism. The absolutism of 'identity' is the engine of history, what Derrida in autobiographical terms of being Franco-Maghrebian once described as 'a disorder of identity', but questioning these cultural processes as processes, one suspects, will have a negligible effect on the relentless sectarianism of conflicts in the world today.[90] How many tribal or ethnic particularities behind civil wars are going to receive serious consideration by diplomats in New York, representatives of polities with the indelible imprimatur of colonial pasts, wars which the most powerful of the assembly of United Nations are responsible for? This perspicacity on the condition of Being is a legacy of Enlightenment thinking and I will return to this development below. As the tone adopted by Derrida shows, these thoughts belong to the province of private retrospection. On the one hand, there is Selim II and the seizing of Cyprus in 1571 to prove the pious injunction to extend the Domain of Peace by ritually flaying, stuffing and parading the sewn-up carcass of Bragadino, the Venetian senator and governor of Famagusta, to exact a spectacularly theatrical revenge for the loss of 50,000 Turkish men in capturing Nicosia and Famagusta; on the other, the protection of peasant rights to land under Islamic law's rule of *waqf*, which allowed them to export surplus wheat for the empire and the European markets, that reveals a latent 'tension between the state and the church, between the authority of the Sultan and that of the quadi [Muslim jurist], constituting a sort of 'parcellized sovereignty'.[91] The memory of Famagusta would have been alive when Pedraça was writing his history of Granada. Gellner's essentialist view of the Ottoman hegemon ignores the conditions that produce this dichotomy.

If the act of documenting the past, then, is an institutional type of behaviour without which the cultural and linguistic souls of individuals cannot be claimed, this past is inevitably going to be an idealisation of the real conditions of existence. Even if the clerics may be ignored at their *minbar* or the uses of the utopian desire for social order in religious doctrine is realised in the most brutal programmes of cultural transformation, this is no reason to believe that an 'ideologically uninfected' order ever existed. To suggest this is to conclude that the Ottoman order was established schizophrenically. And this is actually Gellner's conclusion: '[T]he Turkish commitment to modernization of the polity and society has, or initially had, both an Ottoman and a Koranic quality.'[92] The same conclusion might be reached about the shastric elements, of service and *khadi*, in Congress's avowed ideology of secularism for India's multifarious society.

Islam is the generic explanation for Gellner. In the medieval past, the religious system allowed the bloody Ottoman succession to be conducted according to harem politics but these intimate details have now to be isolated from the martial prowess that led to the fall of the capital of the Eastern Christian empire in 1453 and the various Mediterranean theatres which proved a particular obstacle for the Sultan – wars for which he had spent his life being trained. Gellner's idea about the Ottoman Turks 'keeping the peace', then, is a euphemism in strictly historical terms. One Vinayak Damodar Savarkar sums up the logic of *justum bellum*: 'For the excited logic of those who committed the massacres naturally began to say, "oppose illegal force by righteous force!"'. He uses the violence in Granada to end the *convivium* and the massacre of 21,000 Turkish peasants by Greeks in 1821 as examples to show how the offspring of the black snake [meaning Muslims] ought not to be allowed to live.'[93] The Circle of Equity for one man is a pretext for a tendentious logic in the context of India's pre-colonial history for another.

To use Althusser's celebrated idea, the ideological state apparatuses of the past often charged themselves with the moral duty of reproducing the past of the people for them. For Gellner, since capital and capitalism are now irrelevant, we cannot describe the groups who consider it their privileged destiny to fashion these symbols for the people as a nationalist class, let alone a feudal clerisy. In contrast to the minatory rhetoric of the feudals, 'modernization' is essentially hieratic but in a neutral form; it will perforce put pay to any elite that describes its superiority in terms of tradition, whether this superiority is founded on tribal, ethnic and racial differences, imperialist rule or on communalism–caste grounds. In the new formulation of Marx's classic statement about the transition of modes, each subsequent transformation, especially in pre-capitalist formations, is now determined not by the monopoly on production by a class but by the utilitarian consequences of a division of labour. Gellner concludes how 'Mankind moved from a hunting–gathering state when all had leisure, to an agrarian one when only some (the ruling elite) had it, to an industrial age governed by the work ethic, when none have it. Or you might say we moved from no delay in gratification to some delay and finally to eternal delay.'[94] For Imperia, Nature is one vast latifundium from which the fundamental riches of civilisation may be mined; yet it is the accident of history or the hidden work of Providence that has designated the sole individual to show

Historiography and narrative 29

the word of God acting in human affairs that would otherwise remain obscure in the mundane necessities of existence to the unlettered shepherd or myopic village burgher. Braudel's great meditation confines the matter of history to the former processes, tracing the migration pattern of shepherds on the Iberian peninsula, for example, to register the 'almost motionless' variations 'of the general relation between man and his environment', pictured as slow waves superimposed on one another.[95] We saw how the urge to disturb this pastoral process was itself a natural inkling in the social psyche. Nevertheless, this was the feat Foucault admired where the peculiar subterranean discontinuities of material civilisation *appear* static: 'Beneath the rapidly changing history of governments, wars, and famines, there emerge other, apparently unmoving histories: the history of sea routes, the history of corn or of gold-mining, the history of drought and of irrigation, the history of crop rotation, the history of the balance achieved between by the human species between hunger and abundance.'[96] This attempt to write the 'material civilisation' of Europe in the sixteenth century means relegating to a footnote the victory of the Christian Armada under Philip II's half-brother Don John over Ali Pasha, Selim II's admiral of the Ottoman fleet, at Lepanto 1571 to partly avenge the atrocity against the Venetian governor Bragadino at Famagusta by Lala Mustafa.[97] Don John's war with the *Moriscos* (forced converts to Christianity), conducted from village to village in the Alpujarras mountains, succeeded in expelling the last remnants of Muslim Spain to Morocco by 1615. The mountains in this instance were no protection to their inhabitants. Of this 'ideologically infected' and clamorous fact of history we find not a word in Braudel's account. In the preface to the first edition, Braudel describes the reason for this conspicuous absence in his encyclopaedic treatment of his theme, acknowledging that 'Philip II or a Don John of Austria ... despite their illusions, [were] more acted upon than actors', or we might say, more sinned against than sinning by the measure of posterity. Braudel's elegant apologia is substantially about the danger of distraction in historiography: '[W]hen I began to ask myself finally whether the Mediterranean did not possess, beyond the long-distance and irregular actions of Spain (a rather arid topic apart from the dramatic confrontation at Lepanto), a history of its own, a powerful vitality, and whether this vitality did not in fact deserve something better than the role of a picturesque background, I was already succumbing to the temptation of the immense subject that was finally to hold my attention.'[98] Instead of the glittering pennants, the galleasses, priest-craft or more effectively, Greek Fire, treacherous embassies, the sieges and Quixotic dramatisations after the event, Braudel provides his avid reader with the minute details of irrigation schemes in Lombardy or the 'ecology', of 'capital importance' he states, of dromedaries and camels. Braudel is aware of the idiosyncrasy of his method, concluding: 'In fact, neither the plateaux of Anatolia nor the Iranian highlands were really open to it, and if Arab conquest failed in Asia Minor, if it was never very assured in Persia, the reason is largely to be sought in the inferiority of the dromedary.'[99] It is an incongruent image, the cosmopolitan splendour of the Ottoman court or the hieratic rituals of Persian sovereignty resisting Arabic because of the sensitivities of the humble dromedary. In Shi'a mythology, the animal and living icon at the centre of Muharram rites is a horse, Zuljenah, which arrived without Husayn ibn Ali, its master, from the battlefields of Karbala in 680 CE, the most dramatic instance for Muslims of the Arab conquest beyond the Hijaz. Gellner's dream of an ideologically uninfected past reflects the optimism of discerning 'individual entities as components of processes which aggregate into wholes that are greater than, or qualitatively different from, the sum of their parts'; it is a perfect encapsulation of his metaphysical commitment to Ottoman hegemony and differs from Braudel's history which, in contrast, in its self-proclaimed modest ambition reflects the ambiguity of the Contextualist attitude to 'the problem of constructing a narrative model of the *processes* discerned in the historical field'.[100] Indeed, Braudel's prefatory comments to his encyclopaedic chronicle without a sovereign consciousness reveal how difficult it is to successfully resist the tendency of a Mechanistic reduction of data in terms of regularities of 'material civilisation' conceived as revolutions at the surface of human history and, on the other hand, 'an Organicist synthesis of those data in terms of the "principles" that are presumed to reveal the *telos* [Ottoman 'civilisation' in Gellner's analysis] toward which the whole process is tending over the long haul'.[101] Braudel's narrative adopts the tropes of wave and stasis that dominate Jacob Burckhardt's conception of the historical understanding. Braudel's text *The Mediterranean* owes its narratological aspect to the conservative vision adumbrated in Burckhardt's lectures on the sixteenth century at Basel from 1865 to 1885, a time of inauguration followed by metastases (in a comment on the revolutionary upheavals of his own times).[102]

To the modern eye, a ruling elite is only conspicuous in the *Agraria* of non-capitalist life in the fast-vanishing past. Even where the agrarian source of legendary riches seems invisible, the lords of humankind presided over the toil of others that constitutes the material bases of civilisation. Public theatre where the Doge came out of his palace to give ritual benediction to the merchants, the symbolic marriage not between land and peasant but between money and sea, reinforced the gradations of the mercantilist Republic. Patronage to the great artists in whose productions the dynamic of suffering remained a matter of *style* and the conspicuous consumption of credit that precluded the spirit of acquisitiveness from bearing the Puritan mark of the capitalist mode, the mirror of Caliban that was Caravaggio's canvas, all this meant that nobody could mistake the rude individual hailing from a family of pastoralists, who might be employed to dig the *canale*, from the de Medici who felt he was emulating Caesar by having his tomb carved in marble.[103] The lowlands upon which the artisan of the city felt himself subject to the 'great and unremitting malice of fortune' were not merely a figment of his imagination.[104]

The dominant ideology thesis finds its inherent limit as an explanatory model with the universalising of a work ethic in the industrial age. This conclusion is hostile to the Marxist or subaltern interpretation of the role that nationalist ideology plays in Indian historiography. And it is liberal bourgeois in the sense that industrialisation, at first and later, 'output' in a mixed economy for the emergent Indian state, will subject the masses to the eternal delay of gratification that characterises production in the backward zones. This 'morality of postponed gratification' as the fundamental of any emergent capitalist order motivated the early architects of the Indian state; describing the disparity between the state-nationalist ideology and the reality it met, Ayesha Jalal concludes by noting the similarity between the two visions: 'This is not to imply that the Gandhian ideal of self-sufficient village communities was a closer approximation of Indian realities, but to suggest that although the Nehruvian agenda kept abreast with the more focused, if broadly, construed requirements of the centre it was quite as ahistorical as that of the Mahatma's borrowings from Western misperceptions about an unchanging past.'[105] The realisation that Indian life is village life and the rapid transformation of the social order achieved by industrialisation is 'gigantism' came to Nehru late in his ordained destiny as nationalist leader with his creation and enthusiastic support for small-scale initiatives fostered by a Ministry of Community Development in 1956.[106]

Barring the obscure ontological differences that Jameson analyses, with the universality of literacy we are all capable of moving within the dominant class from our relatively passive attitude of languishing in a mean social existence to a more active career as conceptive ideologists.[107] No longer does the unconscious reproduction of our lives according to the poetry of religious existence result in the loss of life. It is in this precise sense that all cultural forms in Third World society are conceived in terms of the national allegory. This is the reason why Western thinkers place such Romantic hope in the maturation of the technologies of representation dealing with the self. In Abrams' words and in Hegel's opinion, the 'theodicy of the private life' is the natural conclusion of revolutionary upheaval. Whether this faith in the aesthetic exactly reflected Gramsci's assertive conclusions about the integrating role of the intellectual in the context of Italian history is a moot point. At any moment, the individual overburdened by the corruption of the despotic regime discovers a ferocious eloquence in listing all the wrongs of everyday life. Doubtless, like the Gramscian hero in the rural hinterlands, the traditional intellectual in Indian modernity is best represented by the figure of Gandhi himself. However, since knowledge is subjection, as we will see with Partha Chatterjee's problematic view of Gandhism, the requirement of universal literacy by the modern nation-state can now be dispensed with in reaching some identical conclusions about Indian history.

That the symbolic mode inherent within the historical situation itself cannot be asserted with any confidence and that doubt now replaces the certainty that 'in their origin, all objects have a human meaning' are not factored into the rather glib categorisation of the historical task by the postmodernist position. This symptomatic anxiety about the meaning and value of history goes beyond interpreting the symbolic mode as the result of the writer's personal aesthetic, even where this mode is regarded as an essentially mediated form of reality (ideology) – whether this form is progressive or not. For Jameson

> This original meaningfulness of objects ... becomes visible only when their link with human labour and production is unconcealed. But in modern industrial civilisation this link is hard to find: objects appear to lead an independent life of their own, and it is precisely this illusion which is the source of the symbolic.[108]

The task facing the modern historian, then, is no longer to relate how the random series of events were disciplined by the genius of any individual but to restore the lost link between objects and human labour. The illusion at the source of the symbolic was never as colourful or, as Shakespeare's characters Othello and Shylock reveal, as spectacularly violent as in the Early Modern. If history is very little more than narrative and this narrative function replaces the specific forensic ability of documenting 'real' events, how might the demystification Jameson thinks vital be carried out by historiography as a purely symbolic mode? There is a paradox in treating narrative synonymous with 'the symbolic'. If the symbolic is at the source of this illusion, as Jameson implies, and if *grands récits* including national myths persist in a sort of half-life according to an '*unconscious* effectivity', how might historiography uncover the secret life of objects to dispel the illusion of their autonomy from human processes and yet remain faithful to its most ancient duty to remind the present of the power of human achievements in the past?[109] Apparently, there is a moral imperative to relieve the countless millions in the backward zones of their aspirations towards modernity because this separation between objects and reality, reality and language, spells disaster. The Comintern solution presents itself for the Third World Other even as it is adapted to the needs of late capitalism. Let us leave aside this Kantian-sounding problem. Historiography must be able to describe the objective relationship between things in the past, despite the fact that this relationship is itself symptomatic of the symbolic, in Jameson's elegant formulation. We are returning albeit in a very circuitous way back to the familiar claim that historiography is essentially ideological. It will take Michel Foucault's *Annales* school explanation to see how historiography emerges as *the* symbolic mode of explanation as soon as production itself becomes a discursive object. In Gellner's alternative explanation, this phenomenal change reflecting the increasing specialisation of labour in modern society would not penetrate very deeply to the rest of society with its ponderous base, or if it did, the dream of the economist as technician (if economists dream) would be perfectly circumscribed by the realities of pre-existent and general patterns of need. To quote a tenet from *The Wealth of Nations*, 'the division of labour is limited by the extent of the market'. And Nature herself affords London and Calcutta the means of mutual enrichment by gifting England and India the sea upon whose benign surface so few *civilised* nations of Europe of course ever imagined staging expensive wars.[110] Before the historic defeat of Waterloo, Smith's confidence in Britain's maritime ambition after the waning of the Iberian kingdoms' monopoly over the sea two centuries earlier is due to two factors. First, trade is the result of a favourable economic climate of a century before, brought about by the breaking of the Dutch monopoly in the mid-sixteenth century with the help of France's Louis XIV.[111] Second, the *Navigation Act* of 1660 established a rigorous policy of protectionism by preventing any goods from being imported into England and Ireland that were not the freight of ships belonging to Englishmen, Irishmen or colonists; it also stipulated that this commercial fleet be manned by 75 per cent English crew.[112]

In any case, 'narrative' is now the relatively straightforward sounding answer to any epistemological questions that might arise every time history is considered

Historiography and narrative 33

to be about the translation of 'knowing into telling', or more grandly, the 'fashioning [of] human experience into a form assimilable to structures of meaning that are generally human rather than culture-specific'.[113] These valorising claims about historicity need to be examined in a more straightforward context. The working assumption for us is that historiography is realist. In other words, as a theory of knowledge about the past it is an analogical procedure that aims to inscribe, however imperfectly, a reality that is not itself an imaginary or ideological construction. A problem now arises according to the idea that interpretive strategies in historiography differ from those found in other narrative traditions. The modern historian's ambition is to incorporate various *modus operandi* that determine the sum of human experience as both knowledge and practice.

We need to consider our analysis of the same set of issues arising in Indian historiography *qua* historiography in general by concentrating on the last two columns in Hayden White's scheme when referring to the translation of problems in historiography into narrative solutions. These columns are respectively named 'Mode of Explanation' and 'Mode of Ideological Implication'. The items in the latter column are as follows: 'Anarchist', 'Conservative', 'Radical' and 'Liberal'. There is a caveat as to the generic specificity of these typologies when it comes to how they are to be combined with those under the positivist, less political and more neutral-sounding heading of Explanation. White's emphasis on historiography as a centred discourse treats the parallelogram of forces that constitute any event in terms of their relationship to a legitimating authority, but what form he gives this authority remains obscure for the moment. Let us look more closely at White's scheme. The implications of a Radical mode of interpretation will render, according to White, a Mechanistic explanation. The rest of the epistemological modes identified for each ideological tendency (Anarchist, Conservative and Liberal explanations) are, respectively, 'Idiographic', 'Organicist' and 'Contextualist'. Despite the note of caution, White concludes that 'in fact, the tension at the heart of every historical masterpiece is created in part by a conflict between a given modality of emplotment or explanation and the specific ideological commitment of its author'.[114] There is a tautology here: unless the modality of an historical explanation belongs to some archetypal impersonal source, is not the given quality of it a reflection of the particular ideological commitment to which an individual interpretation of events is dedicated? The secondary point still stands. History is the inevitable outcome of a priori factors, the 'given modality of emplotment', but these prefigurative determinants of historicity reflect the aesthetic judgements that the historian chooses to give to their political interpretation of events.

The dream of discovering a virginal event whose limits exceed the modality of human comprehension often turns out to be nightmarish. The Nazis' 'Final Solution' for Europe's Jews is one such event; an historical happening that challenges the historian's ability to give any prefigurative form that is not essentially the inarticulate human cry. The repression of utopian thinking, whether of the Left or the Right, is inherent in the professionalising of history for White so that it can faithfully serve as 'custodian of realism in political thought and action in general'.[115] Only the historian is supposed to be capable of arbitrating between partisan interest in the welter of blood and violence to harvest knowledge. Kant's passion for schematising knowledge is the model for White's own deliberations on the narrative character of historiography. For the sage of Konigsberg, the evolution of historical process implied three general tendencies: 'eudamonism' or progress, 'terrorism' or decline, and 'farce' or statis. The political nature of all historiography can be militated against by using Aristotelian judgements about the types of event that can be admitted into historical judgements to distinguish it from romance or fiction. White's conclusions at face value seem deliberately contrary: the narrative function in historical interpretation precludes history from being scientific and so helps it avoid the twin dangers of positivism in liberal thinking and radicalism in Marxian analysis. The *aurea mediocritas* is to be achieved by submitting the interpretation of events to the eighteenth-century ideal of common sense. Avoiding the excesses of moralism or political bias involves a disciplining of the imagination. In White's summary of complex intellectual developments, since Burke's essay *Reflections on the Revolution in France*, historical judgement involves the discrimination of that which potentially defeats human comprehension, the category of the 'sublime', a negative, in moral terms, from that which reflects the capabilities of the human mind, 'the beautiful'. This is not quite accurate. The didactic uses to be made of 'disasters in the moral, as we should behold a miracle in the physical order of things', events which reveal 'the unstable condition of mortal prosperity ... the tremendous uncertainty of human greatness' in the human cosmic drama, enable our minds to be 'alarmed into reflexion'; the Aristotelian conception of tragic catharsis with its constituents of the discursive sublime, terror and pity, *purify* the mind.[116] The tutelary potential of historical events such as the Terror is only realised once the mind reflects on it according to 'the guiding thread of reason'.[117] The 'aimless play of nature' that causes indignation in the witnessing intelligence 'nonetheless finds in the hearts of all spectators (*who are not engaged in this game themselves*) a wishful participation that borders closely on enthusiasm, the very expression of which is fraught with danger; this sympathy, therefore, can have no other cause than a moral predisposition in the human race'.[118] Now we understand the unconscious effectivity of the grand narratives that Jameson alludes to. In White's interpretation, what threatens the golden mean of historical understanding is the demotion of the sublime for the beautiful. White twice asserts the infection of Marxist as well as conservative thinking by this domestication of the chaotic, contingent element in history.[119] However, he singles out the reformist impulse inherent within Marxist thought: 'This understanding may account in part for the weak psychological appeal of the "beautiful life" as a project to be realized in political struggles and, what is more important, for the apparent incapacity of political regimes founded on Marxist principles to sustain their professed programs for the radical transformation of society in anything but the most banal ways.'[120] I do not recognise the totalitarianism of Soviet or Maoist society, with their culmination in 'sublime' episodes of mass purging and organised terrorism, in this conclusion. More historically, Marx and Engels addressed the banality of mandarin reform by committee to achieve the beautiful life in Lassallean terms of the equal distribution of undiminished proceeds of labour to all members of society

Historiography and narrative 35

or indeed the limitations in realising the kingdom of reason on the cotton mill floor of 'New Lanarkshire'.[121] But the problem of interpretation for historical narratives comes to the fore with the efforts of ideologists to both deny and use the Holocaust. The objectivity question in historiography loses its moorings somewhere between a fascist revisionism and Zionist-nationalist opportunism. Callinicos is clear about White's shortcomings in providing a narrative solution to these problems in epistemology. White is susceptible to the rhetorical devices in Romanticism that he identifies as a bulwark against the essentially meaningless quality of history (he is said to toy 'with what one might call the fascist sublime') and, 'by identifying the truth of nationalist histories with their effectiveness in promoting the power of a particular nation-state' (the pragmatic translation of the genre with which White is engaging theoretically), 'White removes any basis on which the crimes committed in the name of such projects can be criticized'.[122] As if to remind us of the reality of events, Callinicos dutifully provides a corrective to the aestheticising of history in White's theory by reminding us that in the year of publication of White's essay, 1982, the Israeli Army besieged and indiscriminately bombed Beirut, and after the withdrawal of the Palestinians from Lebanon, allowed the massacring of Muslims in the refugee camps at Sabra and Chatila by their Christian fascist allies. But is he aware that the truth of nationalist histories – in this case, between Israelis and the Christian Lebanese, as a project designed to exclude and if possible exterminate the Arab presence – relies on a shared experience of genocide? I am alluding to the events of 1914–1916 and the Ottoman government's killing of a million Christian Armenians.

Where does this 'fascist sublime' take White? Rather like the speculative intelligence that is invited to reflect on the nature of historical events implied by Burke's idea of the atrocious realities behind the ideals of the French Revolution, White is emphatic about the inherent plotting of historical realities: 'Stories, like factual statements, are linguistic entities and belong to the order of discourse.'[123] The illustrative example to show how a satirical representation more plausibly conveys the pathos of the Holocaust is Art Spiegelman's comic book allegory of cats (Germans), mice (Jews) and pigs (Poles). White is eager to convey the figurative possibilities of *any* event. For White, Andreas Hillgruber's double essay *Two Kinds of Ruin: The Shattering of the German Reich and the End of European Jewry*, the first being an attempt to rehabilitate the tragic sentiment for the Wehrmacht's defence of the Eastern Front in 1944–1945, oughtn't to stop with noble resignation at the second account: 'In forgoing the impulse to name the kind of story that should be told about the Jews in Hitler's Reich, Hillgruber approaches the position of a number of scholars and writers who view the Holocaust as virtually unrepresentable in language.'[124] We ought to resist the figurative impulse for genocide and try to maintain the austerity of a chronicle. This objective is achieved, according to Berel Lang – whose prescriptions are being critically appraised by White – with the use of Barthes' semiotic concept of the intransitive or middle voice. This needn't necessarily imply 'a genial pluralism' in matters ethical rather than epistemological; rather, it compels a reflection on the unrepresentable nature of the Nazi policy of mass murder in terms that characterise modernist practice.[125] Using Auerbach's characterisation of modern realism as the emergence of 'socially inferior human groups to the position of subject matter for problematic-existential representation' and the 'embedding of random persons and events in the course of contemporary history', White concludes the appropriateness of identifying the genocide of Jews in the twentieth century as typical of the age that produced cultural modernism: 'And this is because the social order which is the subject of this history has undergone a radical transformation – a change which permitted the crystallization of the totalitarian form that Western society assumed in the twentieth century.'[126] Carlo Ginzburg's use of White in this essay as an heuristic device to conclude the political genealogy for the enthusiasm of one Giovanni Gentile, disciple of the idealist philosopher of history Benedetto Croce, is excessive when White, albeit with a heavy emphasis on the 'effectiveness' of both the interpretation of the Holocaust as the founding ideology of the Israeli state *and* the Palestinians' obligation to produce a similar counter-argument about their history, suggests a latent moral confusion about the narrative component of historiography. Ginzburg concludes: 'In fact, White's argument connecting truth and effectiveness inevitably reminds us not of tolerance but of its opposite – Gentile's evaluation of a blackjack as a moral force.'[127] I will be returning in the next chapter to the narrative innovation on the classical mode of historiography by Auerbach's representation of the problem.

The heterogeneity implied by the use of the plural in the context of Indian pasts acknowledges the difficulties faced each time we attempt to isolate ourselves from the modular influences that White lists in order to restore a discursive authenticity to a single, essentially Indian past. A radical mode of historical interpretation is homologous to a mechanistic explanation; the mode of emplotment identified by White for this interpretive scheme is tragic. Although after the foregoing remarks, we might more appropriately identify the mode of emplotment for a Marxist historiography in terms of a subgenre of comedy, namely farce, the inference is that the trajectory of a Marxist historiography ought to be interpreted in terms of a tragic conception of human endeavour. How plausible is this characterisation for Indian historiography? For Ranajit Guha and his school of 'Marxian' historians, the grid upon which historiography can be defined is relatively simple in its dichotomy: the history of Indian nationalism has up until their productions been dominated by 'colonialist elitism and bourgeois elitism'.[128] For the subalternists, the way to avoid writing the history of Indian nationalism as if it were the spiritual biography of the Indian elite is to define an autonomous realm of consciousness that mobilised more spontaneously, more violently than the 'relatively more legalistic and constitutionalist' orientation of anti-colonial resistance by elite mobilisation. Let us examine this idea more closely. We are told that the distinctive features of subaltern resistance to colonial rule 'endowed this politics with many [inexhaustible] idioms, norms and values which put it in a category apart from elite politics'. This manifold idiom of subaltern resistance, Guha continues, was modified under the impact of 'living contradictions' but nevertheless managed to help 'demarcate the domain of subaltern politics from that of elite politics'. Guha continues:

The coexistence of these two domains or streams, which can be sensed by intuition and proved by demonstration as well, was the index of an important historical truth, that is, the failure of the Indian bourgeoisie to speak for the nation. There were vast areas in the life and consciousness of the people which were never integrated into their hegemony.[129]

Guha's definition of 'subaltern' – in the active sense of subaltern classes in revolutionary resistance to the colonial regime – is the product of a demographic equation and its differential between dominant indigenous groups at a national level (epitomised, we assume, by both Gandhi and Nehru) and local groups, 'the lowest strata of the rural gentry, impoverished landlords, rich peasants and upper-middle peasants all of whom belong, ideally speaking, to the category of "people" or "subaltern classes" …' What was the tragic quality of this process in White's definition for a Marxist historical modality? Guha's answer is 'circular' and Lukácsian: 'The working class was still not sufficiently mature in the objective conditions of its social being and in its consciousness as a class-for-itself, nor was it firmly allied yet with the peasantry. As a result it could do nothing to take over and complete the mission which the bourgeoisie had failed to realize.'[130] The hazard of mixing the autonomous streams of elite and subaltern historical phenomena that Guha warns against is amply testified by the narrative elements in which the tragic conception of 'missed opportunity' is differentiated from those ideological implications that result in either a Romantic (Idiographic–Anarchist), Conservative (Comedic–Organicist) and Liberal (Satiric–Contextualist) interpretation of Indian history.

These are the obstacles arranged against the individual's effort of producing a coherent narrative about Indian pasts that is free of any modular influences. The historiography of Indian nationalism, if it is not to remain ideal (elite) and if it is to attain Marxist objectivity, has to include necessarily the idiographic failure of the revolutionary class as well as the more subjective task of realising and announcing *where* in the multifarious sites of complicity of groups failing to act 'in conformity to interests corresponding truly to their own social being' the historian's own alternative discourse is emerging. Is it any wonder that the Indian historian's ability is being tested to the limit where the cognate difficulties of producing an history dominated by the influence of colonialism, communalism and nationalism begin to intrude even before a single statement is produced? These 'given modalities' or pre-figurative instances of intelligibility when writing Indian historiography are about having to acknowledge, first, the historical reality of British rule (colonialism), second, sectarian divisions that are 'pre-colonial' or 'pre-political' in origin, including pre-Mughal and Mughal rule (communalism) and last, the epistemological rules governing the formation of a modern nation-state (nationalism).

Indian historiography, perhaps more than any other national tradition, is the generic comparison of modalities: no matter how complex the minutiae of personalities, texts, practices and events, for Indian historians, these interpretations are all necessarily to be governed by implications that are 'superstructural' in order. The historical masterpiece, to use White's phrase, in Indian historiography is not guaranteed until the historian subjects their material to an interpretation that is kinetic and related to these configurations. This dynamic feature of interpretation for Indian historiography is the conflict between colonialism, communalism and nationalism. The net effect of having to subject every interpretation to the ever-moving configuration of modular influences or a conflict between colonialism, communalism and nationalism is that even the most basic epistemological categories of analysis have to problematised: '"Europe" and "India" are treated ... as hyperreal terms in that they refer to certain figures of the imagination whose geographical referents remain somewhat indeterminate.'[131] The sceptical tenor of postcolonial historiography is a conscious reflection of the preceding investigative modalities of colonial knowledge. In this sense, the epistemological modes of Indian historiography are all essentially 'idiographic'. These modalities – historiographic, observational, enumerative, museological – while 'quite general' in orientation (civilisational), were specific in their aim: 'History in its broadest sense was a zone of debate over the ends and means of [British] rulership in India.'[132] A modern Indian historiography – that is, a postcolonial historiography – is typified either by the impulse to discover 'selfish group-ends' hidden beneath the transition of sovereignty among elites ('Animal Politics') or a critique of both colonialism and its obverse, nationalism, especially from the microcosmic perspective of peasant groups.[133] This is the 'mechanistic' character of radical historiography. These commentaries on the national past do not concern themselves with restoring historical objectivity in the aesthetic terms conceived by Jameson or, more importantly, with the universal anarchism beneath the transition of productive modes in the Indian case. Having said this, Hayden White's meticulous insight into the uses to which iteration may be put in order to account for the meaning of an event in and for history apparently has been instrumental in Ranajit Guha's formulation of the relationship between Indian and English histories. Despite the anarchism implicit in the Romanticist recovery of *the* Indian past, historiography requires formal coherence. White's programmatic idea of the 'pastness' of the present helps us to understand how subaltern historiography characterises the dialectical relationship between dominance and subordination where Indian and English histories are said to cohere around an organising *telos*. Guha names literature alongside historiography as the principal instrument for the way in which a national past is syncretically reclaimed for modernity.[134] White states:

> There does, in fact, appear to be an irreducible ideological component in every historical account of reality ... the very claim to have discerned some kind of formal coherence in the historical record brings with it theories of the historical world and of the historical knowledge itself which have ideological implications for attempts to understand 'the present', however this 'present' is defined.

Commitment to a particular *form* of knowledge, White contends, is indispensable for either 'legitimately' changing our present or maintaining it 'indefinitely' as a reflection of the past world.[135] Whither Cohn's confidence in the valid use of the past now?

Let me summarise our progress. The singular if complex elements in the analytical distinction between history and narrative do not allow for the kinds of pure possibilities of which Lyotard dreamt. Orature and other forms of narrative knowledge in traditional (a euphemism for 'primitive') societies, when they come into contact with a systematic will for objectivity, instantly become politicised. The speculations of the Enlighteners about the relationship between the individual mind and the succession of events comprising the past showed this. The syntactical or as White would say the Synechdocal features of emplotment in the fictive-folkloric are a reflection of the hierarchical social organisation of groups. More simply, the process of adapting reality into narrative form is the means by which mystification to maintain this hierarchical social organisation comes about. Nevertheless, history here meets the universal human need to narrate; it is concomitant with sociality in the anthropological sense. Alasdair MacIntyre notes the indispensable role that narrative plays in the formation of sociality; 'man is in his actions and practice, as well as in his fictions, essentially a story-telling animal'.[136] MacIntyre's conventional idea of 'virtue' in this context essentially means conjuring up 'the vision of the polis, a determinate political community institutionalising the practices, goals, and tradition of a moral community'. It is also the prerequisite of imperialist expansion. Despite earlier enthusiasm for Foucault's conception of resistance as 'an insurrection of subjugated knowledges', Chatterjee's comments on this conventional wisdom expressed by MacIntyre represent an attempt to endorse a perspective that we would critically describe as 'nativist', 'the fact that by its very nature, the idea of community marks a limit to the realm of disciplinary power'. In more polite terms, this is Gandhian. He goes on to conclude: 'My hypothesis, then, is that an investigation into the idea of the nation, by uncovering a necessary contradiction between capital and community, is likely to lead us to a fundamental critique of modernity from within itself.'[137] I am trying to achieve the same conclusion by examining the modality of historiography. Chatterjee is now conforming to Gellner's problematic. A critique of nationalism on these lines is now about capitalism without class. The communitarian ideal is the vital realm where the individual discovers their own essential mark of cultural identity.

Hayden White's formulation as it emerges in his generic distinction between history and narrative will help us to understand more clearly how some of the profounder issues such as 'otherness' or alterity still play a fundamental role in postmodern defences of historiography. Let us look at a specific instance in White's reflections on the problematic of narrative in historiography. Even where it is arguably absent, the chief metaphor of the civic imagination, the *polis*, finds itself recurring as the minimum of historical consciousness. A *kind* of realism which 'a disciplined historical knowledge' is said to conduce, White asserts, ought to function as a guiding principle for the disinterested intellect, one which *may* ultimately be impossible to reproduce in a value-free way but nevertheless helps him to remain 'against revolutions, whether launched from "above" or "below" in the social hierarchy and whether directed by leaders who profess to possess a science of society and history or be celebrators of political "spontaneity"'.[138] In the context of these remarks, Guha's choice of White to characterise subaltern historiography in terms which the latter sketched in *Metahistory* seems incongruent. Surely, White would refuse to extend his blessings to the political project as conceived by Guha? This is the customary liberalism of the pragmatic tradition whose original proponents, like Auerbach, still had the ability to maintain a tenable humanist vision. White takes the interrupted recording of an event for his example, the repulsion of a Saracen force by Gaulish knights in a three-hundred-year-long chronicle, 'Annals of Saint Gall', from the eighth century CE. The Christian *mythos*, White asserts, is not the natural context for all narrative in this society; it is, if you like, not its defining formulaic constraint. 'The calendar locates events', he notes, 'not in the time of eternity, not in *kairotic* time, but in chronological time, in time as it is humanly experienced.' This is why the chronicle is a more plausible instrument by which we might glean the life of community in the Dark Ages since the demise of the classical era with the fall of Rome. However, this narrative conformity is impossible, White ventures, 'since there is no central subject about which a story could be told'.[139] This is an obvious practical consideration. White goes on to assert how the maintenance of the narrative component in historiography is also a reflection of how robust the social order is. This is no longer about the technical capability of historical narrative to represent reality. The fact that the annalist has failed to record the outcome of Charles' battle with the Saracens at Poitiers in 725 is of singular importance to White. This minimum still appears in the description of a skirmish eleven years earlier with the Saxons who, the chronicle simply notes, were driven out of Aquitaine. The lack of narratological detail in this text interests White because it defies our expectations of historicism. We are tantalised by the omission.

In anthropological terms, narrative gives events 'regularity and fullness' and the absence of it or a central subject reflects the periodic economy of scarcity which must have afflicted groups in this society. This is again a tenet of Nietzschean thinking. White goes on to say how a narrative-rich history can only happen with the 'notion of a social centre by which to locate [events] with respect to one another and to charge them with ethical or moral significance'.[140] This point of view explains White's hostility to the thesis of the death of the subject, propounded in the least phenomenological, historicist way by Foucault. Narrative, in other words, is the defining form of community. The chaotic stream of events produced by interminable and internecine conflicts among this relatively 'tribal' collection of individuals can only be ordered into ethical or moral significance by a narrating centre of consciousness. It does not take much to interpret these observations about narrativity in historiography in a conservative frame. We are returning to a similar operation for historiography to the one Jameson argued for more generally for the rest of society. Narrative is the conservative function for historiography and, White claims, this is indispensable: 'It is the absence of any consciousness of a social centre that prohibits the annalist from ranking the events he treats as elements of a historical field of occurrence.' Let us examine this conclusion more closely. If we look at the nominal entries made by the annalist, this view isn't quite accurate. The annalist does perform the task of diachrony in the list by placing each event in a temporal sequence. The sequence may be inaccurate, but to suggest that the entries fail to meet the basic syntagmatic function of historical discourse is simply wrong.

What lies behind White's assertions about the scarcity of narratological detail in 'Annals of Saint Gall', the issue of 'ranking', has more to do with the a priori teleology of Christian narrative that he outwardly denied had any relevance to his interpretation (Creation, Fall, Incarnation, Resurrection, Second Coming). However, we see how this teleology informs his interpretation in the odd humanist language he uses. If the annalist lacked piety, the historian will supply the deficit in his 'intention to deal in real rather than ideal events'. The desire for historicity as something more than an organising principle for this fragile Celtic community who, like us, experience chronological time 'humanly' goes along with all manner of assumptions about what constitutes a harmonious social order; it is signalling some of the reasons why these Gauls were vulnerable to attack from their neighbours and, more controversially of course, from those more alien others of Christendom, the 'Saracens'. This analysis more generally symbolises the kind of representative fear about the value of historiographic knowledge; it is not just about the scarcity of evidence when attempting to reconstruct past societies. This is the fear that historiography might degenerate into *Gesellschaft*. In other words, it is having to face the implacable fact that there are some discursive practices that actually escape historiography. Why else would the historian-theorist feel the need to appeal to the specifically 'human' dimension in the production of historical knowledge? Why is this not a self-evident fact?

Indian historians as well as nationalists have responded in a variety of ways to the epistemological challenges that Foucault's observations represent. The stability of the Indian social order did not imply – as it did for nationalists (I will return to this point) – an epistemological revolution in the interpretation of institutions. Why is this the case? I want to turn to a theoretical description of the problematic status of historiography as narrative that will help to answer this question. This account informs my investigation of the modalities that determine a specifically Indian historiography.

In the new combination that emerges, Lyotard tells us, 'the name of the hero is the people' and 'the sign of legitimacy is the people's consensus, and their mode of creating norms is deliberation'. This more democratic arrangement in the revolutionary nineteenth century sounds appealing. History has a specific investment in this constellation. Why then does this combination present a threat to historiography? After all, is not history's objective to investigate the changing forms of this constellation over time? The essential work of the historian is to analyse the peculiar conditions that determine the deliberative or normative form society takes. Here the narratological, the folkloric, the human cultural attitude on the one hand and, on the other, the 'new scientific attitude' make inquiring into the 'sociopolitical legitimacy' of authority conform to a particular mode. Lyotard states the cost of this conformity as follows:

> It is clear that what is meant ... by the 'the people' is entirely different from what is implied by traditional narrative knowledge, which ... requires no instituting deliberation, no cumulative progression, no pretension to universality; these are the operators of scientific knowledge. It is therefore not at all

surprising that the representatives of the new process of legitimation by 'the people' should be at the same time actively involved in destroying the traditional knowledge of peoples, perceived from that point forward as minorities or potential separatist movements destined only to spread obscurantism.[141]

How can the recuperative task of historiography remain free of the pressures Lyotard describes above? In other words, how do the 'operators of scientific knowledge' intrude into historical discourse and arrange its elements? The figurative form of the ideological process that institutionalises or preserves the content of history in the vigorous way Lyotard is describing above is more ordinarily known as nationalism. There is an inverse relationship here between society and the individual when it comes to historical discourse. Lyotard again: 'The State resorts to the narrative of freedom every time it assumes direct control over the training of the "people," under the name of the "nation," in order to point them down the path of progress.'[142] This conclusion is the ironic germ within the Enlightener's social imagination. The expediency of training the people by the bourgeoisie assumes an infringement of the ancient privileges bestowed upon the villein by feudal service.

Guha identified the epistemological problems facing a specific school of Indian historiography. The latent tensions in this history of nationalism become readily perceptible in the context of Lyotard's conclusions about the use of nationalist narrative by the emergent postcolonial state. We can explore how these problems in historiography relate to the social uses of history and, more specifically, to the interpretive or essentially discursive modes of Indian historiography and their relationship to ideological nationalism. Can historiography resist the intrusion of competing 'secular' discourses like nationalism? Without specifically stating it, Lyotard is describing the new conditions of possibility for historiography. Lyotard has already made up his mind when it comes to the reinvention of historical narrative as a valid epistemological form, 'depending on whether it represents the subject of narrative as cognitive or practical, as a hero of knowledge or a hero of liberty ... Because of this alternative, not only does the meaning of legitimation vary, but it is already apparent that narrative is *incapable* of describing that meaning adequately.'[143] It is only in relation to the state in the Lyotardian sense of 'the people' as nation that one can feasibly talk about anarchic, conservative, radical and liberal tendencies. The volumes in the medieval source *Monumenta Germaniae historia* from which White takes his Gaulish chronicle are each inscribed with the following Latin: *Sanctus amor patriae dat animum* (The sacred love of the fatherland animates us).

Any individuals who believe they are lucky enough to escape the more violent operations of the complete penetration of capital into the previously free domains of Nature, the Unconscious and Third World agriculture, in a modern world where *amor patriae* is generic false consciousness, do so at the risk of inhabiting a psychological realm of anomic depthlessness and a waning of affect.[144] After White's problematic assertions of the historical consciousness and Gellner's quasi-functionalist account of transition in modes of production, whatever our view of a claim for Third World agriculture as an analogy for the others, Jameson's criticism of postmodernism as the new cultural dominant of late capitalism is a compelling argument.[145] Who else would have characterised the near universal reluctance among social scientists and lay folk alike of comprehending the social form as totality (the class 'subject' is intended but historicity is implied) to the premature drawing to a close of the 'American century' (1945–1973 oil crisis)? This portends the fusing together of the superstructural elements with the base – the constituent antagonisms that formed the Marxian topography of capital. The totality that Jameson thinks ought to be abstracted from the sum of relations is not Hegelian, i.e. intellectual-idealist, but Marxist or materialist. In Althusserian terms, the discrete elements of any social formation (he called them Ideological State Apparatuses) – or the religious, the ethical, the legal ideology of institutions – collapse into each other; specificity, the individual or the monad begins to emerge as an illusory category as the basic processes determining the totality of relations become uniform: pure universality in the absence of particularity. This is the artificial form which the bourgeoisie insists had been an essential to humankind even before the beginning of civilised life. The opacity of the dynastic past in chronicles and annals is due to the absence of this individualism. We discover our objectivity by inviting what Marx in context called 'the sentiment of a heartless world' and by merely surviving in our 'soul of soulless conditions'.[146] In Jameson's modernist diagnosis – which White ostensibly shares – this crystallisation of identity signals the fragmentation of subjectivity. Whatever else the limits of the subaltern school of Indian historians, this logic of the postmodern is quite absent. The specific tonality of a predominant mode Marx thought was perceptible, the 'particular ether which determines the specific gravity of every being which has materialized within it', in the postmodern explanation of things, becomes both absolute and bland.[147] This conception may apply to art as a form of social production but not for social production itself. The original metaphoric rendering of this metaphoric reality can be found in the following famous passage describing the logic of capitalistic expansion into the backward zones:

> All fixed, fast-frozen relations, with their train of ancient and venerable prejudices and opinions are swept away, all new-formed ones become antiquated before they can ossify. All that is solid melts into air, all that is holy is profaned, and man is at last compelled to face with sober senses, his real conditions of life, and his relations with his kind.[148]

This disruptive intrusion of capital and all its momentous consequences for non-Western societies, *including the discursive construction of the nation-state*, now becomes apparent. How does this event take place? According to Jameson's interpretation of the same theoretical moment described above, Indian society would form an exception to this development; this is in addition to the near-pathological complexity of defining ideology as a '"Representation" of the Imaginary Relationship to Their Real Conditions of Existence' that I began with.[149] What is curious about late capitalism as opposed to its earlier manifestation in history is that the nostalgia for totality is equivalent to the *Agraria* of traditional rather than historical societies (in Cohn's terms). For Marx, the individual emerges as a sort of legal fiction coeval for the first time with the emergence or at least universal prevalence of the capitalist mode in the eighteenth century. Marx states the pathological milieu which Althusser delineates for 'subjectivity' in the following historical terms:

> Only in the eighteenth century, in 'civil society', do the various forms of social connectedness confront the individual as a mere means towards his private purposes, as external necessity. But the epoch which produces this standpoint, that of the isolated individual, is also precisely that of the hitherto most developed social (from this standpoint, general) relations.[150]

This is the pragmatic ideal, transplanted to Indian soil in the form of colonial acquisitiveness, challenged by Gandhi's *Hind Swaraj*. The indigenist attack on the concerted efforts of this enterprise, 'the bane of civilisation' resembling a dream in which man believes he is consciously awake, Gandhi writes, is designed to make the contradiction between individualism as self-interest and the health of society more salient. And it is not just the health of Indian society that is at stake from the disease of civilisation.[151] This is the most appealing form of Gandhi's conviction that colonialism is bad for societies; the alternative oceanic vision of social order is an advance. For the ancient past, however, one must resist interpreting the Vedic institution of social order as if it represented the organic totality of any particular community. The further back we go into history, the vaguer seems to be this sense of factors inhibiting the productive capacities of the individual. The problem of individuation in colonised society is given a bourgeois cast by Dipesh Chakrabarty, and I will examine his various anthropological answers to the question of who speaks for Indian pasts in the third chapter. Suffice it to say that capital today is the recognisable means – or, in Hegel's terms for the state, the *material* form – in which all the hitherto immature and incremental forms of the spirit of ages past (Oriental, Greek, Germanic, Christian) realise themselves as the content of history:

> the reality within which the individual has and enjoys his freedom, but only in so far as he knows, believes in and wills the universal. This, then, is the focal point of all the other concrete aspects of the spirit, such as justice, art, ethics, and the amenities of existence.[152]

The realisation of capital, as with historical process itself, was not indigenous to India, like linen; it came to Indians 'as a finished artefact without autonomous beginnings'.[153] The obstacle to its emergence, according to Weber, was the economic traditionalism of Hindu life. What Weber celebrates, Gandhi deplores. The Gandhian ideal of *Ramrajya*, the patriarchal order in which each individual feels himself part of the oceanic social reality of the nation, is threatened by the aggressive individualism of the colonial regime. I want to quote the often-read passages from *The Communist Manifesto* at length because they help us to explain the

Historiography and narrative   45

peculiar predicament of an Indian nationalism. The objective is liberation from the colonial regime conducted in the most 'up to date' bourgeois terms and yet, at the same time, this endeavour is in conflict with the 'ancient and venerable' modes of the past that constitutes the patrician legacy of cultural authenticity. For Gandhi, the latter can only be revived by a return to the indigenous modes of small-scale production. Gandhi's vision of the obstacles meeting *Hind Swaraj* conforms exactly to Marx and Engels' explanation, with one major difference. They write how:

> [t]he bourgeoisie has through its exploitation of the world market given a cosmopolitan character to production and consumption in every country ... All old-established national industries have been destroyed or are daily being destroyed. They are dislodged by new industries, whose introduction becomes a life and death question for all civilized nations, by industries that no longer work up indigenous raw material, but raw material drawn from the remotest zones; industries whose products are consumed, not only at home, but in every quarter of the globe. In place of the old wants, satisfied by the productions of the country, we find new wants, requiring for their satisfaction the products of distant lands and climes. In place of the old local and national seclusion and self-sufficiency, we have intercourse in every direction, universal inter-dependence of nations. And as in material, so also in intellectual production. The intellectual creations of individual nations become common property. National one-sidedness and narrow mindedness become more and more impossible, and from the numerous national and local literatures, there arises a world literature ... The bourgeoisie, by the rapid improvement of all instruments of production, by the immensely facilitated means of communication, draws all, even the most barbarian, nations into civilization. The cheap prices of its commodities are the heavy artillery with which it batters down all Chinese walls, with which it forces the barbarians' intensely obstinate hatred of foreigners to capitulate. It compels all nations, on pain of extinction, to adopt the bourgeois mode of production; it compels them to introduce what it calls civilization into their midst, i.e., to become bourgeois themselves. In one word, it creates a world after its own image.[154]

One of the most attractive but by no means certain prophecies about the promiscuous movement of capital in the *Manifesto* is that chauvinism becomes untenable; the revolutionising of communication makes it ever more impossible for regimes to maintain their isolation from the capitalist order and, it has to be said, great hopes lie with this part of the description of the process as far as the implacability of the Chinese wall is concerned. E. M. S. Namboodripad speaks with a representative voice for Indian Marxists when it comes to the benefits of the timely destruction of indigenous society:

> [S]ince there was no internal force which could destroy the stagnant and decaying old society, the external force that appeared on the scene, the European trading bourgeoisie who came to India in the 15th and 16th centuries, particularly

the most modern and powerful of them, the British trading-cum-industrial bourgeoisie, were the 'unconscious tools of history'. Marx the revolutionary therefore did not shed a single tear at this destruction, though with his deep humanism and love for the people, he had nothing but sympathy for the Indian people who were undergoing – and hatred for the British who were inflicting – immense suffering on them.[155]

The eminent General Secretary of the Communist Party of India-Marxist goes on to assert the boon which colonisation brought to a caste-bound society where the eternal ritual form of existence in the self-sufficient Indian village was destroyed as it became 'a part of the growing world capitalist society'. Even if Marx's knowledge of the material minutiae of the Indian social order was deficient – its static agrarian economy, the hydraulic state founded on the small dam, shallow wells and communal pond built by co-operative labour, its unequal and limited distribution of land as property, and so on – England's role as the 'unconscious tool of history' in bringing a revolution in the social state of Asia remained incomplete because of an essential flaw in the original project, a 'profound hypocrisy and inherent barbarism of bourgeois civilisation'.[156] One of the more colourful instances of the East India Company's governing board and their policy of pragmatism concerning the inviolable culture of Hindu India is in stark contrast to the image Namboodripad conveys, where the evangelising mission 'of the early European trading companies', presumably by Jesuit missionaries at Akbar's court in the sixteenth century, 'and the subsequent measures adopted by the British rulers to establish educational institutions in order to create a stratum of educated employees of the company, led to the development of a language and literature which was as popular in style as the earlier Bhakti works, but free from the limitations of the latter which was, by and large, confined to Hindu society and culture'.[157] Foreign capitalism aided the dissolution of an anachronistic, caste-ridden Indian society, according to this interpretation, and even if we do not spend time questioning either the plausibility of the claim that the British were busy creating a stratum that would disseminate cultural forms that reflect the heterogeneity of native Indian society as well as, more oddly, in typical Whig fashion, of ascribing a function of reform when it comes to the preceding native administration, I do not think that Marx would go as far as saying that British colonialism liberated India from the regressive aspects of Hindu culture. Indeed, Marx argued the opposite about their pecuniary objectives:

> While they combated the French revolution under the pretext of defending 'our holy religion,' did they not forbid, at the same time, Christianity to be propagated in India, and did they not, in order to make money out of pilgrims streaming to the temples of Orissa and Bengal, take up the trade in the murder and prostitution perpetrated in the temple of Juggernaut? These are the men of 'Property, Order, Family, and Religion'.[158]

This conclusion, on the face of it, seems typical of a point of view where 'the collective Orient' predominates over the particularity of 'existential human identities'.[159] However, as we saw with Marx's statements in *Grundrisse* concerning the emergence of individualism in the eighteenth century, his concern with the obstacles capitalism faced in the Asiatic mode of production, I agree, do not represent, like the pilgrims engaging in degenerate practices, 'a precollective, preofficial individuality in Asia' – one which Marx identified with momentarily, authentically, only to surrender it when it came across the stock of prejudices (Said calls it 'vocabulary') constituting Orientalist science, Orientalist lore, Orientalist art. Marx's letter to Danielson in 1881 concerning the annual export of commodities to Britain whose value exceeds the total income of sixty million 'of agricultural and industrial labourers of India', as well as the rent, dividends for 'railways useless for the Hindoos, pensions for the military and civil servicemen, for Afghanistan and other wars, etc., etc,.' is summed up as 'a bleeding process with a vengeance'. Ahmad concludes:

> Between the dispatch of 1853 from which Said quotes and the letter of 1881 cited above, there had also been – in terms of chronology – the great Rebellion of 1857 ... it is worth recalling that [Marx] declared it a 'national revolt' and welcomed it as part of what he took to be a great Asian upheaval, indicated to him by the Taiping Rebellion, against Europe – which was certainly more than what was said by the whole of the emergent modern intelligentsia of Bengal, which remained doggedly pro-British.[160]

Benjamin's fifth and sixth theses reflect the anxiety of the process adumbrated in the *Communist Manifesto*. The bourgeois revolution in values pits itself against the Messianic voice of the historian. The wresting away of tradition 'from a conformism that is about to overpower it' is a precarious skill because the prophetic voice of the historian is 'lost in a void the very moment he opens his mouth'.[161] How is it lost? The danger that the historian must avoid at all costs if he is to capture the fleeting 'true picture of the past' is of 'becoming a tool of the ruling classes'. This was the historical failure of the legatees of 'Reform', of the modern intelligentsia of Bengal of whom Namboodripad was so proud. This is the problem that Ranajit Guha identified in his dialectical interpretation of Indian historiography. For Gandhi, as we will see below, the inevitability of technological revolution spells disaster for Hindu civilisation. In contrast, Nehru's idea of Indian civilisation concludes that the elements of transformation Gandhi feared have *always* been incorporated into Indian life without any fatal disruption to the universal tendency towards progress. For Nehru, the greatest danger to the realisation of modernity is the violence of British imperialism; for Gandhi, this violence is entirely consistent with modernity itself.

As if illustrating the disease by its symptom, Jameson's concluding observations in pastiche, about the relativism of postmodern historiography, warn against the ludic and group-insular reinvention of the past: 'The new free play with the past, however – the delirious non-stop monologue of its postmodern revision into so many in-group narratives – is obviously equally allergic to the priorities and commitments, let alone the responsibilities, of the various tediously committed kinds of partisan history.' Jameson, the aesthetician, cannot resist citing the creative energies of this 'fantastic historiography' which, in its promiscuity, is incapable of delivering the kind of *marxisant* judgement on the totality of relations that Gandhi and Nehru worked with in their visions of a liberated India but resembles instead 'the dynastic annals of small-power kingdoms and realms very far from our own parochial "tradition" (the secret history of the Mongols, for example, or well-nigh extinct Balkan languages which were once the dominant power in their little universe)'.[162] It is unclear whether, if at the end of Time when we have all passed through the homogenising process of the capitalist mode, citizens will realise their potential according to a particularity of their own choosing, Mongolian or Balkan.

2 The historical sense

> The narrative function is redeeming in itself ... The little stories received and bestowed names. The great story of history has its end in the extinction of names (particularisms). At the end of the great story, there will simply be humanity.
>
> Jean-François Lyotard[1]

> The past carries with it a temporal index by which it is referred to redemption.
>
> Walter Benjamin[2]

Introduction

If only history were to remain diligently mimetic in describing how things really were in the past; if Clio were to remain content as the recording angel for humankind, history could avoid giving the impression that it is teleological in the sense noted by the *Oxford Concise Dictionary* as an 'explanation of phenomena by the purpose they serve rather than by postulated causes'. How else, if not by being scientific about events in the human past, by postulating causes rather than being purposive, can history perform its time-honoured function as a moral discourse for our modern age? This definition is important for our examination of the difficulty that Indian historiography has in keeping its explanations about the past according to postulated causes rather than to the 'subterranean' purposes that these might be said to serve. How might the problems in historical interpretation relate to the definition adapted above? This conclusion would include those statements that posit the ideological nature of all historiography. Historiography is ideological in the sense of a limited case. More universally, all narratives are explanations of phenomena by the purpose they serve rather than by the postulated causes. This is what makes narrative a cultural activity. In other words, postulated causes can never be value free. There is no such thing as a value-neutral explanation of reality. This is the postmodern position about the ideological nature of historiography, simply put. The causes of this value neutrality, we might argue, are themselves an expression of *specific* interpretation: 'Possibly no social formation we know of has so systematically eradicated intrinsic value from its culture so much as liberal market capitalism, not through choice, but through the "cultural logic of late-capital".[3] This is in the spirit of the Marxian orthodoxy I have been presenting, but there is a problem in describing *a* logic as cultural yet possessing no purposive element of the kind by which we ordinarily understand cultural activity. The Indian history we have briefly considered asserts that historiography is not free from complicity with this logic. Historical narratives are narratives about culture and they *are* culture. And the uses to which historiography is put is ethical because it is a teleological narrative. In this sense, historiography *is* capable of describing the social formation in deliberative terms. If it were not, categories like 'liberal market capitalism' and 'late-capital' would fail to register as historical typologies. Capitalism is not only historicised but is now a new sociological type: late versus early capitalism, liberal market capitalism as opposed to state-sponsored or nationalised market capitalism. In between elation and despair stands J.-F. Lyotard's original recommendation of a scientific solution, of 'paralogical' thinking and 'heteromorphous' language games, even as he signals the obsolescence of classical didactics and narrative (including history), and where in Foucauldian spirit, if not substance, he asserts how the functionaries of the state/company, '[s]cientists, technicians, and instruments are purchased not to find truth, but to augment power'.[4] In his own anthology of speculations that constitute theses on the philosophy of history, Lyotard describes how the mythical impulse *could have* saved 'a German identity sick from its "historical belatedness," from defeat and from economic crisis'.[5] The Final Solution with its attendant cynicism ('Nazi cynicism') regarding the reality of the gas chambers whose victims cannot logically testify to the chambers' existence, and the parodic element of bringing the immensity of the crime before the irrational, implacable rigour of law that always establishes truth-claims through a series of negations are both symptomatic of decadence.[6] How might myth release us from the spell of the technocrat whose unwitting aim is to establish power? We return to Benjamin's formulation in the *Theses* where, despite the fact that the 'Identificatory force of myth is not debatable', 'a sick person does not get better by looking in the mirror'.[7]

History and the myth of science

There have been perennial attempts in European thinking to establish history-writing according to the absolutism of science. I want to examine these recommendations in a more innocent age, a time when it was still possible to consider history in terms of discovering the truth. This function lay parallel to the activity of augmenting power for the early European modern, an enterprise described with ruthless 'objective' candour in Machiavelli's treatise, *The Prince*. Propositions have been made, as we saw in the survey above, not always by historians, which deal with the nature of historiography as it has hitherto been practised and as it *ought* to be practised. This effort is sometimes about marshalling the complexity of the past geometrically, 'but with greater reality, just as the orders of human affairs are more real than points, lines, surfaces, and figures'.[8] I want to draw some solid lines of exposition in my examination of the relationship between history, narrative forms more generally and the attempt to model historiography according to the standards of objectivity in science. Let us look more closely at Giambattista Vico's method for a new historiography. This method is as idiosyncratic as the formulations in Benjamin, and perhaps it is no wonder that both writers in their lifetimes remained at the margins of all that was intellectually fashionable. Vico still needed to invoke the sobriety of Providence to help his criterion for interpreting the past, namely that *'whatever all or most people feel must be the rule of social life'*.[9] That the intuitive life of people in the past ought to be the foundation of historical inquiry seems a familiar tenet to us but it marked a radical transition in the realm of ideas about the function of historiography. For the first time since Herodotus, the staple of stories that ancient cultures told themselves were revealed to be the material base rather than a merely exotic and skewed reflection of reality to be surpassed by more sophisticated versions of knowledge as civilisations came into closer contact with each other. Williams traces the genealogy of the concept 'culture' from Vico by Herder, dismissing the conflict between the latter's Romantic view of 'organic' peoples and nations with the 'external universalism' of the Enlightenment, concluding that Herder's definitive contribution consists of the idea of a 'fundamental social process' which shapes specific and distinct 'ways of life'.[10] This benign interpretation belies the force of Nature as an analogy for human evolution. The differentiating of cultures according to the development of 'innate psychological peculiarities' in each of them 'is fatal to a true understanding of history'.[11] This is because Herder's Organicist conception of human history is not about contrasting the modalities – economic, political, social – of 'say, medieval and Renaissance culture, but of non-historical differentiations like that between a community of bees and ants'. Collingwood concludes:

> Human nature has been divided up, but it is still human nature, still nature and not mind; and in terms of practical politics this means that the task of creating or improving a breed of domestic animals. Once Herder's theory of race is accepted, there is no escaping the Nazi marriage laws.[12]

It seems that with Vico, the moral function of history, that is, interpreting events in the past as a lesson for the present age, is turning into a more complicated hermeneutical model for understanding the classical age. What is inspirational in Vico's conception of the development of human civilisations is that it remains free of the Organicist fallacy Romantic 'method' of the kind Herder indulges in: '[T]he plan of history is a wholly human plan, but it does not pre-exist in the shape of an unrealized intention to its own gradual realization.'[13] Vico's obscure attention to the mythology of antiquity also says a lot about a will to vitality among the Napolese in the late seventeenth century, as well as revealing a plan for the steady domestication, since the primitive age of Man, of 'thought in powerful surges of violent passion, which is how beasts think'.[14] The labyrinth of ossified remains of just such a history for the kingdom of Naples, a veritable kingdom of the dead, silently waits in the subterranean depths to reclaim any attempt by its citizenry to move all human energy on the bright surface above in a direction according to the dictates of a *'rational civil theology of divine providence'*. This concept of Providence is essentially a disguised form of agency for Vico's New Science; a moral effort or *conatus* – as he puts it – designed to rescue society from two perils: an Epicureanism where 'human affairs are set in motion by the blind collision of atoms' and the 'inexorable chain of causes and effects' that the Stoics identified.[15] This problematic was given its most dense form after Marx by Benjamin in his metanarrative on the philosophy of history, the 'Theses' and, as we have seen, even less reflexive (poetic?) forms of historical interpretation, ones which confidently posit that the stratified dimensions of colonial rule are influenced by this understanding. History is the median development between Epicurean individualism and Stoical *communitas*.

The strategic uses of Indian history examined in this book – politically, imaginatively as well as historically – are all concerned with a goal that has motivated historians from every era since the vague inception of history itself, namely, how to establish an objective view of the past. And some of the historiography I will be looking at also self-consciously proclaims its foundation in the 'irrational' or in the emotive particularity of the past. I want to turn to Johann Herder's reflections on Indian history in his magisterial volume, *Philosophy of the History of Man* (1784). This text contains in embryonic form all the more elaborate epistemologies concerning the origins and form of Vedic culture for nationalist ideology. Herder begins his chapter on 'Hindostan' in his Romantic interpretation of the work of Providence by singling out, like many Europeans before and after him, the division of the 'hindoo nation into four or more casts' and speculates on 'perhaps the most durable government in the World' by the first of these castes, the Brahmins.[16] The rule of the Brahmins has not been established by what Herder calls 'bodily subjugation'. The dominion of the Brahmins over Hindu society reflects how simple societies imitate nature – nature 'that divides trees into branches, people into tribes and families'.[17] Herder's Enlightenment view of human nature under the supervision of the invincible but operating hand of Nature is essentially progressive: '… that the flower of our bud of humanity will certainly appear, in a future state of existence, in a form truly that of god like man which no earthly sense can imagine in all its grandeur and beauty'.[18] A profound self-realisation among the human race remains impossible as long as it remains unimaginable. For Herder, 'plastic Providence' simply *must have* taken the necessary steps, where 'the human spirit is so deeply depressed by the yoke of climate and necessity' to elevate or, as he puts it, to gradually exalt 'inferior powers without their consciousness'.[19] If the natural order of things is to arrive at a providential equity with each other, how does one explain the tenacity of the human race in remaining at an astronomical distance from godlike grandeur and beauty? The answer is typical of the faith held by the *philosophes* in rationality and knowledge. As in Egypt, the monopoly of knowledge or the appropriation of 'almost all political science' by a priestly caste is the natural order of things, because 'wisdom is superior to strength'. What would Collingwood make of this dictum? This monopoly, however, is not benign and the ruling caste of priests, Herder states, 'frequently opposed the enlightening of the people'.[20] What is fascinating in Herder's traditional view is the emphasis on the organic origins of the nation and the People. This reflects the preoccupations of the European bourgeoisie busy revolutionising the nation-state as an instrument of its own hegemony. Herder then moves to a Viconian conception of civilisational development for Indian history (without the latter's acumen) by providing a spurious account of the origin of the Brahmin caste by an ancient king, one 'Crishen'. 'Brama' (Brahma), who invented writing and the arts in Herder's mythology, was 'a vizir' of Crishen (Krishna). The division of ancient Indian society is the work of Brama's son. Crishen established colonies of philosophers and priests on the Ganges, and 'built the town of Bahar for the philosophers'.[21] Herodotus's and the Greeks' knowledge of this arrangement remained a mystery, reaching its limit with some mutilated and obscure relations established concerning these ancient people about 'solitary philosophers living in the manner of talapoins' and 'tales of the Samaneans and Germans on the Ganges, of the division of the people into casts, of their doctrine of the transmigration of souls'. Herder is engaging in an anthropology of this vague land in the classical imagination. These accounts of traditions mutually opaque to each other exist in the ancient Alexander biographers. Arrian recounts Alexander's annexing of one of these gymnosophists – as they were customarily called by the Greeks – to his court. 'Calanus', unlike one Dandamis, the oldest of the ascetics among the naked sages of Taxila, chooses the company of the Macedonian general who, in the end, offers his most unlikely cohort a funerary salute with as much pomp as for any native soldier while the Indian philosopher-warrior climbs his funeral pyre. Alexander's nobility is evident in the scruples he shows in watching Calanus, a friend, climb to his death, an end preferable for the Hindu, Arrian informs us, to a life in perpetual exile from the invigorating soil of his native land.[22] We must not be seduced by this martial display of fraternity between two individuals hailing from different cultures. The subjugation of the Swat Valley in early summer, 327 BCE, and Diodorus's account of the resistance Alexander met there – especially the general's decision to massacre 7,000 mercenaries at Massaga who refused to league with the Greek forces against their own countrymen – represents the spirit of Dandamis's refusal to submit to Alexander's charisma. For Narain, this occasion remains 'really heart-rending' and the 'desperate fight which both men and women gave to meet a glorious death', he continues by quoting from Diodorus' account, that this was an end '"which they would have disdained to exchange for a life of dishonour"'; this dishonour in Arrian's version was the kind Calanus chose for himself by joining Alexander's armies. In contrast, Ambhi at Taxila welcomes Alexander and Hephaestion with a lavish entertainment for three days and the patriotic account of this ancient history continues: '[T]he ambition of the impetuous and aggressive Alexander as well as the brave warrior in him did not wander so far to enjoy stale luxury in the company of cowards and those who did not value freedom.'[23] We will return to this ancient scene as an illustration of how Indian nationalist historiography appropriates events in the distant past in order to achieve the kind of familiarity with mutually opaque traditions that can be described with pathos as 'heart-rending', where conflict is inevitable and the universality to which the narrative genre aspires means engendering a 'human' relationship between narrators and narrates 'from "savage" ("national") narrators and narratees in their particularity and multiplicity'.[24] The outcome of humanising the savage or primitive narrative at the heart of a nationalist paradigm involves a peculiar contradiction. On the one hand, the ethical interpretation reflects a timeless concern for the extinction of peoples and, on the other, a desire to identify with the *glory* of the instance, in this case, personified by the 'brave warrior' in Alexander.

How does Herder meet this challenge? He attempts to figure the particular mentality of Indians. In order to delineate the hold the Brahmins as 'a truly political tribe' have over the minds of the rest of Indian society, Herder adduces his evidence from British officials of the East India Company. Although many parts of the Brahmins' religion 'are extremely troublesome and oppressive, they remain as sacred as the divine laws of Nature, even to the lowest casts'.[25] Any Indians who choose to embrace a foreign religion 'are for the most part only malefactors and outcasts, or poor deserted children'. In contrast: 'All the institutions of Europe float only on the surface of a mind thus profoundly swayed [by the Brahmins].' Herder emphasises the particularity of the Indian/Hindu social order: '... for no people are endowed with more quiet patience, and gentle docility of mind'. This docility is all due to the habit of obedience to the precepts of the Brahmin religion inculcated into the Hindu from birth; it occupies 'his whole mind, and employs his whole life, as to leave no room for any other'. Explaining the durability of the Vedic conception of society, Herder remarks how at first it must have been a good thing. How could it have endured for so long and penetrated so deeply into human consciousness as a way of life had it been inimical to human intelligence? 'The human mind shakes off what is pernicious to it ... and although the hindoo may be capable of bearing more than another, he certainly would never love poison.' Herder continues:

> [T]he Brahmins have formed their people to such a degree of gentleness, courtesy, temperance, and chastity, or at least have so confirmed them in these virtues, that Europeans frequently appear, on comparison with them, as beastly, drunken, or mad. Their air and language are unconstrainedly elegant; their behaviour, friendly; their persons, clean; their way of life simple and harmless. Their children are educated without severity; yet they are not destitute of knowledge, and still less of quiet industry, or nicely imitative art.[26]

The rapturous approval of Brahmin civilisation continues apace. The missionaries report on the 'sound reasoning and benign disposition of the brahmins'. The Hindus do not proselytise or persecute, so 'why should not others allow them the same liberty, and consider them at least as well-meaning people, though misled by the errors of their hereditary traditions?' These traditions and their 'mechanical' transmission of knowledge divided into sciences like astronomy, chronology (history), physic (medicine) and jurisprudence may have been established on discredited grounds or on the ruins of ancient lore but this is adequate to the demands of life the Hindus face. This image of a venerable organic evolution of Hindu life is true because it endures despite 'the oppression of the Mohammedans and Christians'. 'The Mungal [Mughal/Mongolian] yoke' has not succeeded in eradicating the culture of the Hindus. All this so far confirms the typically professional Orientalist species of thinking about Indian pre-history to be found in the mentality of scholar gentlemen like Alexander Dow in his *History of Hindostan* (1770), for whom Indian geography, both physical and human, was a vast field of anthropological evidence of European progress beyond primitive despotism.[27] However, when the ideal picture of a static Sanskritic order turns dark, Herder's interpretation of Indian society grows more interesting. In common with other human institutions, Herder asserts, the functional specialisation of labour in caste society also conceals systematic violence. The confinement of the 'pariars' to the 'basest offices' means the lowest of the 'four or more casts' are 'deprived of the claims of humanity and the rites of religion'.[28] Herder's consternation at this social injustice suffered by the pariah who is no different in appearance from other Hindus, however, gives way to speculation on the origins of this oppression in some orthodoxy in some very distant past that punished the aforementioned 'malefactors and reprobates' but with a rigidity that communicated itself to 'their innocent and numerous descendents [who] have astonishingly submitted'. This historical interpretation of the karmic principle in Hindu life will also inform modern radical interpretations of Puranic history in the *dharma shastras* by B. R. Ambedkar a century-and-a-half later. The vital detail of this radical interpretation of the 'doctrine of metempsychosis' relies on the contemporary concern of discovering evidence for an oppressed people in India's antiquity for the origins of *chaturvarnya* (the four-fold caste system). Herder states: 'Though many reasons are assigned for this abasement, and among others, that the pariars may be a subjugated nation; none of them are sufficiently confirmed by history.'[29] In Herder's Organicist conception of human history, the manifest cruelties of Vedic culture are due to the degrees to which the Brahmin's system fails to conform to Nature. 'Accordingly, a want of sympathy is observed even in the gentle hindoos, which may probably be considered as an effect of their organization'; he goes on to contrast how 'still more of their profound submission to eternal fate; a faith which plunges man into an abyss, and blunts his active feelings'.[30] The precepts of Enlightenment thinking determine Herder's conception of the Hindu social order. In addition to his approval of the *sati* who is compelled to follow her husband into death, Herder's erstwhile celebration of the Hindu civilisation's achievements in astronomy, history, religion and medicine now evaporates because these gifts of knowledge remain 'confined as mysteries to one cast' and this monopoly by the priests is ultimately responsible for the subjugation of the rest of the Hindustanis. The ideal trope of the Utopian imagination, the idea of perfect humanity separated from the travails of brutal history that is an abiding form of the Enlightener's view of human nature, and contrary to Raymond Williams' simple interpretation of a difference between Augustan and Romantic views of culture, now emerges in Herder's interpretation of the reasons *why* Indians were susceptible to colonisation from Europeans 'from whom nothing is remote'. He concludes:

> Happy would it have been for such a peaceful people, to have dwelt on a solitary island, remote from all conquerors: but at the foot of mountains inhabited by those human beasts of prey, the war-like mungals; and near those coasts

abounding with havens, to receive the artful and covetous adventurers of Europe; how could the poor hindoos maintain themselves, and their pacific system? Thus it was with the constitution of Hindostan; it sank under internal and external wars, till at length the maritime power of Europe subjected it to a yoke, under which it is uttering it's [sic] last groans.[31]

The anti-colonial struggles of Third World nationalisms were all predicated on a desire to promote a version of the past that is free of the colonial delineation of events. If Reason rather than divine or 'secularised' Providence was the domain in which capitalist expansion began to modify the cultural forms it came into contact with, then anti-colonial resistance had two paths to pursue. First, nationalist resistance had to appropriate rationality in order to adapt those forms according to the needs of the liberated nation. This is a civic discourse of law and order founded on a very eclectic understanding of the glory of the past civilisation. Second, in dealing with the Enlightenment precepts that gave a spurious legitimacy for the commercial activities of the colonial power, it had to expose the universality of the colonial enterprise as a myth (and hence, nationalism with it). Invariably, it was history that was at stake in these struggles, either as an encumbrance to development and modernisation or as an alternative vision to the monopolising state that continued to appropriate the resources of the people in the interests of elites. Whether the two strategies were deployed mutually or exclusively depended on two factors: the historical phase that colonialism had reached at any particular moment and the violent intensity with which the 'directing will' of the colonising nation had been 'implanted' among the colonised in order to realise its commercial objectives.[32]

Aimé Césaire, while indicting the historians of civilisation or novelists ('it's the same thing', he writes) cites the philosopher Lévy-Bruhl for recanting his law of participation, the conclusion that '[t]he West alone knows how to think; that at the borders of the Western world there begins the shadowy realm of primitive thinking, which, dominated by the notion of participation, incapable of logic, is the very model of faulty thinking'.[33] As we saw with Lyotard, French anthropology was particularly attuned to the order of knowledge in human history and the place that 'myth' was to have in it. Derrida explored the textual condition of this development as 'The Violence of the Letter' back to Rousseau.[34] Even for those Positivists of the newly established science of sociology in France who were unwittingly challenging Lévy-Bruhl's classification of the primitive mentality for current social enterprises, where the prospect of this law of participation dissolving in the face of 'the almost infinite extension of the market' was met with alarm, this process was still worth endorsing, or at least doing nothing about, because it enabled the logical conquest of empirical reality by *metaphor*.[35] Jameson's fastidious judgements about the social value of the literary mode are plausible in this context. For all its concern with social facts, Viconian historiography is not complicit with this development, however much *New Science* might contain allusions throughout to the poetic function of historical interpretation from the 'Homeric' age of primitivism to the ideal of civic order in the present. Césaire notes how the invention of arithmetic and geometry by the Egyptians, of astronomy by the Assyrians, the birth of chemistry among the Arabs, 'the appearance of rationalism in Islam at a time when Western thought had a furiously pre-logical cast to it', are all negligible as mere instances compared to the Europeans' respect for human dignity.[36] But how are ancient myths typical of a pre-logical cast of thought? For Vico, the mystery of the ancients, which the Renaissance celebrated as an emblem of universal dignity for mankind, has to be reducible to the evolution *of the patriarchal nation state*. As we saw above, by the time Herder was deploying the mythology of humanism in his Romantic conception of historical development, this idea had become a veritable fact of nature. In other words, the forms of primitive classification that characterised social hierarchy in human societies were designed to reinforce the unconscious law of participation. It is to Vico's credit to draw our attention to this aspect for the first time. Let us take a typical example to illustrate this insight. Vico interprets the sowing of the serpent's teeth by Cadmus as a foundation myth. The teeth are the wooden teeth of the primitive plough used to sow the earth after clearing the primeval forest. His hurling of a large stone symbolises the hard earth that the heroes' servants attempted to wrest for their own use. Vico continues:

> From the furrows, armed men spring to life. In other words, during the heroic contention over the first agrarian law, the heroes emerge from their estates to assert their dominion. They fight now with each other, as the myth relates, but unite in arms against the rebellious plebeians. The furrows signify the orders in which they unite and by which they form and confirm the earliest cities on the basis of arms. Finally, Cadmus is changed into a serpent, which symbolises the origin of aristocratic senates. The ancient Latins would have said 'Cadmus became the ground,' *Cadmus fundus factus est*. And the Greeks said that Cadmus had changed into Draco, the dragon who wrote laws in blood.[37]

This interpretive procedure that Vico calls 'Epitome of Poetic History' is an early instance in European historiography of an anthropological understanding of textual tradition. We will come across the radical uses of this technique with B. R. Ambedkar when he submits the Puranic tradition to critical scrutiny in modern sociological terms for the origins of *chaturvarnya*. For other commentators, the Vedic past furnishes nationalism with all its foundation myths. V. D. Savarkar's use of the Indian pre-historic past to fashion an exclusive nationalist identity is a similar enterprise. That Savarkar's conception 'Hindutva' conforms precisely to Herder's 'sociological' speculations about the Brahminical past is no accident. For Césaire at least, the present intrudes to contradict the flattering image of humanism that the colonial enterprise adopted in the form of French imperialism in North Africa. Doubtless, the horrors of the Belgian Congo under Leopold and the systematic cruelty in eradicating all indigenous instances of resistance (including the 'lazy' native) that remained an obstacle to the realisation of profit were also envisaged as a great clearing of the primeval forest. This was the place where the Belgian overseer learnt his technique from Arab traders in the past and amputated the hands and limbs of the Congolese natives who dared to be tardy. Marlow expresses the Cadmian impulse, the structure of feeling supplied by 'history', which motivated the pitiless exploitation of labour to realise capital *as* an imperialist adventure in the passive and fertile womb of Nature, in the following terms:

> The conquest of the earth, which mostly means the taking it away from those who have a different complexion or slightly flatter noses than ourselves, is not a pretty thing when you look into it too much. What redeems it is the idea only. An idea at the back of it, not a sentimental pretence but an idea; and an unselfish belief in the idea – something you can set up, and bow down before, and offer a sacrifice to …[38]

Césaire recalls the immensity of violence that this vision of a benign colonial order sought to hide, of *la mission civilisatrice* for the cannibals, dismemberers 'and other lesser breeds':

> But let us move on, and quickly, lest our thoughts wander to Algiers, Morocco, and other places where, as I write these very words, so many valiant sons of the West, in the semi-darkness of dungeons, are lavishing upon their inferior African brothers, with such tireless attention, those authentic marks of respect for human dignity which are called, in technical terms, "electricity", "the bathtub," and "the bottleneck."[39]

As Conrad, Césaire and later, Frantz Fanon's tone in *The Wretched of the Earth* and the principles adumbrated to maintain the Algerian Revolution in *Studies in a Dying Colonialism* all amply testify, these appeals to the glory of African or Asian civilisations in the past constituted a futile attempt to arrest the impulses of capitalism driving European colonialism. If this colonialism, taking its cue from the precepts of revolutions in Europe against traditional despotism in the sixteenth and eighteenth centuries, was a more vigorous reinvention of the past, how is the achievement of ancient societies recorded in Vico's Spinozan tabulation of 'ideal eternal history'? How does Vico's poetic conception of a scientific historiography regard the mythical elements of societies past? The momentous advances in human civilisation are certainly not negligible, but these are no less important than recording the fact that Zoroaster is the first sage in history or that giants existed among early peoples, because of references to natural history in Greek myths as well as from 'physical and natural proofs we find in civil history'; after all, morbid exceptions manifest themselves even in the bright realm of Providence.[40] One of these primeval giants roaming the world was supposed to have originally delivered the central idea of Islam, of monotheism, knowledge of the One God, who replaces the crowds of deities to the inhabitants of the Wadi Hadhramawt before being swallowed whole by the earth. Hud's 'form' is visible along the mausoleum built around the cave he is supposed to have disappeared into in the shape of an outcrop of rock. In the ancient world, history begins through the efforts of types: Herculean heroes and sages. Conflict is inevitable between these warriors of the sWest and the motley group of Zoroasters for the poet archetype who founded the civilisations of the Near East. For Vico, the conceit of scholars has to do with the amalgamation of these types, 'all these many founders', into one: 'And they thrust on this man the philosophical Oracles of Zoroaster, which palm off recent doctrines of Pythagoras and Plato as ancient ones.'[41] The argument is not about excising all the typologies with which the ancients inhabited their experiences of often very alien societies from their own. This intellectual vanity puffed itself up even further by providing a genealogy for the founding of the Greek academy by Orpheus through Hermes Trismegistus in Egypt, the master of a Chaldean named Berosus, who in turn was originally Zoroaster's pupil. This is the moribund realm in which revolution can be precipitated by a queen's voice from inside an idol because, in reality, what is this earth 'but an imperceptible point in the scheme of things' and what are men but 'insects devouring each other upon a tiny speck of dirt'? The nullity of Zadig's being is consistent with the fate of Babylon.[42] It is clear throughout the absurdist vicissitudes of fortune faced by this philosopher-sage-knight that his intelligence is atypical of the Oriental mindset others are benighted with. Voltaire's melancholic hero lectures the Arabians who apparently, instead of being productive, allow the burning of widows on funeral pyres: 'They owed it to Zadig and Zadig alone, to have put an end in one single day to so cruel a custom, and which persisted for so many centuries. And thus did he become the benefactor of Arabia.'[43] The esoteric and the genealogical is an illegitimate variety of Providence: it is the job of historians to dispel this improbable *relation* of ideas, not the ideas themselves. If only Zadig had been truly atypical of the Orientalist mindset, he might have travelled as far as the Ganges where his lesson to degenerate humanity rightly belongs. Historians of this secret explanation for the Hellenic miracle, Vico continues, remain ignorant of the 'sociological' fact of whether these Chaldeans were a tribe, family, an entire people or a nation. In the late nineteenth century, a youthful professor at the University of Basel would still confidently assert to his sparse audience that the true history of a people remains 'an invisible bridge from genius to genius' and the indigenous origins of Greek thinking in Egypt and Asia spelt the *decline* of the philosophical 'type' that the culture was capable of producing: the Eleatic philosophy that adduced immanence in all reality because of the Indians; Heraclitus, because of Iran's Zarathustra; Pythagoras, because of the Chinese; Empedocles, because of the Egyptians and Anaxagoras, because of the Jews.[44] Ambiguities surrounding the relations between different peoples in the ancient world can be cleared up by the application of a principle, Vico states:

> First there were individuals, then whole families, later an entire people, and finally a great nation, on which the Assyrian monarchy was founded. The first wisdom of the Chaldeans lay in the vernacular science of divination, by which they divined the future from the nightly paths of falling stars. Later, it extended to judicial astrology, which is why in Roman law a judicial astrologer was called a Chaldean.[45]

Now we come to understand why the ancient civilisations conquered by the Hellenes were incapable of resistance: it is a question of sociological adaptation. Whether Nietzsche would successfully apply Vico's sociological principle to prove his thesis of decline in the classical age, or whether he would regard it in symptomatic terms of belonging to a contemporary malaise incapable of imagining ancient glories where 'everything else is murky, countless variations in inferior material, copies by unpracticed hands', remains open to debate.[46] The Herculean heroes in Asia Minor, Vico writes, were 'perhaps' regarded as Zoroasters. The task of the *New Science* is to correct the misunderstanding of the ancients: 'The Egyptians' mistaken belief in their own great antiquity sprang from the indeterminacy of the human mind, a property which often causes people to exaggerate immeasurably the magnitude of the unknown.'[47] The new science confronts the magnitude of the unknown essential to mythopoeia, at least until the 'moss and lichens of dogmatic theology' have overgrown and quite obscured the truth of the human condition pronounced by the gnomic Oracle, a truth purveyed by 'narration that only hints at the meaning, not directly proceeding to its goal'.[48] The Macedonian general who ended this dispensation that divided the ancient world into two by inhabiting the archetypal function of both soldier and sage ultimately derived his prowess from the legendary Hercules. In this world, strength is the true manifestation of wisdom. One can only speculate on the analytical uses Aristotle found for the spectacular carnage in the *Iliad*, but it flatters the vanity of the illustrious, world-conquering youth to keep, on his campaigns, under his pillow next to a dagger, a copy of the poem annotated by his tutor.[49] This is not to suggest that the antique world of valour and conquest was entirely absent of moral reflection. Nietzsche describes how the Homeric text with its hexameter already contains an infinite variety of archaic formulations unconsciously assumed as proverbial wisdom by the Greeks – a wisdom that reveals 'ethically conscious thought already long in development'.[50] I doubt whether Vico would have approved of Plutarch's comments concerning the great philosopher's habit of imparting esoteric learning to a select few initiates in addition to the principles of ethics and politics. For those sharing the Viconian criterion but attempting to fashion an empiricism without the aid of Providence or poetry, how relevant it is citing Brahman, Prajapati as 'supreme genera, absolute and pure beings ... mythical figures almost as poor in imagery as the transcendental God of the Christians' is, I imagine, open to conjecture.[51] Nevertheless, we should interpret the following remarks about the displacement of the great still age in which bards sang the origins of their tribe as a theogony in the Viconian spirit – a spirit in which the conquering of political realities by the force of historical *metaphor* was an epistemological necessity. Foucault writes:

> But historical beginnings are lowly: not in the sense of modest or discreet like the steps of a dove, but derisive and ironic, capable of undoing every infatuation. 'We wished to awaken the feeling of man's sovereignty by showing him his divine birth: this path is now forbidden, since a monkey stands at the entrance.' Man originated with a grimace over his future development; and Zarathustra himself is plagued by a monkey who jumps along behind him, pulling his coattails.[52]

This simian menace that checked Zarathustra's progress ought to be magnified by a transformation into Nietzsche's metaphysical solution to the problem of history: the doctrine of Eternal Recurrence. The more scientific historiography can be made to be, the closer we are to the true conditions giving rise to events in the past: such is the idea adopted and repudiated by Nietzsche. The rule of thumb concerning the scientific investigation of the past applies to the interpretation of 'modern' processes like colonialism as well as for the edifying task of documenting the rise and fall of civilisations. Before looking at Indian historiography, therefore, we need to consider how descriptive objectivity about the world, in modern times at least, has come to mean the transformation of a more diffuse historical sense into a science of signs or a 'hard' semiological practice.

This transformation was not a smooth or linear process. It is clear by now that the invention of a regime in historiography that obeys the rules of internal coherency is all too often in conflict with the application of the *very* mode adopted (and subsequently questioned) from historiography itself by the social scientist, namely the production of law-like generalisations. One would have thought that nothing was more straightforward than reproducing the past using all the cognitive resources available to us when analysing the present, even after Newton's *hypotheses non fingo* (I do not forge hypotheses). Slowly, in small incremental steps, History as 'the mother of all the sciences of man', and 'as old as human memory', will assume this task that had been prematurely usurped from her by the other human sciences. After all, like all new ideas, haven't these human sciences eventually failed in comprehending Man in all his infinite complexity by reaching their epistemological limit? Foucault plays great games with the lack of certainty surrounding this limit. Was it inherent in the break from History or did it manifest itself as an essential flaw? By dispelling the illusions of the past to reveal the truth of the human condition, History will overcome the assault made on her by these offspring investigations. The nineteenth century, in which these forms of knowledge matured beyond their infancy as the issue of History, is itself merely the most difficult of passages or streams of time in the evolution of the oldest of new sciences. Only history as the active intelligence of this world is best placed for this work, because it has served a number of vital functions for humankind in the past, as Foucault emphasises, in the West. From the ancient Greek civilisation on, these are:

> ... memory, myth, transmission of the Word and of Example, vehicle of tradition, critical awareness of the present, decipherment of humanity's destiny, anticipation of the future, or promise of a return. What characterised this History ... as opposed to our own – was that by ordering the time of human beings upon the world's development (in a sort of great cosmic chronology such as we find in the works of the Stoics), or inversely by extending the principle and movement of a human destiny to even the smallest particles of nature (rather in the same way as Christian Providence), it was conceived as a vast historical stream, uniform in each of its points, drawing with it in one and the same current, in one and the same fall or ascension, or cycle, all men, and with them things and animals, every living or inert being, even the most unmoved aspects of the earth.[53]

Vico's idea of Epicurean ontology has now become a pretext for Christian Providence. We are reminded how the law 'is a calculated and relentless pleasure', an opportunity 'to delight in the promised blood, which permits the perpetual instigation of new dominations and the staging of meticulously repeated scenes of violence'.[54] The truth of every civilisation to the primitive consciousness is the transformation of the hero into the paterfamilias, of Cadmus, not into the dragon Draco but Draco the Athenian legislator. The substance of history has been characterised in identical terms in Vico's reading of origins. This translation of Epicurean norms for a Christian analogy of existence finds its specific historical expression in the medieval mission to liberate the Holy Land and its more secular shadow, Constantinople. This description of history is the sublime measure of *la mission civilisatrice*. Returning to the relationship between history and the human sciences, all the characteristics defining the content of the latter as irregular domains of knowledge, even before their invention as disciplines, that Foucault interrogates with the encyclopaedic ambition of the Enlightenment *philosophes* – 'Representing', 'Speaking', 'Classifying', 'Exchanging' – as well as the impediments faced by this almost divine ambition from the classical age on, are all to be interpreted as moments in the process of historical becoming. True to the Renaissance humanism that the new epistemologies were *supposed* to have made their break from, Foucault never examines the exterior motivations of the emergent disciplines of economics, biology and philology. He fails to question the enumerating ambition of Europe's gentleman-scholar, one which Césaire and others engaged in anti-colonial resistance, as well as those conscious of their Maghrebi origins, like Derrida, had a particularly immediate conception of through experience. Perhaps we are invited to think that these new sciences unwittingly colonised those absent spaces in the European imagination 'by extending the principle and movement of a human destiny'? Perhaps modernity was only one specific point of origin for this endeavour in history in the West until it encompassed everyone, including insensate Nature? In contrast to Foucault's scrupulous silence over the use of these knowledges by the French Republic, especially in North Africa, the *Annales* school historian Lefebvre boldly asserts how 'the great majority of the earth's population lived and died without suspecting that in one corner of the world, in France, a revolution had occurred which was to leave a spiritual legacy to their descendents'.[55] The Revolution now typifies the spirit of Providence by exalting even those least conscious of their inferiority, with one essential difference: it is not a gradual achievement consistent with the evolution of tradition. What does it matter that the custodians of this legacy, the revolutionaries drafting the Declaration of Rights for the Constituent Assembly committed the sin of omission for a colonial species even as they imagined themselves Lords of Humankind? The Deistic appeal to a Supreme Being in establishing formal equality between men ought to be supplemented by an historic observation, according to Lefebvre's warm paean to the ideals of 1789:

> [I]ndividualism symbolizes European man's impulse to surmount all obstacles and conquer the world, to master nature through knowledge and invention,

ultimately to control his conduct, government, and society. In this sense the new principles defined an ideal – the earthly well-being of man become his own God, a condition slowly drawing near as a reward for centuries of striving.[56]

In one of those protracted hostilities between the European colonial powers, a black Robespierre and a rebellious troop of insurgents enthused by the idea above would be resisted with all the might English constitutionalism could muster in the face of French liberty. Henry Dundas, War Secretary under Pitt, addressing the Commons in a debate against the abolition of slavery, would use a pragmatic line of argument about the dangers to the state, which we would today find familiar. In order to quell rebellions that might harm the plantocracy capitalism upon which England's wealth was founded, he asserts: 'The war in the West Indies on the part of this country was not a war for riches or local aggrandizement, but a war for security.'[57]

The task of making historiography scientific as it penetrates to the heart of spiritual legacies is complicated by two different but related species of methodological inquiry. Historians have to differentiate how faithfully statements reflect the social milieu in which they were produced from the question of their veracity as a pure description of events. This distinction is about analysing the *ideological* nature of history. In this narrow sense, the discursive procedure of historiography becomes a more important consideration than the archaeological function of statements as forms of evidence about what actually happened in the past beyond the veil of ideology. The question is how closely individual instances conform to law-like generalisations that we have discovered (or as Foucault might say, invented) about segments of the human past; hence, the need to re-think historiography as 'a generous series of methodologically reflexive studies of the makings of the histories of post-modernity itself' when the 'epistemological fragility' of history is an opportunity for historians to promote descriptions of the past with many rather than a singular explanation.[58] Instead of sorting the infinite variety of objects according to a sovereign principle of veracity, history must make itself heterogeneous. Peter Novick charts the confused pedagogical climate that such an attempt represents for historiography.[59] The rather prolix phrase 'makings of the histories of post-modernity itself' is nothing more than a tacit acknowledgement that the world of human affairs is more chaotic than the book of Nature. The reflection of human destiny in the mirror of history can never be perfect: we are all aware that perspectives about historical events differ depending on systems of belief, conflicts of interest among social groups, and the evolution of our understanding about social processes and so on. These dilemmas are truisms intrinsic to history, and the interpretive modes of Indian historiography are no exception. Having said this, I want to examine this a priori view of historical practice as having to consider 'the makings of the histories of post-modernity' a little more closely. It will help to explain how history as a cosmic chronology of events or the direction of individuals as atoms in the stream of time by Providence is not only particular to the European imagination.

The methodological issues about the status of historiography as a philosophy of knowledge or the kinds of knowledge it deploys to interpret historical events come into sharp focus when historiography is judged according to the positivism of scientific inquiry – a positivism I described above in terms of 'internal coherency'. According to Foucault, this question arises for history very late after it has formed the staple of biological investigation into the evolution of organisms, the economic interpretation of modes of production, accumulation of capital and fluctuation of prices and lastly, the phonetic and grammatical elements of language according to which it changes *regardless* of the properly historical consequences of migration, trade and wars. History no longer inhabits a realm beyond the sum of human experience as a kind of supervisory gaze adopted by the historian to judge the relative merits of any specific order for its impact upon the world's development. This is why Herder's generalisations about Hindu India analogous to the development of the human race appear to be ahistorical. The Brahmin may be a symbol of the collective conscience of Hindu society, but that does not necessarily mean he is the sole obstacle to the potential of the Indian nation's realising itself in the way Guha and the subaltern historians described, let alone the individual Indian in Deistic terms of godlike grandeur after the European. According to the cosmic chronology of the Stoic Foucault mentions above, 'Plato, at Syracuse, did not become Mohammed'.[60] The kinds of knowledge informing historical investigation may be social, political, ethical and economic (in recognisably modern terms), or more classically, historiography will be typically concerned with the religious, aesthetic or moral aspects of societies in the past. No matter how *passé* this question may seem to be today for some, the problematic status of historiography as a form of scientific knowledge has to do – as Foucault shows – with more than 'historians' relatively cavalier attitude towards theory and introspection'.[61] I want to look at these other reasons.

History as knowledge and sense

Although culminating with him in a particularly rigorous way, the problematic analogy of history with science has a history before Marx. Vico's attempt was an early instance. Waning certainties over the predictive power of law-like generalisations that Jenkins and the postmodernists – an enlightened company of intelligences, indeed – take for granted are themselves derived from the culture of scepticism, prevalent first in seventeenth-century England and then in the long eighteenth century in the rest of Europe. This was a time when the relationship between explanation and prediction had first been given a *socially* and not merely pedagogically decisive significance by, among others, Hobbes and Locke, Comte and Mill, Helvétius and Diderot and Condorcet. For the great minds behind the *Encyclopédie* – d'Alembert, Diderot and so on – the resources of the past are as often contaminating influences on the virginity of the reflecting mind that is comprehending reality as they are a potential guide for a correct understanding of the reality it inhabits. This attitude marked a break from the classicism of the Renaissance. The according of a supernatural value to individualism was entirely new. I will have more to say about this below but I want to cite Marx's famous rejection of the historical sense that he inherited from the French Enlightenment to *criticise* the propagation of the founding myths of the Bonapartist state. Marx famously asserted the stylistic features adopted for the Absolutist state in 1851 as being typical of the original 'bourgeois revolution' carried out by Louis Bonaparte's more illustrious relation, his uncle Napoleon I, in 1799, as follows:

> Men make their own history, but they do not make it just as they please; they do not make it under circumstances chosen by themselves, but under circumstances directly found, given and transmitted from the past. The tradition of all the dead generations weighs like a nightmare on the brain of the living. And just when they seemed engaged in revolutionising themselves and things, in creating something entirely new, precisely in such epochs of revolutionary crisis they anxiously conjure up the spirits of the past to their service and borrow from them names, battle slogans and costumes in order to present the new scene of world history in this time-honoured disguise and this borrowed language.[62]

Marx is identifying the classical modality of the fascist state. There is something comforting rather than salutary in the idea that the upheaval of the social order in which the capacities of humankind come close to destroying it was not an invention of the present, that the yoke of tradition – in Marx's characterisation of it – was also felt keenly enough by those engaging in the revolutionary transformation of this present so these 'godlike' capacities might at last be realised. Tradition is no longer an organic expression, as with Herder, of the particularity of cultures. Marx goes on to describe how this 'world-historical conjuring up of the dead' involves the past as a pretext by the nascent bourgeois class. This class rhetorically reinvents its initiatives ('the conditions under which free competition could first be developed, the parcelled landed property exploited, the unfettered productive power of the nation employed') because it is aware of its mediocrity compared to the glorious past: Rome for the Napoleonic *coup d'état* and in the seventeenth century, Marx concludes, the English under Cromwell and the establishing of bourgeois rule with Puritan allusions to the Old Testament. Once the capitalist revolution had been established, the ideologue of individualism inevitably replaced the prophetic voice of millenarianism, 'Locke supplanted Habakkuk'.[63] This process of deistic transformation as a spurious solution to the hoary problem of sovereignty is beautifully described thus: 'But at the same time, the theory of sovereignty, and the organisation of a legal code centred upon it, have allowed a system of right to be superimposed upon the mechanisms of discipline in such a way as to conceal its actual procedures, the element of domination inherent in its techniques, and to guarantee to everyone, by virtue of the sovereignty of the State, the exercise of his proper sovereign rights.'[64] It was Hegel's task to lend philosophical dignity to this process at its inception. There was nothing contradictory in this reformist intelligence; calling upon a principle that went back to the Stoics, the Enlightenment reintroduced natural law to temper the absolutism of the Second Estate: '[S]ociety, founded to protect the individual, was based on an original contract freely concluded among its citizens; similarly, governmental authority rested upon a contract between the sovereign people and their delegates, who had authority only to protect the inalienable rights conferred upon man by God.' Lefebvre continues:

> The Americans and the French later proclaimed the natural rights of man in the presence of the Supreme Being. Natural law perpetuated the universalism of classic and Christian thought by omitting distinction between the different branches of human kind.[65]

Natural law is the aggressive motor of revolutionary change rather than gradual transformations worked across eons by Providence. If Locke replaced Habakkuk, this was only because contract itself became a religious mystery in the proto-capitalist state. Why does Marx identify historical tradition as an impediment to realising revolutionary change in *Eighteenth Brumaire*? This has to do with the political consequences of the rarefied epistemological debate among Enlightenment thinkers that failed to deliver the freedoms promised by this discourse. Marx would need to develop a systematic alternative to the aspirations of these men. The *philosophe* and revolutionary, Condillac, a nominal member of the First Estate, dealing only with the fallen world in which God has granted man faculties to interpret the reality of his experiences, promotes a surprisingly similar point of view as the postmodern theorist of history. He writes how 'reflection ... makes us begin to discern the capability of the mind' and continues:

> So long as we cannot direct our own attention, the mind is ... ruled by its environment subject to everything that surrounds it, and owes what it is to some extrinsic force. But if we are masters of our attention and direct it as we choose, then the mind is in control of itself, it draws ideas from it that it owes only to itself, and it gains enrichment from its own resources.[66]

Condillac is here describing the flight of mental processes from sensate reality, the way in which the mind frees itself from the subjection of its milieu. Contrary to the preceding tradition of philosophical analysis, typified by John Locke and his *Essay Concerning Human Understanding* (1689) where consciousness is entirely dependent on the environment of sensations through which we come to terms with reality (today, after Herder, we would reduce Locke's elegant argument to a simple formula of Culture over Nature), Condillac is here arguing for an essential autonomy from the environment in which our individuality is formed. A legacy of the medieval principle, the human imagination owes its most essential processes to itself. This has some serious consequences for those who argue that every human endeavour is a product of history. The naturalism in Locke's account is also autonomous, but to a degree: man is a 'succession of fleeting particles' whose identity or personality is guaranteed only by consciousness of its self by 'imputing to *itself* past actions'. In contrast to Condillac's assertion about this freedom of the mind, which is cast in wholly aesthetic terms, for Locke the natural propensity to happiness is concerned with ethical dimensions as the personality extends itself beyond the present to the past.⁶⁷ However, no sooner has Locke argued this point about the moral purpose of history for the individual consciousness, he concludes with Biblical authority, that whatever this consciousness cannot 'reconcile or appropriate', it needn't be concerned with. If the mind discovers an event or personality in history that is alien to it, then the mind is no longer obliged to treat the past as a catechism for behaviour in the present. Here is another dimension of the prescience that Benjamin gave ironic expression to in 'Theses in the Philosophy of History'. In 1688 at least, this *might* have been a useful rule of thumb to follow in order to resist the deadweight of the past from defining the course of events in the present. Over a century later, the eighth stage in Antoine-Nicolas Caritat's (de Condorcet's) *Sketch for a Historical Picture of the Progress of the Human Mind* (1795) aptly reveals the optimistic faith of the intellectuals of the age with 'the natural progress of civilisation': 'From the invention of the printing press to the time philosophy and the sciences shook off the yoke of authority.' Tradition has become synonymous with authority. The tendency towards autonomy of the mind that Condillac discerned from Locke, initially anonymously and with the help of the Encyclopaedist Diderot in 1746, for Condorcet, is now no longer a simple fiat of nature that mankind instinctively obeys as part of its divinely ordained destiny: it is the culmination of collective will. The prophecy for humanity in Vico's 'scientific' method is at last being fulfilled. However, how to account for the world's stubborn insistence in furnishing plenty of evidence to the contrary? Superstition seizes consciousness, corrupts it and makes individuals susceptible to the despotism of others. Condorcet pictures the progress of the human mind as a faltering process; no sooner has it been 'released from the leading-strings of its infancy', than its triumphant achievement of the truth 'encourages tyranny to return, followed by its faithful companion superstition'. He goes on:

> [A]nd the whole of mankind is plunged once more into darkness, which seems as if it must last for ever. Yet, little by little, day breaks again; eyes long condemned to darkness catch a glimpse of the light and close again, then slowly become accustomed to it, and at last gaze on it without flinching; once again genius dares to walk abroad on the earth, from which fanaticism and barbarism had exiled it.⁶⁸

On the third day after the emperor had arrived in Paris from the Russian front on 18 December 1812, having left half a million behind – 400,000 dead and 100,000 prisoners – the *Moniteur* published the speech already delivered before the Council of State. For the general who had crossed the field of battle by stepping through the entrails of his fallen soldiers, the ideologues with their impractical, 'shadowy metaphysics' and dogmatic assertions upon which the legislation of peoples is to be based were easily identifiable as subversives threatening the authority of the nascent Republic and the 'sanctity of laws'. Instead of 'making use of laws known to the human heart and of the lessons of history', the quest for first principles will necessarily result in 'the rule of bloodthirsty men'. Bonaparte continues to emphasise the appeal he answered of the affective force of tradition and the lessons of history as the true foundations of state power. Tacitus, as a type for the 'ideologues', was a slanderer of the Empire, 'a discontented senator' and Destutt de Tracy and the marquis de Lafayette who submitted the Declaration of Rights before the Constituent Assembly in 1789 are also types, 'empty brains ... who cry against despotism as if it existed, when they are allowed to protest, intrigue, criticize as they please'. Napoleon concludes:

> When someone is summoned to revitalise a state, he must follow exactly the opposite principles. History depicts the human heart, and it is in history that we must discover the advantages and disadvantages of different forms of legislation. Such are the principles of which a great empire's Council of State must never lose sight. To these should be added the courage to face any test and the readiness to die in the defence of sovereign, throne and laws.[69]

As Foucault described it, history comes full circle. The meeting of the Estates General was a pretext by a venal cabal who 'proclaimed the principle of insurrection to be a duty ... [who] adulated the people and attributed to it a sovereignty which it was incapable of exercising'. In the symbolic-allegorical terms of Nietzsche's *alter ego* Zarathustra, the ape will always successfully manage to supplant the 'hero'. The ape, let's call it Hercules or Napoleon, can quite easily blot out the democratic light of the sun whose happiness is superabundant because it is for everyone.[70] To conclude, the will of the moderniser is an ascetic attempt to free oneself from the encumbrances of sentiment, of the laws of the human heart that have been fashioned in the furnace of a real experience of history. We will leave aside the idea that France in her long history experimented with different forms of legislation in order to rediscover the sanctity of constitutional monarchy.

When we look at most history writing conducted in most societies during most eras, we quickly discern how its composition as narrative is essentially heterogeneous, hybrid, formally promiscuous. The social and intellectual revolutions in eighteenth- and nineteenth-century Europe that modified or dissolved the *ancien régime*, with the emergence of the *nation* as well as the value 'man' as bourgeois phenomena, have obscured the antecedents of history in less credible forms of knowledge.[71] This is typified by J. B. Bury's declaration that the art of narrative remains the bedrock of history as 'a science, no less and no more'.[72] My purpose in the rest of this chapter is to investigate this claim by examining the peculiar composition of this narrative foundation of historiography. The conclusion is that Indian nationalism, like many other instances of 'imagined community', depends on the deliberate and strategic conflation of history and myth.

This confusion in the modality of history in the early twentieth century was inevitable if historiography, partly reflecting the more ancient function of myth, began to be more or less successfully deployed by the intellectual luminaries of the nineteenth century *as if it had* successfully escaped this function and cohered as *a* philosophy, *a* theory, *a* science. In 1960s France, this methodological question obsessively exercised Althusser's imagination and the strange fruit of this labour, when it came to Marx's reflections on the issues that Bury, in true Anglo-Saxon fashion, had thought he had successfully concluded, was the exegetical or the 'symptomatic reading'. This style or interpretive mode is a matter of examining the textual relationship between Marx's reflections and those of the eighteenth-century authors whom he had read, only to conclude that Marx's scientific historicism (dialectical materialism as a theory of a science called historical materialism) led to the 'paradox of *an answer which does not correspond to any question posed*'.[73] To conclude that this may actually be due to the embryonic nature of the orthodoxy capitalism supplied itself with as a 'science', namely, political economy, is to return to the discredited hopes of the *philosophes*.

No matter how untenable some of the 'solutions' in Althusser's symptomatic analysis of Marx's reflections according to the logic of Marx's thinking, I am suggesting that the narrative or 'mythological' impulse in historiography is largely due to the fact that history concerns itself with 'what was going on inside people's heads'.[74] Lawrence Stone continues to assert how a new vogue (circa 1979) for a 'non-analytical mode of writing history' is detectable, one which takes *mentalité* rather than structural analyses as its object of concern. This recommendation seems modern but a concern with *mentalité* or the sensibility of the age, as we saw above, is an eighteenth-century solution to the modern problem of history. Peter Brown's *The World of Late Antiquity* is Stone's example and in this text the author has apparently pursued a policy of 'deliberate vagueness' which, paradoxically, has successfully produced a vivid portrait of reality; Stone likens the method to a *pointilliste* way of writing history. This successful effect, the optical illusion of proximity to a society very distant from our own, is achieved by 'the intimate juxtaposition of history, literature, religion and art'.[75] Stone's remarks bring to mind the celebrated image of contrasts in historiography. This question of achieving control over the potentially anarchic sequence of events through ironic distance (whether bardic or secular) is expressed metaphorically by Auden in *The Shield of Achilles*. The ideal of *civilitas* we today think synonymous with 'democracy' is a medieval appropriation of Hephaestus' symbol of two scenes, one in which the city is governed according to order and the other, the anarchic state of Man in competition with Nature. Instead of Ionian glory for her warrior son, the poet registers the goddess's dismay at the manner in which the blacksmith to the Olympians, and hence, the real material power addressed by the human suppliant, had depicted the squalor and confusion of modern war. The colourful spectacle of ancient sacrifice of 'White flower-garlanded heifers' in 'Marble well-governed cities' makes room for a scene where bored officials are present to authorise sweating sentries to execute the patriotic duty nobody seems to have much faith in. The ethical cost of gaining historical perspective of contemporary events through the mythical lens of the past, Auden implies, is very great as 'ordinary decent folk' emotionlessly look on with the execution of 'three pale figures' tied to posts.[76]

I want to continue with literary *pensées* to analyse this apparently ecumenical, non-scientific interest in modern historiography. This will necessarily take us to phenomenological assertions about the present. As we saw in the last chapter, the generic link between historiography and narrative has remained a complex issue for historians and lay folk alike in European cultures. The transmutation of the past into the present is so powerful in Indian society, according to Romila Thapar, that the patient documenting of the past to make it amenable to the kind of analytical inquiry Stone suggested no longer interests historians, poses a formidable challenge to Indians who might also be guilty of a deliberate vagueness, 'of bury[ing] their past in forms which are difficult to unravel'.[77] Thapar's point about the transformations in the epic tradition (*katha*) of the *Ramayana* is a quasi-materialist reading of the scene in Indian pre-history: that the productive capacities of an evolving political order are inevitably caught up in these mythical representations. The well-governed city is founded upon the primal violence it likes to think it has exiled beyond its walls.

The implications, then, of the analogy between historiography and narrative form are as vast as the hubris assumed by T. S. Eliot in his description of 'the historical sense'. For Modernism as a literary movement in the early twentieth century, the historical sense was an essential component and Eliot felt that its practitioners, if they wanted to continue in their vocation as poets after reaching twenty-five years of age, needed to possess it as an intuitive virtue before attempting to shape the present by transforming it in words; anatomising the malaise of contemporary existence is useless without it. This skill of the individual in relation to the preceding tradition is to represent their culture as the 'mysterious social personality'; it was the extinction of this personality that troubled Eliot and we are invited to believe that this is the creative mainspring of Eliot's own practice.[78]

The claim on behalf of the historical sense obviously concerns poets, painters, artists, historians, but the implication of Eliot's defence of it is that it is an urgent requirement for us all. In the aftermath of two world wars, for the first time in history, the private apprehension of death can be multiplied to include whole national cultures; where 'unification of the world' appears to be 'desirable for its own sake'.[79] The prospect of mass extinction for cultural life sounds alarming; it conjures up visions of darkness where the specificity of *our* tradition becomes lost and no longer speaks to us. Who or what is the enemy in Eliot's conservative vision? It is something as elusive and concrete as the *social mode* itself. Braudel's history of the sixteenth-century Mediterranean represents the spirit of internationalism that Eliot felt compelled to reject. Eliot speaks of the dissociation of sensibility afflicting the mind of England – a condition of complexity from the sixteenth century to the present where the poet, once capable of rendering experience more truthfully, must now reproduce the difficulty of modern civilisation by becoming 'more comprehensive, more allusive, more indirect, in order to force, to dislocate if necessary, language into his meaning'.[80] This is the policy of deliberate vagueness that Stone recommended for historians. The task of historiography is formidable in a context where the 'internationalization' that Eliot had perhaps only a vague sense of by 1945 becomes a social reality in the form of transnational business practices that give rise not only to new divisions of labour ('the flight of production to advanced Third World areas') but also to new epistemological advances that were initially designed to serve 'a vertiginous new dynamic in international banking and the stock exchanges'. 'Late capitalism' is the name that Frederic Jameson gives to this abstraction. Late capitalism, or more specifically its ideological 'mytheme', postmodernism, is inimical to the historical sense. The technical correlation of Eliot's historical sense is a proper historiographic concern: 'periodicity'. Jameson goes on to state the task facing us all in the amnesiac milieu:

> In periodizing a phenomenon of this kind, we have to complicate the model with all kinds of supplementary epicycles. It is necessary to distinguish between the gradual setting in place of the various (often unrelated) preconditions for the new structure and the 'moment' (not exactly chronological) when they all jell and combine into a functional system. This moment is itself less a matter of chronology than it is of a well-nigh Freudian *Nachträglichkeit*, or retroactivity: people become aware of the dynamics of some new system, in which they are themselves seized, only later on and gradually.[81]

Here we again encounter the dynamic understanding of the relationship between history and culture which Williams expressed behind his notion of 'structure of feeling', but more pessimistically. Is it any wonder that most of us do not feel as capable as Eliot did in casting the encyclopaedic vision to measure the adequacy of the present age? Though Braudel does not examine it, despite the natural propensity for the historical sense which people in earlier, agrarian, traditionally stratified societies may have had in more localised forms (clan genealogies, eulogies to semi-divine kingship, or heterodox religious practices), a pervasive lack of the historical sense may be decisively due to the fact that modern life does not allow every individual to absent themselves from economic necessity either by its suspension if not wholesale removal. This is a prerequisite of gaining sufficient levels of cultural capital.[82] The historical sense in its most straightforward form – that is, as the brilliant radiation of sensuous particularity from the epicentre of an event to personalities far at the margins – may be symptomatic of societies in which the transmission of knowledge can be maintained as an essentially ritual function. Myth is the ancient democracy of knowledge. In other words, the primary function of myth is not the forensic examination of the truth of an event but whether its representation is conducive to the social bond. Lenin's adumbrating of tasks for the Russian proletariat in his 'April Theses' is a celebrated and recent example of this phenomenon, read twice and very slowly.[83] In case we think we have escaped narrative as the primal habit, consider the following assertions in more detail: '[M]an is in his actions and practice, as well as in his fictions, essentially a story-telling animal.' Alasdair MacIntyre presents a strong deterministic vision of the centrality of narrative to social life. This is a healthy corrective to the version of social life where people become aware of the new order only once they have been 'seized' by its effects. MacIntyre writes:

> [Mankind] is not essentially, but becomes through his history, a teller of stories that aspire to truth. But the key question for men is not about their own authorship; I can only answer the question 'What am I to do?' if I can answer the prior question 'Of what story or stories do I find myself a part?' We enter human society, that is, with one or more imputed characters – roles into which

we have been drafted – and we have to learn what they are in order to be able to understand how others respond to us and how we respond to us and how our responses to them are apt to be construed ... Hence there is no way of understanding society, including our own, except through the stock of stories which constitute its initial dramatic resources. Mythology, in its original sense, is at the heart of things. Vico was right and so was Joyce. And so too of course is that moral tradition from heroic society to its medieval heirs according to which the telling of stories has a key part in educating us into the virtues.[84]

Now we understand the dynamic of the individual as well as that individual's talent in relation to tradition; the latter is broadly conceived as a society's 'stock of stories which constitute its initial dramatic resources'. The invocation of history as if it were serving the mythical function has to contend with the more austere reality where the performative aspect of socialisation is itself increasingly outmoded. 'Most people have lost the nostalgia for the lost narrative.' Lyotard does not deny the ethical orientation of historiography whose narrative aspects MacIntyre is describing above and he is emphatic that this incredulity about the solidary function of narrative does not, however, result in anarchy:

It in no way follows that [individuals] are reduced to barbarity. What saves them from it is their knowledge that legitimation can only spring from their own linguistic practice and communication interaction. Science 'smiling into its beard' at every other belief has taught them the harsh austerity of realism.[85]

Condillac's argument for the autonomy of the mind is a pretext for the complacency of scientific knowledge. The French philosopher is reflecting the concerns of another more ostensibly revolutionary age. Stone's seemingly innocent explanation of the new object of historiography represents 'the enormous social and psychological transformations of the 1960s, which swept so much of tradition away on the level of *mentalités*'.[86] Eliot the poet felt this revolution as long ago as the sixteenth century. The activist–critic Edward Said provided us with some compelling, if at times esoteric, reasons for the harmful results inflicted on whole nations and cultures due to the pervasive absence of the historical sense. The historical sense, as we can see, is certainly no longer an organic extension of the *habitus*; most of us cannot claim the whole library of Europe from Homer to the present in 'our bones', but clearly some intuitive ability to reflect on the dilemmas of the present with the mythic resonances of the past is in order: 'the historical sense involves a perception', Eliot writes, 'not only of the pastness of the past, but of its presence'.[87] In Eliot's phenomenological language, the noun 'presence' is synonymous with the adjectival 'present'. Even if we don't live (*pace* Said) in a war zone, most of us are aware that our daily lives have an affiliation to previous modes in the past and that no matter how our existence is modified by the pressure of technocratic fantasies, the kind of historical sense Thapar attributes specifically to Indian society is a phenomenon we all share. Can any Briton confidently assert that he or she has either mastered or struggled against the mystery of their national origins more than has any Indian?[88] The purposive element in Eliot's argument, however, means having to *submit* one's own consciousness of the present to the past. Even if the answer to national origins is contingent on clearly historical events, like migrations and battles, an *ethnic* explanation for a national identity, while it may not be free of these contingencies in the distant past still implies the intuitive use of the historical sense. Despite its mystical quality, Eliot's meditation on the question is worth considering for the limitations he perceives in the forensic recovery of the past to make it present as presence. The hybrid consciousness of time is certainly not reducible to 'a complication in economics and machinery'. If it were, what purpose would there be in the prayers of Sen's pious Bengali householder? The slow transformation of society according to material necessity – 'progressive epochs in the economic formation of society', as Marx's famous doctrine states – is nothing more than a spurious reduction of the complexity Eliot describes in the following terms:

> He [the individual poet] must be aware that the mind of Europe – the mind of his own country – a mind which he learns in time to be much more important than his own private mind – is a mind which changes, and that this change is a development which abandons nothing *en route*, which does not superannuate Shakespeare, or Homer, or the rock drawing of the Magdalenian draughtsmen. This development, refinement perhaps, complication certainly, is not, from the point of view of the artist, any improvement. Perhaps not even an improvement from the point of view of the psychologist or not to the extent which we imagine; perhaps only in the end based upon a complication in economics and machinery. But the difference between the present and the past is that the conscious present is an awareness of the past in a way and to an extent which the past's awareness of itself cannot show.[89]

It is only after possessing this historical sense, an awareness that already concedes a perfect representation of the past *as it actually was* is impossible, that we can identify with the existential predicament of the odd characters and voices that inhabit Eliot's poetry. A singularly psychological view of the Theban prophet Tiresias's sexual boredom on the typist's bed 'At the violet hour' in *The Waste Land* is an insufficient explanation for the morbid decline of society; it is actually symptomatic of it. In a more edifying spirit, an historical sense of the Indic elements of consciousness, alongside the Hebraic and Graeco-Roman cultures that have informed or, more correctly, *failed* to form European identity, will deliver a more coherent meaning to the metaphysical value of the Upanishadic conclusion 'Shantih' to Eliot's masterpiece.[90] Buddha's wisdom about the nature of suffering 'corresponds in importance', Eliot ironically directs his reader, 'to the Sermon on the Mount' and the termination of thought in the Vedic blessing 'Shantih' is equivalent to the Christian meditation of 'The Peace which passeth understanding'.[91] Even if Eliot's kaleidoscopic allusions here are only half-serious, when it comes to the prolific use and abuse of the historical sense for nationalist ideologies, there is little doubt about the labyrinths into which Clio has led *men*; as Eliot puts it: 'Unnatural vices/Are fathered by our heroism.'[92]

My analysis of the problem of writing historically for and in postcolonial India is not chronological in the sense of isolating definitive tendencies of any historical era. I hope it is now clear why, among others, the *modus operandi* of the Cambridge school of Indian historiography now appears quaint or increasingly marginal to the central problem explored in this book. As Eliot's gyno-phobic metaphor suggests, nationalist historiography is by its very nature a promiscuous raid. This book, then, is not a political or administrative history of the modular kind historians produced under the influence of Indian nationalism.[93] I want to resume my explanation of the reasons why this is the case in the general context of historiography *qua* narrative. An examination of the social impulses behind the desire of making history present – in Eliot's sense – despite the fact that the past's awareness of itself can never be represented or realised, will help us to achieve a better understanding of the issues at stake in its ideological appropriation.

By the time Herodotus was compiling his observations about the worldly nexus between 'Europe', 'Asia' and 'Africa' in the fifth century BCE, the use of the Greek term *historiē* – meaning 'investigation' and 'inquiry' – could already be distinguished from that Homeric or epic background of *muthos* that constituted a less credible type of knowledge about the world. *The Histories* famously begin by claiming neutrality between partisan points of view, 'great and marvellous deeds' by both Greeks and barbarians, 'so that human achievements may not become forgotten in time'.[94] Who can fail to identify with the impiety behind Herodotus's project, exemplified by Croesus' rebuke to the Delphic oracle for failing to *philippize* on his behalf in his adventure against the Persians under Cyrus? The defence of Providence as the directing will behind the motives of men sounds weak:

> As to the oracle, Croesus had no right to find fault with it: the god had declared that if he attacked the Persians he would bring down a mighty empire. After an answer like that, the wise thing to do would have been to send again to inquire which empire was meant, Cyrus' or his own. But as he misinterpreted what was said and made no second inquiry, he must admit the fault to have been his own.[95]

Nevertheless, despite the subtle point of interpretation upon which even the will of the gods turns, the Graeco-Roman classical tradition still had its advocates in early modern Europe and these commentators saw 'history as above all a form of rhetoric and a source of exempla – moral and prudential precepts worked out in the concrete form of speeches, trials, and battles'.[96] The profound lesson of Croesus' failure to subdue the Persian Empire is one which Herodotus places in the mouth of the captured king himself on his pyre via the wisdom of Solon that no man is happy until he is dead.[97] Undoubtedly, it is more this comment on the fragility of being in the cruel theatre of existence that would have held its particular appeal to a fatalistic culture rather than the miraculous shower sent by Apollo to douse the flames that impressed Cyrus to spare his vanquished foe. From the late fifteenth century onwards, as we have been exploring throughout, there is still no guarantee that the definite linguistic domains in which history goes seeking to find its contents will deliver the accurate description of events. The weight of this monumental labour still bears down.

In the past, the spectacle of the Homeric hero savouring the simplicity of the present 'between battles and passions, adventures and perils' was about an invitation to identify only with the *processes* that sent 'strong roots down into social usages, landscape and daily life'.[98] Auerbach's modern rendering of realism in mimetic tradition goes against the philosophical defence of antiquity undertaken by Nietzsche. The human geography of events was simpler. The effort of deducing secret motives for this character-type or the haphazard consequences for others around him was futile; this was because his actions were to be confined only to the most universal tendencies of how *he* reacted to his world. This is the Homeric staple of Herodotus's investigations. At best, we found ourselves lured by the narrator of the legend into this emotional reality, a '"real" world existing for itself and containing nothing but itself'. Any attempt to transgress the bounds of the familiar universe in order to discover the meaning of everything in the ancient world is to return, like the Mesopotamian king, Gilgamesh – 'He who saw the Deep' – back again to the confines of a sheep-fold, and 'three square miles and a half [of] Uruk's expanse'.[99] According to the 'Zoroastrian' figure of wisdom in Akkade lore, Uta-napishti the Distant, the occult secret of innocence regained, of 'Old Man Grown Young', is unavailing for anyone who chooses to simply engage in a Herculean feat of toil and travail.

The 'rationalistic interpretation' in historical consciousness, as we will see throughout this book, owes its method to a less immediate conception of existence. The irony in Auerbach's celebrated description of the relationship between styles of representation and reality in the interplay between individual and culture is that the ordinarily crucial historical environment begins to vanish to the exact degree that we concentrate our attention on the definitive part 'psychological and factual cross-purposes' have played in the concrete formation of history as speeches, trials and battles. This is not simply a debate about context. For Auerbach, the Biblical domain is the authentic realm of the *agon* in which these aspects of interiority have a more familiar opportunity to play themselves out. Generations have inhabited this domain because the ordinarily historical background of the events is swallowed up by the symbolic value of the patriarchs' deeds. The historical background of these 'events' vanishes, as it were, by divine mandate.

Let us see where this absence of historical background rather than a quasi-intuitive sense leads. For Nehru, concerned as he was with the secular conditions for the efflorescence and decline of civilisations, Palestine – perhaps because it existed outside Europe and therefore, Indian history – never had 'much historical importance'. He goes on to explain: 'But many people are interested in its ancient history because it is given in the Old Testament. It is the story of some tribes of the Jews, who lived in this little land, and of the troubles they had with their big neighbours on either side – Babylonia and Assyria and Egypt. If the story had not become part of the religion of the Jews and of Christianity, few persons would probably know of it.'[100] This characterisation of Palestine's history at the time

Nehru was drafting these comments to his daughter from prison (January 1931) is itself symptomatic of the eclectic focus through which Indian nationalism perceived British imperialism. The founding of the modern state of Israel is ascribed to ancient factors. The British government were busy failing in their attempts to quell outbreaks of spontaneous violence by more radical elements by inventing and financing the institution of a 'grand *mufti* of Palestine' under the direction of a young cleric, Hajj Amin al-Husayni, after Foreign Secretary Balfour laid the foundation stone of Hebrew University as the new Joshua. An Indian Congress Party-styled boycott of British goods in the early 1930s by the *Hizb al-Istiqlal*, a radical nationalist party composed, among others, of young Palestinian Arabs, hadn't a chance of competing with this patronage of regressive elements in Palestinian society.[101] A recent commentator on British policy of the period states in the same mandarin tone that, led to 'the world's most portentous dispute', '[a]lmost nothing was done to improve Arab backwardness'.[102] Adopting an ahistorical view of insurgent resistance to colonial authority brings together otherwise disparate interests across the colonial divide. Winston Churchill's view of the problem of development in Mandatory Palestine is typical of Nehru's explanation of this 'little land' of ancient nomadic peoples whose claim to history would founder if it looked to the Bible for authority. Speaking of the failure of the Palestinian notables' regime to modernise by bringing irrigation and electricity to the country, he writes how the Arabs of Palestine 'would have been quite content to dwell – a handful of philosophic people – in the wasted sun-scorched plains, letting the waters of the Jordan continue to flow unbridled and unharnessed into the Sea'.[103] Churchill's and Nehru's ideas of progress and the impediments it faces in tradition are identical to the Organic myth of peoples in harmony with their environment introduced into historical consciousness by Herder.

Only when 'Greek culture ... encountered the phenomena of historical becoming and of the "multilayeredness" of the human problem' did events in human history themselves begin to form the staple morality of European culture.[104] The magnificent carnage of ancient history is now the symbolic emblem of human misery intrinsic to history, the material of *Shoah* or *al Nakba*. How can the durability of revelation *qua* narrative as an explanation for the order of things remain intact? In other words, the intrinsic ambiguity of the episodes recounted in the Pentateuch, the Hebrew epic, would relegate the truth of the ordeals suffered by its hero (the tribes of Israel) to the aesthetic realm of personal experience. The mountains of Moriah *become* the self. Nietzsche would rail against this philosophical reinvention of piety. Historical consciousness is to be substituted for by a more refined dialectic now, one which 'has an elevation that I can form a conception of but no more'.[105] The limits of the stylistic conventions of antiquity, which Kierkegaard was not the first to feel (or Eliot, the first to think he had conquered by reproducing in metonymic form) during his meditation on the episode of Abraham's sacrifice in Genesis, first became apparent with the 'deep subsurface movement' in the synoptic Gospels. I want to quote Auerbach's description of this epistemological revolution at some length; as well as being a defining factor in the evolution of European historiography, the explanation is absent from Anthony Grafton's otherwise able account of the influence of the classical tradition on European historiography. More importantly, in Auerbach's method we can discern a poetic analogy of a Viconian kind for historiography. In his remarks about the transition in style we see how the preponderance of the natural law celebrated by the Enlightenment *philosophes* – in Lefebvre's words – obliterates the differences between the different branches of humanity. Auerbach's observations also help us to conclude how the historical sense moved from being a relatively crude didactic device to a more subtle condition of being. 'A Greek or Roman writer describes a popular movement', Auerbach notes, 'only as a reaction to a specific practical complex of events – as Thucydides for instance describes the Athenians' attitude toward the project of an expedition to Sicily ...' He goes on:

> [T]he movement is characterized as a whole – as approving, disapproving, undecided, or perhaps tumultuous – just as the observer sees it, looking, as it were, from above; but it could not possibly occur that reactions so various among so many individuals of the common people should be made a major subject of literary treatment. What considerable portions of the Gospels and the Acts of the Apostles describe, what Paul's Epistles also often reflect, is unmistakably the beginning of a deep subsurface movement, the unfolding of historical forces. For this, it is essential that great numbers of random persons should make their appearance; for it is not possible to bring to life such historical forces in their surging action except by reference to numerous random persons – the term random being here employed to designate people from all classes, occupations, walks of life, people, that is, who owe their place in the account exclusively to the fact that the historical movement engulfs them as it were accidentally, so that they are obliged to react to it one way or another.[106]

These are the original conditions that give birth to an 'ethically oriented historiography'.[107] The humanistic philological tradition Auerbach is associated with is doubtless present. Beyond the Platonic realm of letters which the author found his solace in, from the 'surging action' of forces threatening to obliterate not only his talent but his very life, the genius of this passage is in introducing a kind of historicism that questions the increasing autonomy of the progression of history. This 'narrative' use of history was a fundamental tenet for those, like Nehru, who began to look upon events in the past as a guide for the future evolution of their own societies once they had been liberated from the yoke of colonial power. To Moses and the patriarchs of the Old Testament, the deep subsurface movements determining the odyssey of their people was to be found at an extraterrestrial location: 'And the Lord went before them by day in a pillar of a cloud, to lead them the way, and by night in a pillar of fire, to give them light to go by day and night.' What is truly miraculous about this symbol of Providence, as the text goes on to state, is the Old Testament God's desire not to deprive the children of Israel of his help at this crucial moment in their immanent liberation of bondage to Egypt (Exodus 14: 22). The symbol of God's constancy to his chosen people is eschatological. In the language of asceticism adopted by the Puritan sects during the Reformation, in the secular world where men create their institutions, the elect can no longer discern the outward manifestation of God's grace. In Weber's words: 'In its extreme inhumanity this doctrine must above all have had one consequence for the life of a generation which surrendered to its magnificent consistency. That was a feeling of unprecedented inner loneliness of the single individual.'[108] This was the experience of modern capitalist civilisation under colonialism which Gandhi was reacting to in his communitarian vision of *Hind Swaraj*.

Having reached the field of experimentation where this species of Stoicism became the foundations of the nascent liberated state, a latter-day Ezekiel denunciating at the door of the Temple rather than a suffering Job with potsherds would attempt to imagine a new and invigorated covenant between the individual and tradition. Harold Bloom, Fukuyama's teacher, and erstwhile student of Leo Strauss, the neo-conservative visionary who would help the next generation of oligarchs to steer the ship of state through troubled times, envisaged the defining qualities of greatness as both originality and 'strangeness'. What is clear in Bloom's spirited essay is the erosion of intellectual authority where the university, as an institution charged with defending the storehouse of (mostly) literary high culture, can no longer perform its function. The Great Tradition is endangered by the barbarians, dubbed The School of Resentment, those 'who offer little but the resentment they had developed as part of their sense of identity'.[109] It is with a playful sense of Irony, the favoured trope of the émigré, that Bloom attributes the great events of the Old Testament not to any Israelite 'personality' but to a Hittite woman. The personality of the tribes (priests and cultic scribes described as 'revisionists') is intent on translating the 'neurotic anxiety' of King David's wife, and Solomon's mother Bathsheba – Bathsheba J, after Jehovah, a German misnomer for Yahweh – her 'ironical freedom', and it is out of this tropological inversion (*pace* White) between the divine and the human that something emerges and manages successfully not to be merely a product of 'the most blasphemous of all authors ever'. Bloom continues, 'The J saga as far as we can tell, when Yahweh, with his own hands, buries the prophet Moses in an unmarked grave, after refusing the long-suffering leader of the Israelites more than a glimpse of the Promised Land.' The perversity of J lies in 'a narrative *beyond* irony and tragedy that moves from Yahweh's surprising election of the reluctant prophet to his motiveless attempt to murder Moses, and his chosen instrument'.[110] An itinerant cosmopolitanism might be the order of the day where historiography is 'fantastic' (*pace* Jameson) but Bloom's message to us is that everybody has a duty to protect the particular enclave of their own tradition from assailants. If the archetypal repose is impossible where God keeps company with Man in Canaan, we can all at least attempt the New Jerusalem. Bloom takes it upon himself to proudly display the head of the New Empire; it has been drained of any living culture but what does that signify to the victor with his trophy? We notice the complete absence of dignity in Bloom's satirical evocation of tradition. In contrast to the hermeneutical dilemmas that are at the source of the second most important form of European tradition, there is nothing edifying in the ethnographic motives of 'Plan Dalet' that the new historiography of Israel has revealed for the foundations of the Jewish state.[111] The noble dream not to have one's culture, like Moses, be buried in an unmarked grave *at any cost* will take us the rest of this book to explore.

I want to relate these observations to the relationship between historiography and the mythical narrative in late antiquity whose influence over the European consciousness Auerbach gave such importance to. In his topographical description of the new hermeneutic or problem of history, there is an implicit repudiation of the translation of the religious doctrine of Providence into a philosophy of history. This is namely a rejection of the Hegelian view that autonomy is *intrinsic* to history; as Auerbach states, 'it is not possible to bring to life such historical forces in their surging action except by reference to numerous random persons'. In the problem of history, our attempt to give sociological form to this dynamic relationship between random actors and the direction their reality takes is a foreign importation according to classical norms. The dialectic of history involves (or as Auerbach puts it, 'engulfs') individuals but this *seemingly* accidental involvement is determined by the place history assigns them. Behind the material particularity of Providence with the frenetic activity of individuals from all classes, occupations and walks of life, the pagan register of Fortuna can still be discerned as 'a deep subsurface movement'. Auerbach's conclusion for the rhetorical uses made of historiography is subtle and succinct: '[T]he ethical and even the political concepts of antiquity (aristocracy, democracy, etc.) are fixed, aprioristic model concepts.'[112] This is an important consideration when we look at some of the cruder uses made of millennial history for nationalist ideologies in the twentieth century. Auerbach's astonishing feat is to lend the primal myth of Transhumance a less rigid form. Henceforth, when we examine the past as a rhetorical device for the present, most meditations on the problem of realism in narrative, including Auerbach's own, end up being symptomatic of the following realisation:

> Abraham I cannot understand; in a way all I can learn from him is to be amazed. If one imagines one can be moved to faith by considering the outcome of the story, one deceives oneself, and is out to cheat God of faith's first movement, one is out to suck the life-wisdom out of the paradox. One or another may succeed, for our age does not stop at faith, with its miracle of turning water into wine; it goes further, it turns wine into water.[113]

Let us examine more closely the wisdom of the paradox between Providence and Fortuna; it will help us to characterise the hybrid nature of historiography I alluded to at the beginning. For Kierkegaard's interpretation of the agonistic moment, imagining the outcome of Abraham and his people's destiny by the predictive measure of faith in the restoration of eventual order after travails is misguided. 'How can it be known that Abraham isn't a paranoic subject to homicidal (infanticidal) urges? Or a fake?'[114] One can probably say the same for the outcome of history from this perspective. Homeric life was free of the sterile paradox plaguing individual consciousness, and ancient historiography was never solely about establishing an epistemological regime (literally, an *autopsy*) in which, to adopt the miracle as a metaphor, wine is to be turned into water. To Herodotus, Thucydides, Xenophon and other ancient historians, the 'miraculous' dynamism of history (its *telos*, to adopt the native concept) did not conceal any subterranean forces of the kind modern historiography seeks to reveal. Society is the alternation of one hard brilliant reflection of the civic cosmos after another; it is the job of historians to render these often momentous but sometimes subtle transformations by the use of their disinterested intellect. Herodotus's *Histories* are designed to expel the categorical mystery of otherness by going in the midst of the Persians and the Egyptians. The appropriation of the classical mode in the European early modern as a theory of knowledge could not have been a coherent explanation of social reality without the development described by Auerbach. In the language Auerbach chooses to use, it is an innovation in *style*. 'Discourse' is the contemporary phrase that no longer has a Cartesian innocence of meaning to it. Perhaps we might confidently be able to identify the impulse behind the reduction of the miraculous to the mundane: 'Style', writes Adorno, 'considered as mere aesthetic regularity is a romantic dream of the past'. He continues

> The unity of style not only of the Christian Middle Ages but of the Renaissance expresses in each case the different structure of social power, and not the obscure experience of the oppressed in which the general was enclosed. The great artists were never those who embodied a wholly flawless and perfect style, but those who used style as a way of hardening themselves against the chaotic expression of suffering, as a negative truth.[115]

We see the great spiritual discipline that Eliot perceived as the virtue of simplicity in the Metaphysical poets. For Auerbach, doubtless weary of the fascist appropriation of the classical past, the duty of the Renaissance as well as of the Modern is to liberate the age from history as if it were the procession of different structures of power. This was also the spirit of truth behind Bloom's mischievous reading of the Pentateuch. We were already aware that art for the Socratic Hellenes had been distant from reality, with the painter of this reality at a risible third remove from *physis* both after the originating *demiourgos* and the craftsman.[116] Despite Hayden White's ingenious rendering of Irony as the dominant mode in *Metahistory* as typical of the spirit of our age, Nietzsche first and Heidegger after him projected it as the value of the Socratic innovation in Greek thought. The desire for the Renaissance artist or German philosopher to represent social reality as it truly is is not only an unattainable goal but also no longer even a desirable one; it is a question of returning with 'unity of style' from society. And society is nothing more *at any one moment* but the petrified residue of power. Both Auerbach and Adorno, for good historical reasons, share the latent pessimism in the idea that no Führer was able to control destiny without at the same time reflecting, on the one hand, the obligation to react to emergent irresistible forces of the *demos*, the People, and on the other, the positivist use made of human misery. The Homeric hero did not live this paradox. We would describe the ambiguity of these processes by a single word today: ideology. The reader (or listener) of *The Iliad* would not have, and indeed could not have, expressed any astonishment as the narration of the momentous events of the poem, already legendary elements in collective memory, culminate with Priam's appeal to collect Hector's corpse only after an episode of undignified bickering among the gods. When the founding father of the Roman people tries to avenge the destruction of his city by killing Helen, his divine mother reminds him of his obligations to his own family amidst the annihilation. She also points to the unavailing work of destruction in the panorama below Priam's palace to which Neptune, Juno and Athene are committed in the confused fray of humans.[117] The patron voice of morality and Reason at least attempts to reflect the nascent consciousness of the human community which Achilles, in his revenge on the senseless body of his opponent, surpasses with all the violence that only divine fury can conjure. However, Apollo's resignation reflects the as yet imperfect emergence of individuation from the primal backdrop; the god concludes his appeal for clemency to the rest of the immortals with the homily that 'The Fates have given mortals hearts that can endure'.[118] In contrast to this flawed relationship between the human and the divine in Homeric myth, there is the voice of heaven staying the father's hand from sacrificing his son with the gentle refrain, 'Abraham, Abraham'. The opacity of Abraham's resolution is due to the ease with which the voice commanding him by name to perform this supreme act of selflessness for his god is simultaneously *the mind in conversation with itself*. It is in this spirit that we read of Odysseus' return to Ithaca as a typical bourgeois on an estate managed by a cadre of grateful employees. If they dared to resist, the example meted out to the suitors' mistresses by the heir apparent in Book 22 will suffice to terrorise them into obedience. After all, it is a parable of patriarchal conquest over geography and time. The feet of the women hung in a row, Homer writes, 'kicked out for a short while, but not for long'. Adorno resumes the subtextual flow of narrative by questioning the human *ellipsis* in it, the emotionless quality of the description:

> As a citizen reflecting momentarily upon the nature of hanging, Homer assures himself and his audience (actually readers) that it did not last for long – a moment and then it was all over. But after the 'not for long' the inner flow of the narrative is arrested. *Not for long?* The device poses the question, and belies the author's composure. By cutting short the account, Homer prevents us from forgetting the victims, and reveals the unutterable eternal agony of the few seconds in which the women struggle with death. No echo of the 'not for long' remains except the *Quo usque tandem* that the rhetors of a later period unwittingly devalued themselves laying claim to the long-suffering attitude in question. In the narrative account of atrocity, however, hope attaches to the fact that it happened a long time ago. Homer offers consolation for the entanglement of prehistory, savagery, and culture by recourse to the once-upon-a-time device. Yet the epic is novel first, and fairy tale later.[119]

The interesting question for us is that the veridical procedure in historiography never claimed the same metaphysical value as a religious or epic explanation for the origins of the ethnos. From the beginning, the primary motivation of historiography

82 *Re-thinking Indian histories*

in the rhetorical mode was never to carry the individual to a point where the outcome of the story reduced the moral imagination to a mute silence. The citadel of History is not the 'arbitrary spot' Auden described as being circled by barbed wire from which the indifferent crowd has dispersed, leaving nothing behind but corpses. In addition to the homiletic function, the task of historiography is to give expression to the subtle evolution of social structures. If structure was the essence of classical society, and something the feudal order tried to emulate after the advent of the Holy Roman Empire, one wonders at the occurrence of any radical movement at all in the long passage of time. Perry Anderson describes this as an internal contradiction of the social formation preceding our own, in the following terms: 'There was thus an inbuilt contradiction within feudalism, between its own rigorous tendency to a decomposition of sovereignty [and the eventual emergence of classes, one assumes] and the absolute exigencies of a final centre of authority in which a practical recomposition could occur.'[120] What is certain is that the practical recomposition of the social order, as Anderson euphemistically puts it, by the eighteenth century at least, could not be brought about by the actors involved without a reinvigorating of the modalities of the classical age Auerbach worked with in his sympathetic interpretation of texts. White defined this final centre of authority as the historical consciousness. What is true in this regard of the Renaissance artist in Adorno's description also applies to the historian: the cultivation of the historical sense is a bulwark against the negative truth that suffering is itself the chaotic expression of being human.

How does the narrative style of history contend with the forces which in theological terms at least are responsible for the 'obscure experience of the oppressed?' The abduction of a local king's daughter by Phoenician sailors whilst shopping for wares in a crowded marketplace, Herodotus informs us, that begins the cycle of vendettas in which women are stolen from their communities, is the true event that inspired the Trojan prince to steal a Greek wife for himself, confident in the proverbial wisdom 'that no young woman allows herself to be abducted if she does not wish to be'.[121] The competition for Paris's favour among the Olympian goddesses becomes nothing more than an elegant pastoral conceit and, after Auerbach, we cannot truly blame the prince for being ignorant of the historical consequences that would ensue from his actions. To Nature at least, the distinction between herdsman and burgher to be found much later in 'feudal' Europe is non-existent in primitive society. The audience which has already witnessed the relentless carnage of war detailed by the poet in terrifying detail is reminded in the last book how when Culture came to his shepherd's fold in the guise of Athena and Hera, he chose that which any herdsman or prince would consider his birthright, Nature, and that which Love promised him, 'who dangled before his eyes the lust that loosed disaster'.[122] What force has this assertion as a homily? In the midst of the cataclysm, Achilles taunts Aeneas for being unable to defend himself. The momentarily favoured hero reminds us of the status of women when men go on expeditions for raiding sheep; when Aeneas fled down the slopes of Ida, Achilles sacked the place: 'I tore the day of freedom away from all the women, dragged them off as slaves.'[123] Not for the Trojan prince the paralysis of introspection inflicting the superstitious Hebrew mind at such depredations. Compared to the immediacy of experience (Eros), the search for origins for the ethnos (Genesis) in historiography is like the disguise adopted by Zeus to seduce hapless Io whom the Phoenicians found so irresistible, shrouded in the obscurity of clouds and thick mists.[124] Men are most like the gods when they are victimising women. The Jewish god would never have exercised his potency for such a mean end. If it helps, Herodotus writes how the physical description of the Egyptians he offers from his own eyes for the less remote Colchians, as having black skins and woolly hair, is less important than the *cultural practice* of circumcision the former shared with the Ethiopians in describing their race.[125] The tangible is preferred only as a sign to be scrutinised over the genealogical in penetrating this obscurity. The historian can take a step back from the great order of events that the abduction of womenfolk brings about to remark on the fine anthropological details of everyday existence. Contrary to the mortiferous ritual whose mystery attracted Baudrillard's attention, for the Greek historian, the temple priests of Egypt were engaged in an entirely laudable aim as well as the very mundane procedure of mummification at the behest of the relatives by professional embalmers described in *The Histories*.[126] The Egyptians have made themselves the most learned of any nation 'by their practice of keeping records of the past.'. This passion is coincidental with their dietetic regime, 'a belief that all diseases come from food a man eats; and it is a fact – even apart from this precaution – that next to the Libyans they are the healthiest people in the world'.[127] A people aware of both the good and bad effects of diet and knowledge are sure to flourish.

In the pages that follow, the didactic function of narrative will crop up consistently enough to suggest that Indians shared a similar attitude to their own history as the Europeans who inherited the classical *modus operandi* of antiquity. In examining some of the propositions made about the continuity between communities in the past (some in the long distant past) and the present, Indians are as prone to the reflexivity encountered in attempting to formulate the *narrative* art of recovering the past as the Europeans were for their own history. This reflexivity is doubly ethnic (Hebraic) and scientific (Greek). Whether Indians managed to graduate beyond this attitude to an *ars historica* that might at times challenge the rhetorical model of history and its ethos will depend, I imagine, on the degree to which Indian history began to resemble, like the history of Europe, something more than the epochal version of events containing speeches, trials and battles.

3 *Hindutva* and writing postcolonial India

> Getting its history wrong is part of being a nation.
>
> Ernest Renan[1]

> The facts are beyond dispute, and they point to the inevitable conclusion that national sentiment in India can derive no encouragement from the study of Indian history.
>
> H. Risley[2]

> If it was only to bring back again the same state of affairs as before, the same Moguls, the same Marathas and the same old quarrels – a condition, being tired of which the nation in a moment of mad folly allowed foreigners to come in – if it were only for this, the more ignorant of the populace did not think it worthwhile to shed their blood for it.
>
> Vinayak Damodar Savarkar[3]

Introduction

I began by considering Herder's image of the peaceable Hindu according to his Organic understanding of human nature with a conclusion: that it was a thesis in embryo containing all the elaborate epistemologies later used to transform the Vedic culture of ancient peoples into nationalist ideology. It is time to examine this process in detail. Instead of the individualist emphasis of *Swaraj* that Gandhi placed in his practice of non-violent resistance to colonial domination, an alternative paradigm has aroused the enthusiasms of the Indian masses and come to challenge the hegemony of Congress pluralism since at least the 1980s and 1990s. The political mobilisation of communal pride after independence, as Hindu nationalism legitimates pogroms against a weaker minority through the efforts of *The Rashtriya Swayamsevak Sangh* and its cohort of parties by monopolising state power, entails a coherent vision of the direction the Indian polity ought to take. This chapter considers the historical modality of this contrary vision for postcolonial India. The critical interventions by Vinayak Damodar Savarkar – during the period of organised anti-colonial resistance to colonial rule in the early twentieth century – will help us to explore how the ideological presuppositions of Hindu nationalism were *first of all* about an appropriation of the millennial past. A latent communal dynamic began to overdetermine claims to Indian identity at this time and in the eventual emergence of the conjunction knowledge-power, the discourse of nationalist resistance, it is argued, failed to conform to an essentially ecumenical view of the past. The name of this practice that simultaneously shares and repudiates *Swaraj* is *Hindutva*.

In his last book, *Six Glorious Epochs of Indian History* (1963), after a long career of agitation against British rule, the Hindu nationalist V. D. Savarkar returned to the scene of battle that Herder described in picturesque terms as an encounter with native gymnosophists, between the tribes of the Swat Valley and the Macedonian army. The similarity between the invading Yavanas and the Vedic tribes is important for Indian pre-history. How does a 'Hindu' historiography relate this encounter? The question will help us to illustrate the verifying norms of recovery undertaken by a type of practice that looks beyond the 'moment' India was colonised by British values and yet, as we will see, with its idiom of nationalist resistance and revolution, owes all its impetus to this moment for its cultural awakening. The army of enlightened Greeks are properly called Yavanas, while the later Muslim hordes are 'Mlenchas'. Savarkar mentions the Spartan practice of infanticide by one of these Ganas (republics). The absence of the Buddhist cult in accounts of Alexander's invasion of India 'deserves special notice in the proper interpretation of subsequent history'.[4] This contact between Hellenic culture, personified by Alexander, and Indic peoples is a fortuitous event; it galvanises the Hindu tribes on the frontier into a form of proto-nationalism. The encounter between Europe and Asia in pre-history is a theatre in which tribal chiefs become the representatives of Indian democracies fighting on behalf of a nationalist cause.[5] Savarkar admires the martial prowess of the campaign, describing it as 'a mighty Greek army of a hundred thousand gallant soldiers and their brave, world-famous, captain-general Alexander, who had vowed pompously to trample over the whole of India and conquer the crown of Maghada for himself, and which finally forced him to strike a retreat homeward from the very threshold of India'.[6] There is even the historically implausible suggestion that this vanguard reached the eternal hinterlands of Mathura where one of the 'leaders' of these republics belonging to the Vrishni dynasty once lifted a mountain to protect his cowherding disciples from a deluge released by an angry rain god after preaching an antinomian lesson on the significance of one's own actions over ritual.[7] Leaving aside the Kafirs of Nuristan as proto-Hellenes, Savarkar might have emphasised the resemblance between mighty Krishna worshipped by the lionskin-clad Gujars of Pir Sar and the ancestry to Heracles claimed by the Greeks. Arrian maintains neutrality over the question of a Theban Dionysus worshipped by the inhabitants after the god had conquered India on his return home 'toward the Grecian sea' – a tribe who incidentally are made to glorify Alexander's dominion as greater than the god's.[8] The accretions of time gather into a complex residue of tradition. An English version of the *Romance of Alexander* (*c.* 1400) contains an illumination depicting the world-famous general as a crowned and ermined king emerging from a pavilion. He is beckoning a company of naked Brahmin sages to cross the Indus. The wildness of the scene is emphasised by fabulous griffins that guard the gymnosophists.[9] The Kalash people in Chitral, Pakistan, can still be seen preserving their pre-Hindu way of life even today. The Kalash graveyards in Bumboret village still contain a profusion of wooden coffins that Alexander's army broke up and used as firewood.

For those, like the Nanda ruler of Maghada who refused to join the Massagans' cause by sending reinforcements, or those who aided the Greek incursion, like the ruler of Gandhara, Ambhi, at his capital Taxila, is reserved all the opprobrium attached to someone who fails to participate in a nationalist war of liberation against the colonial regime: 'This cowardliness on his [Mahapadmanand, the last of the Nanda rulers] part, made on the one hand, every self-respecting and nationalist Indian despise him, on the other, made him crafty. He hated the selfless national politicians.'[10] It would be Mahapadmanand's illegitimate son Chandragupta who realises the Hindu nation's being by deposing his father from his throne at Pataliputra (Patna) between 324 and 322 BCE, but more importantly in the context of Savarkar's nationalist reading of events, the Mauryan dynast defeats the invasion by Seleucus Nicator in 305 BCE after the death of Alexander in order to reclaim the Punjab from the Achaemenid/Macedonian Empire. Let us pause. Even before the Greeks, the tribes along the Indus had to capitulate to foreign domination, according to the eminent historian Hemachandra Raychaudhuri's thesis *Political History of Ancient India* (1923). An early instance of iconoclasm forced upon the inhabitants of Gandhara rather than those inhabiting the lower Indus region has been cited: 'One of the newly discovered stone-tablets at Persepolis records that Xerxes "By Ahuramazda's will" sapped the foundations of certain temples of the Daivas and ordained that "the Daivas shall not be worshipped", the king worshipped Ahuramazda together with Rtam (divine world order).' Raychaudhuri concludes, '"India" may have been the lands which witnessed the outcome of the religious zeal of the Persian king'.[11] Was the syncretism of the Greeks any defence for the inhabitants of Swat against the violence of Alexander's army?

In contrast to the cautious pace of Raychaudhuri's patient use of archaeological evidence to combat Vincent Smith's conclusion in *Early History of India*, that a political history before Alexander's invasion was impossible to write, for Savarkar, an encounter between the founder of the future Mauryan dynasty – called 'Sandrocottus' by Justin and Plutarch, then a 'young stripling' and student at the university at Taxila – and the Macedonian general is the meeting of equals in 'A Marvellous Half Hour in History': 'It appeared as if two lustrous suns, one fast approaching his zenith and the other not as yet risen fully out of the misty shroud of the early dawn, were staring at each other.'[12] Though Savarkar is dismissive of the canonising of Alexander in Islam, here it seems that the general is represented as one of the Suryavansh Kshatriyas belonging to the solar line. Taxila, with its Hindu teachers and doctors, was the place where the young Chandragupta must have familiarised himself with the precepts of governance contained in the *Arthashastra* ('Science of Material Gain') authored in tradition by Kautilya (or Chanakya), one of the exiles from Maghada. The Pali and Jain versions of the legend in which the Brahmin preceptor discovers the boy playing king among the village children resembles the staple of miraculous discovery-myths – say of Cyrus in Herodotus's *Histories* or, come to that, of Moses in the Hebrew tradition.[13] The *Arthashastra* is the text from which Savarkar draws a quote about the liberation of Bharatbhumi by 'national armed strength' and 'national scientific advance' that had decayed under the Nandas.[14] Modern scholarship has shown that Kautilya could not have been the single author of the *Arthashastra* and this instance would now read as an interpolated commentary on the text. The unprepossessing Brahmin whom the Nanda ruler had pulled by his tuft of hair eventually avenges himself by invading the Maghada capital with his protégé. Kautilya's ugliness in the Jain version is attributed to a pious if inexplicable act, his having his teeth ground down by his father to guard him against hubris. Apparently, vengeance is more edifying than pride. In *Six Glorious Epochs*, we are treated to an analogy for the moment of dissidence at court, with another in the seventeenth century. Kautilya's motives were no more personal than Shivaji's when he had been invited and insulted at Aurangzeb's court at Agra; both Kautilya and Shivaji were inspired by the 'emancipation of his religion and country'.[15] One might again note how the Jain version's psychologically more sophisticated version, where a *dasi* or slavegirl turns him out of his seat in the almshouse for encroaching on the Nanda king's shadow, also goes against the spirit of Savarkar's appropriation of these events. This nationalist version of events in the fourth century BCE means that Taxila is the hidden fulcrum of revolution (of 'the deep-laid Indian plot') during the last few years of Alexander's life.[16] Here Kautilya returned to its university, where his fame 'amongst the learned circles of India as a great scholar' first grew and caught the attention of the Nanda king. According to Savarkar, Kautilya was inspired by the Macedonian unification of the failing city-states and this vision took him as a secret mission to Magadha, visiting poor huts to the royal palace. No historical document confirms this interpretation. Taxila is where the future 'For the Entire Undivided India' was first determined by a Brahmin scholar and his (albeit illegitimate) royal student. It is through the august portals of the university of Ambhi's city Taxila that Chandragupta passed through by learning the sciences of war and politics under the tutelage of the Brahmin Kautilya, the brilliant youth who 'was destined to carve a glorious page in the history of India'.[17] Both John Marshall and Auriel Stein in their archaeological studies of the area for the Indian Archaeological Survey in the early twentieth century fail to find any evidence for the physical site of this great institution. Savarkar puts Vincent Smith's history to good use in *Six Glorious Epochs* to paint a picture of nationalist resistance to foreign invasion. We find photographs of armed *Pukhtun* clansmen and Hindu shopkeepers in Stein's survey of the topography of this region. This is the time and place where we would find Mahbub Khan, horse-dealer and British agent in Rudyard Kipling's 'Great Game'. It is in this spirit that we should read Stein's conclusion about contemporary events in comparison to the ferocity of Alexander's actions with the ancient frontiersmen on his campaign:

One mention [in Arrian and Curtius] is made of seven thousand Indian mercenaries, brought from a distance, who shared in its defence and after its capitulation made a vain endeavour to regain their homes and in that attempt were exterminated. The employment of so large a paid contingent from outside clearly indicates command of extensive material resources. At the same time it shows that the organized defence which the settled population of ancient Swāt opposed to Alexander was of a very different character from that with which a modern invader of tribal Pathān territories on the North-West Frontier has to reckon, as illustrated by the severe fighting on the Malakand in 1905 and 1907 or in the memorable Ambēla campaign of 1862. In the second place it deserves to be noted that, in spite of the valour shown by the defenders, Arrian puts the total loss suffered by the besiegers at only twenty-five men ... In this cheap price paid for the success we may recognize a proof of the ascendency which Alexander's highly trained and war-hardened veterans derived from the possession of superior armament; for both Arrian and Curtius bear testimony to the overmastering effect upon the defenders of the besiegers' war engines, including moveable towers and powerful ballistae.[18]

For Stein's expedition through this hard zone fabled even today, noting the topographical similarities with Alexander's campaign, being a guest of the ruler of Swat or 'Badshah' Miangul Abdul Wahab Gul-Shahzada much like Alexander was the guest of Ambhi at Taxila, the journey from the Kabul River or the Kush that the Macedonian armies made is a feat to be emulated, 'a matter well worthy of the attention of the modern military student interested in these regions'. This hagiography is in contrast to Savarkar's depiction of the 'colonial' encounter in ancient history between Indians and the Macedonian army. For Stein, the pathans of Swat represent a race of men who are indistinguishable from the cruel terrain of these fastnesses. In Savarkar's recovery of this ancient moment for his monumental style of history-writing, the valorous self of 'Hindu' resistance has to be summoned in order to defeat the foe. Instead of the august portals of Taxila university, Alexander's generals encountered primitive windowless mudbrick dwellings lining a crooked avenue to a hall supported by wooden rafters. To the left and right, communal dustbins added their charm to the narrow lanes of a slum. This is not to gainsay the private wealth of the citizens who hid their Hellenic-styled jewellery in the earthen grounds of their homes when the Sakas and Parthians eventually replaced the rule of Archebius, the last Greek ruler after 100 CE. An object depicting the balding head of a bearded man holding a double-handled wine cup with a curved staff ending in a bulbous design (the *thyrsus* or wand), identified as Dionysus, has also been found at the site.[19] Marshall makes a generous concession regarding the cosmopolitanism of Taxila, one which Savarkar would not second because of its foreign origins: '[W]e can hardly doubt that the interchange of eastern and western ideas during the period following the Persian conquest must have done much to stimulate the spread of knowledge, and that this stimulus became increasingly stronger under Maurya and Greek rule in the third and second centuries BC.'[20] The pre-Buddhist and Jain Brahmin orders to which Kautilya must have belonged formed fraternities or *sabhas* but, Marshall notes, '[t]here is no reason, however, to suppose that, apart possibly from a common assembly hall, they possessed either property or endowments, or that they enjoyed the use of common lecture halls, libraries or the like'.[21] In the second appendix to his rather magnificent volume, Marshall lists the opinion of three authorities on the question of Indian universities to corroborate his conclusion.

These conclusions about the homiletic use made of traditions in claiming singular and exclusive (ethnic) identity from the heterogeneous – that is to say violent – fray of history reflects the experiences of anti-colonial resistance for nations in the Third World. We examined in the previous chapter how the historical sense can be mobilised to achieve this objective. This dynamic can be illustrated by the following assertion made by Savarkar in the prologue to his account *Hindu Pad Padashahi – Story of the Maratha Struggle to Re-establish Sovereign Hindu Power* (1925):

> It would be as suicidal and as ridiculous to borrow hostilities and combats of the past only to fight them out into the present, as it would be for a Hindu and a Muhammadan to lock each other suddenly in a death-grip while embracing, only because Shivaji and Afzalkhan had done so hundreds of years ago.[22]

There is some latent confusion in this historiography. For Savarkar, there is no doubt; there are individuals in Indian history who *have* embodied the rhetorical model of history by reacting to events in a way which ordinary individuals of the kind Auerbach thought constituted an unconscious realism can only aspire to. As we will shortly see with Nehru, even gifted individuals have to perform to the choreography of Providence to secure their name to history. Contrary to the assertions in his last book, Puranic texts, like those celebrating the greatness of other civilisations, the Chinese, Babylonian and the Greek, are not history, 'replete' as they are 'with anecdotes, folk-lore and the deification of national heroes and heroines'.[23] Savarkar mentions Lord Shri Krishna of the *Bhagavat Puranas* and his sons among the leaders and state officials of these Gunas encountered by the West.[24] The task of amending the milieu in which Indians perceive their history from a foreign bias, in common with Savarkar's account of the 1857 Uprising against the colonial regime, is about the 're-orientation of our historical concepts and accepted theories'.[25] Historiography here is insufficient if it means a dispassionate account of what actually occurred in the past. The Puranic tradition precedes the glorious ephocal account of national life for Savarkar. What makes an epoch glorious, then, is not the artefacts of a civilised state of being, poetry, music, philosophy and theology (*accoutrements* to the cult of beauty amongst the *Vrishnis*) but the successful repulsion of invasions and the liberation of the nation from foreign domination. This anarchist conception of historiography lends itself to situations in which figures can behave according to the Romantic mode. Savarkar's analogy for Indian history is 1775 and the North American colonists' war with England. Though America's history is short, the war for liberation provided it as yet with its single instance of glory. Propaganda for Savarkar is 'a national duty' if the Hindu race is to counter its history as a narrative of serial defeats.[26]

Like others before him, the leader of the Maratha confederacy against Aurangzeb, Shivaji, is an avatar of the archetypal deliverer for the Hindu nation/race. In other words, the customary pathos of distance that divides the practice of writing history as a prudent and accurate description of the past from the biases and inclinations of its author-rhetor is now crossable by making a profound, albeit symbolic, identification with actors and events in the interests of the nation. The Romantic mode in which the ironic conception of history manifests itself in a self-conscious 'naive' counterpart, for the reasons gone into in Chapter 1 and Chapter 2, may not have been consistently worked out in any uniform way by the critics of the Enlightenment (in Gandhi's case more strongly, less so for Savarkar) but, in the Indian case, involved an often dogmatic adherence to rationalism as a standard by which to measure the development of society in history. That said, in contrast to the evolution of European historiography, the 'empathetic' response to the contents of the past needn't necessarily imply scorn and condescension of the kind White attributes to the Enlighteners.[27]

Nehru's views on historical development figure as a peculiar example of the nineteenth-century crisis that White charts in his account. Nehru's views are an attempt to liberate his conception of the Indian past from the anarchist impulses in the Romantic mode identified in Savarkar. Nehru *attempts* to subordinate the idiographic explanation of heroic example to the mechanistic process of historical becoming. This is not merely the idiosyncratic outcome of Nehru's complicity with reformism, noted by Chatterjee as the maturing of nationalist discourse into a discourse of order. In India, with the transformation of nationalism from 1870 on as an ideology competing with other lateral claims on the masses (especially after revolutionary internationalism in Soviet Russia), Nehru's acuity of vision about the postcolonial direction of Indian nationalism had to be carefully and strategically misaligned from the 'overlap between the appeals of national and social discontent, which Lenin with his usual piercing eye for political realities, was to make into one of the foundations of communist policy in the colonial world'.[28] The new world order for Nehru meant, above all, maintaining India's neutrality. He was not going to be guilty of delivering India to the thrall of one order after delivering it from another. With his eye on both Stalinist Russia and capitalist America, he writes:

> Co-operation can only be on a basis of equality and mutual welfare, on a pulling-up of the backward nations and peoples to a common level of well-being and cultural advancement, on an elimination of racialism and domination. No nation and no people are going to tolerate domination and exploitation by another, even though this is given some more pleasant name. Nor will they remain indifferent to their own poverty and misery when other parts of the world are flourishing. That was only possible when there was ignorance of what was happening elsewhere.[29]

Industrial power was the material means through which the great reservoir of human and natural energies were to be deployed to achieve general well-being and cultural advancement. Utilitarianism was the residue left to the nationalist elites in their experience of colonialism. Chatterjee notes: 'Within the ideological framework of mature nationalism ... the path of economic development was clearly set out in terms of the "scientific" understanding of society and history.' The problem with Nehru's conception of modernity is that when nationalist understanding appealed to 'the scientific outlook of Marxism' as the fundamental requirements of technological development became apparent, he failed to replicate the political values.[30] For Chatterjee, Nehru's Socialist revolution is now typical of the failings Engels noted in the Utopians, that '[n]ot one of them appears as a representative of the interests of that proletariat which historical development had, in the meantime, produced'.[31] We note how historical development produces needs independently of class interests in Engels' metaphysical interpretation of Marx's idea. This problem is something Chatterjee's Marxian analysis of the situation with Indian nationalism has to set aside. Gellner's distinction between the use of the state to promote industrialisation and the requirement that institutions be 'ethnic' ones is also unhelpful here.[32] For Chatterjee and the *bhadraloki* (literally, respectable folk) Marxism of Bengal that truly represents the communitarian ideals that Nehru gives a merely rhetorical voice to, all that matters is that Nehru's nationalist vision 'did not necessarily mean a fundamental reallocation of rights in society, or a revolution in the nature of property. It did not mean an equalization of incomes either.'[33]

Men who perceive the manifest destiny of their people and those who, like Nehru, regard it as their life's goal to realise this destiny, are apt to a peevish reluctance to share their greatness in the company of others. The helmsman of the ship of state will only look for captains if they are distant enough on the horizon. From his prison cell in the district gaol of Dehra Dun in September 1932, this is how Nehru characterises Alamgir the First's (Aurangzeb's title, meaning World-conqueror) grandfather, Akbar, as a 'wise despot [who] ... worked hard for the welfare of the Indian people'. Reflecting Nehru's own vision of secular modernity, Akbar's rule represents a kind of proto-nationalism at a time when this ideology had not been as urgent for the technicians of the constitutional reckoning after the departure of the British to combat the divisive tendencies of religion that had led to colonial rule in the first place. We will see what Savarkar makes of this detail soon. Akbar, who may be considered 'the father of Indian nationalism', however was not alone. There was an example of univocity in Indian history before Akbar:

> Akbar's name stands out in Indian history, and sometimes, and in some ways, he reminds one of Ashoka. It is a strange thing that a Buddhist Emperor of the third century before Christ, and a Muslim Emperor of India of the sixteenth century after Christ, should speak in the same manner and almost in the same voice. One wonders if this is not perhaps the voice of India herself speaking through two of her great sons. Of Ashoka we know little enough, except what he has himself left carved in stone. Of Akbar we know a great deal. Two contemporary historians of his Court have left long accounts, and the foreigners who visited him, and especially the Jesuits who tried hard to convert him to Christianity, have written at length.[34]

The idea that a Buddhist or Muslim should be the authentic voice of India in her long history would be anathema to Savarkar and his Hindu nationalist following.

For Nehru, the historical moment of India's self-realisation in Maratha resistance to Aurangzeb – the moment Savarkar concentrates on – is an opportunity to resuscitate a Whig tradition of the past. And in the best tradition, Nehru's encyclopaedic interpretation of events in his letters to his daughter as well as the autobiographical compendium represents a desire to speak in oracular fashion in the temple of History. Nietzsche represents this impatient desire in the memorable terms of the 'man of action' whose goal is not his own happiness but that of a nation or of mankind as a whole. In the temple of history, the role this consciousness carves for itself is that of teacher, comforter and admonisher to those following him. The figures in Nehru's history are separated by others by centuries and resemble each other in the following constellation:

> That the great moments in the struggle of the human individual constitute a chain, that this chain unites mankind across the millennia like a range of human mountain peaks, that the summit of such a long-ago moment shall be for me still living, bright and great – that is the fundamental idea of the faith in humanity which finds expression in the demand for a *monumental* history.[35]

The details of economic planning that might involve a radical implementation of price and wage policy to achieve the kind of equity Nehru doubtless desired seem a very mandarin affair set against the spirit of magnificent hubris informing the attitude to the past suggested above. The chapter headings nevertheless represent revolutionary aspirations reflecting the determinism of modernity first encountered in the French Encyclopaedists: 'Aurangzeb puts the clock back. Growth of Hindu Nationalism. Shivaji.' Hindu nationalism is an atavistic reaction. In contrast to Alamgir, Nehru continues to write:

> Only Akbar might have understood the situation and controlled the new forces that were rising. Perhaps even he could only have postponed the dissolution of his empire unless his curiosity and thirst for knowledge led him to understand the significance of the new techniques that were arising, and of the shift in economic conditions that was taking place.[36]

The implications of Nehru's expository mode are clear. Although it may at first sight appear as an essentially capitalist bourgeois *modus operandi*, the ability to perceive the importance of technological advancements will enable an individual to embody the spirit of the age and, by doing so, to transcend it. This spirit is by its very nature teleological. 'No man can succeed in great tasks unless the time is ripe and the atmosphere is favourable' Nehru continues to note in *Glimpses of World History*. The horizon of Indian history for Nehru, unlike that for Savarkar, remains temporal and not cultural. In other words, the conception of the providential role history played in forming the Indian nation is as organic and undifferentiated as the matrix of Nature, the kind Herder imagined for humankind. There is a vital difference though: for Nehru, the course of an individual civilisation grows moribund if it is not invigorated by contact with others. Nehru would not care to live in the eternal *Ganas* at the foot of the Himalayas, as if protected from the depredations of foreign invasion. If only these invaders would send an embassy of technocrats rather than armies! 'Contact' for Nehru's discourse is not the social Darwinist conception to be found in the anarchic conception of a war for survival of cultures in competition unto death. He is to be congratulated for resisting the spirit of this interpretation found in Savarkar, as we shall see below, as well as in the revolutionary policies of the Ottoman government, the Committee of Union and Progress (CUP). To give contact a technological character reflects Nehru's faith in the incremental advance of humankind. This technocratic view of human history concentrates more on the sanitary rules enforced at Maghada's Pataliputra concerning the condition of the streets than the evanescent glory of Alexander.[37] While from the mid-1950s on, having realised the limits of a Socialist revolution in the social state of India and having repudiated the 'disease of giganticism' (although not in symptomatic terms of a colonial legacy but of utility) that was now interpreted as foreign to Indian life in its actuality, when it came to the workings of the speculative intellect whose habit Nietzsche described, Nehru could still be said to formally typify the passionate adherence to a monumental historiography.[38] This attempt to resurrect the totality of the past in all its great complexity he shared with the Hindu nationalist appropriation but, unlike the combination of an authoritarian idealisation of 'a *remote past* of natural-human innocence from which men have fallen into the corrupt "social" state in which they currently find themselves', Nehru's observations represent a rather moving optimism in the genera of historical development.[39] Let us explore his characterisation of one such element in India's history: Islam. 'Like a meteor in the sky he came and went, and left little of himself behind him except a memory.'[40] In contrast to the admiring tone Savarkar adopts for albeit an abortive attempt by Alexander to conquer India, for Nehru his violent campaigns inspire repulsion and disgust.[41] Islam, in contrast, was an *idea* rather than an individual's attempt to attract the gaze of posterity and, as such, it 'brought a new impulse for human progress to India'. Nehru continues:

> To some extent it served as a tonic. It shook up India. But it did less good than it might have done because of two reasons. It came in the wrong way, and it came rather late. For hundreds of years before Mahmud of Ghazni raided India, Muslim missionaries had wandered about India and had been welcomed. They came in peace and had some success. There was little, if any, ill-feeling against Islam. Then came Mahmud with fire and sword, and the manner of his coming as a conqueror and a plunderer and killer injured the reputation of Islam in India more than anything else. He was, of course, just like any other great conqueror, killing and plundering, and caring little for religion. But for a very long time his raids overshadowed Islam in India and made it difficult for people to consider it dispassionately, as they might otherwise have done.[42]

That Islam should democratise the conditions prevailing before the Ghaznid invasion, like a kind of monotheistic Buddhism, goes along with the transcendental value Nehru attributes to forms of belief in the revolutionary conditions of societies that are themselves *supposed to pass* from obsolete to more vital forms. And in the culmination of this process, the essential heterogeneity of Indian society, – rather like Michelet's Romantic ambitions for the great Platonic year 1789 in France – also represents the amalgamation of potentially inimical forces into a pacific unity; 'We worshippers of the future, who put our faith in hope, and look towards the East', as Michelet put it, except Nehru was looking West in this instance.[43] Nehru's Romantic emplotment of the history of India continues to emphasise the lateness of Islam's arrival to India as the cause of conflict. Again reflecting his faith in the vitality of ideas before they become embroiled in the substance of history as the excreta of ambitious men like Alexander and Mahmud of Ghazni, 'the rising Arabian culture' implied by Islam's manifestation 'would have mixed with the old Indian culture'. Nehru continues to give a proleptic shape to events in the past: 'It would have been the mixing of two cultured races; and the Arabs were well known for their toleration and rationalism in religion'; Nehru goes on to note how in Baghdad the Caliph, like Akbar later, was the patron of discussions between religious and atheistic men alike meeting 'together to discuss and debate all matters from the point of view of rationalism alone'.[44] The Turkic conquest of India, unlike the 'culture of the Arab', was military, but even here, the eudemonic tendency predominates and Nehru alludes to Akbar as the realisation of 'progress and creative effort' *working itself out*.[45] That it is a natural tendency in the evolution of human history is revealed by the autonomy he perceives in the historical purpose, and we saw above how this autonomy can move beyond the control of even the glorious individual. This organic insight, however, unlike the tragic trope associated with a mechanistic understanding of historical process, operates in an atmosphere where the harmonious resolution of problems is always at the forefront of interpretation. Nehru's observations about the rationalist element in Islamic consciousness in an alien environment do not stop at the physical manifestation of conflict. Neither is he prone to a crudely dialectical reductionism of a kind we might discern between rationality on the one side and reason on the other. In this specific regard, one would have thought Nehru's conspicuous departure from the form in which the late nineteenth-century phase of Hindu revivalism had degenerated (*Hindutva*), his confident if a little arid appropriation of the 'religious semiotic' would be welcome, but no.[46] Rationalism is a law unto itself or rather reason is the ore to emerge from the dross of superstition in religious belief. Chatterjee's deeply ironic interpretation of Nehru's betrayal of that authentic religious semiotic concerning a remark the first Prime Minister makes to his audience when opening a train-making factory on Gandhi's birthday is typical of the way the moral element of Hindu consciousness has been 'subsumed under the rational monism of historical progress': 'For now, Gandhi's Truth had surrendered the specificity of its moral critique: it had been cleansed of its religious idiom.'[47] Chatterjee's response, I am sure, would be that modalities of Gandhi's *Swaraj* are in no way identical to those of Savarkar's *Hindutva* but we will see how, especially from Ambedkar's perspective, the 'semiotic' or historical interpretation of these contrary visions in Hindu consciousness for postcolonial India are identical. The conclusion of this examination of comparative development and retardation between Asia and Europe in which the goal of history is universal freedom – in the best Liberal tradition of the Enlighteners – is that the contrary to freedom, stagnation and decay, appears only when Indian civilisation began to imprison itself by 'building a shell round itself'. The metaphor is organic but properly belongs to the economic realm of the eighteenth-century debate between Mercantilists and Physiocrats over how to produce an infinite supply of 'specie' or capital. And sure enough, economic isolationism is equivalent to cultural decay in Nehru's examples of China and Japan. No doubt reflecting on his own physical confinement, Nehru concludes:

> It is a little dangerous to live in a society which is closed up like a shell. We petrify there and grow unaccustomed to fresh air and fresh ideas. Fresh air is as necessary for societies as for individuals.

Savarkar's history *Hindu Pad Padashahi* is the weakest of his works; this history is intended in the mode of vindication. In contrast to Nehru's observations, where the line between history and the present is only blurred to endorse a eudemonic view, the rhetorical version of the past as the preferred mode for Savarkar is not to foster solidarity among individuals in the face of colonial realities but as a means of justifiable protest against the ancestry of India's Muslims. Shivaji's resistance against Aurangzeb's forces is an exemplary model of courageous conduct for the Hindu community. This, however, does *not* mean Hindus ought to precisely emulate this figure from the seventeenth century in their reaction to the challenges of modern times. Why would this course of action be suicidal? After the events portrayed in *Hindu Pad Padashahi*, when the Marathas had razed the Mughal (Savarkar writes 'Muslim') throne and placed it at the feet of Bhau and Vishvas in 1761, the enmity between the two religious communities had been set aside. Resistance to British domination complicates the otherwise simple trajectories of identification that communities ought to make between themselves and historical figures: Muslims for Aurangzeb, Hindus for Shivaji. Incursions into the national past ought to be made carefully in the context of actual past realities. After all, the sages or 'Haribhaktis' of 'Hindudom' had entered Delhi during the Uprising in 1857 against the British and, Savarkar concludes, '[v]iewed in this light, the history of the Marathas is so far from standing in the way of any real and honourable unity between our Hindus and our Muhammadan countrymen'.[48]

To what do we owe the conclusion that Nehru's nationalism marked a departure from Gandhi's Truth? I stated that the religious semiotic had degenerated into a minatory discourse by the early twentieth century, with the implication that the Gandhian undertaking of peaceful resistance to the colonial regime met its terminus in the idiom of *Ramrajya* that informed his metaphysical understanding of what needs to be done. It is easy to characterise the anarchism resulting from a Romantic evocation of martial prowess as a native solution to a foreign problem, but this would be an interpretation in a vacuum. Ranajit Guha explains how the 'only way the indigenous bourgeoisie could hope ... to compete for hegemony was to mobilize the people in a political space of its own making – that is, to enlist their support for its programs, activate them in its campaigns and generally organize them under its leadership'.[49] We will see below *how* nationalist discourse used the past to create that indigenous political space but I will state at the outset, with Guha, that in the course of its encounter with dominance by the colonial power, 'the leading bloc within Indian nationalism must have met with the resistance of a political culture in which force had been privileged over consent by virtue of an age-old and nearly sacrosanct tradition'.[50] How long could the nationalist bourgeoisie have resisted the use of the powerful instrumentality of the state apparatus in imposing its own native version of colonial sovereignty on the masses?

This instrumentality that takes 'sacrosanct tradition' as its guise is not simply the classical analogy of battles in the Puranic past that we also find in European historiography in the Renaissance. British pragmatic rule hid within itself the means to actualise juridical power. For the first time, Indian nationalists were faced with the grim choices of the form in which juridical power was to be exercised in achieving the objectives of a unitary postcolonial state. It is Edmund Burke who gives the best expression of Guha's idea of sacrosanct tradition that motivates a colonial 'governmentality'. Speaking at the impeachment of Warren Hastings as Governor-General of India for abuses of power, Burke identifies Hastings' remit in the following terms:

> He have arbitrary power. My Lords, the East India Company have not arbitrary power to give him; the King has no arbitrary power to give him; your Lordships have not, nor the Commons, nor the whole Legislature. We have no arbitrary power to give, because Arbitrary power is a thing which neither any man can hold nor any man can give away. No man can govern himself by his own will, much less can he be governed by the will of others. We are all born in subjection, all born equally, high and low, governors and governed, in subjection to one great, immutable, pre-existent law, prior to all our devices, and prior to all our contrivances, paramount to our very being itself, by which we are knit and connected in the eternal frame of the universe, out of which we cannot stir.[51]

The English jurist's conception of power perfectly represents the universality of force. Let us look at Burke's speech closely. It illustrates how the lineaments of state power emerge out of the more obscure backdrop of feudal society. This form cannot yet be categorised as the nation. The first thing to note is that Burke's conception of sovereignty is pre-capitalist. If power is not restricted, as it is in Hobbes' theory of the leviathan-state, in, for example, the wholly metaphoric body of the King, how is it to exact duties from its subjects? Contract is impossible on this ever receding but bounded horizon of power where no private individuals can practice or measure their will against a parallelogram of forces. The first duty of this relatively primitive function of the law was to decipher this pattern. It is no wonder that one such atom, namely Hastings, gets lost in 'the eternal frame of the universe'. This conception of power that exceeds the pragmatic application of force to punish any individual is the reason why Hastings escapes the charges laid against him by Burke rather than any psychologistic motive of 'colonial guilt to emerge from the colonization of India' or, a little more plausibly, than any 'subterranean admission that it was indeed too facile to assume that Hastings alone could be held responsible for the exigencies of what it means to colonize'.[52] These are retrospective projections. The dark age of guilt and exigencies of colonialism that nationalists will respond to with their own version of order has not yet enveloped the advanced particularistic individualism of the French Enlightenment. For Burke, and therefore a colonised India's conception of history, the individual is a bright atom in the Great Chain of Being. Every instance of self-interest is an incomprehensible infraction of a sublime law which is sublime because it is a state of nature: '[W]e are all born in subjection.'

When set against the infinity of law, the demands of a population are all petty instances. What is peculiar in Burke's conception of power is that a Brahmin priest interpreting the responsibilities of *dharma* (ethics) and *niti* (politics) in shastric sources could not have expressed the foundation and source of authority in better terms. Native and foreign modalities of rule coalesce even as the latter finds itself expressed in a discourse of improvement and reform. This is consistent with the project of reform of native Hindu and Muslim legal practice undertaken by Hastings, resulting for the former in N. B. Halhed's text *A Code of Gentoo Laws; or, Ordination of the Pundits* (1776), reform continued by men like William Jones and his successor, Colebrooke, who (incorrectly) identified by analogy the regional differentiations in *Dayanaga* and *Mitakshara* types of Hindu law with the *Hanafi*, *Shafai*, *Maliki* and *Hanbali* interpretive traditions of *shariati* practice in Sunni Islam.[53] With the help of the *pandit* for Hindu litigants and a *maulvi* for Muslims, Collector Sahib would sit in *Dewani* (civil and revenue litigation) and *Faujdari* (civil order and criminal) courts to impartially rule in Ashokan style on the respective testimonies presented to him by the different parties.

Burke's Augustan or conservative vision of law in the late eighteenth century has a profounder affinity to native conceptions of sovereignty. Jones, the 'Justinian of India', was in regular correspondence with Burke shortly after his arrival in India, sending him his ideas for the inviolability of the laws of the natives in 'Best Practicable System of Judicature'.[54] We have a parallel in *Rajniti* (statecraft) in the immutable law that is prior to all inferior human practice and 'paramount to our very being', a force which restricts and contains every individual in 'the eternal frame of the universe … out of which we cannot stir'. Although the great Mauryan ruler Ashoka does not describe himself as such in any of his rock-hewn Edicts, 'Buddhist tradition depicts him as the *chakkavatti* – the universal monarch who ensures the turning of the wheel of law is the essence of his rule'.[55] Foucault identifies the patristic essence behind the modern discipline of governmentality in the following terms: 'To govern a state will therefore mean to apply economy, to set up an economy at the level of the entire state, which means exercising towards its inhabitants, and the wealth and behaviour of each and all, a form of surveillance and control as attentive as that of the head of a family over his household and goods.'[56] 'All men are my children' was the rallying cry by the king as nucleus of the Mauryan system in the classical age of India's millennial past.[57] The spirit of Ashokan rule, paternalistic in essence though originally Buddhist, would also inspire Gandhi's Hindu ideal of non-violent resistance (*ahimsa*). The best guarantor of the lives of those least able to defend their interests could never be left to the moral conscience of Hinduism for those who desire a radical transformation of Indian society on egalitarian terms with no inherited forms of oppression. The Great Chain of Being could never be malleable enough to form a perfect Circle of Equity by the native principles of Hindu belief.

Burke's conception then actually exceeds the terms of sovereignty established in the classical sense of order; it makes even the paternalistic exercise of power in the interests of the subordinated a mythical process. This transcendental Force which in the native lexicon is called *Danda* – whose origins are mythical and whose effects are diffuse enough to impact beyond the actions of individuals – binds 'high and low' together in sociality. 'The sacral aspect of the idiom allowed such exercise [of coercive authority by the dominant over the subordinate in every walk of life] to justify itself by a morality conforming fully to the semi-feudal values still pronounced in our culture.' Guha goes on to state: 'Armed with this doctrine, every landlord could indeed play "maharaj" to his tenants in extracting *begar* [forced labour] from them or setting his *lathi*-wielding myrmidons on them if they refused to oblige.'[58] What happens when human society is struck by Nature's equivalent of the divine *Danda*? How does British power respond in saving the most vulnerable and abject *praja* (people)? Is order excited into kindness by the adversity of fortune, so that at the most critical moment improvement and progress means maintaining the precarious balance between life and death for a subject population? Wolpert notes how, by the end of 1769

> when the monsoon rains failed, Bengal was left naked, stripped of its surplus wealth and grain. In the wake of British spoliation, famine struck and in 1770 alone took the lives of an estimated one-third of Bengal's peasantry. The company stored enough grain to feed its servants and soldiers, however, and merchant speculators made fortunes on the hunger and terror of less fortunate people, who bought handfuls of rice for treasures and were eventually driven to cannibalism.[59]

Despite the owners cultivating their estates along with the help of migrant labourers, the shortage of labour actually preceded the famine of 1769–1770. The increased revenue demand by 53.8 per cent by alien *ijaradars* (revenue farmers) and *amils* (revenue collectors), 'with the increasing predominance of Europeans as the zamindars' creditors', worsened the crisis.[60] The Indian *gomasthas* (the speculators noted above) that monopolised the supply of grain, one of the means by which the Company's private servants made their fortunes, in addition to the intervention of the government with its large cash reserve buying 120,000 *maunds* for its armies and servants, would prompt the following observations by Richard Becher for the Court of Directors in London: '[S]ince the accession of the Company to the Diwani [revenue collection] the condition of the people of this Country has been worse than it was before ... this fine country, which flourished under the most despotic and arbitrary Government, is verging towards its Ruin.'[61] The novel *Anandamath* by the nationalist Bankim Chandra Chatterjee allegorises the fortunes of the country under the British by recounting this predicament faced by the *bhadraloki zamindar* Mahendra Singh, his wife Kalyani and their small daughter during the famine. The novel also best represents the historical conditions for the religious semiotic in practice in Gandhi's moral vision of a liberated country. A more modest rise of 10 per cent by the government collector 'to advance his personal prestige' than the increase noted in economic histories is enough to deprive the couple of their subsistence living during the famine. The propagandist flavour of the text from 1882 is given by the following episode. Mahendra Singh is being shown 'a gigantic, imposing, resplendent, yes, almost living map of India' by a sage called Mahatma Satya (*satya* is truth), who belongs to an outlawed sect. In a dark room, with a single shaft of light Mahendra is shown a map of India in rags and tatters. 'The gloom over this map was beyond description.' Bankim goes on

> 'This is what our Mother India is today,' the Mahatma said. 'She is in the gloom of famine, disease, death, humiliation and destruction.'
> 'Why does a sword hang over Mother India of today?' Mahendra asked.
> 'Because the British keep India in subjection by the sword. And she can be freed only by the sword. Those who talk of winning India's independence by peaceful means do not know the British, I am sure. Please say Bande Mataram.'[62]

The Mahatma's recommendation of violence is not a nationalist myth. The statue of the viceroy Sir John Lawrence (1864–1869), erstwhile celebrated chief commissioner who thwarted the Mutiny of 1857 with his Sikh regiments, would have looked down on Bankim in his native Calcutta. The motto beneath the statue reads: 'The British conquered India by the sword and they will hold it by the sword.' To reinforce the message, another statue of Lawrence was erected in front of the Lahore High Court in 1887 at whose base the natives would be asked a rhetorical question: 'Will you be governed by the pen or the sword?' We are reminded that 'The split between law and violence is false even, or above all, with regard to the modern State. For unlike its pre-capitalist counterparts, this supremely juridical State holds a monopoly of violence and ultimate terror, a monopoly of war.'[63] In native terms, this is the *danda* (order) behind *dharma* (improvement).

The attempt by Indians to resist the code of organised public violence of the British state, along with the pre-capitalist arbitrariness of terror that accompanies this resistance, first manifested itself in a similarly organised and less 'spontaneous' way in the Sepoy Rebellion of 1857. These inscriptions are designed to reinforce the tough paternalistic order epitomised, for example, by Bankim's contemporary, Rudyard Kipling. The old Punjabi soldier in Kipling's adventure tale *Kim* recounts the mutiny of the native troops to the boy hero and his venerable lama in terms of 'madness'. Having turned against their officers, 'the first evil, but not past remedy if they had held their hands', the soldiers 'chose to kill the Sahib's wives and children. Then came the Sahibs from over the sea and called them to most strict account.'[64] The soundness and permanence of colonial rule, post-1857, is founded on having a monopoly of war rather than the elegant question of 'equity' of economic interests and rights between landlords and tenants in the political economy of Permanent Settlement of the kind promoted by John Company a mere sixty-four years before. The monuments are an attempt to give metaphoric form to state violence in terms of a civil discourse of law and order. Edward Said correctly identifies the true motivations behind the ideological manoeuvre in Kipling's novel and therefore, to Bankim's novel of anti-colonial resistance: 'To reduce Indian resentment, Indian resistance (as it might have been called) to British insensitivity to "madness", to represent Indian actions as mainly the congenital choice of killing British women and children – these are not merely innocent reductions of the nationalist Indian case but tendentious ones.'[65] Kipling's soldier is referring to the loss of English lives all over North India with the capture of Delhi, the killing of 125 women and children in the Bibigarh at Kanpur, the massacring of the rest of their fleeing kin at Sati Chowda Ghat, the siege of the Residency at Lucknow by mutinous troops and so on. Residues of the paternalism of colonial rule, no matter how tendentious, still remain. The valorous measures of Sir Henry Lawrence, elder brother of John Lawrence and 'one of the company's wisest servants' and lately chief commissioner of Oudh province, is described as having 'herded *his* flock of Europeans and Indians into the residency'.[66] Bankim's novel, then, is responding to the dynamics of an event in recent memory rather than to the Bengal famine of a century before.

The episode with Mahendra and the Mahatma's exhortation of *Bande Mataram* (Hail the Motherland) is part of the nationalist discourse of the late nineteenth century and properly belongs to the strategic concerns of resistance to colonial rule at 'its moment of departure'. The novel is a perfect vehicle for what Partha Chatterjee describes as 'a specific subjectivity of the nation'. This subjectivity is ahistorical and the reason for this ahistoricity is, he explains, because it is circumscribed

> within an essentialist typology of cultures in which this specificity can never be truly historical. Within the domain of thought thus defined [nationalist thought in opposition to colonialist Orientalist thought], however, it seems a valid answer. The West has a superior culture, but only partially; spiritually, the East is superior. What is needed, now, is the creation of a cultural ideal in which the industries and the sciences of the West can be learnt and emulated while retaining the spiritual greatness of Eastern culture. This is the national-cultural project at its moment of departure.[67]

We now understand why the scene from *Anandamath* lacks historical verisimilitude. Any attempt to create a historically faithful representation of what native Bengalis might actually have felt or said about Company Bahadur during the famine of 1769–1770 is subordinate to the obligation to represent the specific subjectivity, the 'cultural ideal' of India a century later. This strategic omission of an historical sense is emblematic of the decision to cast the Bengali bourgeois couple at the centre of the narrative. Bankim's bourgeois nationalist mode as well as his cultural religious identity prevent him from enacting a drama in which the magnates of Burdwan, Rajshahi or the banking families of Seths and Omichands would play their role of intrigue with the British to challenge the authority of the Muslim Nawab Siraj-ud-Daulah to rule. A conspiracy in 1757 against the Mughal appointment, 'led by several of the great men, at the head of which is Jugget Seit himself', is commented on approvingly by Clive in a letter. Speaking of Jagat Seth, 'as he is a person of the greatest property and influence in the three subas [Bengal, Bihar and Orissa] and of no inconsiderable weight at the Mogul's court, it was natural to determine him, as the properest person to settle the affairs of this Government'.[68] The principally hegemonic project of nationalism, Chatterjee writes, is borne out of a conflict of loyalties for the Calcutta middle class. The collaborating class of the mid-eighteenth century faced no such dilemma and were not 'created in a relation of subordination'. There are a number of reasons for this. The colonial dialectic of dominance and subordination/resistance had not emerged in the critical way it did by 1857. Only by the late-nineteenth century, when 'political and economic domination by a British colonial elite was a fact', could the small *zamindar* Mahendra Singh and others of his class undertake the task of creating a cultural ideal around which the rest of the nation is invited to respond.[69] Bankim belongs to this class. The problem of *Anandamath* is that the elites in the mid-eighteenth century, where this cultural ideal had not yet been formalised as a political strategy, were, as the excerpt of Clive's letter shows, busy collaborating with the nascent successor power to the Mughals in Bengal. The nascent nationalist consciousness that perfectly suits the atypical (for 1769) figures of Mahendra and Kalyani is entirely imaginary, which is why it has been projected back into the mid-eighteenth century.

The most that could have been expected from the Jagat Seths or Pran Bose, an *ijaradar* of Rajshahi, or the Rani Bhabani is 'a benevolent despotism, living in splendid isolation from the subject people, but sternly exacting from them obedience and tribute'.[70] In feudal society, *danda* is synonymous with *dharma*. It is only later in the nationalist imagination of Bankim that this class of individuals were invested with 'the mantle of peasant-resisters'.[71] In this imaginative reconstruction of the nation's past we can see Mahendra Singh and Kalyani working unyielding fields with their *ryots* (tenants). This picture is far from the contest of elites that establish British colonial rule. Kalyani would have sacrificed her wedding jewellery to the *gomastha* for a little rice to save her family and so on. Had some of John Company's British detractors peopled Bankim's novel with their voice, it would not have read so much as a late nineteenth-century polemic for a situation a century earlier.

This is not to suggest that the idiom of the Indian nation was absent in the dissenting voices to British policy. After expressing a pecuniary interest in reducing the national debt and protecting assets in 'those distant parts of the world', a witness as partial as a stockholder in the East India Company would allude to the arbitrary nature of the economic doctrine where the 'great territorial revenues in Bengal ... have, of late, been so extravagantly accumulated in the coffers of private men, for trifling or destructive purposes'. The subordination of Indian trading capital to the Company and European private capital solely devoted to mulberry cultivation to meet the increasing demand for silk in the London market, together with a small decrease of only 5.08 per cent in the revenue collection just two years after the devastating effect of depopulation from famine, sets the tone for the following sentiment.[72] In 1772, the English gentleman exhorts his Majesty to 'resume' the sword from the rapacious merchants of the Company, only then can justice be restored to end the frenzied competition of private capitalists. He continues

> We might then hope to see an impartial administration of justice in India, without its being subject to the control of those who are most likely to be the greatest delinquents. We might then hope to see an end to those cruel monopolies, carried on by the Servants of the Company, in the necessaries of life, and to which the wretched natives are obliged to submit, with the bayonet at their throats: and we might then hope to see those Servants once more attentive to the commercial interests of their employers; without attempting to equal, in riches and splendour, the first nobility of the kingdom.[73]

The employees of John Company, protected as they are by a standing army, are to be secluded from the allure of violence by the King's nominal authority. Captain Thomas, who is guarding a silk factory from rebel attack, is ambushed by one of the Children of the secret order when he goes hunting in a dense forest. Enchanted by the beauty of a *sanyasi*, he threatens to kill the ascetic (as Englishmen are wont to do). The *sanyasi* 'fell like lightning upon the Englishman' and dropping his skin and his matted wig, 'the English captain found himself confronted by a ravishingly beautiful Hindu woman'. What is the Englishman to do with Shanti, the female *sanyasi* who is the wife of one of the rebels he has been billeted to defend the factory from? The ravishing epitome of Hindu womanhood, Shanti, assures the captivated (in both senses) Englishman that she will not harm him. She exhorts him to leave the Motherland over which he has no 'moral or legal right to rule' and return as a true Christian back to England. Captain Thomas offers Shanti his bed as his mistress. A bizarre exchange ensues in which she agrees to his offer if, when the 'inevitable' war is over, she is still living. She asks him: 'And if we win, will you live in my monkey cage and eat bananas as a monkey?'

> 'I love to eat bananas. Have you any now with you?'
> 'Here you better take back your rifle! It is difficult to talk with such savages!'
> Shanti threw away the rifle, and walked away smiling.[74]

The militancy of the insurgents does not actually extend to killing this Captain Thomas who has been sent by the Governor-General Warren Hastings 'to crush the Children'. Perhaps the role of Hindu womanhood is not to emulate the Kshatriya or warrior ideal the Mahatma was inculcating in Mahendra Singh? There is an important point to conclude from this romantic-melodramatic encounter: it is clear that the role of the Bengali woman is to uphold the native social order and, in this spiritual task, only moral victories are available to Indian womanhood; it is the work of Indian men to defend the purity of Mother India from the alien aggressor.

In Partha Chatterjee's terms, Shanti represents a spiritual superiority over the British. The question is why *Anandamath* is set in the eighteenth century in a context where the nationalist movement by Congress was establishing its ideological answer to British colonial rule on the terms of native culture that Chatterjee identifies above.

One of the reasons why the novel does not reflect a contemporary concern to resist colonisation is because of the complicity of the native Indian social elites to which, Chatterjee reminds us, Bankim as an upper caste Bengali actually belonged. Writing about Cornwallis's land revenue reforms in Bengal of 1793, known as the Permanent Settlement, Bankim thinks these unjust because it was an arrangement that the British came to with the *zamindar* rather than the tenant. Again, there is the characteristic note against 'feudalism' by the nascent nationalist bourgeoisie. The reforms failed because of the greed and rapacity of a section of the landlords. Turning to the present, Bankim is not arguing for the reversal of the reforms of the late eighteenth century to cure the maladies that beset the Bengali peasantry (and by implication, the Indian peasantry) in the late nineteenth. 'We request the British Indian Association' to exhort the landlords to mend their ways. 'If they can control the wicked landlords, they will do a service to the country which will be remembered in history for all time to come ... If this is not done, there is no hope for the prosperity of Bengal.' Bankim can only arrive at the colonial solution of benevolent despotism at the problem of his own class. Chatterjee concludes: 'That is all [Bankim] could suggest as a remedy for the poverty of Bengal's peasants.'[75]

There is no doubt that no nationalist historiography was ever an invention *ex nihilo*. In this limited sense, nationalist ideology is identical to the other more traditional species of dominance that made free use of history writing in feudal society. If classic and Arab-Persian chronicles before the British served to legitimate the vision of any dynast, nationalism also required history to lend authority to the stamp of its 'modernity'. This is what I mean by normative assumptions in Indian historiography. Chatterjee partially ascribes Bankim's hostility to Islam (after all, half the population of the Mahatma Satya's Bengal would be Muslim) to a post-Enlightenment view by European historiography of Islam as 'being devoid of spiritual or ethical qualities, a complete antithesis to his ideal religion, irrational, bigoted, devious, sensual and immoral'. This is a dubious conclusion for reasons I will soon turn to. For Chatterjee, Bankim's attempt at a unitarian ideal of nationalist culture (typified, it has to be said by *Bande Mataram*, the call of arms to defend the Motherland) in a Hinduism that is to be disseminated among the people after it has been purified of folk religion, does not reflect rationalistic tendencies he rather conventionally identifies in 'early medieval Islamic scholarship and its explorations in Greek philosophy'.[76] Ernest Gellner would have something to say about the relationship between Islam and Hinduism as social systems but it is not safely relegated to 'the European Renaissance of which Bankim was so appreciative' or to the early medieval scholasticism which Chatterjee similarly finds an edifying moment in history. Hinduism as a political ideology aspiring to the condition of nationalism is a late arrival compared to Islam: 'The mechanisms which underlie Muslim fundamentalism, of an identification with an anonymous

Umma, are similar to those which underlie modern nationalism: men leaving, or deprived of places in a local social structure, are attracted by identification with a community defined by a shared High Culture.'[77] The failed theodicy of Marxist societies that were 'the first secular *Umma* or sacramental community' is similar to 'a kind of prefabricated Constitutional Law, which sits in judgement on their own rulers, and obliges them at least to enforce the Law, even if not to refrain from Mafioso-style politics'.[78] How does Islam manage to inoculate societies of the recurring decimal of nationalism, where 'every national flea has smaller fleas to plague it in turn, not to mention the fact that fleas of the same size also torment each other?'[79] The anthropologist in Gellner cannot resist the conclusion that modernity posed no inherent problem for Islam and that 'Islamic society was ever ideally prepared, by an accident of history, for this development'.[80] This is the problem that Kemalism faces and addresses with its peculiar repetition of the Decembrist solution. Gellner goes on to state how Islamic society is immune from the accident of history because

> [i]t possessed within itself both a high and low culture. They had the same name, and were not always carefully distinguished, and were often deliberately conflated and fused; they were linked to each other. Both, in the past, could be and were the means of a whole-hearted, passionate identification with a (supposedly unique) Islam, as an absolute, uncompromising and final revelation. Islam had no church perhaps, but the church it did not have was a broad one. In the modern world, the low or folk variant can be and is disavowed, as a corruption, exploited if not actually invented or instigated by the alien colonialist enemy, while the high variant becomes the culture around which a new nationalism can crystallize.[81]

Hindutva as a defining modality for Indian historicity arises against this pragmatic background where Islam manifests itself as infinitely capable of combining its essential millenarianism with the demands of history. Nehru's odd remarks of a belated Islam arriving in India have to be understood in the context of its appeal as 'Reformation-prone', as 'Permanent Reformation'.[82] Apocryphal notions about the perfect social order in religious texts are given new life, 'needing argument, persuasion, evidences of many kinds; what seems simple and transparent is really obscure and contrived, the outcome of circumstances now forgotten and preoccupations now academic, the residue of metaphysical systems sometimes incompatible and even contradictory'.[83] If in the early twentieth-century insurgents against British colonialism looked to Mehmed V, the puppet of the military *pashas*, to revive hopes of a Caliphate, the lesson was not lost on V. D. Savarkar. Despite the fact that 'some deeply engrained religious-cultural habits possess a vigour and tenacity which can virtually equal those which are rooted in our genetic constitution … the price these high cultures pay for becoming the idiom of entire territorial nations, instead of appertaining to a clerkly stratum only, is that they become secularized'.[84] For Khilnani, in contrast to Chatterjee's critique of Nehru's nationalist discourse, the attempt to 'remould Indian society' by the state was a form of benign trusteeship. The state is a guardian against the ignorance of the masses: after all, '[p]olitics was still being played by men who were not professionals but had come to politics through the nationalist movement'. Any deformities resulting from the secularising of high culture when history is made to serve the discourse of power are symptomatic of 'a genuine idealism'. This is Khilnani's conclusion:

> Yet most citizens remained outside this conversation [turn-taking in the exercise of power] altogether, and were increasingly puzzled by its terms. Nehru himself was aware of this, and insisted constantly on the need to explain the operations of the state, and of democratic politics, to them: but he was caught by his own conceptual language, restricted by the boundaries of intelligibility set by the English language of power. Little was done to widen the circles of deliberation, to establish a public vocabulary through which Indians could talk to one another as Indians.[85]

Nehru has now become the unwitting victim of the colonial discourse of order. This discourse by definition was undemocratic. The implication is that a native alternative beyond the bounds of intelligibility set by the English *actually* existed, if only Nehru had deployed the means to realise it. Khilnani does not state any obstacles in vestigial tradition that this ever-widening circle of light will inevitably dissolve. No matter how hesitantly, Indian life has to be made to conform to the movement of universal history. In order to prevent the tendency towards an outright despotism, the 'constitutional' nature of democracy is used by the state for a perpetual transfer of power between oligarchs who, by the way, are innocent of the characteristic modalities of the state despite these forms being inherited from the preceding colonial regime. It was because Nehru aspired to the summit of political power that he was touched by colonial history; the rest remain particularly immune. We will return to this idealised view of power in the next chapter. Suffice to say here that if the subaltern masses are mystified by the mechanisms of the state, the responsible politician does not draw the conclusions Gandhi did, that is, state power is essentially alien to the *Lebenswelt* of the people. Consensus is the destiny of the hazardous play of power exercised by the proto-capitalist state. Structural inequalities are not responsible for the discursive bounds of intelligibility in which the conversation between Indians is supposed to take place. We are entitled to ask 'why is it that non-European colonial countries have no historical alternative but to try to approximate the given attributes of modernity when that very process of approximation means their continued subjection under a world order which only sets their tasks for them and over which they have no control?'[86] For Khilnani, Nehru, Congress, Bharatiya Janata Party (BJP), and all participants in the democratic process, the allying of Reason with capitalism is the natural outcome of a mature political life. In this sense, Gandhi's vision of a return to *panchayati raj* or a rule of village republics after freedom from colonial rule is a radical alternative.

Interpretive modes

As the general observations in preceding chapters shows, the dilemmas of a reflexive historical practice (under the generic misnomer 'postmodern') do not end by presenting reality as an antidote to history as ideological practice. Two theorists feel obliged to recommend something called a 'dynamic relation of the common' because, to them at least, India represents, in singular terms, a reality different from the species which most Europeans share and take for granted. The analysis deliberately lacks any historical sense and perhaps this contributes to its novelty. In the sophisticated naiveté only postmodern reflections seem to be able to get away with, we are told that 'we share capitalist production and exploitation' as well as individually two eyes, ten fingers and ten toes.[87] They go on to describe how Indian realities differ from the rest of the world after this salutary reminder about the sensuous particularity of social formations to which we are all obviously prone as humans. The ideal of the 'multitude' manifests itself more comprehensively in the peculiarly empirical domain ('every local reality within India') of Indian life. Indians, Indonesians, Peruvians and Nigerians are the nationalities actually cited; Italians and Americans, one assumes, are also implied in this phenomenology *qua* homily.

This avant-garde intervention is actually a very traditional view of Indian unity-in-diversity; one which formed the staple of Congress politicians as the nationalist party and others until quite recently. However, since the state sanctioned pogroms by Hindus against Muslims in Gujarat in 2002 that in their violence were reminiscent of communal conflict during Partition, even the Indian diaspora is being taught the lesson about the invaluable role of secularism for the Indian polity.[88] Secularism is the political doctrine of pragmatism equivalent to (as Hardt and Negri fancifully put it) the shared and produced in common. This twenty-first century ideal looks back to the turmoil of Europe in ages past caused by the aspirations of Charles V, Phillip II, Louis XIV, the Jacobins and Napoleon. We saw how Nehru resolved any hostile tendencies in Indian history in the Romantic doctrine of freedom. This idea of Indian unity-in-diversity was always an ideological conception to maintain hegemony by political elites. Reflecting the vicissitudes of the European experience in the nineteenth century, Indian nationalism's bid for political hegemony under Nehru was also motivated by the Prussian orthodoxy that Leopold von Ranke represented for the systematic emergence of the historical ground decried by Chatterjee, to legitimise the marriage between Reason and capital by 'absorbing the political life of the nation into the body of the state'.[89] White describes the imperialist tendencies of this process:

> But these bids for political hegemony were frustrated by the operations of the principle of diversity-in-unity which Ranke took to be the distinct mode of social organization of the European system of nation-states. This mode found its overt expression in the emergence of the principle of *balance of power* as the corollary of national differentiation.[90]

Nehru's historicism in *Discovery of India* and *Glimpses of World History* is an attempt to treat nationalism as if it were a plausible *substitute* for the federal arrangement Ranke posited as an antidote to conflict in Europe. Gyanendra Pandey reminds us about the obsolescence of unity-in-diversity for state ideology today, and how inimical it is for the 'Brahminical Hindu consumerist' class: '[A]ll that belongs to any minority other than the ruling class – all that is challenging, singular, local – not to say, all difference – appears threatening, intrusive, even "foreign" to this nationalism.'[91] It is in this sense that I will be deploying '*Hindutva*' as an exclusive designation of nationalism.[92] I will return to Pandey's more ambiguous rendering of this generic difference between singular points of view that claim the universality of nationalist self-realisation when it functions as historicism below. I first want to cite an instance where the limits of secularism envisaged as unity-in-diversity are all too apparent for the implicit ideology of the ruling bloc in the way Pandey characterises above. The *Times of India* (21 March), reflecting the collective hysteria in 1981, warned the population of a London-based Muslim organisation's 'plan to convert 80 million out of 120 million Harijans of India'. What actually happened was the 'conversion of a mere couple of hundred untouchables unable to bear the Hindu torture' in a small village called Meenakshipuram in Tamil Nadu.[93] This report, albeit by a partisan voice on behalf of the Dalit cause, goes on to describe how this turmoil touched those in the highest places, and where

> [e]ven Prime Minister Indira Gandhi forgot she was heading a 'secular Government' unable to get over her Kashmiri Brahmin background, and tried her best to prevent conversions using her Govt. agencies. Muslim and untouchable leaders of her party told us that when they met her, she looked worried over the conversions and asked them to rush to Meenakshipuram 'and do something.'

Questions still abound concerning the motivations of conversion 'as a deliberate practice of cultural criticism' by tribal peoples and Dalits against the 'oppression and exclusionary features of Brahminical Hinduism propounded by the upper caste Hindu elite'.[94] Far from being the exclusive concern of the BJP and the global activities of the World Hindu Council of the Vishwa Hindu Parisad, since the decision of the state judiciary of Uttar Pradesh, in March 2003, to allow an archaeological dig by the Archaeological Survey of India to corroborate the evidential merit of a case arguing the original existence of an ancient Ram temple at a site in Ayodhya, conversion still constitutes an irrational fear for the majority Hindu population. This is even the case where, in contrast to the policies of the Ottoman CUP in the early twentieth century, 'the pace of conversion has no realistic possibilities of altering the numerical balance among religious groups'.[95] If there is any doubt about the decline of Indian plurality implied in the classical universality-in-diversity theme, the Indian political scientist established in Western institutions cannot escape the tendentious logic whose historical modality I will be exploring below. The distinction between activists and intellectuals alike is cosmetic in this argument. The dream of avenging themselves on the Muslim population is now described in terms of individuals being *ontologically* incapable of sharing the commonality celebrated by Negri, Nehru and the political class. Historical realities recede from view as the diagnostic process of comprehending the spirit of violence is now cast as a troubled species of 'masculinity'. Pandey compellingly signals this negating spirit at the beginning of the article cited. A symptomology ordinarily to be found in psychoanalytical discourse can now instead be used to explain how the state, itself now 'embodying' nationalism and masculinity, is essentially incapable of preventing the critical mass of *Hindutva* from reaching the level of 'lethality'.[96] This conclusion about 'anxious' masculinity, if it is designed to reveal the defensive nature of the collective *Hindutva* response, also functions as a normative explanation for the monopoly of violence held by the state. *Pace* Poulantzas, the institutional materiality of the Indian state is a modified form of awareness (a certain nativist light-mindedness, we might say) when it comes to the exercise of violence.[97] Part of my objective here is to restore the historical sense to these *modi vivendi*.

I want to continue investigating the historical conditions that made the problem of Hindu nationalism first arise. If Indira Gandhi's reaction to the conversion crisis in Tamilnad was colluding with the forces that produced moral panic, her father's response in history attributes the growth of Hindu nationalism in the seventeenth century successor state of Muslim sultanates to both state and economy. Nehruvian discourse is as certain about quelling communalism, of controlling forces, as Indira Gandhi was in her policy of despatching Muslim and Dalit leaders to the troubled region.

In the first chapter of her classic account of early India, Romila Thapar states how the 'close relationship between power and knowledge was being tacitly recognized' in historical theories by Indian historians in the late nineteenth century. Nehru's emphasis on the structural constraints that any individual might face, no matter how great, and on the instrumental role that knowledge plays with the intrusion of European colonialism in the evolution of any epoch, is the perfect expression of the new modality Thapar is describing. Even if this relationship between power and knowledge was defined more than intuitively in the late nineteenth century for the first time, I am exploring the problematic of history writing from a perspective after this conjunction has become a commonplace. Some historians regard this new aggregation typically in terms of the Orientalist thematic, but originality is not my concern here.[98] That historiography might contain an assemblage of normative assumptions and that it should be an ideological 'discourse' (in addition to the Foucauldian sense Thapar intends), in common with other narrative representations, is taken for granted. I examine, instead, some of the presuppositions informing the species of political or administrative history of the modular kind that historians produced under the influence of Indian nationalism.[99] The conjunction between power and knowledge to which Thapar is alluding as an event in academic history also has, as we have seen, its correlative in the more 'political' realm.

The question centres on the a priori of nationalist historiography rather than, say, on any individual epochal account typified by the Cambridge School or a history of the Indian National Congress. Anil Seal, J. P. Narayan or V. P. Menon, in their various accounts of the political climate of the 1920s and 1930s and the eventual 'Gandhian' form Indian nationalism took (*swaraj*), each fail to consider the role of the kind of practice I will be investigating, though they were all writing after the moment Thapar cites. The kind of ideological nationalism (*Hindutva*) that has been crucial in hegemonising segments of India's millennial past isn't named as a vital tendency that even more moderate Congress members sought to combat.[100] The presuppositions of this conception of Indian history and Indianness might have been 'adroitly marginalized' by a Gandhian Congress, but 'these were never erased: many nationalists outside Congress, and even some within it, shared them'.[101]

The survey of the problem of writing historically in postcolonial India is not chronological, in the sense of isolating definitive tendencies of any historical era. What is the central problem explored here? Even if the title of this book signals a tautology and even if (or because) new explanations have not been forthcoming from nationalist history, the tacit relationship between power and knowledge that is made explicit in postcolonial historiography means having to acknowledge that nationalist history, as Thapar concludes, was and still remains 'a powerful voice in the debate on the past'.[102] We can modify the unitary conception of an Indian past in Thapar's assertion for a postcolonial historiography and describe the source of this potent debate by professional historians and laymen alike in terms of there being a competition between different pasts. It is hoped that in revealing the subterranean motivations informing India's nationalist historiography, we do not reproduce the dialectical argument where this history is itself a homogenised 'subaltern' reflection of 'a master narrative that could be called "the history of Europe"'.[103]

Let us see where such a 'dialectical' view takes us. The problem in adopting various strategic positions from, say, a bourgeois Bengali perspective of the *bhadralok* where 'Nationalist thought was premised precisely on the assumed universality of the project of becoming individuals', is that the subalternity of nationalist historiography seems to be symptomatic of the same modern purview whose 'contradictions' Chakrabarty wants to make salient in terms of 'developing the problematic of nonmetropolitan histories'.[104] Jameson reserved his particular antipathy to this narrative-invigorating impulse in postmodern historiography. Modernity here implies that individualism is only embryonic with the disappearance of the *Agraria*. Examining the problematic of Indian historiography in these 'micrological' terms, that is, of the *bhadralok* class as the site where '"Indians" challenged ... received ideas in such a way as to put in question two fundamental tenets underlying the idea of "modernity" – the nuclear family based on companionate marriage and the secular, historical construction of time' – I argue, itself rests on the assumption that history is 'a discursive practice that enables present-minded people(s) to go to the past' for the moment *their* individuation first came about.[105] When it comes the discursive creation of Hindu India, the desire of discovering one's identity according to the patriarchal essence of Hindu life is not seriously questionable from the two fundamental tenets identified by Chakrabarty. It is as if the metaphysical realm, 'the vital zone of belief and practice' in which 'the new disciplinary culture of a modernizing elite' is supposed to discover a form of self-discipline, first perceives its destiny in expurgating all forms of social existence alien to it.[106] In other words, by the early twentieth century this cathartic moment in the self-realisation of a nationalist elite had itself discovered a project beyond the sedate purview of Bengali syncretism. When it comes to discovering hard, physical evidence for the *Ramjanmabhumi* (birthplace of Ram), Sudeshna Guha signals the problem with the most empirical modality of historical enquiry in archaeological practice: 'By choosing to keep the public ignorant of the methodologies through which corroborative analogies [whether morphological, ethnographic or stratographical] are commonly derived to interpret material finds, the officers of the Survey seem to have willingly complied with the myth implicit in the judiciary's decision, that historical truth exists "somewhere out there" waiting to be unearthed.'[107] Nevertheless, we are told that the 'radical cogency' of the revisionist enterprise is about making those aspects of the past visible in order to make a difference to these individuals in search for an origin for their modernity: it is optimistically described as making 'emancipatory material differences to and within the present'.[108] I will be challenging this view below. This eclectic search for a paradigm by Chakrabarty for universality, whether 'assumed' or not, that might exhaust all the various possibilities in describing the moment in which a nationalist class became conscious of itself as such, is an essentially *anthropological* idea of modernity. The conjunction between power and knowledge in historical practice now enables the historian to detail the emergence of individuality from the unconscious net of native kinship that makes historicity both possible and problematic. This holistic endeavour takes Chakrabarty to literary and biographical texts, postmodern theorisations as well as European continental phenomenology.[109] My points of reference are more conservative, if only because the answer to the question Chakrabarty, in common with many other voices, has posed about the representative voice of Indian pasts has grown increasingly urgent. Before leaving Chakrabarty's type of analysis, I want to emphasise a possible reason why the recourse to anthropological categories is problematic, albeit in more sophisticated terms than the nineteenth-century social evolutionary type. Hayden White's magisterial volume *Metahistory*, concerned with the archetypal tendencies of nineteenth-century historical consciousness, does not address its impact upon the colonisation of the globe by European states. One might almost believe that there *was no* impact and that the promiscuous combination of ideas about humankind's evolution remains locked in the historian's brain. Indian historians as well as visionaries had to readily submit these developments to the most exacting empiricial examination: how do they apply to life as it is lived? Chakrabarty's micrological historicism (whether metropolitan or peripheral) is confined to *anuloma* or the isogamous marriage customs of the Bengal bourgeois elite. It is a narrative describing the coming-into-consciousness of this class *as* a class in privative terms. My differences from Chakrabarty's conception of cultural resistance to colonial authority, as we will see, are about how national consciousness in the Indian case relied on a series of universals about the Indian past where this resistance – in the form of maintaining the slender line of tradition from some archaic origins – goes beyond the native Indian's realisation of his or her identity (the Indian's 'unhappy consciousness' is Chakrabarty's Hegelian phrase) as part of a class. Indeed, we will discover how this consciousness reverts to a historical mode that has very little to do with the modest scale Chakrabarty identifies in the drab ideology of domesticity and 'the voice of the colonial modern looking to orient domesticity to the requirements of the civil-political'.[110] What complicates the link between the cultural genesis of individuality (in terms of colonisation) and a radical individuation that only emerges – in Chakrabarty's stylisation – as the product of 'nonmetropolitan histories'? I now want to move in the direction of this doubt about the historical scope of universality.

An anthropologist's ambition for his own endeavours will help us to define the general problem of Indian historiography for historians. Let us look at Lévi-Strauss's formulation. It will help to explain the appetitive element in even divergent epistemologies of the Indian past. If the Jesuits rediscovered a new history in Greco-Roman antiquity for their own way of life in the European early modern, and if the Renaissance portended 'the means of putting its own culture in perspective – by confronting contemporary concepts with those of other times and places', a non-classical humanism extends itself in a more *inferior* mode for more geographically distant civilisations. The Indian, Chinese, Middle and Far Eastern, when it comes to the 'technique of estrangement', Lévi-Strauss notes, 'merited our interest only by their most scholarly and refined productions'.[111] In being able to capture in a living culture 'the slightest nuances of the natives' psychic life', ethnologists will go far beyond the Jesuits to contrive an epistemological intimacy with otherness for their own age; for Lévi-Strauss, the method will usher in a truly democratic humanism. Even when the encounter between the classically European and classically Indian civilisations furnishes us with contrary evidence, I will soon investigate some of the reasons why, in the aftermath of the 'aristocratic' and 'bourgeois' humanisms, 'a doubly universal humanism' is unlikely to result for all Indians. That it failed in the instance of North Africans, Césaire already noted. For the West, Lévi-Strauss tells us, civilisation was founded by the completion of these humanisms. There is a hidden motivation in bringing these more distant but temporally more proximate civilisations to closer scrutiny. Lévi-Strauss's conclusion that is typically in the spirit of the anthropological descriptive modality is euphemistic in the context of colonial history; for him, it is an investigation into how historiography helped to keep the 'exotic humanism of the nineteenth century ... tied to the industrial and commercial interests which supported it and to which it owed its existence'.[112] This is the pragmatic nature of the conjunction Thapar noted between power and knowledge; it is at the same time the dynamic legacy of colonialism which Nehru wanted to protect from the atavistic forces of Hindu nationalism.

The site of complicity Lévi-Strauss identifies between historical analyses of civilisations and their usefulness for industrial and commercial interests extends beyond the European impulse to colonise these inferior but immediate civilisations with their own values. This ambition is coincidental with a desire to subject these other modes of being to 'scientific' scrutiny to explain the eventual shape these civilisations took. The association between epistemological value about India's past and the utilitarian interests that looked anew at her future destiny in the modern industrialised comity of nations was too precious to be destroyed along with the departure of the colonial power; on the contrary, it was to be given a *pneumato-logical* or spiritual colour. Towards the end of the nineteenth century, the primary modality of these values found themselves coalescing in a *reaction* to colonial rule. The cult of individuality that Chakrabarty explores in Bengali civil society is an epiphenomenon of this historical process. We find that the kind of universality associated with the greatness of ancient civilisations, and with which semi-feudal elites were very much enamoured as an ancestral golden age, cannot be clinically separated out from the kind of bourgeois universality that promoted its industrial and commercial interests in a newly combined revolutionary humanism. Whether it was retrospective-traditional or futurist-progressive in orientation, this vision united the traditional echelons and the urban middle classes. All strata of Indian society subscribed to this 'hybrid' humanism. The new ideology proved serviceable *pace* the 'illusion' of India as a factious society bequeathed to us from the positivism of European liberal thinking, at the intermediate level of feudal elites as well as at the 'all India' level of indigenous classes comprising 'the biggest feudal magnates' and 'the most important *representatives* of the industrial and mercantile bourgeoisie'.[113] B. R. Ambedkar, using some colourful language in making his *ad hominem* attack on Gandhi and the monopoly Congress had over the national question, especially Gandhi's refusal to grant the depressed classes separate representation to safeguard their interests after the British have departed, would describe the emergent polity as a Brahmin–Bania combine to replace the Brahmin–Kashatriya governing class of ages past.[114] We still find an echo of Ambedkar's language in the description used by Pandey to characterise this 'spurious' dominant class.

This exotic humanism that is capable of galvanising, for a limited period at least, lateral interests across different social strata has a name – I call it *nationalism*. In other words, an interest in India's most scholarly and refined productions, or the rediscovery of these, would now be put to use for a more political objective than the kind of prolix interest in 'civilisation', borrowed from a century earlier, that motivated the Victorian missionary, the provincial *Gazetteer*, Collector or for that matter, the subaltern historian today in putting their own culture into an evolutionary-historical context. However, this 'humanist' ideology was conditional and of service to the colonised only as far as the development of society was to be undertaken after 'native' society was emancipated from identifiably foreign industrial and commercial interests. The objective was to rediscover in one's own culture the conditions that best served this purpose in the wake of the colonial era. In sum, the anthropological modality of nationalism is not museological but tactical. The key features of the campaign by the Indian National Congress for self-rule or *Swadeshi*, through boycotts on imported goods and non-cooperation, are expressed by a leading nationalist politician, Bal Gangadhar Tilak:

> The whole Government is carried on with our assistance and then [the rulers] try and keep us in ignorance of our power of cooperation ... We shall not give them assistance to collect revenue and keep peace. We shall not assist them in fighting beyond our frontiers or outside India with Indian blood and money.

We shall not assist them in carrying on the administration of justice. We shall have our own courts, and when the time comes we shall not pay taxes. Can you do that by your united efforts? If you can, you are free from tomorrow.[115]

Despite history's time-honoured function of producing evidence from the past about the evolution of societies, the practice itself is 'discursive'; it can no longer perform its forensic function without the reorganisation of some occluded elements first taking place according to the political needs of the present. Even after relegating this need (the social agenda of reform) to the realm of politics proper, in pedagogy this seemingly radical interpretation of the need to promote a corrective to elite historiography in terms of minority discourses looks forward to the Enlightenment business of recovering origins in terms of relating 'the official papers of the scribe' to 'the pleadings of the lawyer ... in their apparently disinterested attention, in the "pure" devotion to objectivity'.[116] We saw how in the realm of politics proper this juridical endeavour was met by the 'Napoleonic' evocation of history as the law of the heart. This is all implied in the historically momentous endeavour for the postcolonial state that Tilak describes above; it is also the reason why Chakrabarty and associated subaltern historians are concerned with the colonial archive: only in the prose of counter-insurgency might they discover the 'objective' conditions that made the realisation of an authentic nationalism possible, if only fleetingly.[117] Tilak's summation of the task ahead is the programme of passive revolution described as a particular feature of anti-colonial resistance in the Indian case. The difference between this 'proto-Nehruvian' and the later form Gandhian *swaraj* took is that the salient features of the colonial state identified by Tilak are infinitely adaptable to the needs of the liberated nation: 'The specific ideological form of the passive revolution in India was an *étatisme*, explicitly recognizing a central, autonomous and directing role of the state and legitimizing it by a specifically nationalist marriage between the ideas of progress and social justice.'[118] Napoleon made plain what role he thought the ideologues were to play in this epithalamion in his speech to the Constituent Assembly. To Gandhi in his *Hind Swaraj*, the conjunction between progress and social justice – or more correctly, the realisation of the latter with the former – is essentially incompatible.

What possibilities are available in attempting to found an authentic Indian identity in micrological terms when the sphere of action in anti-colonial resistance was determined by questions that were essentially about the form universality took in the long Indian past? The discursive nature of historiography makes it ideological, whether this is in the sense of rediscovering one's essential self from an alien perspective amid the undifferentiated milieu or whether it is a related task, of identifying the proud beginnings of one's own culture in a pristine historical event. In this description, some of the natural limitations we examined in the last two chapters, limitations that are inherent in emancipatory projects, have now to be underplayed. After all, what does it mean to make 'material' differences (the choice of word is itself revealing) in the present where there is at the same time, according to the author, a pervasive and systematic eradication of intrinsic value in capitalist society?[119] In the case of colonialism, Indian capitalism (late or otherwise) is not exoteric to the coalition of classes that formed the nucleus of the state: it 'is not independently dominant in Indian society and state ... [and is actually] *the only truly universalising element* in the ruling bloc'.[120] This is the reason why Jameson's 'empirical' observations about Third World literatures are far off the mark. Let us for a moment accept the effort of the theorist and historian in recasting the ethical significance of historiography proportionate to the decline of its descriptive function, 'in its traditional guise as a subject discipline aiming at a real knowledge of the past'. In a context without a social consensus about the value of value, what possibilities are there for a radical historiography of the kind envisaged even in purportedly micrological terms? There are a series of related concerns. What happens if history is unavailing when it comes to providing a motivation or voice for minorities? Does the radical cogency of the discourse about the past automatically serve the needs of the present? If this 'relativism', whether cultural or forensic, is impossible, what choices are left to minorities? These questions are not peripheral for the individual living Third World 'otherness' but central for Indian historiography.

Perhaps these 'present-minded people' are not looking for a curative in history, for the precise moment when individuals similar to themselves were first dominated or celebrated for their particularity? The risk of conceiving history in identitarian terms – more traditionally in terms of ethnicity or racially, latterly in terms of gender, sex or class – is that a series of very contemporary reflections become imported within the rubric of the past. I will give an example. Resistance to the ideality of patriarchy can now be conceived itself ahistorically where women's struggles are said to be synonymous or in conjunction with those continued against authority in general by the subaltern classes.[121] For Gayatri Spivak, any conceptual observations about the transition from communal to feudal 'social organization of production' in Indian pre-history fails to foreground how 'communal control of sexual relations' (the ahistoricism of the patriarchal household noted by Chakrabarty) might affect sociality – a sociality that is instead figured as 'considerable co-operation and mutual aid in productive activities'.[122] If peasant insurgents in the colonial era refused to be led by women, it is also plausible to question the kind of co-operation between women and the subaltern classes that Chakrabarty envisages against patriarchal authority: this is in terms of the difference where women are figured as 'man-eating goddesses, objects of reverence and generators of solidarity on the one hand, and secular daughters and widows, unacceptable as leaders, on the other'.[123] The benefits of a reflexive historiography that is attuned to the needs of the present are not in reproducing an unconvincingly Whig paradigm for the past and more in detecting the relative strengths of solidary bonds in any social formation that, in the end, define the particular form domination takes. In my opinion, this is the best use to be made of 'postmodern' historiography. We will examine the adapted revisionism of a truly 'anarchic' form of historiography when it comes to the use of pre-political religious consciousness in Indian nationalism below.

Nationalist historiography, I repeat, is by its very nature a promiscuous raid. No matter how sterile nationalist historiography is (and we will see why this is the case for Romila Thapar), when it comes to producing a fresh insight into civilisations past, the debate about the past along the lines she mentions of the conjunction between knowledge and power informs even histories that are written in explicit opposition to nationalist histories today. The investigation into how nationalism *qua* ideology makes a transformative use of the conjunction between power and knowledge means analysing Thapar's understated conclusion that nationalist histories (she has now introduced a plural view) in the subcontinent are the articulation of interests singly in terms of monolithic religious identities following the 'success of anti-colonial nationalism'. In the preface, I began by saying how this is a characteristic understatement for a historian who deals in epochal terms with the 'pre-historical' past. Indeed, the ideographic nature of this view about the uses made of India's past challenges the micrological processes Chakrabarty thinks were essential in the formation of modern classes in colonial society. More importantly, in the following sections I will examine how the 'intellectual foundations of historical discourse' are threatened by this communal ordering of the past.[124]

A nation is born

Partha Chatterjee distinguishes between other species of fundamentalism in the subcontinent and *Hindutva*. *Hindutva* is not the clumsy transposition of unconscious idolatry for saffron-clad leaders in cultic practices; it is not merely to be explained in terms of 'collective malady', the crude expression of which entails the onslaught of a violent and amorphous mass 'charged, pickaxe and shovel in hand [with] "Jai Shri Ram" in their voices' to demolish a mosque on the site where, Hindu legend has it, Mir Baqi – one of Babur's generals – destroyed a Ram temple commemorating *Ramjanmabhumi*. Even the modern historian – one who, it has to be said, has a reputation for demystifying communalism in colonial accounts – is reluctant to negate the appropriation of an inimical, more heterogeneous element of modern historiography by a monistic discourse of *Hindutva*, preferring instead to relate conflict of this particular site in Ayodhya in dyadic (and occasionally, dialogic) terms of the 'coexistence in these two accounts of two different notions of time, two discourses, two "histories"'.[125] Chatterjee is less equivocal in his conclusions. The systematic terrorising of the Muslim Indian by the legal state apparatus by promulgating a series of stereotypical features, 'now sickeningly familiar in their repetitiveness', is the effect of a larger policy. The *Hindutva* Right is designed 'to mobilise on its *behalf* the will of an interventionist modernising state' so that it can more effectively 'erase the presence of religious or ethnic particularisms from the domains of law or public life, and [come to] to supply, in the name of "national culture", a homogenised content to the notion of citizenship'.[126] We saw with Gellner's anthropological assertions about the compatibility of Islam with nationalism how this is not a novel development. As Chatterjee notes, even if we accept the plausibility of Pandey's analyses of the reactive tendency in communal conflicts, *Hindutva* is also a positivist project for the state. This is secular modernity colluding with atavistic forces: as we saw with Kaviraj's characterisation of modernist development in the postcolonial state, no dominant bloc could resist the instrumental use of capital to hegemonise itself. A cartoon in

Punch for 28 November 1896 shows a perplexed Sultan gazing at a poster reading 'Reorganisation of the Ottoman Empire – Capital £5,000,000' with Russia, France and England as acting directors of 'Turkey Limited'.[127] In 1881 the Ottoman Public Debt Administration authorised French and British control of Ottoman fiscal policy in order to ensure the modernisation desired by edict (the *Tanzimat*), so desperate were France and Britain to defend the bulwark against Tsarist incursions in the south and southwest of Russia's demesne. The satire goes on to state the purpose of raising the loan of five million pounds: 'to be applied to the cost of the judiciary, revenue, and police service "under European control"'. The British Imperial policy of adapting the needs of 'pre-colonial' fiscal forms to new modernising needs had, of course, already been tried out in India nearly a century before with the Permanent Settlement in Bengal. Whether or not this capital had been successfully 'indigenised' is still a disputed point.[128]

The ideologue of this tendency where (*pace* Kaviraj) pre-capitalist elements both collude with the ideology of industrial-capitalist development and ensure a comfortable survival plan for their own class is one Vinayak Damodar Savarkar.[129] Savarkar, a passionate biographer of Mazzini and president of the Hindu nationalist Mahasabha, won his spurs by being an erstwhile leader of a militant subterranean organisation, the Abhi Navat Bharat (ANB). Members of the ANB travelled to Paris to learn how to make bombs from a Russian revolutionary in order to assassinate the Viceroy, Lord Curzon. I want to continue exploring how the conjunction power/knowledge that Thapar posited for Indian historiography manifests itself in the communal realities facing Indians at a transitional moment. Curzon survived but with him so did the Hindu nationalist legacy of the Chatpavan Brahmin for whom *ahimsa* or non-violent resistance are 'mealy-mouthed formulas' derived from European ideas about India's glorious past. How plausible is this claim? 'The political consequences', Savarkar concludes 'of the Buddhistic expansion has been disastrous to the national virility and even to the national existence of our race'.[130] Events in pre-history resonate boldly as an explanation for the colonial predicament. Tilak presented a similar view in 1906 to an audience at Benaras in his address to the Bharata Dharma Mahamandala (All-India Religious Association). The disunity at the root of India's colonial state under the British also occurred in the ancient past. The Hindu religion was under attack from Buddhists and Jains 'for some two hundred years'. It was only under the unifying influence of 'the great leader, Shankaracharya' after '600 years of chaos ... that Buddhism was swept away from the land'.[131] Tilak's Romantic views about the confirmation of scientific discoveries in Vedic metaphysics apart (a view Gandhi would inherit and adapt in his own vision of Indian self-rule), Savarkar's more aggressive use of 'efficiency political, social, and above all military and aerial' in order for the Hindu kingdom – he is using Nepal as his pretext – to defend itself in an omnipresent climate of struggle for existence establishes himself as a new Shankaracharya modelled after the ninth-century original.[132] What all Indians must do is delve within themselves to discover the nation's reality, not halting at the accretions of the past until they rediscover the primal civilisation given majestic form by Aryan 'ancestors'. Gandhi in his vision of independence from colonial rule also shares

Hindutva *and writing postcolonial India* 117

this nostalgia for *Ramrajya* but for him, in contrast to Savarkar, scientific modernity and technological advancements are inimical to the realisation of its spirit.[133] I want to now explore how *Hindutva* makes its recourse to India's millennial history in order to realise, as Chatterjee notes, 'in rational and sophisticated terms [*pace* Thapar] its impatient dream of turning India into a world power'. An examination of the uses made of historiography for Indian nationalism cannot afford to ignore how the rationative element in nationalist propaganda is the exact antithesis to the micrological 'cultural' instances adduced by Chakrabarty or, for that matter, of the spiritual ideal of withdrawal from the traumatising competition of a colonised civil order in which the Bengali middle class discovered its authentic identity. The prison house of Reason as a foreign and alienating idiom for life is apparent in a dialogue between Dr Mahendralal Sarkar (1833–1904), the founder of the first institution for modern scientific research in India, and the disciples of Ramakrishnan, Girish and Narendra. The tract *Kathamrta* records:

DOCTOR: One has to control these feelings. It is not proper to express them in public. No one understands my feelings. *My best friends* think I am devoid of passion ... My son, wife, even they think I am *hard-hearted*, because my fault is that I don't express my feelings to anyone ... My *feelings* get *worked up* even more than yours do. *I shed tears in solitude ...*

NARENDRA: Think of this. You have *devoted* your life to the cause of *scientific discovery*. You risk your health. The knowledge of God is *the grandest of all sciences*. Why should he [Ramakrishnan] not *risk* his *health* for it?

DOCTOR: All religious reformers – Jesus, Chaitanya, Buddha, Muhammad – each one in the end comes out as self-opinionated: 'This I have said, this is the final truth!' What sort of attitude is that?

GIRISH: Sir, you are guilty of the same crime. When you say they are self-opinionated, you make the same error.[134]

There is that delicious barb against the ecumenicism of Ramakrishnan's syncretic cult and the aspirations of the Arya Samajists. In our context, the spiritual ideal of devotion according to the precept of religious figures in India's own history, including Buddha whom Girish describes as helping 'us cross the oceans of worldly living and scepticism', is set against the repressed violence of Dr Sarkar's own devotion to a rational existence. For the doctor, Buddha as Prince Gautama having eaten pork took opium to relieve cholic. 'Do you know what nirvana is?' he asks. 'Drugged by opium, drugged senseless – that's nirvana.' It is in *this* sense that *ahimsa* manifests itself as a disabling condition for colonised Indians. In contrast, alongside Gandhi, Ashis Nandy describes how the rationative tendency, 'the ancient forces of human greed and violence ... have merely found a new legitimacy in anthropocentric doctrines of salvation, in the ideologies of progress, normality and hyper-masculinity, and in theories of cumulative growth of science and technology'.[135] Nandy would be an ideal disciple alongside Narendra and Girish. When Savarkar looks forward to the world-historical role that Indians will play in the impending struggle for existence and power, he expresses a desire to return to a mythical or Puranic past in order to source those forces of violence, salvation, progress and hyper-masculinity which, he states, have been nullified by Buddhistic 'reform' and later, with the Muslim and British conquests. We find the purest expression of *ressentiment* in Savarkar's *Hindutva*, his manifesto from 1923. Inspired by the fifty years' life sentence imposed on him in a prison cell by the colonial government for sedition, Savarkar in the Andamans dreams how Indians like himself '[W]ith India for their basis of operation, for their Father land and for their Holyland with such history behind them, bound together by ties of common blood and common culture can dictate their terms to the whole world. A day will come when mankind will have to face the force.'[136] Let us see how this totalising doctrine of common blood and common culture deforms the content of India's long history. In a sense, the ideological mystification of historical conditions is readily apparent in the way Savarkar puts the 'historicism' of *Hindutva* to use in describing Indian realities. Those Congressmen who fail to conceive these realities in the monistic terms Savarkar argues for, 'unity-hankers', are obstacles to the somewhat spurious vision (considering the means by which it is to achieved) of an impartial Indian State: '[T]he mission and policy of the Hindu Mahasabha ... have been more rational than the present day policies of the Indian National Congress itself.'[137] Moreover, the Muslim League politicians, under their leader Mohammad Ali Jinnah (and founding father of Pakistan) at the Lucknow session in the same year, in 1937, call for the imposition of Urdu as the national language. Responding to the threat reported from the Muslim League's Karachi session calling for their co-religionists over the border to aid them in combating Hindu rule, analogous to the appeal Sudetan Germans made to their countrymen from Czechoslovakia, Savarkar ominously concludes that 'if we Hindus in India grow stronger in time these Moslem friends of the League type will have to play the part of German-Jews instead. We Hindus have taught the Shakas and the Huns already to play that part pretty well.'[138] A primal Indian essence from the accretions and 'refinement' that Lévi-Strauss thought typified Orientalist scholarship serves more than an epistemological function for Hindu nationalists. Savarkar lists the 'pre-historical' conquests Hindus/Indians made over Daityas and Asuras, from 2000 CE. In the incessant struggle for survival of the fittest, where Incan, Egyptian and Babylonian civilisations failed, and when 'this very England which rules today over an Empire' had fallen prey to the Romans, Danes, Dutch and Norwegians, 'after some centuries of life and death struggle' against Greek and Hun invasion, the Hindu nation vanquished 'the avalanche of Huns under Vikramaditya the Great'.[139] The distinction Lévi-Strauss makes in the progress of Enlightenment, one which was indispensable for the emergence of European humanism, is too subtle in the pneumatic interpretation of Indian history by nationalists.

Congressite nationalism (of a legal-constitutional variety, as we saw with Tilak's exhortation) is an inadequate solution to the colonial problem in the morbid interregnum between the two world wars. Latent within Congress campaigns of civil disobedience against colonial domination are the same reasons for India's or Bharatvarsha's external vulnerability to Hun conquest in the distant past. 'Hindutva

Hindutva *and writing postcolonial India* 119

is not a word but a history.' This is as well as the threat from Buddhism that originally arose internal to the nation. From the very outset then, Savarkar announces the terms on which his disciples will learn to interpret the emergence of India's own 'organic order' from the backdrop of 'chaos of castes and creeds'. For 'as long as the whole world was red in tooth and claw' in the morbid period of contemporary world history, with the two visions of capitalism and state socialism competing for dominance, the Hindu nation could not afford to dispense with the unifying force of national and racial cohesion.[140] This is the right to live both spiritual and political life according to the right of her soul.

Dharma is no longer the individualising principle brought to theoretical attention by Célestine Bouglé in 1908. Buddhism in India's millennial past, for Bouglé, would inevitably give way to the restoration of the cultic elements of 'Hindu' belief. For Bouglé, Indians were peculiarly susceptible to the eternal flow of the Ganges, rather picturesquely imagined as 'the powerful and troubled waters of traditional emanatism, this Lethe of the Orient which pours out for the living who drink it, disdain for the injustices of life'.[141] This mystical Heraclitean element in which the primal consciousness of the people is lost can only be awakened by the opening-up of 'the mines of Vedic fields for steel', in Savarkar's interpretation. For Gandhi, individuals lived under the sacred penumbra of this once-bright Vedic reality, at least for as long as they remained within the orbit of their inherited profession or life's task (*varna*) within the Hindu social order.[142] The potentially disintegrative forces of caste consciousness in producing the Hindu nation are innocuous elements of the primal social order. 'Indiscriminate racial amalgamation' was discouraged by the patristic authority of the Aryan founding fathers of the Hindu nation, in another milder exposition of the identical terms Savarkar uses to describe the origins of the nation's life. Radhakrishnan's Oxford audience is urged not to be detained by

> the stagnation of the aboriginal tribes. They were also raised above the welter of savagery and imbued with the spirit of gentleness. Sheltered on the same soil, bound together by common interests, evolving under the influence of common psychic and moral surroundings, the different component tribes not only improved in their level but became adapted to each other in spite of diversity of origin.[143]

Even Herder's image of the peace-loving Hindu did not describe the Brahmin monopoly over the life of Indians as a civilising mission. The egregious fact of caste conflict – that Gandhi would later appropriate as his own private cause in his own vision of a freed Indian culture – has an analogous voice in Radhakrishnan's idea of Hinduism as protonationalism. The *dharmic* eternity that Europeans are invited to gaze into by French anthropologists and these Hindu thinkers alike, which is responsible for the Hindu soul's having 'no place for dogmatic intolerance', is also, frustratingly for Savarkar, the same reason for the lack of political unity without which no major persecution is possible.[144] Even as Indians formerly considered their history as beginning properly from the 'Mohammedan invasion', the Buddhistic period is erroneously considered 'the most glorious epoch of our history' as well as constituting the outer threshold of the mythical past.[145] Let us examine this conflation. Savarkar goes on to state that, no matter how great Ashoka and the Mauryas were, 'the political virility or the manly nobility of our race' could only combat the 'strange Bible of Fire and Steel' of invading barbarian hordes by sharpening the Vedic sword on the altar of Kali the Terrible, so that Mahakal, the '"Spirit of Time" be appeased'. Ashoka as Thapar's heroic dynast and, for Radhakrishnan and Nehru, the enlightened convert to Buddhism representing an invaluably ecumenical dispensation, in Savarkarite terms is emblematic of decline from the martial ethos in Puranic history. Not for Savarkar the inspirational ideal of a world-commonwealth, in which self-realisation and self-determination for communities is consistent with *karma* and *dharma* as precepts of Hindu belief.[146] This idea of cathartic violence is at the origins of the temporality in which Pandey examines the timelessness of *Ramjanmabhumi*. The appeasement of Mahakal is the symbolic form that Savarkar gives to the duty all Indians owe to their own history. Both Gandhi's and Radhakrishnan's ideas of the millennial past are rejected. Muslims and Christians are the enemies of Mahakal. I will return to the monarch of the pastoral kingdom of Ayodhya below.

If Indian Muslims and Christians regard Hindustan as their Fatherland, why are they outside the bounds to which Savarkar is seeking to give a historical significance in his concept of *Hindutva*? Even if, as the inscription to his text implies, a person regards the land of Bharatvarsha, 'from the Indus to the Seas as his Father-Land', he or she can never be described as Hindu unless they also regard this geopolitical entity as the cradle of their religion. For these Indians, 'their holyland is far off in Arabia and Palestine' and this symbolic but highly crucial attachment to a sacred land is only natural and deserving of neither condemnation nor regret. In case we think this proposition is typical of the strategic interests of a political doctrine, despite her note concerning the genocide of Indian Muslims by Hindu extremists since 1992, Spivak as one of the most reflexive theorists of Indian history and culture cannot resist describing the 'dilemma' of Islamic India in identical terms to those used by Savarkar of a generic Islam as having its head turned away from the subcontinent, across the Arabian sea, 'perpetually emigrant toward Mecca'.[147] Maria Misra plausibly describes how Savarkar's militant vision of nationalist identity – based on common nationality (*Rashtra*), common race (*Jati*) and common civilisation (*Sanskriti*) – is itself based on the reactive tendencies he came across among Pan-Islamic Khilafatists in prison in the early 1920s. Savarkar denounces Islam as alien, where it is Mecca and not the seats of once-flourishing Mughal power in Delhi and Agra that constitutes a 'sterner reality' for Muslims.[148] In a highly tendentious interpretation, we also find present in V. S. Naipaul's writing that Indian Muslims are casualties of being won by a cult at the point of a sword.[149] What Savarkar does admire in Islam and Christianity, in contrast to Naipaul and others, is the 'fierce unity of faith, social cohesion and valorous fervour' they inspire.[150] The greatest threat, Misra notes, was not the disintegrative forces of individual liberty, elaborate philosophising and arcane traditions in establishing a theocratic patriotism. We've found each of these evident in, respectively, the Bengali Babu, Ramakrishnan's ascetic creed, and Bouglé, Thapar and Radhakrishnan's idea of

Hindutva *and writing postcolonial India* 121

the impact of Buddhistic reform of a shastric martial ethos. Only the state is powerful enough to 'weld [Hindus] into an organic whole'. Hindus, she goes on, 'had to embrace modernity, western science, European forms of the state and military organization. The greatest threat to this militant integration, in their [Savarkar and his Fascist disciple and leader of a Hindu Right party, one M. Golwalkar] opinion, was Gandhi, with his wishy-washy dogmas of non-violence and love of the primitive.'[151]

The fierce unity and social cohesion of Indian Muslims was nowhere more evident to Savarkar than in the elements organising as if spontaneously to overthrow the Feringhi (Frankish, foreign) Raj. In his history of the 1857 Uprising, published in 1908, the youthful twenty-four-year-old would describe the events as 'The Story of History as a programme of organisation and action ... for the future war of liberation'.[152] The outcome of this story of history as a mechanistic programme of freedom, complete with its satellite of events all conforming to the inevitable tendency within the national idea itself is entirely different from the kind Savarkar eventually propounded in his books *Hindutva* and *Hindu Sanghathan*. The restoration of Bahadur Shah on the Delhi throne, a throne which had already been 'smashed to pieces by the hammer of the Maharattas' (actually, it had been looted by Nadir Shah, the king of Persia in his invasion of North India in 1793) by the mutinous sepoys, is a figurehead whose lineage goes back to the barbarians Changez (Genghis) Khan and Timur (Tamburlaine), decried as the enemy in the manifesto *Hindutva*. Nevertheless, Bahadur Shah as the repository of hope is now a 'freely chosen monarch of a people battling for freedom against the foreign intruder'. Savarkar continues to exhort: 'Hindus and Mahomedans send forth their hearty, conscientious, and most loyal homage to this elected or freely accepted Emperor of their native soil on the 11th of May, 1857!'[153] Hankering after unity is apparently symptomatic only of historic realities.

Some individuals will shine forth in this comic mode of emplotment in which the only tragic component of history is the insistence by the design of Providence (the spirit of Mahakal) that each person sacrifice themselves so that the essential harmony of the natural order disturbed by the British intrusion can be restored. Thus, one of the revolutionaries, a cleric called Moulvie Ahmad Shah, 'Patriot of Fyzabad', has an honourable place in Savarkar's history. Even Malleson, a British historian of the 1857 'mutiny', has to acknowledge this man's bravery to the last stand, and praises him for not staining his sword with assassination, or conniving at murders, choosing instead to fight manfully against strangers who have seized his country. He is in the end betrayed in ambush by the colluding, native Hindu aristocrat Raja Powess whose brother shoots him as he attempts to escape in a mahout on an elephant. The actual contents of history contradict the assertions in Savarkar's manifesto *Hindutva* and Ahmad Shah is praised in the following terms: 'The life of this brave Mohamedan shows that a rational faith in the doctrines of Islam is in no way inconsistent with, or antagonistic to, a deep and all powerful love of the Indian soil, and that the true believer in Islam will feel it a pride to belong to and a privilege to die for his mother country!'[154] In the book *Hindu Sanghathan* nearly thirty years later, the 'Mohamedan' is 'nowhere to be found while the national struggle goes on and [is] everywhere to be found in the forefront at the time of reaping the fruits of that struggle'.[155]

The concept of *Hindutva* as the primitive sublime

In this section I will explore some of the ontological features that determine the concept *Hindutva*: it will be inevitable that the claims of a seamless continuity in the terms Savarkar wishes to claim an homogenous Hindu identity for Indians will conflict with the eventuality of history itself. The temporality of *Hindutva* is *kairotic*; events are the result of an efflorescence where there is an essential 'simultaneity of past and future in an instantaneous present'.[156] These are the terms in which Savarkar's own love of the pre-historical and the 'primitive' are to be documented. Even with inconsistencies, there is a more historical element in Savarkar's concept *Hindutva* than there is in any of the more demotic forms to which it has given rise. The pamphlet 'histories' of *Ramjanmabhumi* that inspired the *kar sevaks* (votaries to build the temple) to their destructive work, in *Sri Ram Janmabhumi ka Rakt-Ranjit Itihas. Tala Kaise Khula* ('The Bloodstained History of Sri Ram Janmabhumi. How the Gates were Unlocked') or in *Sri Ram Janmabhumi ka Romanckari Itihas* ('The Horripilating History of Sri Ram Janmabhumi'), mix the miraculous with the plausibly historical. The *Rakt-Ranjit* tells how the Emperor Vikramdtya, inspired by a vision of a blackened Prince Trithraj Prayag who grows white after bathing in the Ganges, erects a temple on the site where a newly delivered cow with a new-born calf starts lactating.[157] The *Romanckari Itihas* details the expiation by Babar for the sin of a faqir at whose instigation the building of the mosque was decided. This faqir, Jalal Shah, abused the esoteric knowledge he inherited from a great yogi, Baba Shyamanand, to summon the corpses of Muslims from far and wide to be buried at the Janmabhumi.[158] After a siege by cannonade by 400,000 Mughal soldiers eventually broke the temple doors protected by 174,000 'Hindu' soldiers for fifteen days, the victorious Babar still has to accede to the priests' stipulation that he allow the consecration of the place at the entrance by inscribing it as *Sita Pak Sthan* ('Spot sanctified by/sacred to Sita').[159]

At the superficial level shared by these populist appropriations, Savarkar's text *Hindutva* is also involved in the conflation of the authentic-canonical with the apocryphal but its defining modality is historical rather than theological. How is the defining modality of the concept of *Hindutva* historical rather than theological? *Hindutva* as a concept is a universal metaphor for not only a religious or spiritual history of 'our people' but, when used synonymously with its metonym 'Hinduism', it becomes 'a history in full'. Let us pause. Next to the inscription defining who a true Hindu is – a person who regards Bharatvarsh as both fatherland (*Pitribhu*) and holy land (*punyabhu*) – there is a quote praising the might of Indra to destroy 'our enemies, the Dasus' with his thunderbolt. This seems to inspire the authority of a quote but it in fact belongs to no Vedic text. There's no room here to explore how the caste consciousness of B. R. Ambedkar or his Dalit followers would respond to this second 'Vedic' inscription, exhorting Indra to destroy the Dasus to aid the Nation of Sapta Sindhus (seven rivers) into identifying with the 'historical' conception of *Hindutva*. I will turn to the legacy of this imagined moment in Indian antiquity for an historical comprehension of India's social order in the next chapter; for now, I want to continue examining the claim of historicity made by Savarkar in his book *Hindutva*.

How is the metaphoric force of the concept *Hindutva kairotic*? *Hindutva* is the residue of at least forty centuries of continuity. 'Hinduism' is metonymous to *Hindutva*. A failure to regard it as such has led, Savarkar states, the sister communities of the Hindu civilisation to 'mutual suspicion'. *Hindutva* is beyond ideology and as the more expansive essence of Hinduism is the expression 'of the thought and activity of the whole Being of our Hindu race'. This metaphysical claim is certainly not reducible to the label used to describe 'any particular theocratic or religious dogma or creed'.[160] *Hindutva* as 'theocratic patriotism' *in its own terms* transcends the Vedic corpus which represents Sanskriti or Hindu civilisation. Hinduism is a lesser, sectarian term.

Etymologically, the name the Persians used to describe the inhabitants of the land of the seven rivers, Sapta Sindhu, transformed into its Prakrit form, Hapta Hindhu: '[T]he cradle name chosen by the patriarchs of our race to designate our nation and our people, is Sapta Sindhu or Hapta Hindu.' This Vedic conception of a geographically located 'community' is already the abstract expression of the Sindhu nation. It is Savarkar's task to make it concrete for Indians today. This area in the consciousness of the neighbouring Persian civilisation, albeit very dimly, was thinly populated by scattered tribes.[161] Let us pause in the exposition. The communitarian model that Savarkar is adopting to describe the tribal peoples of the land the Persians described as Sapta Sindhu is recognisably Semitic. There is the modern idea of a people latent in the aggressive consciousness of a neighbouring civilisation. We saw how Hemachandra Raychaudhuri used some inscriptions on stone tablets recording Xerxes' edict to forbid the worship of 'Daivas' among the Gandharans as an early instance of zealotry that 'Indian' people had to face. While there is no great symbolic exodus from the yoke of an oppressive ruler, the terms are already present to unite an originally diasporic or nomadic peoples. Despite his desire to see Muslims suffer the same fate, Savarkar looks forward to the time when the Jewish diaspora realises itself as a Jewish state from the nation of Palestine. He writes how 'it will gladden us almost as much as our Jewish friends' where, in any conflict between their loyalty to their holy Motherland and America and Europe – like the Muslims of India – they will sympathise with the former 'if indeed they do not bodily go over to it'.[162] *Ressentiment* makes for strange bedfellows. Savarkar ends by furnishing the Crusades as another historical example of a common holy land uniting people separated by race, nationality and language. He means, of course, Christendom and not the Islamicate whose centre of spiritual gravity is not Jerusalem but Mecca.

If the aboriginal inhabitants of this sparsely populated region of Sapta Sindhu, or more correctly Sapta Sindhava, were not themselves displaced from any other kingdom, how did they relate to the carriers of Vedic lore that is the essence of Sanskriti civilisation? This acculturation of values is one to which the aboriginals, variously named by their conquerors as Vidhyadharas, Apsaras, Yakshas,

Rakshas, Gandharvas and Kinnaras (real peoples mixed with the mythical cohorts and enemies of the invading Aryans' pantheon of gods), submitted peaceably over the length of five or so centuries. Savarkar's vision of the inception of the classical golden age that would later be tarnished by Buddhistic reform is one where the real scattered inhabitants of Harrapa and Mohenjo-daro welcome the Aryan magi, acting as their guides. These magi brought along with them their already remote culture as ancestral memory and the power to name the geography anew. In their own version, this advance from the east of the Doab into the Gangetic plain by the Aryan peoples at around 1000 CE is metaphorically rendered by the nuptials of King Santanu, who falls in love with the goddess Ganga. Savarkar does not feel the need to ask the question that baffled Europeans about the origin of the 'Aryan' patriarchs. The question is unimportant; what is vital is the power to name, because naming brings the primeval land into history. 'When the Arabians invaded the Jews and the Parsees', Savarkar writes, 'they left their land and refused to barter away their racial and cultural identity'.[163] In the Puranic past, *Hindutva* created the land and the lesson to be adduced from this moment is contrary to the one Savarkar is alluding to for the exodus of Jews and Zoroastrians due to Islam: a true Hindu is a true nationalist.[164] The intrepid King Santanu and his retinue weren't willing to remain in the Panchanad (Punjab) but carried their ancestral consciousness into the ancient forests, a primitive domain which even the sophisticated technology of the Harappans could not tame. The symbol of this mission was the Sacrificial Fire. It was with the sacred fire and with the discovery of greyware at Hastinapura, Alamgirpur and Kausambi, the metallurgy of iron 'which they may have learned from their Indo-European cousins who ruled the neighbouring Iranian plateau during Sialk VI', that the Aryan peoples brought bloodshed and internecine strife recorded in the Puranic epics.[165]

Even if the original inhabitants of the Panchnad, in Savarkar's attempt to thwart any secessionists from the order he is adumbrating, decide no longer to adhere to the Vedantic 'revelation', choosing instead to define themselves as a community apart, they still remain Hindus. Jati is more vital than Sanskriti. Sikhs remain Hindus because, in the Romantic idiom in which Savarkar interprets the colonisation of the subcontinent, these people are 'almost direct descendents of those ancient Sindhus and can claim to have drunk their being at the very fountain of this Ganges of our Hindu life before she had descended down to the plains'.[166] This immemorial imbibing of the Sindhava spirit, then, does not sit very plausibly with Savarkar's explanation for the susceptibility of the Sikh rajas of Patiala and Umballa to Feringhi rule. These rajas provided the British with resources and safe passage through their lands to thwart the critical focus of the 1857 Uprising in Delhi. Despite the consciousness of 'hated Mohamedan slavery' with which the spirited followers of the Khalsa fought for a hundred years, the peace-hungry *kisan* (agriculturalists) hadn't apparently enough time to realise the ultimate end of the Great Game. A mere decade of English slavery, combined with the venal lie of restoring Ranjit Singh's kingdom to its former glory according to the prophecies in the Sikh holy books while allowing no quarter to the descendents of Akbar, was not sufficient to foster the millennial spirit of Mahakal in the most ancient remnants of *Hindutva*.[167] The martial Sikhs had been fooled by Pax Britannica. The ancient 'colonies' that the Aryan patriarchs founded had names now forgotten – the Kurus, Kashis, Videhas, Maghadas – as all became assimilated. Where is this teleological adumbration of India's millennial past tending?

The institution of Chakravartin or universal ruler is the greatest expression of Savarkar's interpretation of 'natural and cultural unity' to replace Sindhava. The Aryan mission ends with the geographical limit in Ceylon, reached by 'the valorous Prince of Ayodhya'.[168] The glorious ideal of companionate marriage, the perfect cosmic expression of the patriarchal family order, is found in *Ramrajya* (rule of Ram). He is 'the most illustrious representative monarch of our race' and it is only under 'the great white Umbrella of Sovereignty' with the 'Princes of Aryan blood' that the real birthday of the Hindu people comes about; both Aryans and Anaryans (Dravidians?) knit themselves into *a people* and a nation was born.[169] The king of the Raghus is the perfect template for sovereignty. Without speculating about the Vedic or Jain nature of his rule or the exact age of it, the people of Aryawarta (north of the Vindhya range up to the Himalayas) and Daxinapath in the south all delighted, Savarkar writes, in calling their motherland and cultural empire by the name of an ancient king, Bharat. Bharatvarsha is the name given in the *Vishnu Puran*. However, Savarkar describes the parallel name Sindhus with which the people used to evoke their attachment to the Indus. Other civilisations – among whom the Avestan Persians, the Hebrews and the Greeks – all clung to this ancient name to mean 'not merely … the borderland of Indus by this term as in days gone by, but the whole nation into which the ancient Sindhus by expansion and assimilation had grown'.[170] This is the 'historical' modality defining the project of *Hindutva* and, in the postcolonial context, it defines the search for *Ramjanmabhumi*. Non-Hindus are an anachronistic obstacle to this historical progress of self-realisation by Hindustan. Gyanendra Pandey describes how the *kar sevaks* focus on the 'remarkably repetitive' instance of construction/destruction of a temple at one particular site, to liberate the Janmabhumi after 'the coming of the Muslims'.[171] In the last section below I want to explore Savarkar's deployment of this monistic discourse of *Hindutva* purity to see how it conflicts with a more 'scientific' standard of veracity when it comes to the arrival of Muslims as a temporal force.

The concept of *Hindutva* and history

If Savarkar is scornful about the inauguration of a 'modern' historiographic modality for the Indian nation with the invasion of Muslims, there are some very mundane reasons compared to the vanished majesty of the Hindu order for deciding not to dwell on this moment in the nation's past. Even in defeat against the invading King of Persia in 1739, Govindrao Kale, writing to one of the valiant and 'victorious' Marathi agents, a Nana Fadnavis/Farnavis, describes how the smallest victories are 'extolled to the skies' by Muslims while 'we Hindus are inclined not to refer to our exploits however magnificent they may be'.[172] In his speech at Nagpur in 1938, Savarkar would describe this tendency in the Muslim consciousness of India's past in negative terms. It is because Muslims in general and Indian Muslims in particular have not matured out of an intensely religious or theological concept of the state that they are susceptible in their view of the past to defects of collective memory.[173] This 'curious memory that is supremely oblivious of all events which remind them of their defeats and discomfitures' means that '[t]hey will never remember that the Hindus beat them like a chip in a hundred battle-fields in India and had in the long run freed all India from the Muslim yoke and re-established Hindu-pad-pada-shahi'.[174] A recognisably modern temporality is intruding in Savarkar's mythopoeic conception of *Hindutva*.

Prithviraj Chauhan's defeat in 1192 on the battlefields of Tarain, 120 kilometres northwest of modern Delhi, by Shahabuddin (Muhammad Ghuri, or Shihab al-Din Muhammad bin Sam), established a permanent Muslim presence in the subcontinent. How does the Savarkarite mode of interpretation treat this important event rather than the more symbolic spoliation of the hollow Shiv lingam of its treasure by Mahmud of Ghazni (Mahmud Ghaznavi) at Somnath, over a century-and-a-half earlier, in 1025? Today there is an obvious desire to ameliorate this iconoclastic fervour by describing the inception of the Delhi sultanate as the successful fashioning of 'Indo-Islamic Cultures', as the 'pre-modern accommodation of differences'.[175] Ghazni, in present-day Afghanistan, instead of being a Buddhist region in the seventh century before it became the Turkic capital of the Ghaznavid Empire, is described as being Hindu. Conversion to Islam by 'Hindu communities' is the motive Savarkar ascribes to Muhammad Ghuri's foray into Haryana. *En route* through Multan, a Hindu queen offers her daughter in marriage to the Sur Pathan after killing her husband for his cowardice.[176] The citing of a fascinating anecdote in a native history that suggests that the large, sacred idol was once housed in Mecca itself and was brought to Somnath by a Hindu king 4,000 years after the time the Yavanas (foreigners, Greeks) say the human race was born, is a laudable corrective to the paradigm of nationalist history I am analysing here.[177] Researches into Deobandi syncretism, in one Shams Usmani's attempt to provide Hindus and Muslims with a common codifying ancestor identified as Manu/Noah, is another more recent attempt to mitigate communalism.[178] In the Savarkarite paradigm, the outcome at Tarain is transformed into a moral victory for the Hindu faith. What is the first troubling difference that has to be occluded in this interpretation? Savarkar fails to mention the defeat of Prithviraj in the plausible tactical context of his failing to unite with a neighbouring Hindu king, Jayachandra Gahadavala of Kanauj, in order to repulse the Ghurid invasion. Without the commonality identified by Savarkar's interpretation of events as *Hindutva*, 'for the notion of a unified Hinduism is a modern one', actual history finds the two kings mortal enemies of each other.[179] One can only speculate on the banal reasons for this enmity where Jayachandra decides to side with Muhammad Ghuri against Prithviraj, his son-in-law. Suffice to say accommodations of difference are usually motivated by more pragmatic reasons on the field of History rather than the desire to found cultures that will outlast the passing of the ages.

'Hindu activities from AD 1300 to 1800', we are invited to think, ought to be seen in the context of *Hindutva* as 'a vital spinal cord through the whole body politic and made the Nayars of Malabar weep at the sufferings of the Brahmins of Kashmir'.[180] Again, we are to miss the vertebrae or the substantial elements of history. Savarkar is referring to the defiant message given by the Sikh Guru, Tegabahadur, to the Brahmins, that they go and tell the Turks (Savarkar parenthetically adds 'Mohammedans') to make their great Hindu leader convert to Islam first. These events are happening in *kairotic* or millennial time. Any real animosity among Hindu kings is simply inconceivable. The concept of *Hindutva* is not equivalent to history; it is an attempt to lend ontological force in order to discover beyond the elements of any received 'tradition' a moment where it might perceive a ground of its own to stand on. It fosters the same sceptical attitude to temporality where the self-evident nature of historical tradition actually 'blocks our access to those primordial "sources" from which categories and concepts handed down to us have been in part genuinely drawn'.[181] Savarkar goes further; he wants us to regard the profusion of elements that constitute the nation's past as a fictional creation inimical to the spirit of Hindu identity. Since the traumatising intrusion of Mahmud Ghazni or the victory of Muhammad Ghuri over Prithviraj

> [n]othing makes Self conscious of itself so much as a conflict with a non-self. Nothing can weld peoples into a nation and nations into a state as the pressure of a common foe.[182]

Instead of strategic failures by individuals by the standard of modern historiography, we have the disturbance of a primal golden age, 'the long reign of plenty and peace from Ceylon to Kashmir' established by a dynasty of Rajputs. Savarkar continues: 'The moral victory was won when Akbar came to the throne and Darashukoh was born.' How did Akbar ascend the throne? The first 3,044 years of *Kaliyuga* and the prevailing age (*saka*) of King Yudhisthira of the *Mahabharata* is the closing era of King Vikramaditya, comprising 135 years. To be sure *Kaliyuga* is not exhausted by the Vikramaditya *saka*. When Islam Shah died, heir of the Afghan dynasty whose father Sher Khan Sur Humayun failed to rout from the throne in Delhi, his Hindu *Vaisya* minister Hemu proclaimed himself Raja Vikramaditya. Mrityunjay's *Rajabali*, in Abul Fazl's Jain account his contemporaries are inhabiting the fifth *ara* Dukhman, an era of 21,000 years of which just over 2,000 have lapsed.[183] Hemu was soon fatally wounded at Panipat by Bairam Khan, regent on behalf of the newly crowned teenager Jalal-ud-din Muhammad Akbar. The Mughal campaign would put an end to the Afghan Sur-sponsored age of Vikramaditya in the next two years. Abul Fazl attributes this early victory over Hemu, the 'self-conceited self-worshipper', to his emperor's famed virtue of self-restraint and his ability to master passion.[184] Hemu does maintain a dignified silence when questioned after victory. The chronicler describes his silence as *jahalat* (ignorance) but, when it comes to the choice about whether to imprison or to execute Akbar's enemy, he acknowledges Hemu's record of service to the Sur dynasty and his lofty spirit.[185] Though urged by Bairam Khan to kill him by his own hand, Akbar's exemplary self-restraint is visible in the decision to visit Hemu with the more politically spectacular punishment of dismembering. Abul Fazl concludes: 'In order to display the Majesty of the Shahinshah, and to give a lesson to the superficial they sent his head to Kabul, while his trunk was conveyed to Delhi and placed on the gibbet of warning. The world had rest from strife and tumult, and mortals obtained happiness and tranquillity.'[186] Savarkarite *Hindutva*, if not from the long point of view of Brahminical eternity, would probably explain the brevity of the Vikramaditya *saka* in terms of the fatal admixture of the *dharmic* with the Yavana Sur power that propelled Hemu onto the throne of Delhi. Hemu's decision to crown himself Vikramaditya recalls the Gupta dynasty in the fifth century CE and their identification of Ayodhya as *Ramjanabhumi*, birthplace of Lord Ram. King Chandra Vikramaditya II was the last attempt to realise the golden time of *Ramrajya*, the patriarchal ideal of just rule.

Dara Shikoh, who among others was sponsored by the Sikhs, lost the bitter succession struggle to his younger brother Aurangzeb in 1658. 'The frantic efforts of Aurangzeb to retrieve their fortunes lost in the moral field only hastened the loss of the military fortunes as well.' Savarkar is alluding to Aurangzeb's re-imposing of the *jizya* tax on non-Muslims, abolished by Akbar. This sweep culminates with moral victory despite 'Hindus' losing the battle of Panipat by forces loyal to Muslim rulers. The Hindu banner is carried to Attock by Marathas and Sikhs, to the banks of Kabul and where '[n]ever again had an Afghan dared to penetrate to Delhi'.[187] We have now left the field of history entirely and instead find ourselves in the realm of propaganda.

In Savarkar's *Hindutva*, Vikramdtiya 'who drove the foreigners from the Indian soil and Lalitaditya who caught and chastised them in their very dens from Tartary to Mongolia were but complements of each other'.[188] They are also the mythical complement that substitutes the real failure of Prithviraj and Jayachandra to unite. In Indian pre-history, the invasions that dimmed the glory of Sanskriti were caused by the 'opiates of Universalism and non-violence' and the 'secret agents in sympathy with foreign Buddhist powers'. These invasions from China, Savarkar continues to expound from the *Bhavishya Purana* and the *Pratisargha Parva*, were successfully repelled and the defeated armies, comprising millions, swore never to return to the Aryadesh 'with any territorial designs'. These same texts that record the undertaking of foreign Buddhist armies never to invade India also cite an edict of Shalivahan, Vikramditya's grandson. Having been victorious over the Shakas, Chinese, Tartars, Balhikas, Kamrupas, Romans, Khojas and Shathas, it was this edict that established an ancient line of control beyond the Indus as belonging to the Mlecchas (infidels).[189] It ought to be no surprise, then, in Savarkar's Hindu history that an eleventh-century text by one Chand Baradai, like the *Bhavishya Purana* describes how Shahabuddin was released on condition he renounce his intention to attack the Hindus who are ruled by a noble and generous Hindu monarch. Shahabuddin fails to heed this gesture and, after being taken prisoner a second time, is offered the same reconciliatory terms before being released again. However, on this occasion Shahabuddin, the recidivist, defeats the Hindu forces and has the Hindapi Prithviraj murdered using a plot.[190] We now turn to the central problem of the *Hindutva* concept's expository mode as a faithful representation of historical events. This problem also concerns the modality of 'Hindu history', at least in more sophisticated terms than the type Pandey examined about *Ramjanmabhumi*.

Hindutva *and writing postcolonial India* 129

In the footnote to his main argument, Savarkar draws our attention to the veracity of the contents in the *Bhavishya Purana*. It must not be forgotten that he has been relying upon these contents to give his idealist conception of the Hindu past some historical ballast. All the defining elements of modern historiography are now to be rejected outright. The accuracy of dates for decrees and edicts or even for the dispensations of individual kings that gave birth to these are now described as necessities that are alien to the native tradition. Here we find the ontological plain upon which the Being of Hindu selfhood discovers its authenticity. Properly historical details are now to be conceived in the same theological terms as the encounter of this self with its antithetical other, the 'non-self'; in other words, they are to be subordinated to the more vital drama where the Hindu is to appease the spirit of Mahakal. Savarkar is intellectually conscious of the problem of historiography *qua Hindutva*. Brevity is not the only consideration present in the following assertion about the foreign origins of a secular 'Indian' identity: 'It must be emphasised here that all these our remarks are true in their collective sense only. It is not possible to deal with details and exceptions either individual or actional [sic] in such a short address as this.'[191]

Facticity ('details and exceptions') is superfluous to this agonistic ('collective') version of events. What does a 'native' tradition rely on then? This is where the answer is no crude conflation of the authorised and the apocryphal. For Savarkar, the modalities of modern historiography are alien to the native tradition that instead relies on *memory* for its ground. 'The habit of doubting everything in the Puranas', Savarkar concludes, 'till it has been corroborated by some foreign evidence is absurd'. The preservation of a national tradition has helped Indians to survive the depredations of invasions and revolutions that have 'effaced the very traces of whole nations and whole civilizations elsewhere in the world'.[192] Sacrificing historical veracity is a small price in order to maintain this spiritual bulwark against the forces that have threatened Sanskriti. The 'modern up-to-date puranas' are a meagre achievement in contrast and also, we are told, anachronistic. The foundations of the sixteenth-century city of Vijayanagar in these secular interpretations of Sanskriti are said to be described in the far more ancient *Ramayan*.

The term 'Puranic' is used by Savarkar in a generic way for all historiography. This use points to the competitive nature of any account that might challenge the epistemological foundation of the concept of *Hindutva*. Indeed, this is history that is self-consciously clinging to the threshold of modernity at the same time it seeks to mobilise events, in Partha Chatterjee's phrase, according to history as 'the play of power'.[193] If the demotic narratives surrounding the *Ramjanmabhumi* are mixtures of the mythic and the communal/colonial, one Mrityunjay Vidyalankar's history, a history that is the story of 'the Rajas and Badshahs and Nawabs who have occupied the throne in Delhi and Bengal', deals with the defeat of Prithviraj from a radically different albeit native perspective to *Hindutva*. This is what Mrityunjay's *Rajabali* (1808) has to say about the Hindapi's response to the news that Yavanas (in this instance, Muhammad Ghuri and his forces) are arrayed for battle at Thanesar:

When the King heard of the threatening moves of the Yavanas, he called a number of scholars learned in the Vedas and said, 'Oh learned men! Arrange a sacrifice which will dissipate the prowess and the threats of the Yavanas.' The learned men said, 'O King! There is such a sacrifice and we can perform it. And if the sacrificial block [*yupa*] can be laid at the prescribed moment, then the Yavanas can never enter this land.' The King was greatly reassured by these words and arranged for the sacrifice to be performed with much pomp. When the learned men declared that the time had come to lay the block, much efforts were made but no one could move the sacrificial block to its assigned place. Then the learned men said, 'Oh King! What Isvara desires, happens. Men cannot override his wishes, but can only act in accordance with them. So, desist in your efforts. It seems this throne will be attacked by the Yavanas.'[194]

In the East India Company's Orientalist sponsorship of a 'Brahminical' view of the venerable past (Mrityunjay taught Sanskrit to British officials at Fort William College), Prithviraj's defeat is not concerned with the moral failings of his enemy. Instead, we have the idea that no amount of earthly splendour can bribe Providence or Divine Grace to work in its favour. The *dharmaraj* sit implacably above in cosmic indifference to the particular denomination of history. Chatterjee reminds us that 'in Mrityunjay's scheme of history, dynasties are founded by the grace of the divine power, and kingdoms are retained only as long as the ruler is true to dharma'.[195] With this Puranic or native version of events and in contrast to Savarkar's paradigm of *Hindutva*, *dharma* exceeds the order by which we arrange history. Let us recall how, in Savarkar's Aryan view, the original inhabitants of Bharatvarsha mingled with 'Apsaras' (celestial beings) and 'Rakshasas' (demons). Mrityunjay's *Rajabali* gives us the esoteric reason only the priests can decipher for the historic defeat and also the failure of the sacrifice:

Prithviraj's father had two wives, one of whom was a demoness (*rakshasi*) who ate human flesh. She had also introduced her husband into this evil practice. One day the *rakshasi* ate the son of the other queen who, taken by fright, ran away to her brother. There she gave birth to a son who was called Prthu. On growing up, Prthu met his father. At his request, Prthu cut off his father's head and fed the flesh to twenty-one women belonging to his *jati*. Later, when Prthu became king, the sons of those twenty-one women became his feudatories (*samanta*). 'Because Prthu killed his father, the story of his infamy spread far and wide. Kings who paid tribute to him stopped doing so.' In other words, Prithviraj was not a ruler who enjoyed much respect among his peers.[196]

Clearly Jayachandra of Kanauj did not fear for his daughter when he contracted the union with the fratricidal and cannibalistic Chauhan. Savarkar would dismiss these supernatural elements from the legend of Prithviraj as accretions of folkloric knowledge. However, in one very important respect the corroborative norms of modern historiography he dismisses serve a vital importance for the appropriation of the Puranic past. In Chand Baradai's eleventh-century text, Prithviraj is assassinated in a plot. The Hindapi Rajput is not given an opportunity to test his prowess on the battlefield by the cowardly Shahabuddin. In Savarkar's preferred account, Shahabuddin is given not one but two chances to renounce his avaricious claims to the Chauhan's territory. In Mrityunjay's *Rajabali*, the eventual fate of Prithviraj is different:

> [Prithviraj] emerged from his quarters and engaged Sahabuddin in a ferocious battle. But by the grace of Isvara, the Yavana Sahabuddin made a prisoner of Prithuraja. On being reminded that Prithuraja was son-in-law of King Jayacandra ... he did not execute him but sent him as a prisoner to his own country of Ghaznin.[197]

In *Rajabali*, the grace of Isvara is not conditional upon the religious caste of the actor. That this lesson Mrityunjay is offering his compatriots is also convenient for his employers is incidental. Bengal bewails Prithviraj's fall, as do the Sikhs. According to Savarkar, these communities share with all other Indians 'the fate of a conquered people [who] suffer together as Hindus'.[198] Thanesar is not only a battleground in history where two individuals arrayed with their respective armies fought for victory. For Savarkar, the 'veritable human multitude' of Hindustan contracts with Muhammad of Ghazni's attack and Thanesar becomes a symbolic field where the Hindu self discovers itself in an ontological conflict with a negating otherness (the non-self). So it is a matter of no small importance that we find which figure, Muhammad of Ghazni or Prithviraj, practices a just restraint in dealing with his defeated foe. Savarkar's use of Chand Baradai's conclusion of Thanesar is an inversion of the traditional history recorded in Mrityunjay's *Rajabali*. Shahabuddin at Thanesar is not the same as at Ooch. In contrast to the magnanimity of Prithviraj, he *would* have enslaved the Rajput princes and taken the most beautiful captive women into his harem to ravage them.[199] There is a variant conclusion according to a folkloric account by a poet called Chand Bhat in his 'Prithviraj Raso'. The Bhat visits the blinded king at Ghazni 'in order to do his traditional duty as a Bhat of laying down his life for his emperor'. Sat next to the last Hindu emperor of Delhi where Shahabuddin had been intrigued to witness Prithviraj's ability to strike a mark by sound, the poet composes a couplet instructing the blind man to aim for their foe. The sultan is killed and, before the guards reach the two Hindu captives, they decapitate themselves with their own swords.[200]

When it comes to their nation's past, typical Indians are as symptomatic, in *amor intellectualis* at least, as the *kar sevaks* of the condition Savarkar describes as 'Hindutva'. Each is busy engaged in the labour of disinterring this history as 'the story of the Eternal City' Freud once described as a metaphor for the life of the unconscious itself, in his late essay *Civilisation and Its Discontents*. And like Freud, reflecting on his childhood, each of us is also the object of an emotive hold where in history we might find ourselves belonging not to the imperial dispensation, Aryan or Roman, but to the barbarian train of Hannibal 'the semitic general' and the Carthaginian hordes.[201] Radhakrishnan's twentieth-century interpretation is a culmination of the Enlightenment epistemologies that only naively informed Vidyalankar's idea of the role of history for the British in the early nineteenth century. The conclusion of this view about the organic *telos* of Hinduism is that the attempt to *make* Hindu faith consistent with the organic evolution of human nature, where Hinduism is 'a slow growth across the centuries incorporating ... good and true things as well as much that is evil and erroneous', especially by an endeavour that often fails 'to throw out the unsatisfactory elements', is only to acknowledge that the 'subconscious heritage' is not amenable to the kind of adaptation that Savarkar and *Hindutva* ideologues seek to promote.[202]

4 B. R. Ambedkar and the Hindu past

[A]n historian ought to be exact, sincere and impartial; free from passion, unbiased by interest, fear, resentment or affection; and faithful to the truth, which is the mother of history, the preserver of great actions, the enemy of oblivion, the witness of the past, the director of the future.

B. R. Ambedkar[1]

The truth is that good government depends as much on circumstances as on a desire for freedom and there are regions of the globe which may never know its blessings. But it is a characteristic of doctrines such as self-determination to disregard the limits imposed by nature and history, and to believe that a good will alone can accomplish miracles.

Elie Kedourie[2]

We have turned the caste of servants, the Sudras, into our middle class, our '*Volk*', those who make political decisions.

Friedrich Nietzsche[3]

Introduction

What were the circumstances the Untouchable leader Bhimrao Ramji Ambedkar (1891–1956) encountered during the years preceding Independence that might dim if not entirely vanquish the reformer's will when it comes to realising the modern dream of a society free of domination by the strong? This chapter seeks to answer this question by examining the hermeneutical strategies Ambedkar used to interpret the Puranic past for his followers. After the last chapter, we might leave the issue of anarchist appropriations of India's antiquity to the retrograde objectives of the concept of *Hindutva*. This would be a mistake. I drew attention to the moment in Herder's account of Hindu society where he casts doubt over the authenticity of a claim by 'pariars' as a subjugated nation. In the late 1940s, Ambedkar had looked to India's past for an explanation by formal argument for the origins of those unfortunate enough to comprise the lower and lowest strata of India's social order. And in this long-distant past Ambedkar discovered traces of events that go beyond the conventional wisdom Herder expressed for the predicament of the pariah in the monopoly over knowledge possessed by the Brahmin cabal. Ambedkar's conclusions about the mundane circumstances for the eventual emergence of this fatal division of Indian society into four castes (*chaturvarnya*) on the face of it represent the diametric opposite of the attention to the fabulist or mythic in Savarkar's ideology of *Hindutva*. One would have thought that Ambedkar's sociological interpretation of India's millennial past would render a purely realist, functional origin of untouchability in the spirit of Rankean objectivity, that there would be no room for heroic *dramatis personae* from whose actions and intentions the tragic dimensions of the Dalit experience flow to the present. These questions were at the foreground of Ambedkar's mind when he hypothesised about the origins of untouchability. In *Who Were the Shudras?* (1946), Ambedkar described his obligation to submit theological principles to the secular standards of historical veracity in terms of producing 'pure history'. And yet in the sequel to this volume, *The Untouchables* (1948), he goes further by acknowledging the limits of a scientific objectivity and the instrumental role of the imagination in discovering the origins of the social practice 'buried in a dead past which nobody knows'. Allusions to time-honoured analogies for the historical task follow: the classical analogy of disinterring a city in its original state to reclaim it for history, the palaeontologist's delicate labour of constructing an extinct species and, perhaps more problematic, the painter who creates a scene by discerning objects on the distant horizon.[4] In other words, patient analysis will release the secret of things considered the natural order in humankind's cultural memory. For Ambedkar, the historical process is conceived as furnishing the historian with incomplete fragments of evidential fact. He provisionally quotes Goethe's observation that the historian must conceive his task as a juror summoned to hear a trial. Where fact fails, the imagination has to be used to fill in the space or, in his words, to construct the links.[5] The inferential method implies that the missing links exist outside this synthesising activity. What people think is a sociological fact. The Vedic corpus of text in Indian antiquity does not supply us with direct evidence for the question of *origins* and, unlike Gibbon's celebration of Roman prosperity, the thicker texture of pagan mythology for Ambedkar was woven of various discordant materials that had to be dissolved in order to reveal the truth.[6] The astonishing feat that ordered the segregation of humanity beyond the precincts of village life to make a world of paler reflection to the Vedic order, for itself, unlike the temporary defilement to which primitive man was prone, will turn on the question of whether eating beef was taboo. By emulating the asceticism of the Buddhist way of life, the Brahmanic order hoped to retrieve its lost fold. The cosmic act of sacrifice or *Yajna* that sanctified the practice of slaughtering cattle for ritual in India's antiquity is reduced to the universal motive of self-preservation once 'the masses' were persuaded of its ineffectual and even immoral character. The Brahmin priests 'wanted to oust the Buddhists from the place of honour and respect which they had acquired in the minds of the masses by their opposition to the killing of the cow for sacrificial purposes'.

Ambedkar concludes:

> To achieve their purpose the Brahmins had to adopt the usual tactics of a wreckless adventurer. It is to beat extremism by extremism. It is the strategy which all rightists use to overcome the leftists. The only way to beat the Buddhists was to go a step further and be vegetarians.[7]

All the contradictions of ancient lore are given a contemporary meaning. One can describe the conflict between the orthodoxy of king and priest and the antinomian revelation, even where the former allowed commensality by necessity and excluded fraternisation by choice, as a political problem of ideologies. Indian society had been incapable of evolving the autonomous city-states of late medieval Europe because of the strict application of the hereditary principle and the forbidding of 'fraternization of its productive citizenry'.[8] One instant of this tragic element of ritual barriers between castes manifests itself in the policy of drawing chalk circles around utensils used by those receiving food by the colonial government during periods of famine.[9] Even Nature was powerless in forcing commensality between tribes in Hindu culture. Before Ambedkar draws attention to the opportunism of the Brahmin priest in depriving the pious sacrifice-giver (*jajmani*) of most of the carcass hidden in the instructions of the *Atreya Brahmana* ('true orgies of covetousness' as Weber quotes), or the first appearance in 412 CE of an edict outlawing the killing of a cow as equivalent to the murder of a Brahmin, he deploys the explanatory mechanism of neutral terms in anthropology.[10] The argument is that when nomadism ended, the settled tribes expelled groups epitomising the older way of subsistence by animal husbandry to the periphery of collective life. Ambedkar's thesis gives colour to the functional place Weber gives to helot handicraft by the Shudra castes – a subsistence living etched out because of the deprivation of rights to village lands, the 'pillars of Indian industry' that later allowed the spires of temples to rise which probably soon followed the establishment of permanent settlement.[11] The glories of Hindu civilisation were impossible without the nine-fold Sat-Shudra (pure Shudra) caste of artisanal labour. Ambedkar goes to Henry Maine and Frederic Seebohm to adduce evidence for the broken character of the outcastes from Hindu sociality. In the evolutionist paradigm to which these anthropologies of Celtic community were prone, the integration of the Broken Men (Maine's term) as tenants was inevitable as the Irish chief extended his sway to the border area where the 'cultivators and servile states were permitted to squat'.[12] The implication in Maine's theory is that this integration was a prerequisite of establishing social order after the ensuing chaos as these individuals sought protection from tribal internecine conflict. No such largesse was extended to the Untouchables in India:

> [T]he notion of Untouchability supervened and perpetuated difference between kindred and non-kindred, tribesmen and non-tribesmen in another form, namely, between Touchables and Untouchables. It is this new factor which prevented the amalgamation taking place in the way in which it took place in Ireland and Wales, with the result that the system of separate quarters has become a perpetual and permanent feature of the Indian village.[13]

The revival of Hinduism is founded on an exodus narrative where Buddha's disciples after his death started erecting stupas: 'The Brahmins followed it [and] in their turn, built temples and installed in them images of Shiva, Vishnu and Ram and Krishna etc., – all with the object of drawing away the crowd that was attracted by the image worship of Buddha. That is how temples and images came into Hinduism.'[14] In marked contrast, after the defeat of the Greek convert to Buddhism, Menander, by the Maghadan king Pushyamitra and the ensuing 'persecution' of the Buddhists, the establishment of the great Vedic horse sacrifice by the latter ('A National Festival' sanctified by the presence of Brahminical sages), the religion of *ahimsa* from the Savarkarite point of view became a pretext for 'treason' whenever India was prone to Hun invasions from the north.[15] The translation of the Buddhist Pali and Prakrit canon into Sanskrit at Kanishka's Buddhist court represented the dominance of 'Indian religion, Indian language, Indian thought and Indian customs' and the great interruption of *Hindutva* suffered by Asokan Buddhist tyranny comes to an end with the formal conversion by Kanishka's grandson to the Vedic religion.[16] For nationalist historiography, all the possible outcomes of historical processes are contracted to the religious affiliation of a ruler as 'the pre-eminent factor of change'.[17] How could it have been otherwise? The following conclusion is typical of the orientation given to the complexity involved in determining the political value of the Indian past. The context for these assertions is Ambedkar's conversion to Buddhism in 1956. Quoting the activist's comments in his essay *The Untouchables*, on the origins of untouchability, the authors remark how Buddhism

> is portrayed as the only Indian belief system with an historical tradition of egalitarianism. Buddhism is seen to have been destroyed by a Brahminical counter-revolution which pushed its most determined opponents to the periphery of society and declared them to be unclean. This was the origin of Untouchability. Although Buddhism was to all intents dead in the land of its birth, Ambedkar set out to reclaim it as both spiritual guide and sharp ideological break with Hinduism.[18]

The question I want to ask is: what a priori considerations are involved in any interpretive feat before these can plausibly describe events in Indian history in terms of sociological modalities? The image of the short-lived moment when Buddhism reformed the Hindu social order entails a series of recognisably modern developments: 'egalitarianism', 'counter-revolution', 'periphery', as well the more generic term 'society.' The evolution of *dhamma* in the Mauryan kingdom under Asoka, in contrast to the already nostalgic values of the Hindu patrimonial kingdom reflected in Kautilya's *Arthashastra*, served as an ideal ground for the emergence of mercantilist communities. In marked contrast to the spirit of the interpretation given to them by Savarkar's concept of *Hindutva*, the propagation of Buddhism 'to make it virtually the religion of the Mauryan state' went beyond – as all systems of belief in fact do – the cultic paraphernalia of priests and their congregation. Thapar concludes that this was Asoka's true *intention* (with all that this implies about intentional fallacies for long-dead actors in history):

The edicts would belie such an intention. He appears to have been concerned with using a broader ethic to explore the ways of governance and to reduce social conflict and intolerance. *Dhamma* was aimed at creating an attitude of mind in which the ethical behaviour of one person towards another was primary, and was based on a recognition of the dignity of human beings.[19]

The 'anti-charismatic' charisma of Gautama in the chieftaincy clans, in contrast to the kind in older patrimonial kingdoms whose order the Brahmin caste spent all its energies cultivating, was an ideal expression of the emergent social value of *individualism* that Thapar reads into Asoka's rock-hewn edicts. For Dalit consciousness, Ambedkar's decision to convert to Buddhism involves (Mendelsohn and Vicziany assert) a *reclamation* of this more amenable social order from the long-distant past. Almost all the significant actors involved in anti-colonial resistance, both in the defining Independence movement of the Congress Party and outside it, with more militant elements represented by the Hindu Mahasabha, shared this desire to discover an impulse in the millennial past that might serve to legitimate a claim for equality in the evolving constitutional life of the nation. Whether it was Gandhi's *Swaraj* or V. D. Savarkar's *Hindutva*, the formally democratic arrangement after freedom from British rule had been achieved necessarily involved some historical thesis about the particular character of Indic civilisation. Ambedkar's decision to convert to Buddhism as a political voice of the Dalits would not represent the elegant triumph of scientific objectivity over the partialities in Indian antiquity. Instead, it evokes all the torsions of cultural memory under the duress of foreign domination. The notable exception to this consensus about the generic value of the past as a resource for transforming the *status quo* is Nehru. 'We in India', he writes, 'do not have to go abroad in search of the past and the distant. We have them here in abundance. If we go to foreign countries it is in search of the present. That search is necessary, for isolation from it means backwardness and decay.'[20]

Though sharing Nehru's aspirations for modernity, especially when it came to social reform, it is in the context of a critical historicism that we should interpret Ambedkar's observations about the diasporic indigenous tribes who defended village communities from attack from their victors and whose Buddhist descendants were later the victims of Brahmin persecution for their antinomianism. Historicism was an essential ingredient in fashioning the norms of political and social modernity. Ambedkar's statements about the subaltern role played by the Chandala, Untouchables, Dalits, Harijans or Depressed Classes in pre-history were indeed a strategic attempt to 'build a wider class-based coalition of subordinated peoples'.[21] It is also a metaphoric rendering of the past. More significantly, Ambedkar's interpretation of the microsocial conflicts that led to a universal stigmatising by the Brahmin elite of the indigenous tribes reflects his own caste consciousness as a Mahar for whom the watchman was one among the other traditional occupational roles as village servant (*Balutdar*).[22] From this, we are told that Ambedkar's conversion, while being 'profoundly political', remains incomprehensible in the context of his worldliness and his 'deep sympathy for the forms of western constitutionalism'.[23] The apparently singular act of conversion resonates far beyond the metaphysical desire to identify with a system of beliefs more amenable to an individual's style of being. This style of being always has its correlate in India's long past. The sociologists go on to describe how, on the one hand, there is his historical role as one of the draftsmen of the Indian Constitution and, on the other, an atavistic return to the religious separatism of a movement a few decades earlier, the *Ad Dharm*. The latter, we are told, is symptomatic of 'the depth of his consciousness as an Untouchable'. Mangoo Ram's *Ad Dharmis*, while sharing the political radicalism of Ambedkar's followers, again, from the sociological perspective, had failed to graduate beyond the ritual and ethical elements of *bhakti* (devotion) in their vision of equality. I have been describing the historical conditions for Ambedkar's profound consciousness as an Untouchable. Ambedkar's failure to realise a secular and materialist vision of equality in combating Congress hegemony and Gandhi's personal resistance to the possibility of separate electorates for his followers, discussed in Poona during 1930–1931, is now used to *partly* explain his 'gathering determination to seek a religious way out'.[24] As we will see in the following sections, I want to question this expository mode that detects a conflict between political modernity and religious radicalism in Ambedkar's thinking by closely examining the way Ambedkar conceived the institution of caste or *chaturvarnya*. What we will see is that for Ambedkar, no conflict exists between the urgent contemporary demand for formal equality and the substantive foreclosure of it in 'ritual and ethical' terms in Indian history. Ambedkar characterises the two aspects of conversion as both 'social as well as religious; material as well as spiritual'. He goes on:

> Whatever may be the aspect or line of thinking, it is necessary to understand the beginning, the nature of Untouchability and how it is practised. Without this understanding, you will not be able to realise the real meaning underlying my declaration of conversion.[25]

The sole reason why the Brahmin learned scholar is not able or was unwilling to perform this task of questioning the exceptions that define Hindu civilisation – twenty million comprising criminal tribes, another fifteen million the aboriginals – is because he has failed to emancipate himself from the interests of his class. Voltaire's defiance of Catholicism is the ideal. The terms by which Ambedkar measures the morality of Hindu life are outside the norms of that culture: what does one make 'of a civilisation which has produced a mass of people who are taught to accept crime as an approved means of earning their livelihood [and of the *adivasis*], another mass of people who are left to live in full bloom of their primitive barbarism in the midst of civilisation?'[26] Nothing could be more equivalent to the colonial censure of ages past than describing native practices in terms of the poisonous growth of primitive barbarism in the garden of civilisation. Hindu life failed to realise the terrestrial harmony promised by Buddhism and the result is fatal to its progress. This value judgement, incidentally, would violate the 'scientific' or anthropological objectivity Herder used to describe the organic evolution of different human civilisations. Ambedkar's historical method confirms that the aetiology of the Indian present cannot be eradicated by a purely mechanistic understanding promoted by a tragic conception of the past. The Brahmanic order had been entirely successful in thwarting any consciousness that challenged its hegemony over the minds and souls of Indians. In questioning the social establishment of the current order historically, Ambedkar exceeds the necessity of structural transformation that the radical invests his or her energies in, to *share the same non-temporal plane as the anarchist*. The annihilation of *chaturvarnya* implied the possibility of seizing control of one's humanity *at any time* in the long duration of the Hindu order. Let us see how Ambedkar records the singularity of events outside the monotonous finality of caste.

Improving the apocalyptic present

This attention to the historical dimensions of the 'religious semiotic' was timely. Gandhi had made the question of a separate constitutional arrangement for the 'Harijan' population an occasion to fast unto death in 1932 and 1933. This implied a moral monopoly of the uses to be made of Hindu tradition in fashioning an alternative to the colonial democratic resolution to India's most famous problem, a position that Ambedkar challenged in a dedication to his predecessor, Jotiba Phule: 'The Greatest Shudra of Modern India who made the lower classes of Hindus conscious of their slavery to the higher classes and who preached the gospel that for India social democracy was more vital than independence from foreign rule.'[27] This is the spirit in which we ought to read Ambedkar's highly critical forays into the same long-distant past as Savarkar in order to recover *Homo minor* as the egalitarian foundation of the modern nation. Not for him the oceanic or hierarchical rendering of the anthropological categories 'interdependence and separation', where the individual is essentially a consciousness that transcends the material world of conflict and, therefore, of history. *Chaturvarnya* is instead the fatal outcome of these formative social facts in Hindu tradition. Equity is to be achieved by the individual's intervening to adjust the parameters of economics and politics. In his war against saintliness, Nietzsche confided his thoughts about the spirit of egalitarianism attempting to prevail after the revolutions of the nineteenth century by drawing an analogy between the present and the Puranic; he called it 'the victory of Chandala values'.[28] Ambedkar, who shares the modernising paradigm with Nehru, would have no time for the ludic conception in which democracy is about turning the caste of servants, the Sudras, into a middle class entrusted with the primordial Aryan function of making political decisions in former ages: Nietzsche ironically calls them the 'Improvers of Mankind'.[29] We will see how Ambedkar's desire to achieve this victory takes him to an anomalous destination where he fails to free himself from the Great Chain of Being in which *Homo hierarchicus* maintains its social existence by ritualising inequality as a fact of nature. Having said this, Ambedkar's ethnogenetic account of the appearance of the Shudra stratum in the Hindu social order, as well as his invectives about the present order of things, makes us realise how deficient Gandhi's interpretation of the past was in establishing this objective. For Gandhi, modern civilisation and the means by which it is spread – the railways – by its agents – that is, lawyers and doctors – is responsible for subverting the venerable order of India's past civilisation, to which 'it behoves every lover of India to cling ... even as a child clings to its mother's breast'.[30] The separation of religion and culture from the realm of politics and economy was symptomatic of colonial rule. Bringing them together again was indispensable not only in supplying resistance to colonial power with spiritual and cultural resources but also for 'utilising the new spirit' for criticising defective practices in Indian civilisation.

In Louis Dumont's diagrammatic representation of *Homo major* and *Homo minor*, both the *Hindutva* and *Hind Swaraj* ideologies appear anomalous in terms of the intrusion of the category 'nation' in the hierarchical scheme for social formations.[31] '[T]he spirit of nationality' for Gandhi transcended the communal-religious difference and, if individuals interfere with each others' religion, 'they are not fit to be considered a nation'.[32] For Gandhi, it is only with the onset of British colonial rule that these enmities arose and eventually engulfed any ordered resolution. Nationalism is derivative only to the degree that it can be used as a standard of maturity to measure the conduct of groups. Hypernationalism and totalitarianism by the state are symptomatic of the whole's asserting itself against a process of individualistic atomisation in the organic understanding of a past in which the individual had its existence in a sort of dignified distance outside the world of competing social processes. Ambedkar's ambition was to retrieve the spirit of nationalism of the kind Herder speculated about among the oppressed groups. Gandhi's remarks about British colonial rule were to challenge the extrinsic quality of the idea of nationhood with a conservative organic or synecdochic idea of Indian civilisation: 'There is no reason to believe that there is one law for families and another for nations. History, then, is a record of *an interruption of the course of nature.*'[33] Left to itself, the miracle of Providence would have ameliorated the worst excesses of those investing themselves with the historical destiny of humankind. Herder and Burke would be in agreement. The prerequisite of a civic order based upon an instrumental distinction between the private and public realms in which the individual conceives their rights before the universality of the law is subverted in more conventional terms in the criticism that Gandhi reserves for the legal system in colonial India.[34] Gandhi and Ambedkar occupy entirely different terrains on the pre-figurative understanding of the nation as an historical reality. Gandhi's desire was to see all the tensions of the traditional Hindu order dissipate themselves through the subjective efforts of *satyagraha* (non-violent resistance). This conservative vision subordinates the antagonistic relations of modern society to the primal or comic resolution of conflict. In the course of the confrontation between the individual and the colonial apparatus, the 'non-violent soldier of freedom' is issued with the instruction '[to] write out the slogan "do or die" on a piece of paper or cloth and stick it on his clothes, so that in case he died in the course of offering satyagraha, he might be distinguished by that sign from other elements who do not subscribe to non-violence'.[35] The idea latent within this instruction to the nation before Gandhi's arrest on 9 August 1942 is that the Indian soul should distinguish itself from the violent fray that defines the field of historical action. Let us see how Ambedkar interprets this strategy.

A nationalist historiography furnished Indians with the conceptual tools necessary to fashion a political culture that challenged the imposition of values. B. G. Tilak's celestial explanation for the Aryan origins of the Indian nation – that it originated in the Arctic because of references in the Vedas to the peculiarly long diurnal nature of time – is countered by an almost equally astonishing tradition in the *Ashvamedha Yajna* of queens vying to copulate with the supreme totem of that culture, the horse. Ambedkar reminds us that horses do not roam Arctic wastes, so the theory is implausible.[36] But Tilak's theory is infinitely adaptable concerning the long eras of the world's history for the Hindu nationalist endeavour. The wily Britisher, according to M. S. Golwalkar who inherited the mantle woven by Savarkar, propagated the myth that Indians 'were never the children of the soil but mere upstarts having no better claims than the foreign hordes of Muslim or the British over this country'.[37] Loath to subscribe to the Aryan invasion thesis that Tilak's ideas concluded, the worthy Golwalkar in *We, or Our Nation Defined* (1947) would invoke modern scientific research that had shown the North Pole to be a portable region, and 'that long ago it was in that part of the world ... [which] is called Bihar and Orissa at the present'.[38] By the mid-twentieth century, the imposition of colonial values began to take on an appearance of increasing relative autonomy – in Lévi-Strauss's terms – from the original industrial and commercial interests after 1765 when 'John Company sought to establish its raj over Bengal, and Orissa on as sound and permanent basis as possible'.[39] Universality is the guise of anticipated rather than actualised power for the colonised bourgeoisie. As Tilak's attempt to mobilise the masses shows, although universality is the discourse the colonial power used to give spurious legitimacy to its authority, the mode of dominance still remains intact in nationalism; it is figured here as the strategic deployment of universality in the name of all the people. For the Congress nationalists, as much as the Kantian burgher citizen of the enlightened state: *'Argue as much as you like and about whatever you like, but obey!'*[40] After the British, the demotic masses will not be allowed to engage freely with each other in the 'happy anarchy' of ages past and to level the institutions established with the complicity of the collaborating elites. The native will still stand in the dock to have his punishment meted out to him if he transgresses the penal code and he will still pay taxes to fund the power that has brought him there. Tilak's message to those engaged in the non-violent campaign against the formidable machinery of the colonial state is that soundness and permanence are sober virtues worth inheriting from the British experience, to rationalise Congress power after the British are ejected. As we saw in the last chapter, the creation of a political space in which the people can be mobilised implied a wholesale deformation of history. This was solely the result of Indian nationalism's having to face the irresistible object of *force*.

This fact infected the pacific resistance to colonial authority that Gandhi had imagined as a duty of all Indians. Speaking about the Tilak Swaraj Fund, B. R. Ambedkar draws attention to the 'organized and systematic loot' and the 'reckless plunder committed by the predatory leaders of the Congress of public money for nursing their own constituencies without any qualms of conscience'.[41] Gandhi himself stands accused of not insisting that a substantial portion of the sum of Rs. 1

crore and 25 lakhs 'under his command' go for the betterment of the Untouchables.[42] As well as for propaganda, the fund was 'spent on feeding briefless lawyers who were alleged to have given up practice in the cause of the nation without an inquiry whether they had any'. Credit for the creation of a party machine goes to Gandhi and, for Ambedkar, '[t]he fight between the Congress and the Untouchables was a fight between an army and a crowd'.[43] The instrumentality of Congress as a political movement intent on appropriating the machinery of governance, after Gandhi took charge in 1919, is revealed by its forging of 'sanctions', 'a thing never thought of before'. From passing ineffectual resolutions on the flaws in the British administration, Ambedkar continues, Gandhi's *sataygraha* campaign used non-cooperation, boycott, civil disobedience and fasting as weapons in 'the Congress armoury' to subvert colonial rule.[44] A *satyagrahi* may have 'had to be a *brahmacharya*, supremely self-controlled in his personal habits, behaviour and desire', but this weapon of soul-force to 'infuse manliness in cowards' and allow Indians to 'conquer our conquerors the English [and] make them bow before our tremendous soul-force' was not to be turned on one's own kin and countrymen, unless the objective is to rout any collaborators of the colonial regime.[45] Ambedkar notes the absence of any concrete attempt to politically address the issue of untouchability, gainsaying Gandhi's childhood recollections of having to touch a Muslim, at his mother's behest, to diffuse the polluting effect of touching a latrine cleaner when washing. 'If Mr Gandhi could make the Hindu accept spinning and boycott as franchises for membership of the Congress', he failed to do the same 'to make acceptable the employment of an Untouchable in a Hindu household for membership of the Congress'.[46] When a mass *satyagraha* at Chowder Tank, in Kolaba District, for the right to draw water from public watering places and another for admission into the Kala Ram temple was carried out by thousands, when 'both men and women belonging to the Untouchables were insulted and beaten ... and some were imprisoned by Government on the ground of causing breach of the peace', instead of lending these agitations his support Gandhi denounced the action in the strongest terms.[47] Another incident in Kavitha, Gujarat, where Gandhi advised Harijans to vacate their homes 'in search of self-respect' because they were subjected to boycotts by the caste Hindus for daring to send their children to the same school as the higher-caste Garasias' children rather than to challenge them, gives us an idea of this paradoxical ideal in practice. For Ambedkar, it is evidence that Gandhi did not want to alienate the foundations of his appeal among caste Hindus who dominated the leadership and Provincial Assemblies after the arrival of *Swaraj* in 1937.

Why was Congress eager to co-opt the legal profession, apart from the prestige attached to constitutionalism at the moment of nationalist awakening? *Swadeshi* as the political ethos of nationalism was 'soaked so thoroughly in Hinduism', Guha informs us, that even liberal professions such as doctors and lawyers identified as secular-modern could be mobilised to ostracise those members of society who were seen as not cooperating with the 'weapons' Congress used to challenge the legitimacy of the colonial administration. No matter what shade of political expression, whether conservative, centrist or liberal, Brahminical tradition played the most important role in the ideology of nationalism. The complicity between modernity and tradition was perhaps nowhere more pronounced than with lawyers. Guha notes how '[i]n the politically more active districts they often operated as a well-knit nationalist force, with the local Bar Association assuming some of the functions of caste councils and advising priests, barbers, and washermen not to serve those considered guilty of deviation from the Swadeshi code'.[48] The relatively small numbers of recorded 'Actual or Threatened Withdrawal of Services by Professional and Ritual Agencies from Clients Opposed to Swadeshi', by lawyers, doctors and Brahmins, as well as washermen and barbers, is not important. This is an illustration of how the revolutionary humanism of nationalist resistance used the universality of tradition in the form of caste sanction as a tool. Caste may have been a useful way to isolate those who failed to share the Congress's vision of *swaraj*, but the atomising affect of it, despite the ability of 'oriental societies' to adapt to external change, is antithetical to the nationalist project: 'The sole, intimate, ever present authority that regulates every detail of Hindu life, is precisely that which keeps the Hindus apart from each other, and forbids them to weld themselves into a nation: the authority of caste.'[49] This is the reason for the centrality of caste in Gandhi's vision of *swaraj*. Indeed, in the Round Table Conference organised by the British government in 1930 to frame a constitution for an independent India, Ambedkar submitted a memorandum to outlaw the use of boycotts against the Depressed Classes because '[t]he method of open violence pales away before it'.[50] From the point of view of modern state formation, the subversion of caste authority by Gandhi's sentimental appeal to include the Untouchables in the Hindu fold for the moral good of the caste Indians (to punish them for the 'sin' of untouchability) is an inadequate safeguard against the *raj* of the Bania and the Brahmin. To seek constitutional safeguards for minority rights, including quotas by governmental institutions for members from the Untouchables, is, Ambedkar continues, to make 'demands [that are] ridiculed by Congress as communalism and the leaders of the Untouchables are represented as job hunters. The Congress places its opposition to these guarantees on the high pedestal of nationalism, of which it holds itself as the guardian angel.'[51] Even before the Round Table Conference in 1931 about a constitution for the new state, Gandhi's refusal to grant separate electorates for the Untouchables was based upon a universalist task that only Hindus are capable of taking on to remove untouchability from their religion: 'What I am against is their statutory separation even in a limited form, from the Hindu fold, so long as they choose to belong to it.'[52] That Gandhi chose to submit to the Muslim delegation's demands despite their refusal to join 'the diabolical plot of Mr Gandhi' reveals the essential limitations of Gandhi's holistic vision.[53] Even before the political form that national sovereignty would take became an issue, for B. R. Ambedkar, Congress's spurious attempt at representing the whole Indian nation was evident in the Bardoli resolutions of 1922. I have already cited Ambedkar's meticulous recording of the systematic abuse of funds for party propaganda and the marginalising of the Untouchable problem by relegating it to the militant Hindu organisation, the Hindu Mahasabha.

Dissolving the Hindu past

V. D. Savarkar's argument in *Hindutva – Who Is a Hindu?* attempts to discover the Hindu nation in Indian pre-history. B. R. Ambedkar's question posed in the title of his book *Who Were the Shudras?* is an a alternative history for the concept of *Hindutva*. Passionate admirers have chosen to elevate Ambedkar to a position of lonely eminence: 'Babasaheb was the Other of the nationalist thought and practice which was being forged by Gandhiji and Nehru.'[54] As we saw above, the modality of the question is critical: the great religion of Indic civilisation for Ambedkar is the occurrence of propaganda in the grand manner in the past.[55] This attitude reflects Ambedkar's training under the sociologists Alexander Goldenweiser and E. R. A. Seligman at Columbia University, where he gained an MA in 1916.[56] Ambedkar published his doctoral thesis as *Evolution of British Provincial Finance in British India – A Study in the Provincial Decentralisation of Imperial Finance*, in 1925. Ambedkar's claim of producing a history that is pure of false accretions of dogmatic practice that are millennia old is a high one. It is consistent with the reformist impulse in cultural nationalism and the desire to found a tradition that is free of the taint of domination. For Baxi, Ambedkar's attempt to subvert the normative power of Hindu law by transforming the universality of human needs (a negative or neutral conception *vis-à-vis* encroachments by state power) into rights (a minimum duty to maintain equality) is a heterological practice: 'Ambedkar interrogates the organised millennial lawlessness structured through the "sacred" law of ancient civilisation.'[57] What is interesting for us is that this postulate, in contrast to Savarkar's *Hindutva*, is a logically coherent expression of what Ambedkar characterised as 'pure history': a heterological practice requires a history pure of ideological influence. The paradox is represented succinctly as follows: Ambedkar's critical historiography for Dalit India has to confront the spirit which artificially stemmed the force of life itself and, in this enterprise, it *could* never have 'proceeded out of a pure well of knowledge'. The reason why Ambedkar's strategy is so liable to what Baxi, in psychologistic terms, dubs 'disarticulation', silence or more grandly, in Lacanese, the archetypal expression of a pervasive fear that is 'typical of the structures of paranoid knowledge', is that the following verdict can be pronounced by justice itself – 'For all that exists is *worthy* of perishing' – without culminating in the hiatus of an absolute anarchism where 'it would be better if nothing existed'.[58] Ambedkar's pure history is pure for as long as it is concerned with halting a millennial lawlessness from intruding into the eventual shape of the Indian nation. Perhaps India's first Law minister in Nehru's administration thought he was ideally placed in challenging the nascent discourse of order in protecting the life of his people from the depredations of an ancient regime? He is the Solon of the Dalits. Both Savarkar and Ambedkar's Marathi local cultures would provide the habit of mind for the question concerning the condition of historicity for alternative visions of Indian nationalism.

According to European scholars, *chaturvarnya* is the *social* institution whose individuating force prevents both the consolidation of the Hindu nation in the past or the requisite spirit of modernity in the present. For Savarkar, the ideal separation of the Hindu order into four castes is the single most important principle of cohesion maintained by kings and emperors that preserved Sanskriti or native society despite countless foreign invasions.[59] Beneath the valiant emperor of defiant Indic peoples lies submerged a whole humanity from which the paternalism of the Hindu order derives its moral authority. Dedicated as he is – as a title of one of his essays shows – to the annihilation of caste, we would expect Ambedkar in his 'pure history' of the same institution to exorcise any Puranic element when he criticises the ideality of caste in the *shastric* tradition. This seems to be his intention as he lists the regime of perpetual and 'sanctified' violence meted out to the Shudra as the Aryan's enemy. The *shastric* proscriptions against any contact between the Brahmin's Vedic culture and the Chandala, according to the *Gautama*, *Apastamba* and *Vasishta Dharma sutras*, go to extraordinary lengths in punishing the Shudra. In the first, if a Shudra listens intentionally to the Vedas being recited, molten tin is to be poured into his ears. The injunction continues: 'If he recites [Vedic texts], his tongue shall be cut out. If he remembers them, his body shall be split in twain.'[60] Metaphorically, the Shudra is as polluting as a burial ground, according to the *Apastamba sutra*. In the *Vasishta sutra*, if a Brahmin dies after eating the same food as a Shudra, no sacrificial fire (*Agnihotra*) or prayers will avail him and in the next life he will be born a pig or, analogously, into the family of a Shudra.[61] Even in modern times, Ambedkar notes one Sir P. C. Ray who, in his childhood, used to witness rows of children on the roadside in Calcutta each morning with cups of water waiting for the Brahmin to wash his feet so that they might take it to their parents to sip before eating.[62] The *Apastamba Dharma sutra* ascribes merit for the Shudra who lives according to this pious practice. The Nayars who wept at the fall of Prithviraj by Muhammad Ghuri in Savarkar's tract, according to European travellers to India since the sixteenth century, used to practice *droit de seigneurie* and offer up their new brides for the chief Brahmin priest before their nuptials.[63] The *shastric* injunctions reflect a history of systematic violence rather than a portrait of peaceful expansion until it is met with obstacles, in Savarkar's text. How is systematic violence of this order transformed into the pacific adjustment of culture? The ritual prostitution of wives – practised, Ludovico Di Varthema notes, exclusively by the king who pays the Brahmin 'four to five hundred ducats' – in Savarkar's account is the means by which Sanskriti maintained its *jati* or 'a common flow of blood from a Brahmin to a Chandal'. In the Puranic order he cites from Vyasa, it is Pandu who allows 'his wives to raise issue by resorting to the Niyoga system and they having solicited the love of men of unknown castes, gave birth to the heroes of our great epic'.[64] Gandhi speaks out against the practice of Niyoga that Savarkar thinks is the foundation of Hindu civilisation: where, 'in the name of religion, girls dedicate themselves to prostitution'.[65] A member of the twice-born castes, the *Manusmriti* recounts, loses his position in the *chaturvarnya* if he marries a Shudra woman but not if he commits adultery with her, in which case, the *Apastamba sutra* stipulates, he is banished.[66] The logic of the *shastras* is that an individual who has exiled himself from the terrestrial order by making such a polluting union is no longer a threat to the divine order that maintains the sanctified authority of the priest, very much like the individual who – in Savarkar's autocratic sense – is going to endanger the vital mark of Sanskriti by returning with subversive ideas. In Savarkar's terms, the rulers who lived according to these *dharmic* codes of conduct forbade their subjects from visiting alien shores because these Hindus, he writes, then as now, 'are sure to be subjected to national disabilities and dishonours'.[67] The *sutras* are in agreement over one thing: any Shudra who either commits adultery or cohabits with a twice-born woman outside his caste is to be deprived both of his property and his penis. The rules of caste exogamy, punishing as they do any infraction with castration for Shudra men, are bound to inhibit any of the happy admixture Savarkar identifies as the origins of the panoply of heroes in the *Mahabharata*. If the Rajputs of Oudh 'took their wives from the aborigines without any degradation of their descendents' or the Jats sought 'girls of low caste, [passed] them off as girls of their own blood, and [married] them', these same Rajputs and Jats were and are scrupulous about not offering their daughters to men of lower castes.[68] Ambedkar summarises the subalternity of the Shudra individual, noting that in every aspect of social life, the Shudra 'is of no value and anybody may kill him without having to pay compensation and if at all of small value as compared with that of the Brahmana, Kshatriya and Vaishya'. It is a sin to educate a Shudra, for his holding any office and '[t]hat the higher classes must not inter-marry with the Shudra. They can however keep a Shudra woman as a concubine. But if the Shudra touches a woman of the higher classes he will be liable to dire punishment.'[69]

Like his own relations who achieved modest prosperity by serving in the Bombay army, Ambedkar notes how the education that Untouchable recruits had in the East India Company's army gave them 'a new vision and a new value'. Establishing community with other Hindus in an attempt to realise this new egalitarian vision necessarily meant 'the abolition of the Caste System'.[70] It is interesting to note how, in order to achieve this objective, Ambedkar does not merely remain at the level of sociological explanation in interpreting this extreme inequality in Indian life. He has to undertake an exegetical inquiry into *chaturvarnya* by subjecting the texts of Sanskriti to the methodological process of historical scrutiny. His ambition is to produce a history for the Shudra classes that has been purified of the accretions leant to their history by Brahminical tradition, which is a monopoly *of* history. There is a circularity to this approach. If the author of this pure history were the same man who burnt a copy of the *Manusmriti* at a gathering in 1927, twenty years earlier – a text that 'is still portrayed as the basis of "Hindu law", the gift of the greatest of the Brahmin law givers' because it 'is also a document of profound justification for the idea of pollution and its most perfect realisation in the form of the panchama or Untouchables' – then we ought not to expect his discourse to be about providing evidence for the fact that, in history, Shudras weren't identical to Dasyus but were actually indigenous Arya Kshatriya.[71] If his vision of emancipation was firmly 'terrestrial', unlike the utopianism of Gandhi's *Ramrajya*, in this attempt to discover an origin for the Shudras' predicament, we find elements in Ambedkar's historicism that also escape the bounds of Enlightenment thinking, as do elements of the historicism of his adversary, Gandhi.

However, nobody who has read Ambedkar's texts, especially his criticism of Gandhi's complicity with the traditional origins of his support for Congress (Ambedkar's *ad hominem* terms are the Brahmin-Bania combine of a governing class that has replaced the Brahmin-Kshatriya one of ages past), can fairly describe his attempts at a political solution to the social-cultural problem of untouchability as a 'deplorable failure' or his interventions as symptomatic of 'the traditional Indian way of thinking'.[72] Yet as we will see, the problematic he devoted his entire intellectual career to, the removal of *chaturvarnya* as the essence of *Hindutva* ideology (*pace* Savarkar), never managed to escape cultural nationalism as the thematic of *Hindutva*. In other words, the argument in *Who Were the Shudras?* is for a Dravidian Rajabali. How can this be illustrated?

Though Ambedkar will use the term 'Shudra' rhetorically, let us rid ourselves of the impression that the Shudras constitute a biological race in his etymological account. In this he is line with the critique, established even before Bouglé, of the 'scientific' investigation of the origin of castes by measuring noses and skulls of Bengalis by H. Risley in 1896.[73] For Ambedkar, Vedic literature 'does not support the contention that the Aryas were different in colour from the Dasas and Dasyus'.[74] Etymologically, the root of *varna* in the Persian *Zend Avesta* is not colour but refers instead to the 'particular class holding to a particular faith'.[75] The difference between Aryans and Dasus, therefore, is not racial but cultic. The idea that the Aryans as alien invaders, based on a Western philological argument about the primeval commonality between European and Asiatic 'races', vanquished the aboriginal inhabitants is also mythological for Ambedkar. In this thinking, he is in agreement with Savarkar's view of the primeval past of the Indian nation. Why, then, does the myth persist? Instead of disavowing the Aryan racial theory propagated by colonial knowledge, why does the Brahmin instead 'most willingly' hail it?

> The Brahmin believes in the two-nation theory. He claims to be the representative of the Aryan race and he regards the rest of the Hindus as descendents of the non-Aryans. The theory helps establish his kinship with the European races and share their arrogance and their superiority. He likes particularly that part of the theory which makes the Aryan an invader and a conqueror of the non-Aryan native races. For it helps him to maintain and justify his overlord-ship over the non-Brahmins.[76]

Returning to the native *Rig Veda*, Ambedkar's argument against the congenial theory of foreign Aryan invasion and assimilation through conquest of the aboriginal Dasus continues to adduce that, in fact, the ancient texts suggest a schism in the Aryan camp itself. He notes the formulae of creation in two traditions, one supernatural, concerning the propagation of the human and animal species by a primordial Purusha, and the other, more 'natural', genealogical account of the origins of *chaturvarnya* according to the line of descent from Manu's sons. Using the anthropological part of the Western theory for a common origin of all the races that have differing cephalic indexes (Risley's conclusions), but rejecting its account of invasions from anywhere beyond the Alpine race in the Himalayas, based as it is on 'certain pre-conceived notions about the mentality of the ancient Aryans which they were supposed to have possessed on no other grounds except that their alleged modern descendents ... the Indo-Germanic races are known to possess', Ambedkar concludes that the Puranic *Mahabharata* is an obvious attempt to synthesise two originally conflicting traditions of creation and *chaturvarnya* among a single Aryan people.[77]

A number of things have to be said about Ambedkar's historical method here. Unlike Savarkar's *Hindutva*, these conclusions illustrate that in Ambedkar's analysis of scriptural 'evidence' there is no inherent cultural conflict between a folk tradition and foreign historiography. Where one arrives at any conclusion that differs from the other, the claims of the most plausible must be adapted to the detriment of the other. Where occasionally a flattering portrait of Indic civilisation presents itself in Orientalist scholarship, there is no guarantee that Puranic tradition will not at other times be demystified by the researches of modern historiography to reveal something less edifying. Having challenged the unity of the Aryan ideology by treating Brahmins, *contra* Bouglé, as a church of two denominations, Ambedkar then goes on to conclude that Dasas and Dasyus over whom Indra and the Ashvins are triumphant in the *shastric* sources are not a single but two communities.[78] This comparative analysis has a specific purpose that goes to the heart of the query, namely, that the word 'Shudra' is not an etymological derivation from *shuc* (sorrow) and *dru* (overcome) to denote individuals overcome with sorrow, but is, in fact, a proper name.[79] Shudra is apparently the name of one of several autonomous 'republics' later encountered by Alexander on his conquest East. The Sodari people are identified with the ancient Shudras whom the Vishnu, Markandeya and Brahma Puranas, as well the *Mahabaratha*, all mention by name. This is why Ambedkar's 'pure history' is not subaltern in the modern communitarian sense of the term. He is challenging the normative discourse of the Brahmins but not in any autonomous form. In fact, despite the idea of these Shudra republics, Ambedkar's alternative history of *Hindutva* is cast in identically Puranic terms, that is, in terms of kingship in ancient India.

Perhaps in common with other nationalisms, the thematic of Indian nationalism is supposed to mature in a specific way. Sovereignty passes from the charismatic authority of leaders in traditional communities where a mechanical solidarity is enforced in the repressive way Guha mentioned, to the more 'egalitarian' power of the state. For Partha Chatterjee, this transition was enabled by Gandhi's moment of manoeuvre, a strategic form of passive resistance against the increasingly 'anachronistic' mode of the colonial regime. We saw how, through the use of boycotts for goods and services and a patient but peaceful refusal to acknowledge the authority of the colonial state, its *danda* in the native lexicon, including in Gandhi's own version of *satyagraha*, the hunger strike, this 'weapon' of Congress failed to deliver the promise of authentic citizenship to the subaltern classes. The *Hindutva* Revolution, as Savarkar's history of the 1857 Uprising shows, and also the Hindu conception of 'patriarchal egalitarianism' – where all Indians find a place under the *satyagrahi* or white umbrella of *Ramrayja* in Gandhi's ideology – are particular exceptions to the transition to political 'modernity'. It is surprising, then, to discover Ambedkar going to Sanskriti in order to show the indispensable role the

Shudras played in pre-history: they participated in the coronation of kings; they were kings and ministers in the ancient epics of Puranic history.[80]

Even though the Dasus of Vedic legend in the second epigram from the *Rig Veda* that Savarkar quotes from were not slaves but constituted, in fact, a more superior civilisation than the Brahminical Aryas, this is still no reason to make them identical to the Shudras. Using the same grammatical logic as Savarkar but in an inverted order, Ambedkar posits that 'Dasas' in the *Rig Veda* is derived from the Avestan 'Daha'. The enmity between them and the Aryas in the *Rig Veda*, where Indra deprives the Dasus of their considerable wealth in castles, chariots and jewels and delivers them into bondage to the Aryas, suggests not only a primeval conflict resulting from the narcissism of small differences but also the foreign, that is, Persian, origins of the former. So the Shudras are not identical to the Dasus, the enemies of the Aryas. They are indigenous to India. Ambedkar then goes on to present evidence for the Aryan indigenism of the Shudras. Apart from the *Dharma sutras*, which, he maintains, were authored by the enemies of the Shudra, the fourth in the great order of the *chaturvarnya* did have a right to perform the *Upanayana*, the investiture of the sacred thread that allowed the Brahmin to perform Vedic sacrifice. If the Shudra weren't slaves to the Aryans, who were they? By examining *sloka* 38, from the sixtieth chapter of the 'Shanti' Parvan of the *Mahabharata* in both North and South Indian recession texts, Ambedkar investigates the history of a Shudra king, one Paijavna. Paijavna in the *Rig Veda* appears as Sudas. The Kshatriya king Paijavna/Sudas who is sponsored by the mighty Indra triumphs over the other thirty kings in a war that is larger than its label suggests as the Battle of the Ten Kings.[81] Sudas performed the Ashvamedha, the horse sacrifice that is the highest sacrifice to Indra. This Sudas, son of Divodasa in the *Rig Veda*, belongs to the eponymous Bharat tribe.[82] Here we might find an alternative, more splendid moment for the Untouchables in the Puranic past.

Why then do we find that the Sudras are relegated to the most inferior place in the Vedic order? The 'Purusha Sukta' is, Ambedkar argues, a later interpolation in the *Rig Veda*. Were it not for the 'Purusha Sukta', we would have found that the Vedic order is divided into only three parts, with the Shudra/Sudas clan constituting the Kshatriya warrior caste. Verses in the form of questions about the division of Purusha and the origins of the *varnas* are, Ambedkar concludes, a fraudulent emendation of the original scheme. Following Müller, Ambedkar gives the example of the change made to 'Agre' into 'Agni' in the *Rig Veda* by Brahmin priests to lend support to the practice of *sati*.[83] The next question to ask is why these verses of the 'Purusha Sukta' about *chaturvarnya* were added to the Arya canon to negate the original classification of three *varnas* in the *Satapatha* and *Taittiriya Brahmanas*. Ambedkar's answer is that a primordial conflict did occur but it was not between an aboriginal slave race and invading Aryans. The Shudras were degraded from the Kshatriya caste because of their conflict with the priest caste, the Brahmins.[84] What is the origin of this internecine conflict whose echo reverberates down the ages? When King Sudas whose coronation ceremony was performed by the *purohit* or chaplain Vasishtha replaced him with a Kshatriya priest, Vishvamitra, as well as the king's putting to death of Vasishtha's son Shakti by burning him alive,

Vasishtha's progeny would thereafter swear enmity to the house of the king and its descendents. According to an exegete, Shadgurushishya, the king had Vasishtha's son murdered because he worsted the court favourite, Vishvamitra, in a debate.[85] Ambedkar relates the virility of the Kshatriyas of the solar line, including King Sudas, who equalled and surpassed the Brahmins for authoring Vedic texts, unlike the Kshatriyas of lunar descent, 'an imbecile lot' who succumbed to slavery before the priestly caste.[86] A solar Kshatriya king, Vena, forced the priests to worship him; another called Pururavas despoiled them of treasure; Nahusha yoked them to a chariot like beasts and Nimi challenged their authority to officiate as family *purohits*.[87] When the King of the Raghus, Ram, slayed the Kshatriya and their offspring twenty-one times, the *Mahabharata* relates how the widows appealed for children to the Bhudevas (earthly gods). 'Free from any impulse of lust', the Brahmins duly obliged to bring 'forth valiant kshatriya boys and girls to continue the kshatriya stock'.[88]

What form did this revenge against Sudas's descendants take? 'The denial of *Upanayana* to the Shudras', Ambedkar notes, 'introduced a new factor in the Indo-Aryan society.

> It made the Shudras look up to the higher classes as their superiors and enabled the three higher classes to look down upon the Shudras as their inferiors. This is one way in which the loss of Upanayana brought about the degradation of the Shudras.[89]

The investiture ceremony (*yajnopavita*) is at least initially extraneous to the description of the *Upanayana* in the *Dharmashastras* that inducted the boy into the Brahmin fold. For Ambedkar, the symbolic rite was important because it was the way that the Aryan Brahmin caste ensured the boy was tied to his *gotra* or order. The *Yajnopavita* had nothing to do with the putative ceremonial objective of the *Upanayana*, that is, the right to recite the Vedas. If the right to property and knowledge of the Vedas depend on the *Upanayana*, women and Shudras alike were alienated of such rights when they were debarred from the ritual. 'The stoppage of *Upanayana* was a most deadly weapon – discovered by the Brahmins to avenge themselves against the Shudras. It had the effect of an atom bomb. It did make the Shudra, to use the language of the Brahmins, a graveyard.'[90]

Why should this presence of conflict that has been occluded in the theological tradition have any significance for our consideration of the 'pre-political' form in religious consciousness given to cultural nationalism? First, though he would die a Buddhist it helps Ambedkar to establish the seminal contribution made by his Hindu ancestors to *Bharatvarsh*. Second, if Prithviraj represents an ambiguous focus for Hindu nationalism in the distant or Puranic past of 'Hindu' history, the local Marathi tradition or *bakhars* furnish Savarkar's ideal of *Hindutva* with a modern and more local example in the redoubtable figure of Shivaji (1630–1680), the founder of the Maratha polity. How far does Ambedkar's attempt to write a pure history for the Dalits touch this local tradition?

Ambedkar cites the decision in a civil suit brought by the Receiver of the estate of the Raja of Tanjore (Thanjur) in 1924 against the defendants, the Raja's kin. These are the descendents of the founder of the kingdom of Tanjore, Venkoji or Ekoji, half-brother of Shivaji. The 229-page judgment of the Madras High Court decided that the Mahrattas were Shudras and not Kshatriyas.[91] In marked contrast to the intercaste syncretism through Niyoga that Savarkar piously stated was the foundation of Sanskriti or Hindu civilisation, Ambedkar in *Who Were the Shudras?* undertakes a meticulous analysis to subvert any claim to authority that might be made by a recourse to Vedic tradition as a foundation of a Hindu cultural nationalism. This line of argument culminates in the question Ambedkar asks about Shivaji himself.

There is a tragic note towards the end of Savarkar's nationalist history of the 1857 Uprising. Apart from the illustrious individuals at Brahmavarta, if the 'native' nobility – that is, the Hindu and Sikh rajas – divided according to self-interest in expelling the foreign power, Savarkar with a young man's exasperation at the disorganisation in the rebellious sepoys' ranks asks why Tatia Topé, the valorous lieutenant of the Peshwa Nana Sahib, fought for a country of 'wretched, stupid and treacherous people'.[92] If the people lose their zeal in revolution because revolution in Indian history means the same internecine strife between Mughals and Mahrattas, 'the same old quarrels' that compelled Gandhi to observe that '[t]he English have not taken India; we have given it to them', then how might Indians in resisting colonialism correctly calculate at least the most essential element in the odd arithmetic of revolution?[93] *Hindutva* history provides the answer and Savarkar needn't look to the ambiguous events of the country's Puranic past and the tragic fall of Prithviraj. If this history provides a divinely ordained hero for every instance of villainy, then India need look no further than Savarkar's native Maharashtra for the perfect example. Topé's father, Pandurang Rao Topé, served as a Deshasth Brahmin to the court of the late Bajirao Peshwa at Brahmavarta.[94] The Indian earth mirrors the celestial household of god-kings and their sublime officiating magi.

In Savarkar's *Hindutva*, the Hindu poets Ramdas and Bhushan provide Hindu India with a model aspiration after the defeat of the 'Hindapi' Prithviraj through foul means by the Muslim invader, Muhammad Ghuri. In *Hindutva*, in the age of *Rajdharma*, surely Aurangzeb will be dethroned? Bhushan addresses the Mughal emperor who calls himself Alamgir, 'Conqueror of the World', but refuses to face the 'Hindapati' Shivaji and is instead content to pull down 'unoffending convents, churches and chapels'.[95] Shivaji's correspondence appears as 'evidence' for the workings of divine Providence. After the Sikh martyrs, Savarkar quotes the strictly religious appeals made to Jai Singh, one of the best Mughal generals of the period. The Rajput is exhorted to defend the Hindu religion even as Shivaji is forced to surrender himself and his fortresses. Like the defenders of *Ramjanmabhumi*, the Mughal force of some 14,000–15,000 trained soldiers who brought about Shivaji's surrender by June 1665 is just a terrestrial detail in the divine plan. Jai Singh, 'doubtless touched', replies to Shivaji recommending that he make peace with Aurangzeb 'because he is a powerful sovereign'.[96] In the 'war of independence' with Aurangzeb, Savarkar continues to emphasise the Hindu nature of the Maharatta dispensation. At the instigation of a Maharatta guerrilla leader, Bajirao invites a Brahmendra Swami to his encampment. 'But the swami', Savarkar writes, 'did not think it proper to meet one in whose territory the Hindu Religion was being defiled! ... He impressed upon Shahu's [Shivaji's grandson] mind how disgraceful it was that Deities and Brahmins should be subjected to atrocities in the territory of Hindus!'[97] Let us look closely at this claim. Is Savarkar's native Maharashtra a realm of pure *Hindutva* where the Muslim presence is an impious blot? Earlier in the polity's history, when the Mughal forces led by Aurangzeb's father, the emperor Shah Jahan, captured the fort at Daulatabad in 1632 after a five-month siege, Shivaji's father, Shahji, raised and fought in the name of a boy who was heir to the sultanate of Ahmadnagar. It was only after the conclusion of a peace treaty in 1636 between the neighbouring sultanate of Bijapur and the Mughals that required the cutting-off of all support to Shahji that he surrendered himself and the Ahmadnagar pretender.[98] The *swami*'s antipathy to the pollution of the Deccan by Muslims conforms to the ideological portrait of events that Savarkar is committed to. However, the real historical context of these Muslim sultanates in a Hindu Maharashtra is rather different:

> From early on, various groups of Brahmins served the Muslim states of the Deccan, and were crucial to their functioning. They filled all the middle and lower levels of the tax-collecting administration. After the break-up of the Bahmani kingdom, it was the successor Muslim state of Ahmadnagar which controlled much of Maharashtra (in the fifteenth and sixteenth centuries). Deshasta Brahmins ran virtually the whole administration; they had suffered little under Muslim rule, and probably gained a degree of social mobility.

The image of a timeless Hindu polity threatened by a puritanical emperor from the Mughal North in Delhi is a gross simplification of the syncretism of the age, even before Shivaji began his brief reign as Chatrapati ('Lord of the Universe') of the Rajyabhisheka era from the fort at Raigurh in 1674. As for the *purohit* Brahmendra, Savarkar does not say whether his reluctance to visit Bajirao may have been because of a rather more mundane fear for his life. The scene in the text has shifted from Shivaji's appeal to Jai Singh in order to escape Alamgir to the need of repelling Nadir Shah, the King of Persia, in his invasion of North India in 1739 by preventing his crossing the Chambal River. This is now the Rubicon of the sacred land. A Maratha agent, Dhondo Govind, writes to Bajirao, 'after Shivaji, the most charismatic and dynamic leader in Maratha history', asking for his help to 'unite all the Hindu kings' under Shivaji's auspices, and to install the Rana of Udepur on the 'Imperial throne'.[99] In order to rally the modern spirit of Hinduism, Savarkar goes on to quote a Govindrao Kale to one of the 'victors' (despite his defeat), Nana Fadnavis/Farnavis. Kale mentions the hated *jiziya* tax during the reign of Aurangzeb by all those wearing the *yandyopavita*, the sacred thread. Even the smallest victories for Kale are 'extolled to the skies' by the Muslims, whereas 'we Hindus are inclined not to refer to our exploits however magnificent they may be'.[100]

These odd disparate statements from mystic poets as well as the *swami* do not accord with the millenarian tendencies about the prevailing age under British rule that Savarkar alludes to among Hindus and Muslims at the time of the Uprising.

Instead, we find in the *bhakti* ingredient an attempt to found a new moral order – one where '[o]ne typical response is to adapt what can be tolerated from the incorrect rulers', ranging 'from aspects of the dress of the rulers, through eating habits [perhaps], through revenue and judicial terminology in the ruler's language'. But finally, in the context of seventeenth-century Muslim rather than nineteenth-century British rule, as far as a realistic limitation of the emulation of the conquerors in both Savarkar's more extreme and Chatterjee's milder version of the nationalist ideal is concerned, this falls short of 'full-scale conversion'.[101] Before his legendary re-conquest of the fortresses won by Jai Singh and his active resistance to Bijapur's forces, including revenge for the desecration of Hindu places, especially Pandharpur by the general of the Bijapuri forces, Afzal Khan, Shivaji had appealed to the Mughal power at Ahmadnagar to have his father released from his Bijapuri employer's prison and (again unsuccessfully) to Aurangzeb to have his rights recognised in Pune. He would not have needed reminding of the Mughal sovereign's power. With the Mughal heir turning north to contest his right for the throne, after Bijapur ceded by treaty in 1657 all the territory it had 'conquered from Ahmadnagar', Gordon notes how 'Shivaji ... could claim that he was seizing the territory in the name of the Mughals, on the basis of his offer to serve them'.[102] Savarkar is reinforcing the myth of 'Maharashtra Dharma', a polity organised on caste grounds in a text four hundred years before Shivaji. Shjvaji made no 'democratic' or legal appeal to the *deshmukhs* (village headmen) when he claimed the kingship right to collective revenue, the *sardeshmukhi*. It is hard to see how Shivaji's earlier rise by violent conquest of other Hindu kin in the Desh conforms to any *dharmic* ideal. For Savarkar and the *Hindutva* nationalist, the fact that no evidence has emerged to show that Shivaji surrounded himself by Brahmin advisors like the Hindu kings of yore and that 'to the contrary, recent evidence has shown that he did not meet the main candidate for the role of advisor, Ramdas, until 1672' does not lessen the appeal of the idea that the Chatrapati's realm was a realisation of a kind of proto-nationalism. If Muslims were commanders in Shivaji's army, including in the troops who confronted Afzal Khan, or if Muslim judges who, conforming to the practice of the region, adjudicated on cases, this is a reflection of Shivaji's largesse. The colonial view is typified two centuries later in Grant Duff's remarks that Shivaji's 'territory and treasures were not so formidable to the Mahomedans as the example he had set, the system and habits he introduced, and the spirit he had infused into a large portion of the Mahratta people'.[103] There is no doubting Shivaji's valorous vision of independence from Delhi. If the whole country being for the Hindus, Shivaji exhorts his noblemen, while Muslims desecrate temples, plunder their wealth, 'forcibly converting our countrymen to their religion, kill cows openly', in resisting this despotism '[w]e are as brave and capable as our ancestors of yore'. He concludes: 'There is no such thing as good or bad luck. We are the captains of our soil and the makers of our freedom.'[104] Even if this statement was not a verbatim declaration of independence, in the context of Aurangzeb's destruction of the Vishneshwar temple at Benares in 1669, it is not difficult to see why Shivaji's guerrilla campaigns against Mughal incursions in the Deccan seemed to cohere around an attractive ethos to which Hindu nationalists might rally their followers in the nineteenth, twentieth and twenty-first centuries. However, it 'is only those who must see Shivaji as the perfect Hindu king who will not allow that he learned and absorbed from the Muslim states around him, slowly formulating an idea of freedom and kingship that differed from the surrounding Muslim states'.[105] We will now turn to the ritual that established this ideal of freedom and kingship. What the Cambridge history doesn't mention, concerned as it is with 'Animal Politics' in the seventeenth-century Deccan, is another micrological history, a *bakhra* or chronicle in which the primordial history of conflict that Ambedkar adumbrates has a not too insignificant impact on the decision to cast Shivaji as the perfect Hindu king. The coronation of Govind Dondhu Pant, son of the learned Brahmin Mahadev Rao, and his subsequent adoption of the ancestral name of the Maharatta Peshwas, Nana Sahib, in Savarkar's history of 1857, is a metaphoric episode designed to evoke the glory of Shivaji's investiture as King of the Kshatriyas. In his pure history, Ambedkar also telescopes the classical era with the moment when Indian history became susceptible to colonial rule in the morbid interregnum. He, too, after invoking the solemn genealogy of the Shudra kings in Puranic times – a sort of patriciate capable of resisting the lure of Brahmin priestcraft – turns to the same local episode as Savarkar where the abortive genesis of Hindu nationalism was supposed to have enjoyed a brief efflorescence.

Perhaps because of the depredations of the past that Shivaji had inflicted on other Marathi families in their forts that brought him to eminence, or the claiming of *sardeshmukhi* and *chauth*, a kind of protection money from the populace to fund his raids, Shivaji's status as Kshatriya was disputed among the Maharatta nobles. Despite his plan to bring peace and order to Maharashtra, exhorting the commanders of his standing army not to pillage the scant resources of the poor peasants, who will begin to run away, starve and 'think you are worse than the Mughals who overran the countryside', Shivaji's problems lay with his relations with other armed families who held grants, often older and larger than his, from the sultanates of Ahmadnagar and Bijapur. It is worth noting that despite his sacrilegious behaviour, Afzal Khan and the Bijapuri army who campaigned against Shivaji in 1659–1660 had the remnants of the More family (the father and four sons had been killed by Shivaji in an earlier campaign when the Mores had been ordered to put down his mutinous forays) and other *deshmukhs* from Supe, Utroli, Phaltan and Wai. Marriage into the Shirke, the Mohite and the Nimbalkar families was another solution Shivaji adopted to the problem of his legitimacy among the Maharatta feudals. However, despite the last time-honoured measure, these feudal lords still resented having to look up to Shivaji at state dinners. The idea of taking the crown from a Benarsi priest rather than the Mughal emperor came from his secretary, Balaji Avanji Chitnis.[106] Ambedkar describes how Shivaji's claim to Kshatriya status was problematic for two reasons: the lack of a genealogy proving this, and the Brahmins' proclamation that the caste had disappeared in Kaliyuga. From Ambedkar's 'anti-clerical' point of view, it is quite revealing to witness the cynicism or survival of the Brahmin priests who, despite their ancient traditions, nevertheless 'sold' the status to invaders who offered them eminent positions. It was Balaji Avaji who brought a genealogy connecting him to the Sisodyas of

Mewar who hadn't polluted their lineal descent from Lava, the eldest son of Rama, like the Rajputs of Jaipur and Jodhpur, by marrying into the Mughals. However, were the Sisodyas descended from the legendary prince of Ayodhya or were they the descendents of foreign invading Huns who destroyed the Gupta Empire in 480 CE and were only later assimilated by congenial Brahmins?

For Ambedkar, Shivaji Chatrapati as the emblem of a *Hindutva* cultural nationalism is implausible because of these tortuous attempts by his followers and the officiating *purohit*, Gangabhat, to prove his legitimacy for kingship on caste grounds. Even the repetition of the coronation ceremony in a non-Vedic, Tantric form cannot remove the taint of being Shudra. Drawing on a local Bakhari tradition, Ambedkar relates the perversity of Gangabhat's prior decisions as to the status of Kshatriya for Shivaji, including in one instance his willingness to perform the coronation for Shivaji's secretary, Balaji Avaji, instead because he was a Kayastha (clerkly caste). Ambedkar writes: 'He again turned round and gave his opinion that Shivaji was a Kshatriya and that he was prepared to perform his coronation and even went so far as to write a treatise known as the "Gangabhatti" in which he sought to prove that the Kayasthas were bastards.'[107] It is only in collaboration with another priest, no less than the Prime Minister of Shivaji, that Gangabhat after being provided with grand *dakshanas* or gifts agreed to consecrate Shivaji: 'Balaji being Kayastha and the Kayasthas being the deadliest enemies of the Brahmins, Moropant [who also was vociferously opposed to his employer's Kshatriya status] consented to Shivaji's coronation as a lesser of two evils.'[108] It is out of such mean stuff that a claim to sovereignty in terms of *Hindutva* can be made. Modernity intrudes in the scheme where *Hindutva* is supposed to mirror the lost cultures of the great Hindu patrimonial kingdoms.

In other words, it takes the narrative impulse of *Hindutva* considerable effort to hide any conflicts in history out of which any single instance might be used to challenge an Indian nationalism that sublimates – in hegemonic terms sometimes, and at other times, more unilaterally, that is to say, more violently – the communal and caste differences that gave birth to those conflicts. The colonial divide, as we see with Ambedkar, was not as definitive in producing anti-colonial resistance but neither can we confidently assert with Mahatma Gandhi, Chatterjee and others, that the cultural superiority of native tradition had recourse to a more serene terrain of ideas that Indians could draw on to challenge the authority of colonial rule. The most ecstatic culmination of that tradition cannot free itself from 'an inert mass of feudal culture which had been generating loyalism and depositing it in every kind of power relation for centuries *before* the British conquest'.[109] In V. S. Naipaul, we turn to the most representative contemporary figure of the collaborationist tendency that Guha identifies in his essay. By identifying the Indian present with a lapsed state of being, Naipaul's attempt to reinvigorate the discourse of improvement with colonial values of trusteeship, a reactionary rationalism and an antiquarian's nihilism goes some way to giving ballast to Savarkar's violent dreams of cultural awakening. In doing so, it also exudes 'the heavy and ... for his petty-bourgeois readership, endearing smell of gunpowder' as any eminent Victorian's exhortation of imperialist duty.[110]

Part 2
Re-imagining Indian pasts

5 V. S. Naipaul's 'India'
History and the myth of antiquity

> There is a degree of sleeplessness, of rumination, of the historical sense, which is harmful and ultimately fatal to the living thing, whether this living thing be a man or a people or a culture.
>
> Friedrich Nietzsche[1]

Introduction

In Part 1, we saw how anxieties in historiography about the eventual order of things temporal were pre-figurative. In literary form, these manifest themselves as resolutions that no longer require the *same* species of analytical vigilance about the nature of history and its relationship to the truth that historians have had to grow accustomed to as a kind of sovereign rite for their vocation. Not only are we susceptible to the explicitly fabulist form of literary practice when it uses historical content but the resolution of tendencies ideological – whether formal, rhetorical, mythical, even psychological – that remains an impossible motivating factor for the historian is a prerequisite of novelistic practice. The reasons for this state of affairs among historians have been explored thus far. The truth of historical fictions is not the same as the truth in historiography; yet, as Guha notes, the 'conceptual affinity' between colonial and Indian narratives about the Indian past led to a site of antagonism that left a profound and shaping mark on nationalist thinking.[2] I have examined the reception of these definitive modalities by Indians concerned with formulating visions of freedom from colonial rule when they have gone in search in the long Indian past to 'reclaim' a world and time that is at least *potentially* free of domination. Naipaul's writing is a complication in this enterprise. For Naipaul, colonialism as Pax Britannica is preferable to the native forms of *danda*. He scrupulously ignores the systematic violence that the colonial discourse of improvement implied. Before turning to his non-fiction writing on India, I want to explain a little more of what is meant by the resolution or antagonism between kindred modes where these are conceived first as 'rationalist, evolutionalist and progressivist ideas' and an Indian historical thinking that had assimilated the spirit of these fundamentals of 'the post-Enlightenment view of world and time' without its substance and therefore, tragically, failed to deliver the promise of this teleology under 'the force of nationalism itself'. The implication is that, far from being consistent with each other, as the *philosophes* had imagined, nationalism is a deviation or, at best, an aberrant moment in the career of Reason. Guha concludes:

> Historiography was one of the two principal instruments – the other being literature – which would henceforth be put to increasingly vigorous use for such reclamation [of the Indian past]. In other words, historiography would, from this time onward, construct the Indian past as a *national* past that had been violated and appropriated by colonial discourse. The indigenous historian's mission to recover that past was therefore to acquire the urgency and sanctity of *a struggle for expropriating the expropriators*.[3]

In the preceding chapters we saw how the reconstruction of the national past according to the norms Guha suggests above did not halt at the moment when colonialism began its ignominious career of violence to and appropriation of native culture. It reached further back in discovering the sanctity of the mission in which nationalism is figured as a war for monopolising the historical consciousness itself from the actual material fray of conflict. Instead of the noble spirit of *dharma*, a kind of patience eternally waiting as the divine obligation through which the individual ascends the wheel of Time itself, for *Hindutva* the violence of history requires a millenarian sacrifice of lives. Savarkar evoked *Mahakal* for this task. Naipaul's unique contribution to the end of the proverbial idea of Indian unity-in-diversity of the kind Nehru's discourse of order discovered in *moments* in antiquity is like the nineteenth-century historiography that made Indian nationalism possible. Naipaul's reactivation of a specifically pure vision of India's past operates at two distinctly antithetical levels. The argument here is that at the most general level, Naipaul's antiquarian use of history is complicit with the monistic discourse of belonging that Savarkar fashioned. This regime orders the Indian multitude into collectivism through forms such as religious communitarianism or Empire. At the same time, there is a superficial tension at work in this enterprise where Naipaul attempts to resist forms of social organisation that threaten to subvert *Hindutva* and Empire as discourses of order. Naipaul aspires to the condition of historical objectivity when he presents these forms as communal forces. The names we can give to the forces that are antithetical to *Hindutva* ideology and nationalism as a legacy of British Imperialism are, in the first historical instance, Islam and in the second, subaltern radicalism. The aim of this chapter is to make Naipaul's 'timely' interventions in the Indian present part of a more traditional paradigm about the value of history given to India's past. In the end, Naipaul's objective is to substitute the inclusive nationalism that is the legacy of colonial power in the way Guha interprets above (the idiomatic relationship between dominance and subordination) with an exclusive nationalism whose focus remains the realisation of 'the trajectory which the history of India has pursued since ancient times'.[4] And this trajectory cuts across any complexity, traversing it with the nearly absolute force of the abstraction that meets it by segmenting history into Hindu, Muslim and British parts, but, unlike the goal of emancipation from the condition of historicity set up by the inclusive species of nationalism, the exclusive variety – as we have seen – conceived this historicity as inevitably being about the survival of a discrete form of civilisation after it has contended for mastery over its rivals.[5] For *Hindutva*, in the end *only* Islam in India's history is capable of disrupting the goal of *Hindu Rashtra* (statehood).

The ironic conception in the anarchist mode of historical interpretation leads the protagonists to dispute the content of the past at the most definitive, superficial level of comprehension. Naipaul's antiquarian desire to rediscover the glory of Hindu civilisation, as we will see, is more subtle. Even before he unsheathes his pen, Savarkar's depiction of the 'panorama of Indian history in the rise and fall of the Hindus' is framed by his sympathetic editors and translators as being apart from the conventions of academic history; it is 'a broad survey of the growth and survival of our Hindu race'.[6] That this is ultimately a partial perspective is readily apparent by the qualifications immediately necessary to the 'higher altitude' from which Savarkar is supposed to have provided us with a view of Hindu, 'Pan-Hindu' 'totality'.[7] The failure of this totality to come to fruition in the past is due to the very strength in producing its 'war of emancipation from Moslem suzerainty'. The Maratha Confederacy of Rajputs, Bundelas, Sikhs, Nepalese and other inspired Hindu 'movements', the account continues, 'came occasionally into inevitable conflict with their own co-religionists like Rajputs, Jats and other Hindu powers'. The editorial emphasises the most important 'corrective' to more biased interpretations about the predatory raids undertaken by Shivaji, the looting and banditry of 'Surat' and some towns in Maharashtra 'in defence of Hindudom as a whole'.[8] The preface goes on to provide credibility for the heroic version of events as part of the 'Hindu Sanghatana movement today' by quoting 'savants and scholars of the Press' in the emotive terms Thapar objected to as being alien to historiographic practice.[9] The Savarkarite enterprise of expropriating the expropriator's version of the Indian past acknowledges the ideological impulse of 'the national point of view'; the reconstructive effort challenges orthodoxy or taught history – a history that is debilitating because it is only 'eulogizing the foreigners and deprecating the Hindu race, relying wholly on the biased records of the foreign historians and travellers'.[10] The work of reconstruction involves two types of intellectual labour: challenging the biased versions of the past and amending the contemporary milieu defined by those not belonging to the native Hindu race. The first task, in common with the volume Savarkar produced on the 1857 Uprising, is about starting 'the re-orientation of our historical concepts and the accepted historical theories'.[11] We will see how Naipaul's creative re-imagining of the past adapts to this task. The important point is that Naipaul's unitary vision of India's past, in contrast to the conception in *Hindutva* or the kind propounded by the nationalists, refuses to acknowledge *any* regenerative possibilities. In other words, the problem of rendering the past in language that is reminiscent of truisms about the Indian 'polity' mobilises the historical sense in little more than plausible generalities. The demands made upon subjectivity cannot cope with more. Moving from this style of comprehension, I examine a more detailed consideration of Naipaul's strategic relationship to India as an amorphous but lapidary reality. Naipaul's attitude betrays no sign of the prevarication that some commentators think Indian realities deserve, those singular instances of Indian difference 'in itself' fashioned out of a 'dynamic relation of the common'.[12] Finally, I look at the way the historical example is used in Naipaul's writing and the way this recuperative vision of Indian purity (or 'singularity' in the theoretical idiom) cannot function without differentiating in sectarian terms – that is, in the modality of religious nationalism that Thapar alluded to – some of the 'realities' discerned by Naipaul in these details in India's long-vanished past. This recuperative vision is, I argue, the reason *why* Naipaul does not exhibit the kind of hesitancy in pronouncing on the past that Hardt and Negri think Indian realities deserve.

Figuring a history of the present

The late great Edward Said, though he had more local problems when it came to representing postcolonial realities, was acute when it came to V. S. Naipaul's unembarrassed *modus operandi*. Speaking about the dependency that postcolonial nations still have on the West, Said comments:

> [T]his is the consequence of self-inflicted wounds, critics like V. S. Naipaul are wont to say: they (everyone knows that 'they' means coloureds, wogs, niggers) are to blame for what 'they' are, and it's no use droning on about the legacy of imperialism.[13]

Said treats Naipaul's vision, his 'racial eye' with a simplified idea of how the past infects the present.[14] He has missed what Rob Nixon identifies as the mimetic function of Naipaul's vision, where all, including civil society, is ultimately reducible to the postcolonial state's failure to copy 'the eminent cultural life of the West'.[15] What happens when Naipaul adds to this sought-after *Lebenswelt*, where the West is, in no small part, something Naipaul needs to believe in as something essentially different to the history that Said calls the legacy of imperialism?[16] In the 2001 Nobel lecture, Naipaul begins by speaking in praise of the private virtue of *civilitas*. Quoting Proust in *Against Sainte-Beuve*, Naipaul talks of a 'happy amplitude' by describing it in inverse proportion to Saidian worldliness. Naipaul then goes on to emphasise, paradoxically, the intimate proximity between himself and his books in the context of an 'innermost self which one can only recover by putting aside the world and the self that frequents the world'.[17] All the historiographic assumptions that Naipaul strategically invokes can be questioned on their own terms. Generic questions about the possible uses to which history can and ought to be put naturally arise, even while Naipaul deliberately contrasts the autonomy of vision (his own, Gandhi's) apart from the familiar problematic of postcoloniality, that is, as some essentially random, aberrant mobilisation of the truth about the past to measure the inadequacy of the present age. This approach questions both the value inherent in any historical recuperation of the past (Proustian recuperation of self, in Naipaul's stylisation) and the use to which historical events as facts may be put in order to construct that value. This autocritique already exists in Naipaul's observations about India's past but it lies submerged beneath the discursive construction of items like the 'past', the 'present', as well as modes as complex as identity and textuality. In other words, it will turn out that Naipaul's desire for a sanitary self-referentiality in the world involves all the passions of an antiquarian historicism that Nietzsche summed up for us in his essay 'On the Uses and Disadvantages of History for Life'. Gayatri Spivak effortlessly reminds us that the mission to render a consciousness historically adequate to the polymorphic reality of any present – African, Indian, British, or whatever – by regressing into historiography as a mode for believing and behaving is 'to place [ourselves] in a position of irreducible compromise'. She goes on to say: 'I believe it is because of this double bind that it is possible to unpack the aphoristic remark of Nietzsche's that follows ... "All concepts in which an entire process is comprehended [*sich zusammenfast*] withdraws itself from [*sich entzieht*] definition; *only that which has no history is definable*".'[18]

Edward Said's observations about Joseph Conrad's ability to preserve an ironic distance from the 'machine' of history, of imperialism, apply to Naipaul as well. Said writes:

> [Y]our self-consciousness as an outsider can allow you actively to comprehend how the machine works, given that you and it are fundamentally not in perfect synchrony or correspondence. Never the wholly incorporated and fully acculturated Englishman, Conrad therefore preserved an ironic distance in each of his works.[19]

William Dalrymple's judgement as a latter-day Orientalist, that Naipaul's 'credentials as a historian' are entirely questionable, has to be seen in the larger context of Naipaul's self-conscious literary mode of expression.[20] The prerequisite of treating literary practice as if it were a symptomatic reflection of history is to examine not why this might occur as an ideological process (a self-evident fact) but how it comes about. Otherwise, we may as well line up Conrad, Dalrymple, Naipaul and, of course, Said himself in a list of subjectivities that never quite managed to achieve a perfect synchrony or correspondence with the 'machine' of history that produced them. The only reproof that Dalrymple can effectively make against Naipaul's sense of history is that it is a vision that cannot accommodate a radically heterogeneous and discontinuous process of communal *Erlebnis* (or lived experience); Dalrymple is not questioning the idea of history as vision *in toto*. This is not simply that history is incapable of being, finally, final. Somewhat contrary to Sartre's attempt to prove just that in the projected second volume to the *Critique of Dialectical Reason*, the Nietzschean attitude to a single intelligible form (of unceasing totalisation of multiplicity) is that historical finality is essentially ahistorical.[21]

Postcoloniality, for the societies which Naipaul, Said and Dalrymple have written about, is a deeply historical condition and this is not in spite of but because history is susceptible to less prevaricating forms of intellectual judgement than the kinds furnished by dialectics. This is an important point because Naipaul uses, for example, 'India' and 'Islam' in a subtly confused way: it is as if they were processes comprehensible in their entirety because they are concepts from whose points of view the entire process of history is intelligible. How can intelligibility be possible without dialectical reasoning? In Benedict Anderson's survey of nationalism as 'imagined community', the apprehension of time is doubled, by implication, each informing the other; religions use a 'Messianic time', whereas the modernity of nationalisms is supposedly marked by an empty calendrical conception of time. In the case of India and Islam as thoroughly historical formations, the division of temporality, where Walter Benjamin's 'Messianic time' is 'a simultaneity of past and future in an instantaneous "present", does not offer itself up for as easy a classification as modernity *qua* nationalism'.[22] I will return to the solution provided by Ernest Gellner to this more fundamental problem of difference. Writing more simply and without prevarication towards the end, Sartre boldly asserts that 'the days of colonized laureates are over'.[23] The eminence of the West, reproduced by liberation movements farcically and then tragically all over Africa, is itself a fraud. A nascent but degenerate bourgeoisie, in turn, propagates nationalism as a snare to seize and maintain power.[24] This critical awareness of nationalism may have been prophetic or late and subject to formations of historical action and reaction (a coral-like process, Said says), of domination and subordination, from the organic to the traditional, occurring in every place and time, but the substantial truth of the proposition, that nationalist thought itself, far from being essentially a discourse of freedom, of liberty, operates 'within a discourse of power', remains undeniable.[25] Partha Chatterjee attempts an alternative demarcation of how non-European colonial countries have 'derived' their recognisably modern identities other than from a process of 'approximation'.[26] For Fanon, the solution is at once contemporary, 'the veritable creation of new men', and historical, by involving a decision by the native to 'embody history in his own person'.[27] Fanon's solution would appeal to Sartre for the reason Merleau-Ponty identified where Sartre founded communist action precisely by refusing any productivity to history and by making history, insofar as it is intelligible, the immediate result of our volitions. As for the rest, it is an impenetrable opacity.[28] Naipaul is writing out of the moment of this decision and its consequences.

He can be situated between Sartre/Fanon's conception of *praxis* and Chatterjee's 'problematic' instance of nationalism as it is figured in the life of the state. There is, then, more at stake in Naipaul's writing than any exoteric anxiety of influence arising out of generic forms – say, the nineteenth-century English novel – that might evolve in an alien context because of an 'approximate' modernity. In other words, intertextuality presupposes the 'givenness' of the world, of 'frame', from which Naipaul might be said to produce Third World reality as 'outcome'.[29] This givenness is the historical ground, an idea implied in the writers I have just cited, and this ground ought to be interrogated more closely before we reckon with the 'fabulist' mode with which Naipaul assembles the social realities he encounters. Nonetheless, there is an explicit engagement with Western technologies of the self. For all his scepticism about the uses of biography, Naipaul's authorised biographer Patrick French has been busy disinterring Naipaul's juvenilia for the Western archive.[30] Naipaul's declining of Salman Rushdie's invitation to be anthologised in a book, though his reasons remain his own, shows how sensitive the writer is to the rubrics of canonicity if a generic classification of 'Indian writing' is involved.³¹ What interests me is not the symptomatic nature of Naipaul's anxiety about the English literary tradition, or even the derivative nature of Indian nationalism, but a correlating certainty. This certainty figures in Naipaul's assertions about the Indian condition. What is that essentially disinterested quality that accompanies the claim of unassailable authority about speaking for India founded on? Naipaul's eye discriminates the sublimity, scope and dimension of Indian postcolonial realities that would overwhelm any other ordinary individual. The degree to which this 'apperceptive' genius is colonised by values that are other than objective for some Indian critics, is a claim we will be exploring shortly. In more philosophical language, Naipaul's reproductive imagination is an objective unity of apperception despite the contingent nature of empirical judgement on the conditions it encounters; a contingency that more profound intellects found themselves incapable of wishing away.³² However, what is beyond doubt by both detractors and admirers alike is that India never defeats Naipaul. His uniqueness lies in the ability to fabricate 'India' as a timely generality. We will subject this ability to critical scrutiny here.

India as multitude

Let me state my particular concern clearly: Naipaul has taken to using subalternity to validate his more customary thesis about the 'boon' once offered our cultures by the history of British Imperialism. Alongside this development, there is a dangerously problematic view of India's ancient past. Scores of formerly frozen particularities, Naipaul warns us, are now flowing and threatening to engulf the present.³³ Simply put, Naipaul's didactic vision of India's past in relationship with its present involves a 'suprahistorical' legitimation of that past. In Kantian terms, the unity of Naipaul's imagination has a transcendental relationship to its object. For individuals who might have a less attenuated sense of belonging than the kind Naipaul is able to display, because of his 'at once exceedingly simple and exceedingly confused' background, this is an extraordinarily perilous endeavour.³⁴ Said likens nationalism to the force of gravity when it comes to the 'restoration of community, assertion of identity' and, paradoxically, 'emergence of new cultural practices'; there is no use resisting it.³⁵ Our question is slightly different and concerns the reality of Indian identity. The ferocity of communal violence, recently, between Gujarati Muslims and Hindus testifies to the fact that the reclamation of an Indian past often results in pogroms.³⁶ The fragile *entente* that the British imposed is captured by a small decision in 1885. Two judges, one native and the other English, decided on the installation of a railing to divide the *chabutra* (platform) as the site where Ram was born and the rest of the sixteenth-century mosque built by one of Babur's generals.³⁷ The solution, we note, is as symbolic as the original 'problem' of authentic nationalism. Meanwhile, 'India' as the Sartrean resolution to the 'unceasing' problem of discrepant or multiple experiences in history, grows ever more impossible.

Let us look more closely at Naipaul's symptomological uses of subalternity with all its attendant ambivalences. Naipaul's book *India – A Wounded Civilization*

(1977) has the following neat encapsulation of the dilemma of subalternity *qua* national identity:

> For other people ... who lived in India and felt the new threat of the millions and all the uncertainties that come with Independence and growth, India could no longer be taken for granted. The poor had ceased to be background. Another way of looking was felt to be needed, some profounder acknowledgement of the people of the streets.[38]

It turns out that the profundity of Naipaul's response lies, to use his own phrase, in a 'defect of vision'. The vision, when it comes to meeting Indian realities, is as 'racial' as any Naipaul uses for other societies. The ethical aspect of this exercise in representation might be too apparent to a more nuanced sense. In the almost Greek sense of purpose here, of the need for new visions that are able to arrange the mysteriously shifting *ousia* of its object from the background to a foreground, is a tacit acknowledgement that lives in the subcontinent will often insist on definitions when they attempt to historicise the ahistorical dimension of their own spiritual experiences. Let me make this clear. This tendency is not peculiarly Indian or at the service of regressive political interests that might interpret (*pace* Naipaul) 'Independence and growth' in their own ways and with greater or lesser degrees of 'intensity'.[39] It is the mark of a writer like Naipaul to interpret 'the whole positive human reference' – to use Raymond Williams's phrase – as if it were a totality secured in the nation's past.[40] The defects and whirlpools are symptomatic of the present.

Naipaul moves from 'another way of looking' to the mutinous crowd. Since Elias Canetti described the morphology of the crowd, its propensity toward growth, its love of density, its need for direction, its rhythm, Naipaul's observation that opens *India – A Million Mutinies Now* (1990), that Bombay is a crowd, cannot just be the spontaneous expression of an individual setting himself apart.[41] What has happened to the *res gestus* of India's poor? Is the political fact of visibility at the cost of the sanctity Naipaul desires for these crowds, the amorphous multitude in need of consideration and value?[42] One thing is clear, namely that this collected humanity does not consist of the peasant *kisan* for whom ignorant towny engineers design implements that cannot be put to any use.[43] These are 'the people of the streets' but they no longer offer themselves up for easy moral classification as objects of benevolent but distant concern. India's traditional distinction, between the rural poor and its urban proletariat, is no longer a tenable fact of life; a hybridised civil society challenges Naipaul's idea of India and migrant labour presents an overt challenge to the comfortably complacent hegemonies of her political classes. The crowding poor are organising themselves. Organisation is too optimistically Western a notion to describe how Bombay reacts. We saw how Dipesh Chakrabarty in his essay 'Postcoloniality and the Artifice of History: Who Speaks for "Indian" Pasts?' situates the peculiarly *bhadralok* ethos of self-improvement, the norm to which cultural nationalism will submit the Indian mass, in a derivative vein from colonial discourse.[44] Naipaul propagates a specifically antiquarian value against which the mimicry of Indian culture is being measured. Despite the frustrations, the 'old equilibrium' is favoured when the features of the Enlightenment fail to translate and Naipaul often joins his own voice to the many before him: 'Sometimes old India, the old, eternal India many Indians like to talk about, does seem just to go on'.[45] Naipaul, though he aspires towards the condition of being a 'manager of narrative', is unable to dissociate himself from the force of the antithesis between modernity and tradition.[46] The Indian crowd, from which the writer with acuity is going to select his testimonial accounts, is conjured into existence and then, as promptly, made to return to its essential invisibility. Profounder acknowledgement is a kind of reparative act for Naipaul: India, or rather the more *local* manifestation as Bombay, reacts to forces unintelligently, *en masse*. Naipaul observes: 'All over India scores of particularities that had been frozen by foreign rule, or by poverty or lack of opportunity or abjectness, had begun to flow again.'[47] There is a characteristic series which keeps items discrete. Money is transformed into Bombay's ugly skyscrapers. The magical act, beyond anyone's control of course, isn't given a name (say, finance capitalism) but is characterised by its power alone; how it contributes to the release of 'long-buried particularities', of region, caste and clan, distracting Indians from the greater idea of the nation. These are the 'disruptive, lesser loyalties'. For all the grandeur of this rhetoric, we are not left to imagine the distances, after Fanon, between the *parvenu* middle classes in the high-rises and the crowds in the streets below. It is the antiquarian imagination which will conjure up a vision of a coherent past and treat this symptomatic subalternity in strictly atavistic terms. This thesis can be illustrated by the way in which Naipaul manages the narrative of the Dalit protest against caste oppression. The collaborationist tendency of subaltern formations (the tragic tendency of the nation's failing to realise itself authentically) that Guha described as a natural feature of colonial history goes on into the postcolonial present. Contemporary sociologists have perceived this as a paradox at the heart of Gandhi's ideal of inclusion, 'the inclusion that Gandhi actually achieved was to bind many of the Untouchables to Congress without ending the adverse discrimination against them'.[48] The Congress Party in its most authoritarian guise during Indira Gandhi's tenure absorbed in order to neutralise any dissent that would disrupt the technological advancement that her father's discourse of order first sought to initiate. In Naipaul's text, the subalternity *of* woman *qua* subalternity *to* the state (a negation within a negation) is used to show how this neutralisation of resistance is an inevitable outcome of Indian culture.

The woman is called Mallika and the dissident element, since Ambedkar has passed into the hagiographic incongruence of '[j]acket and tie [making] for an unlikely holy image in India ... but fitting because it went against the homespun and loincloth of the mahatma', is Namdeo Dhasal, her husband and the leader of the Dalit Panther movement.[49] Failing to find Dhasal among criminals and prostitutes, Naipaul interviews Dhasal's wife instead. Using her narrative strategically to describe the cooptation of the Dalit movement as the only possible outcome if this political movement was to survive, he quotes her as saying:

The next year, 1975, there was the Emergency. There were something like

350 court cases against the Dalit Panthers – speeches, fighting, etc. The government withdrew all those cases when the Panthers supported the Emergency. That wasn't what Namdeo wanted to do. And *though he never said anything about it*, I feel that was when he began to feel compromised. But that was when I, too, needed him most – in July of that year I had had my child. I needed Namdeo, and I felt he was neglecting me.[50]

What is happening here? By the time Namdeo enters Naipaul's narrative as someone purportedly ('he said') organising a demonstration by Golpitha district's prostitutes, any political action concerning the negligence of women's lives by the state has already been made analogous to the maltreatment of a woman in private life. There is nothing anomalous in drawing attention to the latent hypocrisy of leadership, were it not for the fact that Naipaul cites Namdeo's 'debilitating illness' as the last explanation for the movement's fragmentation.[51] He earlier describes the efflorescence of Dalit poetry by Namdeo in the unpropitious environs of a brothel district. In contrast, the demise of the movement under Dhasal is attributed to activism without a party or an organised set of aims, a failure to maintain resistance after Dhasal's faction lent its support to Congress in the 1977 election. The void of the movement's failure filled with 'a whole new literature ... sprung up on the common basis of rejection of *varna*'.[52] Naipaul, the self-fashioned writer, does not dwell long on this aspect: 'She had suffered. She had been introduced to shocking things. Namdeo had venereal disease; he continued to go with women from the brothel area.'[53] When describing how her husband would react to her 'frank' autobiography of life with Dhasal, how loyalists to the Dalit cause might describe it as a gift to detractors, instead of its being perhaps a reparative act on his behalf Naipaul interprets it in class terms, of her perception with 'middle-class eyes'; it is an opportunity to attribute another *Realpolitik* motivation to Dhasal, the outworn feminist idiom between them: '... there it was, the social comment, the comment on her family house perhaps, the comment on the way Mallika saw herself in relation to Namdeo, the way he saw her – "his argument is that this woman has every right to express what she feels about the marriage"'.[54] Husband, wife and son all live with Namdeo's mother in a house belonging to Mallika's father. With his keen social consciousness, Naipaul takes in the domestic scene: the father in a photograph, a red flag hung behind the television set and the petrified spiritual leader Ambedkar, grey-toned and wearing colonial jacket and tie. The relevance of Mallika's father being a famous folk singer, a Communist *and* Muslim, is significant when we regard Namdeo's life as poet, leader and politician committed to the rejection of *varna*. Naipaul is as fixed into caste consciousness as are those he is describing. The colonised subject may attempt to resist caste but *it* still attaches to them. We will return to the reasons for this in Naipaul's assertions about the value and form of history in the postcolonial era soon. Mallika is describing her 'Lonavala romance' a year before Dhasal's fatal encounter with Mrs Gandhi and, Naipaul cynically notes, 'its time of glory'. Dhasal appears as a heroic figure for Mallika, having been brutalised by the police and at this juncture Naipaul interrupts her recollections with a question:

'You had no caste feeling about the man?'

'I had no caste prejudices. I didn't know about his caste, and I didn't think it was essential to know that.'

Perhaps her communist father, the folk singer, had trained her that way. *Yet caste would have been in everything Namdeo did.* He was a caste leader, and caste still attached to him. In the house that afternoon, in the front room or hall, which Mallika had decorated with such care, there was a thin dark woman in dark clothes sleeping on a mat. That woman, I now learned from Mallika, was Namdeo's mother.[55]

Naipaul's representation of Mallika as bourgeois is a device to forestall the 'new threat' of the subaltern as a new class. It is contrary to the profound acknowledgement he purports to make on the subaltern classes' behalf. Namdeo and his mother are seen as atoms in a discredited enterprise, an anomalously historical part of the subaltern mass of 'small, dark, patient people, serious, and in their best clothes' queuing (and not rioting) on Ambedkar's birthday. They are the first cast of Bombay's theatre of humanity and form the first obstacle to the nation's historical unity.

The materiality of civilisations exerts a perennial hold on Naipaul. The liminality from which he forms his diasporic view imposes some strictures. Naipaul has a responsibility not only to represent the quality of his own experiences (always ambivalent, never straightforwardly celebratory) to a constituency beyond the nation but also not to present narratives to native intellectuals as if they were veridical. Ashis Nandy has put this obligation succinctly when he writes:

[T]he Chaudhris [Nirad C. Chaudhri of *The Continent of Circe*] and the Naipauls are not only critics of an inevitable mode of self-defence, they are also part of it. They provide 'secondary elaborations' of a culture designed to hide the real self – the deepest social consciousness of the victims – from the outsiders ... The determinate is not that determined after all.[56]

Nandy actually shares Naipaul's historical sense, if only in the form of a verso to his recto. Like Nixon's view of Naipaul's endeavour, the inauthentic nature of India's mimicry of the West, judging her as 'not being ... a true copy (itself, of course, a contradiction) or a true counterplayer of the West', is characterised by a familiar ruse of disinterestedness. What is it about Naipaul's strategic narratives that make them less about strategy (how to play or keep abreast with Western modernity) and more about a kind of inverted metaphysics? Why are people like Naipaul 'inverted modern gurus' while they draw our attention to the hypocrisy of Indian essentialisms? Should one counter these essentialisms by problematising modernity or should we regard these essentialisms as symptomatic of the greatest crisis for native culture, that is, its failure in modernising itself, embarrassingly showing up to this West a 'confused self-definition' of itself?[57]

These are species of inquiry that anyone foolish enough to undertake the task of explaining India, either to herself or to others, is forced to take up. How does

Naipaul take them up or, in other words, how does the Naipaulian fallacy about postcolonial societies pass itself off as a discourse of truth? The answer is simple: by circulating an antiquarian kind of historiography for national culture. No matter who or what we've ended up becoming, if we want to present a coherent version of ourselves that is the essential truth about us, we are inevitably prone to an enabling kind of hubris, the kind of historical sense that is truly symptomatic of Nietzsche's 'suprahistorical man'. Naipaul's use of history is ideological because, as soon as he realises his problematic endeavour (to 'fit' the present to a version of the past that is peculiar to him), he reverts to both social class and religious difference to foreclose the emancipatory logic he identifies in the postcolonial nation-state.

Chakrabarty chiefly associates the problematic nature of writing a 'self' by Indians with a higher purpose 'of making Indian history look like' the eminent life (really, the hoary project of the Enlightenment) Nixon mentions, and this endeavour is inevitably going to be in conflict with the kind of revolutionary impulse epitomised by Fanon, where an architectonic (a 'conscious and organized undertaking') national (and not nationalist) consciousness has to come to terms with itself as the most important cultural form.[58] This political aesthetic is a diagnostic view of what postcolonial writing is encumbered by, where individuals inevitably stall, and of how distant and incomprehensible the conflict over meanings about nationhood appears to be from the people it is most likely to affect. It is not too difficult to see how 'secondary elaborations', or rather, how primary and unresolved narcissisms resulting from colonialism (cultures, like individuals, survive on axes of self-definition) overdetermine both the subject and his theme. Nandy cannot castigate Naipaul if, as he starkly observes, '[a]ll interpretations of India are ultimately autobiographical'.[59] Having said this, Nietzsche's remark about suprahistorical man's historical sense – namely the truth about history, that it happens to things that are by their very nature ahistorical – is tantalisingly close to the more reflexive moments in Naipaul's writing. Let us look at what is going on in the following passage from one of Naipaul's novels, *The Mimic Men* (1969):

> How right our Aryan ancestors were to create gods. We seek sex, and are left with two private bodies on a stained bed. *The larger erotic dream, the god, has eluded us.* It is so whenever, moving out of ourselves, we look for extensions of ourselves. It is with cities as it is with sex. We seek the physical city and find only a conglomeration of private cells. In the city as nowhere else we are reminded that we are individuals, units. *Yet the idea of the city remains; it is the god of the city that we pursue, in vain.*[60]

Nandy would enjoy reading a lot into the curious juxtapositions Naipaul is making here, especially after Naipaul's self-avowed difficulties in writing about sex because of his mother.[61] I would like to draw attention to the specific form that Naipaulian transcendence takes. There is an upward movement from a spurious metropolitan cosmopolitanism but this is conditioned by an historical sense. The antiquarian use of history, journeying back to a long-vanished past, to Aryan ancestors, offers this individual, who is peculiarly marooned in his present, the kinds of sensuous satisfactions which he could not otherwise achieve in this present. The present is also a residual literary modernism because, after all, the flight is from a scene characteristic of T. S. Eliot's London, the 'unreal city'. Nietzsche identifies the 'talents and virtues' of this attempt and, as I shall go on to show, 'Aryan ancestors' offer Naipaul

> ... the soul of his nation across the long dark centuries of confusion as his own soul; an ability to feel his way back and sense how things were, to detect traces almost extinguished, to read the past quickly and correctly no matter how intricate its palimpsest may be.[62]

There is also the undeniably faintly comic image of Naipaul here, with whom a transplanted and elusive god is playing His *yogamaya*. It seems that Naipaul, in London, is looking for a pastoral *Vraj*. Naipaul's chapter 'Synthesis and Mimicry' (identitarian terms in psychoanalytical discourse) opens with a dinner party in Delhi. A skittish foreign academic, talking about the attenuated life of India's 'multitudes', is met by an equally useless but *analogous* attitude in his native wife. Naipaul, the interloper, makes his judgement:

> Her Indian blindness to India, with its roots in caste and religion, was like his foreigner's easy disregard. The combination is not new; it has occurred again and again in the last thousand years of Indian history, the understanding based on Indian misunderstanding; and India has always been the victim.[63]

Naipaul, when it comes to some unpleasant habits of Indians in public places, might not have shared the foreigner's easy disregard of poverty but listed these symptomatically nonetheless as something peculiarly Indian thirteen years before.[64] Like Babur in his *Baburnama*, the kind of historical ruler a Hindu nationalist orthodoxy likes to hate, Naipaul is not averse to an exorbitant narrative of autobiographical impressions. In his short reign as the first Mughal emperor, Babur would decry the natives for 'no genius, no comprehension of mind, no politeness of manner ... no ingenuity or mechanical invention ... no skill or knowledge in design or architecture'. Yet there is lots of gold and money in Hindustan and an available system of guild labour where 'in Agra alone there were 680 Agra stonemasons at work on my building every day'.[65]

However, Naipaul's attitude to India's poor is closer to the way the Indian woman perceived them, as 'people having their being'.[66] For Naipaul, hers is a characteristically Indian 'defect of vision'; despite her distance, she is able to accommodate the demands of 'real' life all too well. There is that post-structuralist incredulity about the greatness of grand narratives and, analogously, towards the lives of great men, and a microcosmic analytics concerned with 'the telling details that emerge as metaphors for national life'.[67] Nonetheless, Homi Bhabha's idea that mimicry is concerned with marginalising 'the monumentality of history' is close to but not a perfect interpretation of Naipaul's discourse on India.[68] The problem of being 'parodists of history', the 'apostasy' of erratic inscription and so on, is not about an ambivalence (to use Bhabha's pet phrase) 'in a narrative that refuses to be representational'; on the contrary, India for Naipaul may certainly be synonymous with, a metaphor for even, the 'great life' of one man. We have seen how Naipaul does not hesitate about summing up Indian realities for his reader. At a time when the consensus about Gandhi's role in India's history was strong enough to capitalise on, it would be interesting to see if the germ of the defective vision Naipaul describes did not begin with Mahatma Gandhi himself. Naipaul's relationship to Gandhi, unlike, say Nandy's or Partha Chatterjee's, is dominated by the kind of ambivalence about the 'writerly' self, incapable of anything but an etiolated lyricism that, Chakrabarty notes, is the mark of an unaccomplished culture of privacy.[69] This is not essentially about the problem of colonial textuality attempting to inscribe itself 'across a body politic that refuses to be representative'.[70] What Bhabha means by a narrative that refuses to be representational, what curious species of authorship is being elided, is a post-structuralist dilemma I do not want to explore here. Neither do I want to explore how Gandhi, for Naipaul, is still tainted by the civic virtues of *bhadraloki* or 'respectability' from which Indian nationalism, as a counter-discourse (or a 'derivative' discourse, as Chatterjee would have it), first emerged in the nineteenth century; why Naipaul likes the idea of India 'individuated' as Gandhi is the more interesting issue. For Naipaul, Gandhi is revolutionary because he is colonialist in outlook. The colonialist outlook answers the needs of the postcolonial nation, which, if it is not careful, will revert to the defective vision responsible for its predicament in the first place. Naipaul, at this point in his career, has not given historical credence to the ideological propositions he will later do in his writings; namely, how a caste-ridden entelechy of 'selfless action' might make India vulnerable to Islam. Gandhi, as 'Indian revolutionary', fulfils an historical role in answer to what he spent his political life resisting. 'Vision' is always part of a specifically monistic discourse and Naipaul will not spare Gandhi this single-mindedness either. I find Naipaul's notional desire to remove *ahimsa* or non-violence from Gandhi's *satyagrahi* creed all the more disturbing, considering the 'analytical' context to which India is being submitted. Naipaul writes:

> The spirit of service, excrement, bread-labour, the dignity of scavenging, and excrement again: Gandhi's obsessions – even when we remove non-violence, when we set aside all that he sought to make of himself, and concentrate on his analysis of India – seem ill-assorted and sometimes unpleasant. But they hang together; they form a logical whole; they answer the directness of his colonial vision.[71]

Naipaul then, is materially part of the secondary elaborations he identifies in Indian society. What do I mean by this? Naipaul is writing about India's millions here, as deserving of a 'profounder acknowledgement'; of a kind presumably different to that meted out to them, not only by the middle class, but also by the coercive and violent political manifestation of this class. In *India – A Wounded Civilization*, he is writing in the aftermath of populism and the way this instrumental use of subalternity by the state saw its logical result in Indira Gandhi's declaration in 1975.

V. S. Naipaul's 'India' 173

In this context, it is a noticeably conservative gesture when Naipaul reverts to antiquity, to 'the last thousand years', as an explanation for why the Indian middle class feels the subaltern classes as a 'new threat'. This gesture, like the one Naipaul notes in the Delhi couple, is a recurrent trope in the writings about Indian society. This is the reason why Naipaul's posture (*pace* Nandy) is deceptive about its own origins. Behind Naipaul's analyses of postcoloniality as a political condition there is a compound figure. This is Naipaul as Nandy's 'modern acarya' *qua* Nietzsche's suprahistorical man.

History and the myth of purity in antiquity

Having described Naipaul's historical sense as something essentially antiquarian, we can ask what ideological importance this conservative deployment of history might have for Indian postcoloniality. In the rest of this chapter, I want to show how Naipaul's invocation of India's antiquity and the quality of being immemorially Indian is nothing more or less than an adherence to a Brahminical purity of origins. The logic latent in Naipaul's atavistic interpretation of contemporary India takes him back to the relative 'safety' of the sixteenth century and 'the great Hindu kingdom of Vijayanagar, destroyed by the Muslims'.[72] Let us consider this choice of 'imagined community'. Naipaul travels south and not, as one might expect, north to Ayodhya where, as Hindu legend has it, Mir Baqi – one of Babur's generals, had destroyed a Ram temple to build a mosque for his emperor. Not Ayodhya, but Vijayanagar is now the ideal moment in India's long history of colonisation. What evidence is there for this proposition? Consider the same space, but remarkable for a nominally different intrusion having taken place:

> During the last war some British soldiers, who were training in chemical warfare, were stationed in the far south of the country, near a thousand-year-old Hindu temple. The temple had a pet crocodile. The soldiers, understandably, shot the crocodile. They also in some way – perhaps by their presence alone – defiled the temple. Soon, however, the soldiers went away and the British left India altogether. Now, more than thirty years after that defilement, and in another season of emergency, the temple has been renovated and a new statue of the temple deity is being installed.[73]

There is the characteristically anomalous but necessary logocentrism of India's polytheistic origins where the installation of the image is accompanied by a twelve-lettered mantra, to be written fifty million times by five thousand volunteers. In Indira Gandhi's Emergency, despite the colonial past, 'India, Hindu India, is eternal: conquests and defilements are but instants in time'.[74] We ought to pause and examine more closely how India's past deviated from its essentially pure beginnings. The British, understandably, Naipaul concedes, correct Hinduism with its superstitious accretion of animism by shooting a crocodile, but Vijayanagar, two hundred years before it became vulnerable to Muslim conquest, successfully managed to fend off Islam. However, in the ideality of Brahminical purity, how might history measure up to Naipaul's interpretation of events? The kingdom was founded, Naipaul notes, in 1336 by a prince who returned after being abducted and converted to Islam by the Tughlaq sultanate at Delhi. Naipaul would give short shrift to Sugata Bose and Ayesha Jalal's characterisation of India's 'pre-modern accommodation of differences' where 'it was in the fourteenth century that a true Indo-Muslim culture was forged, based on Hindu–Muslim alliance-building and reciprocity'.[75] If Naipaul's acuity of vision is in setting himself apart from the crowd, Elias Canetti describes the immoderate uses to which this individuation might be put. We have the lonely paranoid despot, Muhammad 'Tughlak', the sultan with whom Vijayanagar's defilement originates. When the sultan failed to quell myriad insurgencies, he decided that a radical solution was called for. Delhi was emptied of all her inhabitants and the wealthy sultan paid in full the value of each house. Ibn Batuta reports:

> [H]is slaves found two men ... one a cripple and the other blind. They were brought before him and he gave orders that the cripple should be flung from a mangonel and the blind man dragged from Delhi to Daulatabad [the new capital] ... He fell to pieces on the road and all of him that reached Daulatabad was his leg. When the Sultan did this, every person left the town ... and the city remained utterly deserted.[76]

William Dalrymple represents the latest manifestation of a desire and demand for a monumental history which, as Nietzsche says, for the soul seeking a place of honour, means capering on the 'summit of ... a long-ago moment [which] shall be ... still living, bright and great'.[77] For Naipaul, the first wound of a wounded civilisation ought to be attributed to Islam. The new Hindu orthodoxy would be interested in the denomination of Tughlaq's victims. Far from reciprocity, then, in Naipaul's keenly hieratic sense of belief, Islam violates an already decadent culture. After all, didn't the anonymous prince 'in defiance of Hindu caste rules' declare himself Hindu again after returning south from Delhi? Popular Hinduism inevitably declines into barbaric practices like slavery, temple prostitution, *suttee*, and even, with an isolated example, into human sacrifice, authorised by the 'great' Telegu ruler Krishnadeva Raya (1509–1529). Naipaul's passion for Brahminical Hinduism with its incantatory system of metaphysics and the mystifying ritual should be noted here. Naipaul is to contemporary Bombay what Muhammad Tughlaq was to Delhi all those years ago.

Let me now cite a more controversial thesis, where the reciprocity of Hinduism and Islam is not founded purely on political economy and trade, as Bose and Jalal both suggest. Vijayanagar has been judged and found wanting but the reasons for its decline, culminating in its destruction in 1565, are more complicated than the colonial stereotypes of temple prostitutes, widow immolation and human sacrifice offered by Naipaul. The most important phrase in the species of 'ideality' at work in Naipaul's recovery of an archaic past, in his melancholy fantasy of an eternally Hindu India, is of course the 'defilement' to which it has been subjected. There are two things to be done here. First, we have to question the qualitative contribution made by Puranic Brahmanism to the crisis Naipaul is identifying. Second, we have to identify an alternative conception of popular Hinduism other than the axis purity/pollution upon which Naipaul founds his idea of India's past.

Ernest Gellner's idea of a pre-industrial 'agro-literate' society provides, in his own terms, a theoretical explanation for nationalism in the nineteenth and twentieth centuries.[78] Having placed his caveat, Gellner goes on to speculate about the ideological nature of these pre-capitalist formations where 'literacy becomes a badge of rank, as well as constituting a guild mystery'.[79] Rank ensures survival in this subsistence economy, where nature 'somehow underwrites, justifies the social order'.[80] Naipaul mentions the precariousness of this arrangement in Vijayanagar, where auspicious monuments, borne out by artisanal effort in an inhospitable environment, call for the 'sacrifice of some prisoners'. Doubtlessly, these individuals were the unwilling victims of a species of coercion where 'a man is his rank'.[81] We need to ask these questions: How does rank maintain social order in Indian antiquity and what kinds of affiliation does Naipaul have with this order? My purpose is to show how the polymorphic reality of India's present reflects an essentially heterogeneous past, whether this is celebrated or denied. The epochal idiom in which Naipaul denies this paradoxical continuity (how can anything so diffuse produce anything as coherently systematic as history?) of a cracking, wounded civilisation in crisis involves an essentially idealist sense of the past. A material history, of detritus, exemplified for Naipaul in India's Hindu and Muslim monuments, of 'Moslem ruin on Hindu ruin, Moslem on Moslem', has a kind of autonomous relation to the intricate palimpsest of meanings. Naipaul declares: 'In the history books, in the accounts of wars and conquests and plunder, the intellectual depletion passes unnoticed ... '.[82]

Naipaul realises the limitations of a Marxist interpretation of Indian history (*pace* Gellner for all agro-literate societies of caste or rank) but this awareness manifests itself as communalism in his writings. We should be clear that Naipaul is not calling for a Gandhian dissolution of modernity, for the kind of *panchayati raj* which sets itself up against the sterility of modern democracy.[83] Gainsaying the political or economic, Naipaul (untenably) presents India's predicament as being wholly due to an intellectual inadequacy where 'archaic India can provide no substitutes for press, parliament and courts'.[84] Leaving aside the way in which these features of Indian democracy, under Indira Gandhi, were inadequate *loci* of power against the state apparatus, a timid recourse to India's archaic past will not in itself solve the symptoms of the present. Naipaul's symptomatic analyses of Indian society – its characteristic inability to reach an intellectual awareness – coupled with his itinerant caste consciousness complicate a little the two kinds of critique traditionally made of Indian society. Succinctly put, Naipaul simultaneously deploys a theory of universal modernity and a synthetic theory of caste.[85] Marx's article, about the moribund nature of India as the 'Ireland of the East', from 1853, inaugurates the former sentiment.[86] *The Laws of Manu* are a defensive sanctification, by a Brahmin class, of the latter. What these diverse attitudes in India's long past share is their interpretation of Indian society in terms of caste and crisis. This is not the place to compare the exegetical rendering of crisis either in Marx or *Manu*, but

176   Re-imagining Indian pasts

it is important to note how 'extremity', 'emergency', 'crisis' are terms in a recurring trope about Indian postcoloniality. Naipaul's India belongs to this intellectual tradition. This pessimism is the secular component of the modern *acarya* or guru, whose portrait Nandy drew up earlier.

Gellner challenges the hegemony of Puranic Brahmanism by characterising the popular aspect of Hindu belief. I do not want to press into service Gellner's hierarchical characterisation of difference here as the missing dialectical half of Naipaul's story of India's antiquity, tempting as that is. In whatever attenuated sense, writing from within that history, I am concerned with identifying the specifically ideological character of the 'ideality' Naipaul is mobilising *as history*. Gellner then:

> This kind of society is characterized by a tension between a high culture, transmitted by formal education, enshrined in texts, and setting up socially transcendent norms, and, on the other hand, one or more low cultures, incarnated only in living practice, and not in that disembodied form of speech known as writing, and hence incapable of rising above actual practice. So what is typical of this kind of society is a discrepancy, and sometimes conflict, between a high and a low culture, which can of course assume a variety of forms: *the high culture may strive to impose its norms on the low, or the members of the low may strive to assume as many characteristics of the high as possible*, in order to enhance their own standing. The former is typical of Islam, the latter of Hinduism. But neither endeavour is likely to be very successful.[87]

Gellner's bird's-eye view of Indian syncretism sharply distinguishes the *chiaroscuro* shades that Bose and Jalal detect in their history.[88] Evidently, this view of India's past would be anathema for Naipaul. Positing a kind of productive antagonism ('sometimes conflict', Gellner writes) between two great religious communalisms adheres in a mock-heroic way to a Hegelian process where the utility of endeavours can be judged absolutely. Though Gellner and Naipaul might part company over the nature of the process, they are in essential agreement about its end. I want to turn to the second question I raised: the possibility of finding an alternative interpretation of 'popular Hinduism', one that is not predicated either on the recovery of a purity of origins or a deliberate isolation of religious consciousness that would serve this recuperation via an idealist teleology. To do this, we should look at Partha Chatterjee's more plausible thesis about the way in which, within popular Hinduism itself, an idealist teleology for practices (*dharma*, in a word) often betrays marks of subalternity.[89] Moreover, for Chatterjee at least, this analysis of Vaisnav Hinduism and its reformist sects, during the period Naipaul posits as one of a general decline for Hindu India, between 1576 and 1582, is fundamental as 'a critique of Indian tradition that is at the same time a critique of bourgeois equality'.[90]

These six years saw the imposition of Brahminical dominance over Vaisnav Hinduism which, with its emphasis on *sadhana*, has always been able to accommodate both men and women who are prepared to undergo a disciplined regime of spiritualism in order to realise within themselves (*svarupa*) the quality of divine love between the deities Krishna and Radha. Contrary to the failure Gellner notes in both Hinduism and Islam, Chatterjee shows how the syncretism of Vaisnav sects reveal how both systems as practice produce the conditions of possibility whereby the ideality of caste (its *dharma*) remains historically contingent. What do I precisely mean by this claim? After citing the participation of Muslims in Vaisnav festivals, Chatterjee concludes:

> It is, as a matter of fact, merely to recognize that the existence of these sects is itself evidence of an unstable layering of popular consciousness of material drawn from diverse dominant as well as subordinate traditions, the only principle of unity being the contradictory one of simultaneous acceptance and rejection of domination.[91]

For Naipaul, then, 'subordinate traditions' here would include the contribution made by a folk Sufic tradition to a syncretic Hinduism. Speaking about Indonesia, before its conquest by Islam, as 'the most uncompromising kind of imperialism', Naipaul shows himself to be an ideal disciple of that antiquarian use of history described by Nietzsche. Historical memory fails to protect itself from the depredations of an Islam that exists outside history. In *Beyond Belief – Islamic Excursions Among the Converted Peoples* (1998), Naipaul, with his historian's vision and a problematic Brahminical instinct for the value of the text as document, writes about the geography of rice plantations in the following way:

> And yet very little was known of this immense history. There were no documents, no texts; there were only inscriptions, and not many of those. *Writing itself was one of the things that came from India, with religion.* All the Hindu and Buddhist past had been swallowed up. *Without writing, without a literature, the past constantly ate itself up.* People's memories could go back only to their grandparents or great-grandparents. The passing of time could not be gauged; events a hundred years ago would be like events a thousand years old. And all that remained of two thousand years of great social organization here, of a culture, were the taboos and earth rites Dewi had told me about. For instance, before the rice harvest you went out to the ripe field and cut seven stalks. You hung these up on your house. Only then could you start the full cutting. No one knew why. The original prompting had vanished somewhere down the centuries.[92]

Naipaul is, of course, aware of the great communalisms of Indian society and their role in the evolution of the subcontinent's history, so it is not these, in a crudely simple way to which he owes his perception of 'the converted Muslim countries'. Naipaul submits his test of authenticity for these nations that have converted to a new religion by appropriating India's antiquity, as others have done before him. This deployment bears the unmistakeable hallmark of an exclusive nationalist historiography and properly belongs to a 'discourse of order'. Chatterjee notes how, by the 1870s, 'the principal elements' of a nationalist history of India were in place, substituting a more mythical or Puranic genealogy of rule.[93] The stories which became nationalist historiography are currently fashioned into 'materials of Hindu extremist political rhetoric'. Naipaul's attitudes are part of a larger process in postcolonial India's 'history as the play of power'.[94] Naipaul makes a miniscule gesture of resistance against the normative tendency of this appropriation of the past; however, this only occurs to strengthen the orthodoxy of his view. Where Nietzsche sees the intricate palimpsest of history, Naipaul notices only defilement, impurity and decline. In contrast to his earlier observations, Naipaul casts this paradigm and preoccupation of a Hindu past beyond the scope of preserving its monuments. What Nietzsche identified as a monumental species of historiography, for Naipaul is risible because it is too secular an idiom to put to use in answering the crisis of an obliterated Hindu past. This idiom of 'the environment' only works in the *mestizo* or bastard societies of South America. It is proper only for the newness of the New World, of accursed Argentina and 'ravaged places like Brazil'.[95]

In contrast to Islam's dissemination in the subcontinent, Naipaul locates the gentle colonisation of the Indonesian archipelago by Hinduism and his own memory of ghostly literary echoes in Charles Kingsley's account from 1871 of Indian 'aboriginals' crossing the gulf to these islands in canoes, and returning again to the subcontinent with fruit. Chatterjee's exemplary text for a modern nationalist historiography is Tarinicharan Chattopadhyay's *Bharatbarser Ithihas*. This text is contemporary with Kingsley. In Chattopadhyay's sixth chapter, 'The Civilization and Learning of the Ancients', there is a detail about the valour of these aboriginal Indians. In the reformist frame of Indian nationalism, Chattopadhyay celebrates these Hindu men who sailed all the way to Sumatra and Bali. With an eye on both India's Mughal past and the British presence, Chattopadhyay notes how now 'the thought of a sea voyage strikes terror in the heart of a Hindu, and if anyone manages to go, he is immediately ostracized from society'.[96] This ostracism is part of Naipaul's own spiritual itinerary as a diasporic person. Earl Lovelace, the Caribbean writer, beautifully captures the overcompensation that this ostracism engenders in individuals like Naipaul. Sonan Lochan, in Lovelace's novel, is said to have given himself a Brahmin name in Trinidad, 'making it clear that now he was not less than anybody even in the ancient orders of his motherland'.[97]

I conclude by stating that Naipaul's ameliorative vision of a Hindu consciousness now almost faded, of rites once vividly practised but now forgotten by the majority of Indonesian converts to Islam, is his attempt to defend a background that derives from the organicism of historical memory itself. It is left to Naipaul to live up to the social reformer's Aryan ideal of the adventurous Hindu. I am not disputing Naipaul's self-identification here, as overdetermined as this is, but I am drawing attention to the mode of history he chooses in order to accomplish this act of identification. The intervention of Islam in the civilisational career of Hinduism conforms to a very particular nineteenth-century nationalist use of history. As soon as Naipaul grows aware of the ideological implications of this interpretation for postcoloniality, he reverts to the classicism of a European past, to the first-century account by Tacitus. The intransigence of Islam in granting any sacred places outside Arabia is retroactively measured by the aesthetic value of the birth of Venus and the rites associated with this mythical event. Naipaul concludes:

> So it is strange to someone of my background that in the converted Muslim countries – Iran, Pakistan, Indonesia – the fundamentalist rage is against the past, against history, and the impossible dream is of the true faith growing out of a spiritual vacancy.[98]

6 Salman Rushdie and the *agon* of the past

> History is always ambiguous. Facts are hard to establish, and capable of being given many meanings. Reality is built on our prejudices, misconceptions and ignorance as well as on our perceptiveness and knowledge.
>
> Salman Rushdie[1]

> [H]istory is nothing but belief in the senses, belief in falsehood.
>
> Friedrich Nietzsche[2]

Introduction

Reading Rushdie one is quickly aware of how his fictional strategy belongs to the tradition of Enlightenment critique of all given forms. The ostensibly satirical comprehension of historical and social reality gives the impression that his output is typically engaged in the ironic mode. In this limited sense, the prevailing spirit of the postmodern is never far from Rushdie's attitude to the present and that is how he would prefer his reader to interpret his writing. The 'inert mass of feudal culture' even in the post-Revolutionary age weighed down the Romantic reaction to the essential irony in Enlightenment historiography so that 'the ascent of thought in a given line of inquiry [was raised] to a level of self-consciousness on which genuinely "enlightened" – that is to say, self-critical – conceptualization of the world and its processes has become possible.'[3] This reflective mode takes the individual beyond the desirably scientific comprehension of social reality as a sum total of productive processes; it is also the key to understanding Rushdie's historicism. Having turned away from the uxorious afterworld, the writer asserts the stern test of independence by affiliating himself, politically, to socialism and in art, to 'modernism and its offspring ... [as] the driving forces behind much of the history of the twentieth-century.'[4] This 'secular radicalism' comprising socialism and modernism is conceived in terms of 'great traditions'. The veneration of both is already a step beyond the lived experience of either. A reverie in Latin class of four *houris* or female spirits untouched by man or *djinn* is sacrificed for the intemperate maturity of historical processes. Electing for the historical process is no easy choice and Rushdie immediately represents the great traditions in compensatory form for something entirely extra-mundane: 'But perhaps, I write, in part, to fill up that emptied God-chamber with other dreams. Because it is, after all, a room for dreaming in.'[5] At first glance, writing is the *via negativa* or a proximate plenitude designed to fill an emptied subjectivity, but this is only a secondary phenomenon to the way in which figurative language is made to fold back upon its own horizon of possibilities of truthful representation only to return with 'its own potentialities for distorting perception under question'.[6] The agonistic characterisation of the creative faculty illustrates how Rushdie's fictions are more typically Romanticist in orientation, idiographic in their chief mode of argument and anarchist in the conclusions they draw about the relationship between human nature and the forces of history. If we accept the self-fashioning according to this shallow pathos deliberately fostered from – White asserts – an *intrinsically* sophisticated and realistic perspective, the attempt to relativise the symbolic function of prophecy according to the norms of history by novelising the life of the founder of Islam in *The Satanic Verses* is a natural culmination of the tendency. As we will see below, it is not the only means available in revealing how, in the monumental sense of history, individuals mobilise *their* will according to the subtle genius of the conjunction they find themselves in to tame the whim of Providence for their own purpose where others fail.

In what exactly does the effort to achieve this sophisticated perspective on the follies of the world lie? Good writers ought to aspire to a point above history, Rushdie insists, to be able to perceive the simultaneity of Benjamin's 'Messianic time' without dwelling in an inadequate unity of a state based on faith. The holism of faith to found a nation-state is symptomatic of an 'insufficiently imagined' sense of community.[7] The name Rushdie gives to this province of abortive imaginings in one instance is Peccavistan. And what evidence is there of that ironic capacity in bringing home the Enlightener's undertaking of questioning the veracity of historical truth itself? Rushdie answers as follows:

> *Outsider! Trespasser! You have no right to this subject!* ... I know: nobody ever arrested me. Nor are they likely to. *Poacher! Pirate! We reject your authority. We know you, with your foreign language wrapped around you like a flag: speaking about us in your forked tongue, what can you tell but lies?* I reply with more questions: is history to be considered the property of the participants solely? In what courts are such claims staked, what boundary commissions map out the territories?[8]

The jurisdiction of history exceeds the terrestrial bounds of its effects. *Midnight's Children* is playfully recommended to 'future exegetes' as a 'source book', 'Hadith ... Purana or *Grundrisse* for guidance and inspiration'.[9] The literary interpretation of his texts is analogous to the quest for finality in archaeology, history, Islam, Hinduism and Marxism. There is the chief desire to see his own productions as part of a tradition, of continuity, the literary artefact as *scripta manent* loosened from the general life of monuments beyond the decrepitude to which all cultures are destined. Religion proper is conceived as an imposture when it fails to transcend linear temporality. Unlike the vital springs at the birth of Islam where Muhammad's words held the strongest appeal for 'the poor, the people of the bazaar, the lower classes of Meccan society', words designed to alleviate and console those still inhabiting the old nomadic system whose termination is nigh, Rushdie asserts that 'plainly, history did move forward; nomadism did not once again become the Arab norm, nor, obviously was that truly Muhammad's aim'.[10] The obvious quality of Muhammad's aim has exercised the imagination of peoples for over a millennium. However, the trope of the imagination is too imprecise to admit a sociological explanation for structural inequalities despite some salutary reminders of 'description [as] a political act' and, in the Marxian spirit, where 'it is clear that *redescribing* a world is the necessary first step towards changing it'.[11] The forms are already given. Despite the tone of solemnity, the forms that emerge from the Chaos of Being all deserve the contempt of a measure beyond the magnanimous self-control that the man of knowledge thinks he has achieved. Traversing the madhouse-world of entire millennia, despite the care he takes not to make mankind responsible for its insanities, feelings 'burst forth' when entering the modern age.[12] Spontaneity or lack of control is the pallid form of authenticity that Romanticism was bequeathed from Augustan cynicism about the limits of rationality. All that remains is for the individual to isolate themselves in the interests of objectivity, to separate heuristic considerations like the nature of belief from the regulatory system: to 'place themselves *sceptically* between culture as a massive body of self-congratulating ideas and system or method, anything resembling a sovereign technique that claims to be free of history, subjectivity, or circumstance'.[13] The postmodern is surely a realisation of the world after sovereign techniques have failed to deliver the earthly paradise free of history, angst and the essential passivity of modern institutionalised life. This is the fertile impasse of the critical imagination. Islam is conceived by the author 'situationally' less than 'a cultural system than as a series of immutable beliefs that can be universal and transhistorical'.[14] I do not want to enter into the banalities elevated to assertions of personal belief that a critic may choose to give in their reading of 'homoeroticism of the colonial paradigm [when] conflated with the body of the prophet of Islam' by invoking the 'God of Islam'.[15] The important point is the author's choice of transposing the postulates of a monumental historiography onto religion. This act is worthy of the prerogatives of the prince *played at* by the historian in establishing 'the rules of political conduct and the best political institutions' for the topography or 'place of power' – a role we are reminded that is ethical to the degree the historian 'analyzes what the prince *ought* to do'.[16] In Rushdie's hands, Akbar's decision to adhere from 1582 to a mystical set of beliefs called *Din-e-Ilahi* (Divine Faith) becomes a pretext for a revolutionary principle: 'to found the religion of man'.[17] Clearly, the writer prefers the Mughal's pavilion to the Bedouin tent, sharing the idea that it is man and not God at the centre of things in the Tent of the New Worship. In marked contrast to the certitude of the Prophet, Rushdie prefers the questioning imagination of the emperor who did not have answers but only questions that felt like answers. In the first two chapters, we considered the analytical effort of achieving this goal where (*pace* Said) system or scientificity is not to be sacrificed for an historical understanding of cultures.

There is a lot going on in Rushdie's propositions concerning the historical and contemporary relationship between religion and politics. Early Islam is said to *acquire* the characteristics of a subversive, radical movement. A series of questions arise about this secularising radicalism concerning religion. First, the cultic beginnings of any religion will resemble the picture of 'pre-political' consciousness Rushdie is depicting specifically for Islam. It is hard to see how the soteriological aspect of any system of belief can be achieved if it remained confined to the mysteries presided over by priest and king. Islam is ideally suited to a progressive movement in time: it is not about abolishing the mercantilism of the Hijaz only to return to a nomadic life; yet this movement that came to the founder of the religion with a terrifyingly divine clarity in the cave at Mount Hira, partially reflecting 'a return to the code of the nomadic Bedouin', has for some obscure reason degenerated into the theocratic politics of Iran and the Zia dictatorship in Pakistan. The historical consciousness, if it faithfully represents both forward and retrogressive movements, simultaneously typified by the metaphor of Janus, cannot materialise without realising those sociological elements Rushdie attributed to it; the form, as we will see, is both lyrical and modern (social). *The Satanic Verses* stages Islam as 'a history of a progressive degradation', a fact shared – in de Certeau's analysis – with the Lutheran sects.[18] Time in the Muslim world is behemoth, ponderous but pliable to the will of the despot, whether it is Mahound, Akbar, Khomeini or Zia. The implication is that, like Christianity, Islam also evolved beyond its modest ambition of maintaining identity across the different spheres of collective life and the mechanistic solidarity of the Bedouin code into an *imperium* in which the individuating factor of a symbolic hierarchical social organisation threatens the crude positive of the repressive law – a law, the original Abrahamic inheritance the revelation insists it is returning to, that directly joined 'without any intermediary, the individual consciousness to that of society, that is, the individual himself to society'.[19] This logical conclusion dramatised in the novel is played out more dialectically in the essay. The theorising ends by returning to Tom Nairn's image of the *progressus* of nationalism. The resonance of the image, perhaps like the hollow idol in Voltaire's Oriental tale, is heard at the very beginning of Islam; Rushdie concludes: 'The birth of Islam was presided over by two gods: Allah and also Janus.'[20] Placing human beings beneath Janus as the sign of history is a mark of political maturity. While giving due consideration to the transcendental element of religious belief, the erstwhile advertising copywriter likens it to the serial disenchantment of the terrestrial utopia offered by politicians, because religions, in contrast, 'have the great advantage of not having their most important promise tested until after their consumer is dead'.[21] Rushdie's remarks about the historical process and the unconscious motivations that human beings are inevitably prone to when adhering to the sacred are reminiscent of the retrogressive movement of the historical gaze fixed on 'concrete and specific activities', with the historian withdrawing only to return with 'a more complete and richer perspective'.[22] We will see how in Rushdie's ironical borrowing of the 'true two-faced Janus' the result is more nihilistic than the aspirations Lévi-Strauss envisaged where 'solidarity of the two disciplines [anthropology and history] makes it possible to keep the whole road in sight'. In contrast to the mysticism to which Christ's political revolutionary death was interpreted by Pauline Christianity, the overtly social, organising, political creed propagated by Muhammad has never withdrawn from the exclusively public sphere. For Rushdie, Islam never matured beyond perpetual revolution. That societies ought to discover the optimum beyond the turmoil of revolution is a pre-requisite Rushdie shares with Nehru's 'discourse of order'. When religion declined along with the elites that provided 'the underpinning substructure of the great universal faiths' and was replaced by the emergence of a secular ideal, that of the nation-state, the most fundamental change in the world's relationship to religious belief gave an opportunity or made space for the apotheosis of the novelist writer I began with.[23]

The tragic form and its discontents

In an earlier fiction, the author confidently recommends the tenets of 'secular radicalism' of 1798–1799 rather than the revolutionary potential inhering in an absolute vision of social order to be discovered in religious belief. Even God cannot escape the spurious infinity of the theocratic state:

> And then the dictator falls, and it is discovered that he has brought down God with him, that the justifying myth of the nation has been unmade. This leaves only two options: disintegration, or a new dictatorship ... no, there is a third, and I shall not be so pessimistic as to deny its possibility. The third option is a substitution of a new myth for the old one. Here are three such myths, all available from stock at short notice: liberty; equality; fraternity ... I recommend them highly.[24]

What does the actual historical descent of the Enlightener's ideals into the Terror signify for the author? In the eudemonic interpretation or the monumental conception of the past, the great truths of history remain untarnished by the actual passing of events, enough, at least, for them to be circulated as a prophylactic against despotism in Third World nationalisms. Before the supernatural solution presents itself to the problem of autocracy, alluding to a play, *Danton's Death*, on the London stage the author expatiates on the ideal of 'stability' with visiting Pakistanis. They envy Britain its ability to stage political theatre and, in contrast, cite the farcical bowdlerising of *Julius Caesar*. The crux Rushdie presents his reader is a conservative one and worthy of Carlyle's history of the French Revolution. Though the protagonists of the novel are quite beneath the high drama of Danton and Robespierre, the author invites his reader to empathise with an abstraction: forget the usual dichotomies of history, of left–right, capitalism–socialism, black–white, he says, 'the epicure against the puritan ... is the true dialectic of history ... Virtue versus vice, ascetic versus bawd, God against the Devil: that's the game'.[25] Here again, the ironic mode returns from the complex arena of actual or material history to the consoling vagaries of individual temperament. As such, and if Robespierre is the people, why was Danton ever heroic? Reading the famous passage of Robespierre's death, his jaw bound in dirty linen, where the executioner is Samson and a woman leaps, 'Sybil-like', on the tumbrel carrying the prisoners after their seventeen-hour ordeal to castigate the sinister figure, all the elaborate sociological and economic explanation for the apocalyptic events in Febvre disappear, leaving behind the banality of the following assertions about an 'internal dialectic': 'The people are not only like Robespierre. They, we, are Danton, too. We are Robeston and Danpierre. The inconsistency doesn't matter; I myself manage to hold large numbers of wholly irreconcilable views simultaneously, without the least difficulty. I do not think others are less versatile.'[26] This being the case, whither *liberté, egalité, fraternité*? All these remarks suggest that Rushdie is performing the same task for the seventh-century Arabians (and as confusedly) as Voltaire's Zadig. In other words, the ironic, satirical mode is a reaction, or rather, the fictional expression of the Enlightener's ideals after the intrusion of realism in this heroic interpretation of events. Rushdie's anatomising of the past resembles the belletrism of the eighteenth century and the complicated relationship of the *philosophes* to the *ancien régime*. His characterisation of the Crusader other Mahound is an attempt to reinvigorate the redemptive possibilities of the imagination by providing a bounded horizon to the impulse of religion. As such, Rushdie's fictions represent the desire of historical man to raise himself to the *suprahistorical* perspective and, by doing so, recognise 'the essential condition of all happenings'.[27] What does it matter that this boldness of spirit encounters the detail of historical events as a singularly unheroic process – one in which the translation of historical phenomena are resolved into a phenomenon of knowledge? The cost of this perception of historical phenomena, of knowing them 'clearly and completely', is the recognition not of vitality but of death: '[F]or he has recognized in it the delusion, the injustice, the blind passion, and in general the whole earthly and darkening horizon of this phenomenon, and has thereby also understood its power in history.'[28] It is with some surprise then that we learn that religion and politics, or the Messianic and the linear-calendrical, are not antitheses but are both 'manifestations of our dreaming selves'. Though again simplifying, Rushdie expresses the dilemma of our modernity (as well as his own after the edict from Tehran) as follows:

> In political thought we seek to express our dreams of improvement, of betterment, of progress – our dreams, some may feel, of dreams. We seek to give life to these grand visions, and we assume that *we can do so*; that our dreams are attainable, that the world can be made what we wish if we wish it enough, that we are capable of *making history*. Thus most political discourse, because it places the human spirit in a position of power over events, can be seen as a dream of adequacy. An optimistic dream. The great universal religions, by contrast, ask us to accept our inferiority to a non-corporeal, omnipresent, omnipotent supreme being, who is both our creator and judge. The word 'Islam' means submission, and not only Islam and Christianity and Judaism, too, classically require of believers an act of submission to the will of God. That is, religion demands that God's will, not our small vanity, must prevail

over history. To make it plain, we could say that religion places human beings beneath history. In this world we are not masters, but servants; so perhaps we can see religion, in this contrast, as a dream of our inadequacy, as a vision of our lessness.[29]

Whether for Turks or Greeks, Nietzsche proclaims, the historical men express a profound belief in the piecemeal revelation of existence in the course of its unfolding as a process. Although this optimism superficially represents knowledge at the service of history, it is actually an endeavour in the interests of life itself. The often inelegant procession of the idea of freedom *may* inevitably terminate with a cynical reckoning with Power. The representation of the heroic figure beneath the sign of history – and in the end, it matters little who this actual figure is – resembles Voltaire's depiction of Charles XII in this regard; a model not to be emulated either by poet and historian. It is in this spirit that Rushdie's conception remains idiographic in the particular form Jameson stated for Third World literature. The mechanistic processes of groups, classes and institutions that constitute the actual movement of history remain hidden in the metonymic force of the charismatic personality. In short, Rushdie is obsessively concerned with the dissolution of the charismatic personality under the pressure of history. The correlative of elite historiography, Rushdie's formulations about history are reducible to the typologies of Power because the drama of these effects exceeds the labyrinths into which individuals would carefully attempt to place them. The effort of placing these diffuse effects of power into a system that is universally coherent is the prerequisite of the transition from feudal to modern society. One cannot describe these effects as the '*insurrection of subordinated knowledges*' in Rushdie's case because the functionalist coherence or formal systematisation given these in modern capitalist societies allows for a degree of validity that is *independent* of the approval of established regimes of thought.[30] Rushdie's fictions insist that this autonomy is impossible; hence, the Romanticist equivalent of this autonomy of thought that Rushdie has defended with the Enlightener's vigour involves an elaborate 'aesthetics of despair'. Despite calling on the tutelary human spirit where the substance of politics is mastery over events, the making of history – as he puts it – the regenerative possibilities of the social imagination fail to ameliorate the subaltern predicament. The religious dispensation places humankind beneath history. We are returning to the familiarity of the Whig universe in which historical events are capable of being domesticated. Nehru could have authored the assertions Rushdie makes about an optimistic faith in improvement, betterment and progress. However, in Rushdie's hands these ideals take on a nihilistic character and the comic or regenerative possibilities that are the particular gift of socialist consciousness soon evaporate:

> What this [affiliation of Modernism *qua* the decadence of Third World elites] excludes … is the dailiness of lives lived under oppression, and the human bonding – of resistance, of decency, of innumerable heroisms of both ordinary and extraordinary kinds – which makes it possible for large numbers of people to look each other in the eye, without guilt, with affection and solidarity

and humour, and makes life, even under oppression, endurable and frequently joyous.[31]

There is a characteristic antithetical development in reaction to literary high Modernism: the search for a purity of origins that is consistent with lauding the historical sense as a vital measure to remedy the horrors of the present has led to 'an *excess* of belonging by *not* belonging' amongst the globalised intellectual class; it is a class of individuals that can afford to liberate itself from the constraints the humanist of ages past endured or enjoyed.[32] Nietzsche's brilliant evocation of an excess of historicity for this most 'postmodern' of conditions is apt. The riotous clamour of historical knowledge forces itself on the limited capacity of human memory. The latter 'opens all its gates and yet is not open wide enough, nature travails in an effort to receive, arrange and honour these strange guests'. The reception of the quarrelsome contents of history cannot continue long and the habituating of consciousness to this content (the 'conflict-ridden household') as second nature eventually produces a weak nature. Rushdie's inflation of the historical sense propounded by Modernism in his adult fairy tale fictions represents the following symptom:

> In the end, modern man drags around with him a huge quantity of indigestible stones of knowledge, which then, as in a fairy tale, can sometimes be heard rumbling about inside him. And in this rumbling there is betrayed the most characteristic quality of modern man: the remarkable antithesis between an interior which fails to correspond to any exterior which fails to correspond to any interior – an antithesis unknown to the peoples of earlier times.[33]

We saw how the Homeric consciousness repudiated the inwardness of historical becoming to be found in the Biblical tradition. For the nineteenth-century philologist, in contrast to Auerbach's celebration of this inwardness as a pre-requisite of modernity, the strength of Greek 'culture' lay in keeping 'a tenacious hold on their unhistorical sense'.[34] Unlike the archetypal experience of exile in the Homeric epic in which the shores of the Mediterranean represented the mythical, literally, narrative atmosphere and ground in and upon whose bright surface Man conquered both others and himself, the productive capacities in the decision to exile oneself from one's community in modern life necessarily involves the anaemic pleasures of floating *above* history. The refusal to 'authorize any sustained acknowledgement of such pains' by this class of individual in the actual experience of an excess of belonging is entirely due to a characteristic absence of agonistic sentiment.[35] The antidote to the human experience in Rushdie's writing and the tedious emphases invariably on misogynistic sexuality and escalations of venality of motive reflect the scatological origins of this monumental regard for the past. The venerable act is to treat the past as if it were the legacy of collecting 'effects in themselves'; the postcolonial migrant, the new debased Adam, as a creature meditating on its own novelty in the great scale of evolution here 'gathers' itself until it eventually discovers the larger penumbra encircling its own dim point of subjectivity in the idea of the nation as 'a historical fact of singular importance'.[36] This is perhaps why the Homeric odyssey of the Hellenes ended very late in a national consciousness: it had no urgent need for it. The modernist disposition for Rushdie relates to the careful harvesting of fragments. He describes the process:

> The shards of memory acquired greater status, greater resonance, because they were *remains*; fragmentation made trivial things seem like symbols, and the mundane acquired numinous qualities. There is an obvious parallel here with archaeology. The broken pots of antiquity, from which the past can sometimes, but always provisionally, be reconstructed, are exciting to discover, even if they are pieces of the most quotidian objects.[37]

When social reality is perceived by a consciousness such as this, the broad avenue of human progress that Lévi-Strauss believed was the gift of an anthropological and historical understanding in solidarity becomes littered with indigestible objects. The mundane has always acquired numinous qualities but emphasis on the metonymical quality of the experience, paradoxically, considering 'Commemoration is the complement to experience', implies a depressed and hyperconscious vision of things:[38]

> In commemoration there finds expression the increased alienation of human beings, who take inventories of their past as of lifeless merchandise. In the nineteenth century allegory abandons the outside world [Hellenic exteriority], only to colonize the inner. Relics come from the corpse, commemoration from the dead occurrences of the past which are euphemistically known as experience.[39]

Shards of prostitution and fragments of beggary people Moraes Zagoiby's imagination. Having a life that expires at twice the rate of normal development, this priapic narrator represents his mother Aurora's attempt to picture Indian realities with 'a clear-sighted naturalism that would help India describe herself to herself'.[40] Rushdie goes on: 'But Aurora, for whom reportage had never been enough, had pushed her vision several stages further; in her pieces it was the people themselves who were made of rubbish, who were collages composed of what the metropolis did not value: lost buttons, broken windscreen wipers, torn cloth, burned books, exposed camera film.'[41] The artist continues to describe the unregenerative mass of Indians 'scavenging' for their own limbs, pouncing indiscriminately on the wrong parts and wearing in this surrealist tableau two left feet, or having failed to discover buttocks, a pair of amputated breasts in their place. The artistic will forces this subterranean reality into focus and the other half of the Oedipal syzygy realises its failure in producing the noble purity of the new nation out of this human detritus by becoming *itself* a 'semi-allegorical figure of decay'. Rushdie goes on to quote Baudelaire to account for this transformation. The Moor itself is a 'human rag-and-bone yard' and Bombay's landscape a symbol to accommodate 1492 when the last Nasrid ruler of Granada, Abu Abdallah al-Andalus (Boabdil), figures as a palimpsest for loss with the voice of History echoing in the taunt of his mother, the terrible Ayxa the Virtuous: 'Well may you weep like a woman for what you could not defend like a man.'[42] By using Arab Spain to re-imagine India, Aurora's fantasy of a golden age for Jews, Christians, Muslims, Parsis, Sikhs, Buddhists and Jains represents the 'romantic myth of the plural, hybrid nation'.[43] In the family saga, the Jewish matriarch's painfully realised agnosticism reveals in the fabric of the synagogue a message of a moment before 'at *the beginning* of a time of war and massacres'.[44] Amitav Ghosh also goes back to the Mangalore of twelfth-century India for a 'belief in the power of syncretic civilisations', a time when this exemplary commensalism in history before the wholesale plunder of European empires started was stronger than the spirit of conquest to which Flory's ancestors or Ghosh's Arabic Jew, Ben Yiju, and his Indian slave Bomma had to succumb, in their different ways.[45] Rushdie's consistent objective is expressed by a movement beyond the depiction of India's immense life 'by a kind of selfless, dedicated – even patriotic – mimesis' to the realisation of History as tableau without a superintending deity.[46] This endeavour is typified by the index of a 'muscular free line' used to draw 'a metamorphic line of humanity' beyond the august personalities of history, both ancient and modern.

Walter Benjamin's spirit pervades Rushdie's historicism. The denouement of the apocalyptic or tragic comprehension of the past in which the Janus figure is the presiding deity prompts the existential predicament that the human subject faces in the welter of history. The suprahistorical achievement is not synonymous with the realisation of Messianic time. How could it be? If it were, the Platonic image of the constellations returning to their original station would mean the end of history. In the sterile medium of modern life, all we have is the Idea questioning itself. Capitalised, the gift of prophetic vision accursed according to an historical consciousness asks itself what kind of an idea it is.[47] In other words, prophetic vision is a consciousness of Messianic infinity that is fatally free of the anxieties about temporal succession ordinarily encumbering an historical sense. It is as if the historical consciousness can only thrive on a diet of indigestible objects. The suprahistorical sense of the kind typified by an anarchist mode is not synonymous with the divine epiphany. Janus is not an original for Allah. However, the depressed and hyperconscious sensibility affects a kind of attitude that wants to readily substitute the temporal and the transcendent. The effort has been futile for over two hundred years, since '[i]n [time] alone is all actuality of appearances possible' and even '[t]he latter could all disappear, but time itself (as the universal condition of their possibility) cannot be removed'.[48] The hysterical sublime characterised by the hypertrophied virtue of the historical sense is born out of this philosophical moment. The character plagued by this sense is a preternatural 'kaleidoscope endowed with consciousness': Baudelaire is the figure on the terrestrial plane embodying this consciousness as a living metaphor for but not *of* the sterile life of the crowded city.[49] This is the secret reason why modern experience is euphemistic. Benjamin represents all that is *allergic* for Nietzsche: incapable throughout of facing eternity with the knowledge that 'life is at bottom indestructibly powerful and joyful', a primal vitality that remains immutable not only 'regardless of the changing generations and the path of history' is unavailable to him; the fruits and foliage of a crowning legacy throughout the vicissitudes that afflict the individual, Greek cheerfulness as 'an aged and unproductive delight in existence' remained elusive for the Hebraic Messianic consciousness for whom the contemporary age demanded an intolerable toll.[50] Rushdie's fiction plays with the actual ambiguity of the source of apocalypticism in the Uthmanic codex: anonymous in Q 91: 1–10, 103: 1–3, personally in Muhammad's voice, 81: 15–21, God in the third person, 'my lord', 'your lord' (Q 43: 64; 96: 1–8), in the earliest passages, where God speaks (Q 73: 5; 87: 6), and in late Meccan and Medinan verses, God as the author reciting the Qur'an as the *kitab* or book to Muhammad (e.g., Q 2: 252; 3: 108; 45:6). However, an early Medinan verse (Q 2: 97) has dominated the tradition of spiritual autobiography (*sira*) and 'the true spirit' (26: 192–3) and 'the spirit of holiness' (Q 16: 102) have been interpreted as the announcing presence of Gabriel. Although objections to the Gharaniq incident began in the fourth Muslim century, the retraction of verses – first coined by the historian Sir William Muir as satanic – conceding to the pagan worship of female deities in 'Sura Al-Najm' (*ghurnuq, ghirnawq, ghurnayq, ghirniq* meaning crow, bird, eagle or high-flying crane in the singular after 'the exalted birds [*gharaniq*] whose intercession is greatly desired'), despite evidence of *isma* or divine protection against error for Muhammad, forms the fable of the novel. Gerald Hawting draws attention to the incident concerning *mushrikun* or polytheists as hyperbolic and typical of intra-monotheist polemics rather than as evidence of a real pagan background to the revelation, but this proposition nevertheless does not alter the plausible proposition that the incident actually occurred and that 'the doctrine of the Prophet's infallibility and impeccability (the doctrine regarding his *isma*) emerged only slowly'.[51] Al-Tabari around 915 CE describes the agonistic desire to win the Meccans that prompted the deliverer to make the imaginary revelation:

> [H]e longed in himself for something to come from God which would draw him close to them. With his love for his people and his eagerness for them, it would gladden him if some of the things he had found in dealing with them could be alleviated. He pondered this in himself, longed for it, and desired it.[52]

Al-Tabari's portrait of a man susceptible to fear and doubt about his vocation is the doctrinal background to the introduction of Janus or the spirit of history in Rushdie's novelisation of Islam's early moment. Incidentally, in Tabari's psychological portrait there is also to be found the romantic dream of an organic ethnos from which the heroic individual discovers a collective destiny. According to the temporal conditions of this human past, the consolation of a correction where the intensity of doubt in any preceding prophet or apostle had *never* before resulted in a diabolical event (Q 22: 52) reveals the immensity of the forces ranged against the individual who aspires to the condition of history. Neither is Rushdie concerned with the philological debate surrounding the Syriac origins of the Qur'an as *lingua sacra*.[53]

In the first chapter, I cited Benjamin's apocalyptical view of tradition. A tremendous shattering of tradition conceived in terms of a 'far reaching liquidation', however, will make room for a radical resurrection of dead forms or at least, in the name of Shakespeare, Rembrandt and Beethoven, each of which 'will make films ... all legends, all mythologies and all myths, all founders of religion, and the very religions ... await their exposed resurrection, and the heroes crowd each other at the gate'.[54] In contrast to the mortifying procedure in the contemporary reclamation of the past which Baudrillard drew our attention to, or the indigestion that human memory might be prone to if its ambition is to confine this hiatus, for Benjamin at least the polyphonic possibility of rendering the great tradition still remains by destroying its aura: 'unexpected combinations of human beings, cultures, ideas, politics, movies, songs' are capable of being celebrated as 'as a love-song to our mongrel selves'.[55] The value of history in the present age figures as a debilitating condition; it is a false Eden in which Man appears as an idler, a spoiled loafer in the garden of knowledge. More dangerously, the seductive lure of fiction always lies in wait ready to ambush the historical consciousness, the whore called 'Once upon a time' in historicism's bordello.[56] Gibreel Farishta, born as Ismail Najmuddin, tiffin carrier on the streets of Bombay, perceives the unreality of London as a periodic instability in which 'its true, capricious, tormented nature' is revealed. He goes on to describe

> its anguish of a city that had lost its sense of itself and wallowed, accordingly, in the impotence of its selfish, angry present of masks and parodies, stifled and twisted by the insupportable, unrejected burden of its past, staring into the bleakness of its impoverished future. He wandered its streets through that night, and the next day, and the next night, and on until the light and dark ceased to matter. He no longer seemed to need food or rest, but only to move constantly through that tortured metropolis whose fabric was now utterly transformed.[57]

London as 'the true home of fallen humankind' entails a vision of endemic deformity: a place 'we must regard' as possessing 'a human shape with its own laws of life and growth.'[58] This perception is symptomatic of a hypertrophied historical sense in which life becomes impossible without the protection of the pastoral faculty of forgetfulness praised by Nietzsche: 'What you were is forever who you are.'[59] Regenerative possibilities of extracting meaning from History – who 'has many cunning passages, contrived corridors', who 'deceives with whispering ambitions,/ Guides us by vanities' and whose sterile gift to Man is merely that 'Unnatural vices/Are fathered by our heroism' – all but vanish.[60] *She* has a fatal allure, waiting to be noticed by the epicurean: '[A]nd a man who catches History's eye is thereafter bound to a mistress from whom he will never escape'; 'History loves those who dominate her: it is a relationship of mutual enslavement'. And again, she is a fit substitute for the questioning intellect that spurns God to fill 'a vacancy in a vital chamber, leaving him vulnerable to women and history'.[61] For Walter Benjamin in 1940, as the ineluctable fate drew ever near, after the hope of welcoming the Messianic presence in secular temporality had also failed, the regenerative possibility in the historical sense – one that is present as an inadequate metaphor in Rushdie's stories – lay with a peculiarly engendered conception of the Marxist hero; the last revolutionary hope remained with the historical materialist whose virility – unlike the absent potential in the uxorious masses obedient to the overtures of the Führer – has not been 'drained'; he is the figure who is 'man enough' to make a fertile break from the arbitrary signification of the eternally long chain of past events.[62] Rushdie's Farishta (Angel) represents the dark, ironic scepticism of Benjamin's imagination after Paul Klee's painting *Angelus Novus*. The Angel of history suffers under the duress of an impossible force, pinioned to a blind future by the apocalyptic storm of Progress that has freed itself for some obscure reason from Paradise; in a supreme metaphor for the travails of existence fashioned from an obsession with the sign of history, this *acedia* receives the Messianic epiphany not as a serene realisation at a point above history ('awaken the dead, make whole what has been smashed') but '[w]here we perceive a chain of events, he sees one single catastrophe which keeps piling wreckage upon wreckage and hurls it in front of his feet'.[63] Progress is not the fatal but proud attempt to conquer the Empyrean, but the accumulation of debris growing skyward. The doubt that assails the prophet, the post-lapsarian universe of meaning that is the gift of historical comprehension and the participation of the migratory ego, of Anti-Christ and Mahound in history where the 'schizo ... hallucinates and raves universal history, and proliferates the races' – all come to a lyrical stop with Rushdie's use of Faiz Ahmed Faiz's expression of conflict between the eschatology that passion attempts to reach were it not for the terrestrial claim of the historical sense.[64] It is worth noting that Faiz's *ghazal* is not typical of the Urdu form, of the trope of spurning Islam or religion in favour of 'some novel object of epistemological and erotic devotion'.[65] Neither is the quoted extract from Faiz an example of 'taut and ironized submission to the alterities represented by an Islamic culture in a colonial world', whatever these may happen to be.

Let us explore this problem more closely. Witness the prevarication Edward Said displays in recommending a secular interpretation of Salman Rushdie's writing: while this is to be admired as typical of regional aesthetic achievements all over the world, 'as part of a significant formation within Anglophone literature', a 'more realistic and political point of view' of Rushdie's practice would acknowledge the 'threatening coercive, or deeply anti-literary, anti-intellectual formation'.[66] As with the original expression of this sentiment later worked into the ambiguous conflations of *Culture and Imperialism*, what agency the author played in this conjunction of *Gestalt* and the untutored religious consciousness remains unclear, except that he became anathema to admirers who formerly are said to have regarded him as a 'champion of immigrants' rights and a severe critic of nostalgic imperialists'.[67] These assertions remain problematic on empirical grounds but Said's conclusion about Rushdie's representative status is logically inconsistent with the pragmatic norms delineated for the thematic of Orientalism as being an instrumental form of knowledge that is *somehow* concerned with social reality but at a number of removes from '"natural" depictions of the Orient'. Histories, philology, political science are as implicated in the imaginative re-creation of reality as the 'avowedly artistic (i.e., openly imaginative) text'.[68] For Said, Rushdie 'provoked Islamic fundamentalism when *once he had been the virtual representative of Indian Islam* – this testifies to the urgent conjunction of art and politics, which can be explosive'.[69] The reactionary forces of configurations (in themselves empty, ready to be filled with whatever content, nationalism at first, religious fundamentalism later) endemic within non-Western societies are engaged in 'the mobilization of consent [and] the eradication of dissent' against an idealised backdrop of Enlightened literary *communitas*. These forces are sinister because they remain free of the control exerted by a sympathetic and literate intuition that is engaged in hermeneutic investigation.[70] The pre-requisite of historical consciousness and the abstract shape of fiction that uses it ought to be defined by a noble dream once Third Worldist cultural nationalism had finally to be abandoned. 'What, then, to replace it with?' asks Aijaz Ahmad. He continues: 'Socialism had already been renounced as the determinate name of imperialism's negation. Nationalism – the whole of it – also now went. This is the redoubled vacuum which, in the radicalized versions of metropolitan literary theory, poststructuralism is now to fill.'[71] Said's interpretation inspired by a principally literary event is symptomatic of a more conservative version of the moment described. Non-Western readers were alienated by the voice of their religion which they recognised in the novel, and yet the production also transgressed the high purpose represented by a community of readers besieged by dangerously regressive 'underlying configurations' – Islam as a configuration, analogous to other historical deformations in the consciousness of the dominant group like 'Communism', 'Japan' and the heuristic category, the 'West', whose force is novel enough to deform the fragile skein of 'affinities, sympathies and compassion'.[72] A basic question concerning the intentional fallacy now inevitably arises: is the novel for the Islamists or the imperialists? It would be counterintuitive to conclude that the novelisation of Islam's early history represents a need of having it translated for Muslims. The problem with this idealist conception of dialectical conflict is that it conforms to the very same processes investigated by Said of a monolithic Islam that US foreign policy is engaged in producing for domestic consumption.[73] More to our purpose, for Said, Salman Rushdie and the poet Faiz represent a group of scholars *self-consciously* engaged in a vast postcolonial cultural and critical effort.[74] According to this argument, the local conditions informing Faiz's socialist dissidence to Pakistan's autocratic regimes – the paranoid atmosphere after Liaquat Ali Khan's assassination in which a purge of left-wing army officers was seen as expedient, including the imprisoning of Faiz as a former lieutenant-colonel – are to be read on the same plane as Rushdie's 'cosmopolitan' practice.[75]

These conflations of political purpose or the substitution of historical particularity for a sensibility are typical of metropolitan literary theory. That this endeavour is every bit as patristic as in ages past is confirmed by the episode in which the agonistic consciousness encounters its Other in the form of the eternal feminine. Sat on a bench made of cast-iron camels underneath Cleopatra's Needle, the apparition in Gibreel's mind, Rekha Merchant, repeats the hiatus in Faiz's poem: 'There are also sorrows beyond the sadness of love/and pleasures beyond the joy of our union.'[76] Rushdie playfully alludes to the fictional rendering of his cast of characters, where it is not Faiz but the Jahilian poet Baal who intervenes to challenge the terrible singularity of Islam's god. At the moment of Mahound's death, the apparition, now metamorphosed as Al-Lat, one of the Jahilian ornithological divinities, returns and Gibreel imagines her evaporation into the light of the sun after she has been denuded of her silks and brocades, her flesh and her very skeleton. The terrestrial claim of history – in the 'ālam-e-mojūd' or the present world, in Faiz's untitled poem about Bangladesh, 1971 – means having to turn one's consciousness from the radiant beloved to the welter of sin and suffering that Hegel thought intrinsic to historical consciousness; it is having to witness the bondage of humankind, of bodies smeared in ash and bathed in blood where the spell of history pretends since time immemorial that the life of the most powerful is the sportive array on a rich tapestry (the brocades worn by the female *daimon*).[77] In Rushdie's novel, this apostrophising of the past as the anonymous experience of the subaltern masses is reduced to the misogynist fantasy of feminine evil. The *houri* or *apsara* returns to haunt the pupil of Cleo. A history of subjection rather than a history of struggle would inevitably lead to the very pleasures Faiz's poem abjures.[78] When Fatima is dying a mere six months after her father ends his vocation as Messiah on earth, a woman among the Medinese women, including the retinue of wives, is admitted into her company. Umar, the second *khalifa* has disinherited her by using Muhammad's words regarding his possessions in common ownership for the *Umma* or community of believers. The mother of the *Umma* invokes the contract that Jehovah made with Jacob and his heirs and Assia Djebar's realism captures the tragic impatience of women in the new dispensation – who have been forced into a sort of half-life 'outside a place of temporal power, which is moving irreversibly away from its original source of light'– in the following words:

> 'This morning', Fatima replied, 'I feel that I am at last becoming detached from this your world, and I am about to rid of all your men! For I have so often witnessed their wrongdoings, for I have had so many occasions to examine them, that I finally reject them all henceforth! From now on, how burdensome all these men seem to me, these hosts of men of indecision!'[79]

This albeit conservative rendering of Islam's history represents the 'phenomenological universe' of the religion without a recourse to a metonymous comprehension of the past where the part-to-whole relationship of the novel to the sacred book threatens 'the logic, propriety, and indeed property of the "proper" name'.[80] Djebar tells us of Muhammad's forbidding Ali the taking of another wife. The eulogy he makes over Fatima's still-open grave echoes the decline of the pristine event: 'Thy daughter will report to thee how thy community has disregarded thy law!' Ali, appointed the spiritual leader of the *Umma* only five years before his death, having lived a whole three decades after his first wife's death, taking eight more wives in all 'thus enjoying his right to polygamy, within the limits and the prescribed forms', represents the distance history has to travel from the original Messianic moment in Djebar's exegesis of Ibn Hisham, Ibn Sa'd and Al-Tabari.[81] The belletrism of Rushdie's satire where a 'postmodern' species of irony has accomplished the existential task of reflexivity that White thought typical of the Romanticist progression is typically illustrated by the allegorical treatment of a woman's renegade decision to oppose the assumption of Ali as caliph by mustering forces to battle on 5 December 656 CE on the plains of Basra. The confrontation between the exiled Imam and 'the Empress', 'the Babylonian whore', 'Al-Lat queen of the night', is a parody of the 'Night Journey' made by Allah's beloved messenger to the Empyrean from al-Quds or Jerusalem on the shoulders of the *Burakh*, a mythical animal, half-woman, half-Pegasus (Q 53). The Imam is the legatee of Ali and Shi'a Islam and the composite figure Ayesha is therefore his natural enemy. There is a sociological analogue for these allegorical happenings. The female prophet Ayesha in the novel who has led a company of devotees to the Arabian Sea to their deaths is based upon miraculous visitations by one Bibi Roqayya, kin to Imam Hussain, the grandson of Muhammad, to a young woman called Naseem Fatma in Chakwal. This rural milieu is the stage for an anthropological drama between myth and modernity:

> The revelations were calculated to disturb the social equations [between landlord and tenant, Sunni and Shi'a] of the village forever. Naseem dominated not only the social but also, and more importantly, the religious life of the area. Willayat Shah [her father] had finally arrived. Both he and Naseem now reached out towards the better, truer world, that, for Muslims, lies beyond death. Through their deaths they would gain an ascendency which would be final and unassailable. They would triumph through the Shia themes of death, martyrdom and sacrifice.[82]

What we have in Rushdie's play with taxonomies in his historical fiction, as well as the general remarks he makes about the emergence of the nation as a form of legitimate historical consciousness, in comparison to the instrumental purpose in shaping society which religious consciousness had performed in the past, is a realisation that the 'calm persistence' and 'indeed, the objective extension, of religious practices in the mass of the nation' during a period of revolution necessarily meant, rather than brought about, 'the rapid autonomy of the "philosophes" in respect to religious criteria'.[83] The novelisation of the Hawkes Bay case in *The Satanic Verses* dramatises this calm persistence of religious consciousness which – in terms of capitalistic expansion in the backward zones – ought to have forever (as the interpretation above goes) transformed the material lives of the rural masses. This is actually wish-fulfilment; it is itself symptomatic of nostalgia for the simple peasant order before it was disturbed by the imperative of capitalism, the 'Gulf Syndrome' or the prevalent emigration of Muslim men to the Gulf states in search of a better life typified by the call to Dubai ('Dubai Chalo'). The termination of the disbeliever's hope where Mirza Akhtar in the Arabian Sea opens at Ayesha's command and the rending of the astonished resistant body 'from his Adam's apple to his groin' represents the original moment the prophet encounters the Otherness of God. For the feminist reading, this episode is the feminising of the prophet, an entering into 'dubiety', where 'the figurative miracle of their union points less to Mecca than to Rushdie's need to articulate openings in the structure of male desire'.[84] For me, this is the natural counterpart to the Romanticist comprehension of the historical task as it arises in writers like Benjamin and Eliot. Whatever else Rushdie's needs may be, whatever the structures and potential openings of masculine desire might imply for a feminist understanding of the mystical relationship between Man and *his* God, the historical representation of this agonistic doubt in Islam occupies a time-honoured place in the Orientalist projection of the Christian imagination. The gynophobia in the Modernist historical consciousness is a natural fable of patriarchy. The dubiety of the figure Mahound that interests me as an epitome of the great burden of history is the historical origins of Rushdie's visiting upon the atheist the visceral revenge for heresy. Ali goes before Muhammad, written upon his face is the fate of schismatics who tempt souls from the consolations of Christ's grace: 'his whole face slit/By one great stroke upward from chin to crest'.[85] Despite the theological anomaly of Saladin's place among the virtuous pagans perhaps born out of Dante's political affiliations to a subversive rationalist scholasticism, Muhammad as the progenitor of Islam, and the caliph's father-in-law and master, follows with a more gruesome affliction, being split from chin to anus as if by a cleaver. Dante's desire to represent the sin of apostasy includes an anatomical description for the contents of the rent body, including the stomach as the sordid organ that turns food to excrement. It is only in Gustave Doré's illustration that the agonistic spirit Rushdie wants to convey in his novelisation of Islam's origins *as a metaphor for the modern historical consciousness itself* truly comes alive. With the poets looking down, the archetypal figure for Ali hiding his face and with the figure for Muhammad looking up, Dante reports how the false prophet opens his *own* bosom, saying 'See how I rend me'.[86] There is no greater expression of the bad faith the Romanticist sense of the monumental past found itself in after the logical hiatus of absolute reform has failed to deliver the Enlightener his dream of the perfect social order.

History as the tragic form

The idiographic mode of historical argument that concludes in an anarchic comprehension of the past is bound to treat religious consciousness as a mentality that functions as 'delay', 'resistance' or, if it is used singularly as a coherent explanation for phenomena that are in the process of being superseded, an inadequate system. This idea forms the background of Rushdie's conclusions about the instrumental role that religion plays in the formation of national consciousness, and Nehru's summation of progress for India to be achieved by freedom from moribund social forms is the political correlation. In this last section I want to test the viability of this view by looking at two fictional interpretations of a single historical event. The theft and subsequent restoration of a relic, the *Mu-i-Mubarak*, would seem to belong to the bucolic realm of happenings of little concern to civic consciousness. Indeed, the force of events in the week during the disappearance of a strand of hair purportedly belonging to the Prophet Muhammad and its restoration by the Indian state's Central Bureau of Intelligence on 4 January 1964 to the place of its sojourn at the Hazratbal mosque for 263 years ought to be typical of a process dismissed by a diplomat's daughter in Amitav Ghosh's novel where nothing really important happens, and where, 'of course, there are famines and riots and disasters … But those are local things … not like revolutions or anti-fascist wars, nothing that sets a political example to the world, nothing that's really remembered.'[87] For the nameless narrator who represents the private consciousness of memory in the face of historical events, this attitude about what constitutes an event for world historical importance is an importation of norms outside the Indian experience. Rushdie starts his novelisation of the episode in Kashmir by anonymising the year to '19 –', to a time in modernity but ideally belonging to a dispensation where individuals are overwhelmed by the fatal workings of Fortune: Hashim's antiquarian mania represents something nascent ('Naturally, I don't want it for its religious value … I'm a man of the world, of this world', the moneylender thinks to himself) and Rushdie's story, as with his observations about the impulses informing his novelisation of Islam's history, is a fable concerning the disappearance of an 'integrative virtue that the religious frame of reference had represented until this time'.[88] De Certeau continues:

> It is here that this principle of unity turns out to be lacking. In each respective group its uncertainty is marked, by 'libertine' critical doubt, by returns in sorcery of the 'pagan' repressed, or by voyages toward the invisible secrets of received language which the absence of God instigates. The *loss of the absolute object* is inscribed within these movements, although in characters relative to what specifies each of these groups. It is the question to which they will respond differently.[89]

It is in this spirit of mock medievalism fostered by a libertine Enlightener's view of religious consciousness that the gelatinous bosom of Lake Dal delivers the 'secular object of great rarity and blinding beauty' to the man who prizes the silver case rather than the 'magical' object inside. Nevertheless, the relic exerts its catastrophic influence on the fragile constitution of family life in the sense of one system's invading another. The family are described as belonging to a 'thunderstruck clan'. The moneylender is transformed into a figure of tyrannical piety. There follow various comic developments as all those who played their minor parts in the attempt to restore the relic from the vigilant moneylender are visited by death. Hashim's son and daughter, in their futile attempts to restore harmony in the house by returning the relic to the shrine, traverse the valley's streets by a phrase recurrently used: 'entering the most wretched and disreputable parts of the city'. Rushdie's Srinagar may be Basra, Damascus, Cairo or Baghdad, but the troping of the place as any in *The Arabian Nights* should not distract us from the 'radical realist' tenor given to the place since the splendour of colonial days where 'the British held power beyond the mountains'. This is manifest in the commercial buildings and villas, whose material is supplied from the Army and Navy Stores catalogue of 1930: 'This phantasmagoric city, an unimaginable mixture of Isfahan, Lhasa, Sunningdale and the Underworld, which seemed … on earlier visits to be suspended for ever in its particularity has altered out of recognition. No doubt all famous cities should be imagined in their ruin.'[90] This pathos of de-chronology, as we saw with Naipaul's travel writing, is an inevitability and represents the following observation:

> This effect is the work of the so-called 'organization shifters' which help the author to superimpose a temporality of his own on that of his theme, that is to 'dechronologize' the historical thread and restore, if only by way of reminiscence or nostalgia, a Time at once complex, parametric, and non-linear ... braiding the chronology of the subject-matter with that of the language-act which reports it.[91]

The superimposing of a temporality of one's own on historical circumstance to make sense and therefore produce the hierarchy and order of events is the idiographic skill of *every* historical endeavour; as the first part showed, it is an indispensable element in all historiography. Interestingly, for Barthes, the synthesising activity latent in all historical discourse means that the historian shares the predictive function with the 'myth-bearer', with the seer. In terms of the slow revolution coming to an abrupt realisation by 1789 of religious practices since the seventeenth century, where 'sorcery and scepticism ... outline the void that a universal Reason or a natural Law will have to fill', this indispensably idiographic element in all historiography leads to a general methodological impasse:

> [R]esearch on *what must have taken place* in the seventeenth and eighteenth centuries in order to produce what undeniably happened at the end of the eighteenth century will normally call for reflection on *what must take place* today and what must be changed in our historiographical procedures in order for these procedures to cast light upon this or that series of elements which have not yet entered into the field of analytical procedures used until now.[92]

This ethical dilemma opened our consideration of historical practice. What *is* undeniable is that the historian, by making these recommendations, continues with the project whose objective conditions he or she is historicising; in other words, he or she, too, is extending the domain of Reason on the hidden elements whose combination up until the present remained the obscure province of superstition about *what actually happened*.

A Bengali family journeying to their old home in Dhaka to save an elderly relative become involved in the centripetal force of events that ensue after, outside the valley and the precincts of the shrine, the 'thin ... belief in the power of syncretic civilisations' was attested to by communal rioting.[93] Ghosh as an Hindu Arabist from Bengal has an historical sense of this syncretism. The narrator makes an experiment. He draws a circular line on an atlas with Khulna at its epicentre where Tridib and fourteen other real people lost their lives all the way to Srinagar and this circumference has a radius of 1,200 miles. The Far East comes within this amazing circle: Chiang Mai in Thailand is nearer to Calcutta than is Delhi;

Chengdu in China nearer than is Srinagar; the inhabitants of Hanoi and Chungking nearer to Khulna than is Srinagar and the narrator reflects on why the congregation in mosques failed to be roused into fatal action.[94] The disinterested intellect that regards nationalist history as a new moment in the self-realisation of humankind would treat the politicisation of space as an anomaly. In contrast to the Orientalist mode, in which elements in the colonial prose of counter-insurgency surface to interpret this event, in Ghosh's fictional interpretation the formative problem of historiography as to what actually happens in the nation's history is given a more radical cast than it is in the Romantic conception offered by Rushdie's monumental view of the Indian past. All the traits of Romanticism are there in Ghosh's novelisation. The silent nuclei of memory are disturbed into action where the ability to impose a scale to historical events can often seem incongruent to the formal recollection of events. The Indo-Chinese War of 1962 compared to the riots of 1964 caused by the disappearance of the relic is symptomatic of collective amnesia, but it is typical of the fact that 'within [the] circle there were only states and citizens; [and where] there were no people at all'.[95] Ghosh's historical sense is a critical practice where the irrationality of communal conflicts invisibly but fatally motivate the movement of people on a stage anterior to the official consensus concerning the materiality of events. The innate anarchism of history is a pretext for nationalist history: 'The theatre of war, where generals meet, is the stage on which states disport themselves: they have no use for memories of riots.'[96] In his witty record of fieldwork among Egyptian peasants, Ghosh expatiates on an 'Indian's terror of symbols' prompted by the curiosity of folk at a wedding about cows, cremation and circumcision.[97] The account suggests that the disabling silence surrounding the events of 1964 lie in the author's own childhood. In erstwhile East Pakistan, on a January day in 1964, a mob of rioters are forestalled in their desire to smoke out Hindus taking refuge in an ancestral home housing the author's father who has been sent on a diplomatic mission. Questioning the whereabouts of silent memory in the narrator's consciousness is not an entirely rhetorical endeavour despite the fact that his memory 'in an act of benign protection has excised every single sound' from the scene.[98] As with all memory, something tangible excites the consciousness into an act of recovery of the contents of the past and, for the six-year-old author-to-be, it is the dark metallic object of a pistol in his father's pillowcase. A Muslim friend calls the police to frustrate the menacing mob and Ghosh concludes:

> I was to recognize those stories years later, when reading through a collection of old newspapers, I discovered that on the very night I'd seen those flames dancing around the walls of our house, there had been a riot in Calcutta too, similar in every respect except that there it was Muslims who had been attacked by Hindus. But equally, in both cities – *and this must be said, it must always be said*, for it is the incantation that redeems our sanity – in both Dhaka and Calcutta, there were exactly mirrored stories of Hindus and Muslims coming to each others' rescue, so that many more people were saved than killed.[99]

This faith in the subaltern detail of historical circumstance is in contrast with the epicurean (de Certeau dubbed it 'libertine') belief of a superintending *terrestrial* totalising Power as the mirror of an individual consciousness of history that will sort out all the interests that are warring within a landscape of disorder because it is looking for a principle of coherence. Buchan evokes this image in his version of the episode coming to a close with Nehru, serenely sitting under a tree at Teen Murti, wearing a white shawl waiting to receive the report of the Indian intelligence officer with the following words: 'God bless you, Mullick, you have saved Kashmir for us.'[100]

Conclusion

> Thus learning and the degeneration or downfall of a nation always go hand in hand.
>
> Hegel[1]

> India has never had a real sense of nationalism ... The educated Indian at present is trying to absorb some lessons from history contrary to the lessons of our ancestors.
>
> Rabindranath Tagore[2]

There are a number of ways we can interpret the conclusion that the 'cunning of reason' operating at the heart of nationalist consciousness, in so far as it was defined by its opposition to colonial rule, 'administered a check on a specific political form of metropolitan capitalist dominance'.[3] Chatterjee beautifully goes on to adumbrate the peculiar contradiction this liberating consciousness is prone to between 'metropolitan capital and the people-nation' for all postcolonial nationalisms, where the passive revolution of the former continues to realise itself through the spurious agency of the state as a substitute for an authentic politics of the latter. He casts this Hegelian dance to his own neo-Gandhian music where 'ethnic separatism or peasant populism' *in principle* is 'capable of being appropriated by the passive revolution by means of yet another manoeuvre'.[4] Only by a critique of nationalist ideology can the way be prepared to divorce capital from reason. And the reader is invited to reflect that this noble task is being carried out up to and perhaps beyond the final page of Chatterjee's learned analysis.

The ambition of this book has been more modest: it is an acknowledgement, for all the reasons explored hitherto, that history by itself cannot perform the task endowed upon it by historians like Thapar and Chatterjee, if it only remained, as the *philosophes* desired, within the sober orbit of rational thought (in Thapar's characterisation) or the pretext of a new universality to replace the disappointing copula capital-Reason (in Chatterjee's). For Chatterjee, this organisation of power by the incipient postcolonial state as a discourse is not only conducted in a single, consistent, unambiguous voice, it also succeeds in glossing over all earlier contradictions, divergences and differences and incorporating within the body of a unified discourse every aspect and stage in the history of its formation.[5]

I have drawn attention to the 'contradictions, divergences and differences' in terms of the communal dynamics informing nationalist discourse throughout. There are disturbances in the glorious passage of the nation realising its spirit by becoming free. The question is whether the nation has managed to achieve this self-realisation by overcoming the limits of temporal existence or whether this potential necessarily involves a conservation of regressive elements on the way to transfiguration; as the analogies from Nature illustrate, Hegel shares Herder's optimism when concluding that 'History is the process whereby the spirit discovers itself and its own concept'.[6] The first thing to note in Chatterjee's description is the unmistakable mark of Hegelian idealism in the incremental character of this self-actualisation of national consciousness. What do we make of the assertion that this immanent discourse of the nation's past incorporates within itself contradictions in every aspect and stage? In a sense, to give this process the name of an individual is itself writing the alternative in symptomatic terms. Even Hegel regards the evolution of the nationalist consciousness as being hampered when it is defined 'by the particular interests of individuals, and no longer by the interests of the nation itself'.[7] The ostensible object of Chatterjee's attack is Nehru and the alternative narrative the statist discourse occludes is 'a politics of the subaltern classes'.[8] In other words, if Nehru typifies the accomplished discourse of order ('mature nationalist thought'), Gandhi's 'passive revolution' could never survive the rational scrutiny Chatterjee thinks it deserves without resembling it as a formative stage in the development of the idea of Indian modernity. The 'split between the two domains' of elite and subaltern politics implies that there were some points of contact, or to put it in more conventional terms, the two domains are nothing but dialectical forms of the same process.[9] The 'specific subjectivity' of the subaltern classes, from the procedures adopted by an elite politics, could only be interpreted in terms of the genius of Gandhi.

An anti-nationalist tract might attribute this charismatic appeal to the 'mythopoeic imagination of the childlike peasant' in symptomatic terms of 'an unhealthy nervous excitement'. This morbid tendency surfaces in India's inevitable transition to rational modernity 'such as often passed through the peasant classes of Europe in the Middle Ages'.[10] Another way of putting the same thing is to say that history 'is always richer in content, more varied, more many-sided, more lively and "subtle"' than any pretensions at a solution to its problems.[11] Describing the state apparatus's ability to recognise the subaltern classes as the Other and, in doing so, to 'efface' the Other, is not an entirely new metaphysical importation, despite Chatterjee's fulsome credit to Gadamer, Ricoeur, Barthes, Foucault and Derrida in a footnote.[12] The concrete image of Chatterjee's analysis is succinctly expressed in the following formula: 'Not only do class struggles have primacy over, and stretch far beyond, the State, but the relations of power do not exhaust class relations and may go a certain way beyond them.'[13] Post-structuralist arguments enable the subaltern historian to reach this secluded meridian but the first Enlightenment thinker to give poetic expression to this momentous process, is, of course, Hegel.

This book obviously could not have identified all the historiographic elements that nationalism monopolised or marginalised in order to achieve its discursive unity. This is partly to do with the fact that an examination of suppressed elements – where the universal urge for liberty and progress finds itself figured in nationalist thinking as 'Romance', 'Comedy', 'Tragedy' and 'Satire' – and this narrative emplotment of the random and crude material of history are inseparable from the explanatory mode Chatterjee thinks is indispensable in describing historical modes like class. 'Figures of speech', White reminds us, 'are the very marrow of the historian's individual style. Remove them from his discourse, and you destroy much of its impact as an "explanation" in the form of an "idiographic" description.'[14] It is ironic then that an idiographic description of Indian historiography of the kind the European thinkers Chatterjee lists above might help us to promote, would remove us from the very conditions that make historiography intelligible.

It is in this sense that nationalism is to be explained sociologically as a deviation from the 'story of liberty'. Let us end by exploring the 'idiographic' nature of Chatterjee's reading of nationalist discourse by looking at how a sociological account of Indian culture fares in his hands. Chatterjee explains how the liberal model of ideological explanation, typified by the 'self-complacent judgement of Ernest Gellner', fails to give any substance to nationalism. He describes the problems that beset this spurious and tautological 'contextualism' as follows:

> Thus nationalist thought did not even need to investigate 'the general logic' of the kind of society it was trying to build: that logic was given to it objectively. It did, of course, have to confront the problem of selecting from pre-existing cultures in agrarian society some of the distinctive elements of this new homogeneous national culture.

The instrumental project of nationalism has to contend with a limited set of possibilities. My argument against Chatterjee's interpretation of Indian nationalism is identical. It 'uses some of the pre-existent cultures, generally transforming them in the process, but it cannot possibly use them all'. Nationalism emerges from the backdrop of incoherent folk culture. In more temperate language, the devotion of the subaltern classes evident throughout Gandhi's *satyagraha* campaign contained 'room for political mediation by the economically better off and socially more powerful followers'.[15] This was the elitism Ambedkar detected in Gandhi's nationalist project of *Swaraj*. Chatterjee emphasises the limitations of this mythical background for Gellner, where folk culture is 'a piece of self-deception' and (he goes on to quote Gellner's account)

> in reality, nationalism is, essentially, the general imposition of a high culture on society, whose previously low cultures had taken up the lives of the majority, and in some cases of the totality, of the population. It means that

generalized diffusion of a school mediated academy-supervised idiom, codified for the requirements of reasonably precise bureaucratic and technological communication. It is the establishment of an anonymous, impersonal society, with mutually substitutable atomized individuals, held together above all by a shared culture of this kind, in place of a previous complex structure of local groups, sustained by folk cultures reproduced locally and idiosyncratically by the micro-groups themselves. That is what *really* happens.[16]

Gellner's argument is self-avowedly theoretical: it is true that the conclusion hides the need to provide any empirical evidence about the transition to nationalist modernity from an 'agro-literate' form of primitive association. Perhaps Gellner is giving a more dignified interpretation of historical teleology found in the editorial from 1921? Gellner's method as well as his conclusions about the real conditions in which Indian nationalism emerges can lend themselves to the satirical mode which White identifies in liberal historiography. Where Gellner describes the evolution of rural practices as 'idiosyncratic', the editor of the *Pioneer* speaks of Gandhi's subversive influence on 'all the neurotic girls of the countryside'. The point is that Indian as well as other postcolonial aspirations are now generic species of 'National Irredentism triumphant and self-defeating', for Gellner. Chatterjee is right to question the mythical origins of this irredentist belief. The paradoxical result of this belief is a transcendental category called the nation: it is transcendent in the restricted sense that resistance to colonial authority now furnishes the cabal that legitimised the old social order an opportunity to modify its adroit use of external coercion and internal moral restraint (culture) to extract the surpluses required for the new regime. In spite of Chatterjee's objection, however, the wider implications of Gellner's analysis are particularly well suited to the conclusions he draws about the conditions in which Indian nationalism matured into a statist discourse. The nationalist class is now poised for its nefarious historical role and, Gellner writes

> It is only in the transition from agrarian to industrial society that culture ceases to be a device which defines specific social positions and allocates individuals to them, and becomes instead, the boundary-demarcation of large internally mobile social unity, within which individuals have no fixed position, and are rotated in the light of the requirements of production.[17]

The spirit of Chatterjee's interpretation emerges more clearly: we understand Nehru's role in fabricating the mythology of the 'Indian national movement in its mature phase'. Chatterjee's antipathy for Nehru's model of progress is the analytical equivalent of a sentiment that was widespread in the early twentieth century. In the most articulate expression of the problem of modern civilisation as a negation of India's organic life, Nehru's vision of the postcolonial nation is of a vast engine of organisation whose abstract, tentacle-like reach even into the faraway future thwarts and entangles the impulses of the human heart 'into some tortured shape of result'.[18] The historian is in consternation at the fact that Nehru achieved his objective out of the odds and ends, the fragments of folkloric belief. Only Gandhi managed to give these random elements of the *Agraria* the kind of authentic unity possible in order to challenge the hegemony of the nationalist elites. The effete Cambridge graduate writing dispatches to his father's newspaper about agrarian revolt by peasants in Rae Bareli in 1921 against rapacious *zamindars* fails to equal the existential adaptations as a critique of modernity Gandhi gave to village life.[19] The note of admiration for Gandhi's appropriation of the subaltern classes falls on the more positive side where 'the specific political demands' of the nascent elites perhaps accidentally also give figurative expression for the first time in history to 'the modalities of thought of a peasant-communal consciousness'.[20] As we have seen, Chatterjee's own interpretive procedure isn't free of the specific dilemmas reproduced in Gandhi's Tolstoyan logic about the possibilities of subaltern consciousness.

The irredentism is self-deceptive as well as self-defeating, in the sense that it is a foreign device that Nehru and the Congress elites make strategic use of when they are manipulating the masses. To Nehru and Congress, Mother India is nothing more or less than that large reserve of labour 'rotated in the light of the requirements of production'. In the single concept of *Bharat Mata*, Mother India, Nehru discovers the magical incantation by which India's infinite complexity throughout her long history can be brought under control. Nehru talks about the 'particular village patch, or all the patches in the district or province' that the Punjabi *Jat* displays such an intense attachment to. Chatterjee concludes:

> The nation as Mother comes to him as part of a political language he has taught himself to use; it is just another political slogan which gained currency and established itself in the meeting-grounds of the Congress. It does not figure in his own 'scientific' vocabulary of politics. But he can use it, because it has become part of the language which the masses speak when they come to political meetings. So he interprets the word, giving it his own rationalist construction: the nation was the whole people, the victory of the nation meant the victory of the whole people, 'people like them and me'.[21]

The portrait isn't very flattering. The best analogy of the dynamic emerging in Chatterjee's description is found in A. J. P Taylor's historical account of another, more regressive nationalism. India was to play not too small a part in challenging the latest manifestation of this type and the *Nacht und Nebel* soon to engulf Europe a second time. Nehru's *Jat* is like the Junker agrarian class to whose philistine conservative heart, a century before, Bismarck would periodically make his sentimental and fictitious appeal.[22] The objectives are identical, how 'to situate nationalism within the domain of a state ideology', and so is the chicanery.[23] The constitutionalism of the Frankfurt Assembly yielded to the might of Prussian militarism, leaving nothing behind but the small voices, in the contemporary context of 1848 and German unification, of Marx and Engels.[24] The analogy at first sight between Nehru and Bismarck might seem outlandish. From Chatterjee's perspective, however, we see the germ of nationalist ideology first planted when, a generation earlier, the spurious nature of the absolutist state's appeal to Junker sentiment as an abstract ideal would go over the heads of the rural farmers' more brilliant sons. The Kaul-Nehru Brahmins descended from Kashmir to join the eminent class of judges, leading landlords and industrialists of the United Provinces. These were the same *parvenu* social types, academics whose exclusive (the liberals excluded the masses) deliberations ended up in a collaborationist solution.

With their hubris of self-determination, all nationalists necessarily fail to graduate beyond the immaturity of Kant's kingdom of ends; or rather, the nationalist, his head 'bloody but unbowed' joins with his cohorts in fashioning this Spartan utopia into the republican state.[25] The European tradition, Kedourie goes on to convincingly note in Rousseau, Fichte and Schleiermacher, culminates in a vision of the state that is, essentially speaking, totalitarian. The *trahison des clercs* under the ominous threat of Prussia consists in the belief that 'the end of politics and the vocation of all citizens was that absorption into the universal consciousness which hitherto had been the ambition only of a few philosophers and mystics'.[26] Nehru's nationalist discourse resembles the Fichtean premise: it is the state's prerogative 'to apply the whole surplus power of all its citizens, without exception, for the furtherance of its own purposes'.[27] This was the historical realisation of the nation bequeathed to Asia from Europe that Tagore regarded as the greatest evil to afflict Indians. From Chatterjee's critical perspective, Nehru is culpable not in spite but because of his awareness of this tendency. We saw how Nehru inveighed against his critics in his prison notebook published as *The Discovery of India*, pointing to the absurdity of claiming that the state planning required to ameliorate the iniquitous effects of colonial rule resembled taking life in a socialist direction: '[I]t is absurd to talk of socialism in a country dominated by an alien power.'[28] After surveying the latent contradictions of the nationalist project in its appropriation of the past, especially in Savarkar's and Ambedkar's thinking, we are entitled to question the feasibility of any project that deliberately sacrifices a reversion to totalitarian measures once the British policy of maintaining its capitalist ideology of surplus extraction as a tenable vision of the direction India ought to take had been discredited in the hearts and minds of Indian people.

Notes

Preface

1. R. K. Narayan, preface, *The Mahabharata – A Shortened Modern Prose Version* (2001).
2. Romila Thapar, *The Penguin History of Early India – From the Origins to AD 1300* (2002), p. 20.
3. Ibid., p. 20.
4. Ibid., p. 19.
5. Ranajit Guha, 'Dominance Without Hegemony and Its Historiography', *Subaltern Studies 6 – Writings on South Asian History and Society*, ed. Ranajit Guha (1999), p. 271, emphasis in original.

1 Historiography and narrative

1. Erich Auerbach, *Mimesis – The Representation of Reality in Western Literature*, trans. Willard Trask (2003), p. 19.
2. Jean-François Lyotard, *The Postmodern Condition – A Report on Knowledge*, trans. Geoff Bennington and Brian Massumi (1997), p. xxiv.
3. Robert Eagleton and Susan Pitt, 'The Good of History: Ethics, Post-structuralism and the Representation of the Past', *Rethinking History* 2: 3, 1998, p. 309.
4. Thomas Carlyle, 'On History', *A Carlyle Reader – Selections from the Writings of Thomas Carlyle*, ed. G. B. Tennyson (1969), pp. 59–60.
5. A. J. P. Taylor, *The Origins of the Second World War* (1991), p. 36.
6. Northrop Frye, *Anatomy of Criticism – Four Essays* (1990), p. 12.
7. Ibid., p. 7.
8. Eagleton and Pitt, 'The Good of History', p. 310.
9. Michel Foucault, *Power/Knowledge – Selected Interviews and Other Writings 1972–1977 by Michel Foucault*, ed. Colin Gordon (1980), p. 69.
10. Ibid., p. 98.
11. Georg Wilhelm Friedrich Hegel, *The Philosophy of History*, trans. J. Sibree (1956), p. 20.
12. Slavoj Žižek, *Violence* (2008), p. 12.
13. Hegel, *Philosophy of History*, p. 21.
14. G. W. F. Hegel, *Phenomenology of Spirit*, trans. A. V. Miller (1977), p. 119, emphasis in original.
15. Rabindranath Tagore, *Nationalism* (1917), p. 7.
16. For Michel Foucault's idea of the regime of 'Bio-power', see the last part of *The History of Sexuality, An Introduction*, trans. Robert Hurley (1990).
17. See Judith Butler, *The Psychic Life of Power – Theories in Subjection* (1997).

18 The young Marx in *Economic and Philosophic Manuscripts of 1844* would investigate Hegel's propositions concerning the nullity of objectivity on the way to achieving the apotheosis of Absolute Knowledge. *The Marx and Engels Reader*, ed. Robert Tucker (1978). Gayatri Spivak concludes: 'Marx's own ostensible project, in this early phase, seems to be to establish self-identity [in contrast to self-alienation in the Hegelian totality] through access to a self-determination that will annul the difference established by history.' *A Critique of Postcolonial Reason – Toward a History of the Vanishing Present* (1999), p. 78.
19 Hayden White, *Tropics of Discourse – Essays in Cultural Criticism* (1985), pp. 2–3.
20 Hannah Arendt, *Eichmann in Jerusalem – A Report on the Banality of Evil* (2006).
21 Louis Althusser, *The Humanist Controversy and Other Writings*, trans. G. M. Goshgarian, ed. François Matheron (2003), p. 20.
22 For a basic comprehensive account of the various sides of the debate, see Richard Evans, *In Defence of History* (2000).
23 Hayden White, *Metahistory – The Historical Imagination in Nineteenth-century Europe* (1975), p. xii.
24 Walter Benjamin, 'Theses on the Philosophy of History', *Illuminations*, trans. Harry Zohn (1992), p. 247.
25 Edward Said, *Culture and Imperialism* (1993), p. 327.
26 White, *Tropics of Discourse*, p. 4.
27 White, *Metahistory*, p. 108.
28 Hayden White, *The Content of the Form – Narrative Discourse and Historical Representation* (1987), p. 115.
29 Benjamin, 'Theses on the Philosophy of History', p. 247.
30 Ibid., p. 255.
31 See *The Correspondence of Walter Benjamin and Gershom Scholem, 1932–1940*, ed. Gershom Scholem, trans. Gary Smith and André Lefevere (1992).
32 Jean Baudrillard, *Simulacra and Simulation*, trans. Sheila Glaser (1994), pp. 9–10, emphases in original.
33 W. B. Yeats, 'Sailing to Byzantium', *Yeats's Poems*, ed. A. Norman Jeffares (1991), p. 302.
34 Friedrich Nietzsche, *The Birth of Tragedy Out of the Spirit of Music*, trans. Shaun Whiteside (2003), p. 110.
35 Benjamin, 'The Work of Art in the Age of Mechanical Reproduction', *Illuminations*, p. 215.
36 Nietzsche, *Birth of Tragedy*, p. 81.
37 Amartya Sen, *The Argumentative Indian – Writings on Indian History, Culture and Identity* (2005), p. 332.
38 Louis Dumont, *La Civilization indienne et nous* (1964).
39 Lyotard, *Postmodern Condition*, p. 21.
40 Ibid., p. 27.
41 Benjamin, *Illuminations*, p. 247, emphasis in original.
42 See Alex Callinicos's *Making History – Agency, Structure and Change in Social Theory* (1987) and *Theory and Narratives – Reflections on the Philosophy of History* (1997).
43 See Richard Ellmann, *Yeats – The Man and the Masks* (1987).
44 Raymond Williams, *Marxism and Literature* (1977), p. 128.
45 Ibid., p. 132, emphasis in original.
46 Bernard Cohn, 'The Pasts of an Indian Village', *An Anthropologist amongst the Historians and Other Essays*, ed. Ranajit Guha (2006), p. 98.
47 Louis Althusser, *Lenin and Philosophy and Other Essays*, trans. Ben Brewster (2001), pp. 109–10.
48 Michel Foucault, *The Order of Things – An Archaeology of the Human Sciences* (2003), p. xvi.

49 Abu al-Fazl, *The Akbar-Nama*, trans. Henry Beveridge (1972), p. 179.
50 Ibid., p. 180.
51 Frances Yates, *The Rosicrucian Enlightenment* (2004), p. 57.
52 White, *Metahistory*, p. 306.
53 M. K. Gandhi, *Hind Swaraj and Other Writings* (1997), p. 189.
54 Williams, *Marxism and Literature*, p. 130.
55 Thomas Trautmann, 'Indian Time, European Time', *Time – Histories and Ethnologies*, eds Diane Hughs and Thomas Trautmann (1998), p. 167.
56 Plutarch, *The Age of Alexander – Nine Greek Lives by Plutarch*, trans. Ian Scott-Kilvert (1973), p. 254.
57 *Ephesians* 3: 21, 1: 21.
58 Francis Fukuyama, *The End of History and the Last Man* (1992), p. 50.
59 See Samuel Huntingdon, *The Clash of Civilisations and the Remaking of the World Order* (2002).
60 Frederic Jameson, *Marxism and Form – Twentieth Century Dialectical Theories of Literature* (1974), pp. 34–5, 168.
61 Ibid., p. 105.
62 Alex Callinicos, *Against Postmodernism – A Marxist Critique* (2002), pp. 128–32.
63 See Jameson's conclusion to the debates among Ernst Bloch, Georg Lukács, Bertolt Brecht, Walter Benjamin, Theodor Adorno, *Aesthetics and Politics* (1992), p. 207.
64 See M. H. Abrams, *Natural Supernaturalism – Tradition and Revolution in Romantic Literature* (1973).
65 Jameson, *Aesthetics and Politics*, p. 203.
66 Ernest Gellner, *Nations and Nationalism* (2007), pp. 93–4.
67 Ernest Gellner, *Encounters with Nationalism* (1995), p. 3.
68 The rest of T. S. Eliot's 1923 review of James Joyce's novel *Ulysses* is to be found in *Selected Prose*, ed. Frank Kermode (1975), p. 177.
69 Frederic Jameson, 'Third World Literature in the Era of Multinational Capital', *Social Text* 15, 1986, p. 66, emphasis in original.
70 Ibid., emphasis in original.
71 Marshall Berman, *All That Is Solid Melts into Air* (1983), p. 17.
72 Jameson, 'Third World Literature', p. 68.
73 Homi Bhabha, *The Location of Culture* (1995), p. 219, emphases in original.
74 Jameson, 'Third World Literature', p. 69.
75 Gellner, *Nations and Nationalism*, p. 92.
76 Gellner, *Encounters with Nationalism*, p. 18.
77 Fernand Braudel, *The Mediterranean and the Mediterranean World in the Age of Philip II*, vol. 1, trans. Siân Reynolds (1995), p. 41.
78 Ibid., p. 35.
79 Gellner, *Nations and Nationalism*, p. 44.
80 Donald Bloxham, *The Great Game of Genocide – Imperialism, Nationalism, and the Destruction of the Ottoman Armenians* (2007), p. 62.
81 Ibid., p. 54.
82 Kwame Nkrumah, *Class Struggle in Africa* (1970), p. 83.
83 See Handan Nezir Akmeşe, *The Birth of Modern Turkey – The Ottoman Military and the March to World War I* (2005).
84 Typically, see Bhabha, 'Interrogating Identity – Frantz Fanon and the Postcolonial Prerogative', *Location of Culture*.
85 Partha Chatterjee, *The Nation and Its Fragments – Colonial and Postcolonial Histories* (1993), p. 3.
86 Jack Goody, *The Theft of History* (2006), p. 105.
87 Andrew Wheatcroft, *Infidels – A History of the Conflict between Christendom and Islam* (2004), p. 125.
88 Ibid., p. 130.

Notes

89 See Charles-Louis de Secondat, Baron de la Brède et de Montesquieu's *The Persian Letters* (1758 edition), trans. George Healey (1999).
90 Jacques Derrida, *Monolingualism of the Other: Or, the Prosthesis of Origin*, trans. Patrick Mensah (1998), p. 14.
91 Wheatcroft, *Infidels*, p. 22. Goody, *The Theft of History*, p. 108.
92 Gellner, *Encounters with Nationalism*, p. 83.
93 Vinayak Damodar Savarkar, *Indian War of Independence – 1857* (1947), p. 276.
94 Gellner, *Nations and Nationalism*, p. 111.
95 Braudel, *The Mediterranean*, p. 102.
96 Michel Foucault, *The Archaeology of Knowledge*, trans. Alan Sheridan (1995), p. 3.
97 Braudel, *The Mediterranean*, p. 104.
98 Ibid., p. 20.
99 Ibid., p. 96.
100 White, *Metahistory*, p. 15, 19.
101 Ibid., p. 19.
102 See the following: Jacob Burkhardt's, *Force and Freedom: An Interpretation of History* and *Judgements on History and Historians*.
103 'It is worlds removed from that spirit of proud worldliness which Machiavelli expresses in relating the fame of those Florentine citizens who, in their struggle against the Pope and his excommunication, had "Love of their native city higher than the fear for the salvation of their souls".' Max Weber, *The Protestant Ethic and the Spirit of Capitalism*, trans. Talcott Parsons (2004), p. 63.
104 Niccolò Machiavelli, *The Prince*, trans. George Bull (2003), p. 4.
105 Ayesha Jalal, *Democracy and Authoritarianism in South Asia – A Comparative and Historical Perspective* (1998), p. 128.
106 Bhiku Parekh, 'Jawaharlal Nehru and the Crisis of Modernisation', *Crisis and Change in Contemporary India*, eds Upendra Baxi and Bhiku Parekh (1995), p. 47.
107 Marx and Engels, *The German Ideology*, ed. C. J. Arthur (1999), p. 65.
108 Jameson, *Marxism and Form*, p. 197.
109 See Jameson's foreword to Lyotard, *The Postmodern Condition*, p. xii.
110 Adam Smith, *The Wealth of Nations, Books 1 to 3* (1999), p. 123.
111 Christopher Hill, *The Century of Revolution, 1603–1714* (2002), p. 211.
112 Ibid., p. 209.
113 White, *Content of the Form*, p. 1.
114 White, *Tropics of Discourse*, p. 70. The Idiographic mode of explanation in the essay published in this anthology earlier featured as the Formist theory in *Metahistory* (pp. 13–15).
115 White, *Content of the Form*, p. 61.
116 Edmund Burke, 'Reflections on the Revolution in France', *Burke, Paine, Godwin and the Revolution Controversy*, ed. Marilyn Butler (1993), p. 47.
117 Immanuel Kant, 'The Idea for a Universal History from a Cosmopolitical Point of View', *Toward Perpetual Peace and Other Writings on Politics, Peace, and History*, ed. Pauline Kleingeld, trans. David Colclasure (2006), p. 5.
118 Immanuel Kant, 'Conflict of the Philosophy Faculty with the Faculty of Law', *Toward Perpetual Peace*, p. 155, emphasis added.
119 White, *Content of the Form*, p. 69, 70.
120 Ibid., p. 70.
121 See 'Critique of the Gotha Program' and 'Socialism: Utopian and Scientific', *The Marx and Engels Reader*.
122 Callinicos, *Theories and Narratives*, p. 70, 72.
123 Hayden White, 'Historical Emplotment and the Problem of Truth', *Probing the Limit of Representation – Nazism and the 'Final Solution'*, ed. Saul Friedlander (1996), p. 37.
124 Ibid., p. 43.

125 White, *Content of the Form*, p. 71.
126 White, *Probing the Limits*, p. 50, 51.
127 Ibid., p. 94.
128 Ranajit Guha, 'On Some Aspects of the Historiography of Colonial India', *Subaltern Studies 1 – Writings on South Asian History and Society*, ed. Ranajit Guha (1999), p. 1.
129 Ibid., pp. 5–6, emphasis in original.
130 Guha, 'Historiography of Colonial India', p. 6.
131 Dipesh Chakrabarty, 'Postcoloniality and the Artifice of History: Who Speaks for "Indian" Pasts?' *Representations* 37: 1992, p. 1.
132 Bernard S. Cohn, *Colonialism and Its Forms of Knowledge – The British in India* (1996), p. 5.
133 G. Aloysius quotes T. Raychaudhuri's characterisation of Cambridge historiography as Animal Politics in his account *Nationalism without a Nation in India* (2005), p. 5.
134 'Dominance without Hegemony and Its Historiography', Ranajit Guha, *Subaltern Studies 6 – Writings on South Asian History and Society*, ed. Ranajit Guha (1989), p. 271, 309.
135 Ibid., p. 215, emphases in original.
136 Alasdair MacIntyre, *After Virtue* (1981), p. 201.
137 Chatterjee, *Nation and Its Fragments*, p. 237.
138 White, *Content of the Form*, p. 63.
139 Ibid., p. 9.
140 White, *Content of the Form*, p. 11.
141 Lyotard, *Postmodern Condition*, p. 30.
142 Ibid., p. 32.
143 Ibid., p. 31, emphasis added.
144 Frederic Jameson, *Postmodernism, or, the Cultural Logic of Late Capitalism* (1996), p. 36.
145 See Aijaz Ahmad's masterly critique of Jameson's essay 'Third World Literature in the Era of Multinational Capital' as a product of this nostalgic style of thought: *In Theory – Classes, Nations, Literatures* (1994).
146 Karl Marx, 'Contribution to the Critique of Hegel's *Philosophy of Right*', *Marx and Engels Reader*, p. 54.
147 Karl Marx, *Grundrisse*, trans. Martin Nicolaus (1993), p. 107.
148 Karl Marx and Friedrich Engels, *The Communist Manifesto* (1985), p. 83.
149 Althusser, *Lenin and Philosophy and Other Essays*, p. 109.
150 Marx, *Grundrisse*, p. 84.
151 Gandhi, *Hind Swaraj*, p. 38.
152 G. W. F. Hegel, *Lectures on the Philosophy of World History*, trans. H. B. Nisbet (1993), p. 93.
153 Max Weber, *The Religion of India – The Sociology of Hinduism and Buddhism*, trans. Hans Gerth and Don Martindale (1960), p. 18.
154 Marx and Engels, *Communist Manifesto*, pp. 83–4.
155 E. M. S. Namboodripad, 'Evolution of Society, Language and Literature', *Marxism and Indology*, ed. Debiprasad Chattopadhyaya (1981), pp. 35–44.
156 Ahmad, *In Theory*, p. 241, Karl Marx, 'The British Rule in India', 'The Future Results of British Rule in India', *Marx and Engels Reader*, p. 658, 663.
157 Namboodripad, *Marxism and Indology*, p. 42.
158 Marx, 'The Future Results of British Rule in India', p. 663.
159 Edward Said, *Orientalism – Western Conceptions of the Orient* (1991), p. 155.
160 Ahmad, *In Theory*, p. 229.
161 Benjamin, *Illuminations*, p. 247.
162 Jameson, *Cultural Logic of Late Capitalism*, pp. 368–9.

2 The historical sense

1. Jean-François Lyotard, *The Differend – Phrases in Dispute*, trans. Georges Van Den Abbeele (1988), p. 151, 155.
2. Walter Benjamin, 'Theses on the Philosophy of History', *Illuminations*, trans. Harry Zohn (1992), p. 245.
3. Keith Jenkins, *Re-thinking History* (2003), p. 75.
4. Jean-François Lyotard, *The Postmodern Condition – A Report on Knowledge*, trans. Geoff Bennington and Brian Massumi (1997), p. 56, 65, 66.
5. Lyotard, *Differend*, p. 152.
6. 'If one wishes to establish the existence of gas chambers, the four silent negations must be withdrawn: There were no gas chambers, were there? Yes, there were. – But even if there were, that cannot be formulated, can it? Yes, it can. – But even if it can be formulated, there is no one, at least, who has the authority to formulate it, and no one with the authority to hear it (it is not communicable), is there? Yes, there is.' Lyotard, *Differend*, p. 14.
7. Ibid., p. 152.
8. Giambattista Vico, *New Science – Principles of the New Science Concerning the Common Nature of Nations*, trans. David Marsh (2001), p. 129.
9. Ibid., p. 131, emphasis in original.
10. Raymond Williams, *Marxism and Literature* (1977), p. 17.
11. R. G. Collingwood, *The Idea of History* (1994), p. 92.
12. Ibid., p. 92.
13. Ibid., p. 65.
14. Vico, *New Science*, p. 125.
15. Ibid., p. 126.
16. Johann Gottfried Herder, *Philosophy of the History of Man*, trans. T. Churchill (1800), p. 305.
17. Herder, op. cit., p. 305.
18. Ibid., p. 125.
19. Ibid., p. 123.
20. Ibid., p. 306.
21. Herder, op. cit., p. 306.
22. Arrian, *The Campaigns of Alexander*, trans. Aubrey de Sélincourt (1971), pp. 351–2.
23. A. K. Narain, 'Alexander and India', *Greece and Rome*, 12: 2, 1965, p. 157.
24. Lyotard, *Differend*, p. 157.
25. Herder, *Philosophy of History*, p. 307.
26. Ibid., pp. 307–308.
27. See the survey in Thomas Metcalf's *Ideologies of the Raj* (1998).
28. Herder, *Philosophy of History*, p. 308.
29. Ibid.
30. Ibid., p. 309.
31. Ibid., p. 310.
32. King Leopold II, 'The Sacred Mission of Civilization'; the title of a pamphlet prepared in 1953 for the United Nations by the Belgian government. For Leopold's original adumbration of tasks for the Belgian soldiers of the state in the Congo, see Guy Burrows, *The Land of the Pigmies* (1898), p. 286.
33. Aimé Césaire, *Discourse on Colonialism*, trans. Joan Pinkham (1972), p. 51.
34. Jacques Derrida, *Of Grammatology*, trans. Gayatri Spivak (1976).
35. Emile Durkheim, *Suicide – A Study in Sociology*, trans. John Spaulding and George Simpson (2002), p. 216. Emile Durkheim and Marcel Mauss, *Primitive Classification*, trans. Rodney Needham (1963), p. 84.
36. Césaire, *Discourse on Colonialism*, p. 52.

37 Vico, *New Science*, p. 306.
38 Joseph Conrad, *Heart of Darkness* (1988), p. 10.
39 Césaire, *Discourse on Colonialism*, p. 53.
40 Vico, *New Science*, p. 48.
41 Ibid., p. 47.
42 François-Marie Aroet, Voltaire, *Candide and Other Stories*, trans. Roger Pearson (1998), p. 151.
43 Ibid., p. 160.
44 Friedrich Nietzsche, *The Pre-Platonic Philosophers*, trans. Greg Whitlock (2006), p. 3.
45 Vico, *New Science*, p. 48.
46 Nietzsche, *Pre-Platonic Philosophers*.
47 Ibid., p. 42.
48 Nietzsche, *Pre-Platonic Philosophers*, p. 15.
49 Plutarch, *Age of Alexander*, pp. 259–60.
50 Nietzsche, *Pre-Platonic Philosophers*, p. 14.
51 Durkheim and Mauss, *Primitive Classification*, p. 79.
52 Michel Foucault, 'Nietzsche, Genealogy, History', *Language, Counter-memory, Practice – Selected Essays and Interviews by Michel Foucault*, trans. Donald Bouchard and Sherry Simon (1980), p. 143.
53 Michel Foucault, *The Order of Things – An Archaeology of the Human Sciences* (2003), pp. 400–401.
54 Michel Foucault, *Language, Counter-memory, Practice – Selected Essays and Interviews by Michel Foucault*, trans. Donald Bouchard and Sherry Simon (1980), p. 151.
55 Georges Lefebvre, *The French Revolution*, trans. Elizabeth Evanson (2005), p. 18.
56 Ibid., p. 141.
57 C. L. R. James, *The Black Jacobins – Toussaint L'Ouverture and the San Domingo Revolution* (2001), p. 163.
58 Jenkins, *Re-thinking History*, p. 84, 13.
59 Peter Novick, *That Noble Dream – The 'Objectivity Question' and the American Historical Profession* (1999).
60 Foucault, *Language, Counter-memory, Practice*, p. 140.
61 Jenkins, *Re-thinking History*, p. 66.
62 Karl Marx, 'The Eighteenth Brumaire of Louis Bonaparte,' *The Marx and Engels Reader*, ed. Robert Tucker (1978), p. 595.
63 Ibid., p. 596.
64 Foucault, *Power/Knowledge*, p. 105.
65 Lefebvre, *The French Revolution*, p. 58.
66 Étienne Bonnot de Condillac, *Essay on the Origin of Human Knowledge*, trans. Hans Aaarsleff (2001), p. 42.
67 John Locke, *An Essay Concerning Human Understanding*, ed. Kenneth Winkler (1996), p. 148.
68 Jean-Antonine-Nicholas de Caritat, marquis de Condorcet, *Sketch for a Historical Picture of the Progress of the Human Mind*, trans. June Barraclough (1955), p. 124.
69 Emmet Kennedy, *A Philosophe in the Age of Revolution – Destutt de Tracy and the Origins of 'Ideology'* (1978), p. 215.
70 Friedrich Nietzsche, *Thus Spoke Zarathustra – A Book for Everyone and No One*, trans. R. J. Hollingdale (2003), p. 39.
71 Césaire, *Discourse on Colonialism*, p. 57.
72 J. B. Bury, 'The Science of History', *The Varieties of History: From Voltaire to the Present*, ed. Fritz Stern (1973), p. 223.
73 Louis Althusser and Étienne Balibar, *Reading Capital*, trans. Ben Brewster (2004), p. 28, emphasis in original.

74 For '"Determination by the Economic": The Althusserian Solution', see S. H. Rigby, *Marxism and History – A Critical Introduction* (1998), pp. 194–9.
75 Lawrence Stone, 'The Revival of Narrative', *Past and Present*, 85 (1979), p. 17.
76 W. H. Auden, *Selected Poems*, ed. Edward Mendelson (1979), p. 199.
77 Romila Thapar, 'Epic and History', *Past and Present*, 125 (1989), p. 3.
78 T. S. Eliot, 'The Social Function of Poetry', *On Poetry and Poets* (1990), p. 23.
79 Ibid., p. 25.
80 T. S. Eliot, *Selected Prose*, ed. Frank Kermode (1975), p. 65.
81 Frederic Jameson, *Postmodernism, or, the Cultural Logic of Late Capitalism* (1996), p. xix.
82 Pierre Bourdieu, *Distinction – A Social Critique of the Judgement of Taste*, trans. Richard Nice (2003), p. 54.
83 V. I. Lenin, *Revolution at the Gates – A Selection of Writings from February to October 1917*, ed. Slavoj Žižek (2002), p. 56.
84 MacIntyre, Alasdair, *After Virtue* (1981), p. 216.
85 Lyotard, *The Postmodern Condition*, p. 41.
86 Jameson, *Postmodernism, or, the Cultural Logic of Late Capitalism*, p. xx.
87 Eliot, 'Tradition and the Individual Talent', *Selected Prose*, p. 38.
88 See Antoinette Burton, 'Who Needs the Nation? Interrogating "British" History', *Journal of Historical Sociology*, 10: 3, 1997, pp. 227–48.
89 Eliot, *Selected Prose*, p. 39.
90 T. S. Eliot, 'The Wasteland', *Selected Poems* (1961), p. 60, 67.
91 Ibid., p. 72, 74.
92 Eliot, 'Gerontion', *Selected Poems*, p. 32.
93 Romila Thapar, *Early India*, p. 16.
94 Herodotus, *The Histories*, trans. Aubrey de Sélincourt (2003), p. 1.
95 Ibid., p. 43.
96 Anthony Grafton, *What Was History? The Art of History in Early Modern Europe* (2007), p. 31.
97 Herodotus, *Histories*, p. 40.
98 Eric Auerbach, *Mimesis – The Representation of Reality in Western Literature*, trans. Willard Trask (2003), p. 13.
99 *The Epic of Gilgamesh*, trans. Andrew George (2003), p. 99.
100 Jawaharlal Nehru, *Glimpses of World History* (2004), p. 19.
101 See Rashid Khalidi's account, *The Iron Cage – The Story of Palestinian Struggle for Statehood* (2006).
102 Ronald Hyam, *Britain's Declining Empire – The Road to Decolonisation, 1918–1968* (2006), p. 50, 57.
103 Churchill quoted by Hyam, *Britain's Declining Empire*, p. 55.
104 Auerbach, *Mimesis*, p. 23.
105 Soren Kierkegaard, *Fear and Trembling*, trans. Alastair Hannay (2003), p. 66.
106 Auerbach, *Mimesis*, pp. 43–4.
107 Ibid., p. 38.
108 Max Weber, *The Protestant Ethic and the Spirit of Capitalism*, trans. Talcott Parsons (2004), p. 60.
109 Harold Bloom, *The Western Canon – The Books and School of the Ages* (1996), p. 7.
110 Ibid., p. 6, emphasis added.
111 See Chapter 5 of Ilan Pappe's *The Ethnic Cleansing of Palestine* (2007) for the trail of responsibility of mass expulsions and systematic extermination of Palestinian villagers in Operation Naschon during April 1948.
112 Auerbach, *Mimesis*, p. 39.
113 Kierkegaard, *Fear and Trembling*, pp. 66–7.
114 Lyotard, *The Differend*, p. 107.

115 Theodor Adorno and Max Horkheimer, *Dialectic of Enlightenment*, trans. John Cumming (1999), p. 130.
116 See Heidegger's interpretation of this problem in 'Plato's *Republic*: The Distance of the Art (*Mimesis*) from Truth (*Idea*)', *Nietzsche – The Will to Power as Art; The Eternal Recurrence of the Same*, trans. David Krell (1991).
117 Virgil, *The Aeneid*, trans. David West (1991), p. 42.
118 Homer, *The Iliad*, trans. Robert Fagles (1991), p. 590.
119 Adorno and Horkheimer, *Dialectic of Enlightenment*, pp. 79–80.
120 Perry Anderson, *Passages from Antiquity to Feudalism* (2006), p. 152.
121 Herodotus, *The Histories*, p. 4.
122 Homer, *The Iliad*, p. 589.
123 Ibid., p. 509.
124 John Lemprière, *Lemprière's Classical Dictionary* (1987), p. 297.
125 Herodotus, *The Histories*, p. 134.
126 Ibid., p. 128.
127 Herodotus, *The Histories*, p. 125.

3 *Hindutva* and writing postcolonial India

1 Ernest Renan, 'Qu'est qu'une nation?' (Conference faite en Sorbonne le mars 1882, Paris, 1882), pp. 7–8: 'L'oubli et je dirai même l'erreur historique, sont un facteur essentiel de la formation d'une nation et c'est ainsi que le progrès des études historiques est souvent pour la nationalité un danger' ('Amnesia and even historical error are an essential part of the formation of a nation, thus progress in historical writing often represents a danger for nationality'), quoted by E. J. Hobsbawm, *Nation and Nationalism since 1780 – Programme, Myth, Reality* (2005), p. 12. My translation.
2 H. H. Risley, *The People of India* (London: W. Thacker, 1915), p. 291.
3 Vinayak Damodar Savarkar, *Indian War of Independence – 1857* (1947), p. 542.
4 Vinayak Damodar Savarkar, *Six Glorious Epochs of Indian History*, trans. S. T. Godbole (Bombay: Bal Savarkar, 1971), p. 8.
5 Ibid., p. 24.
6 Savarkar, *Six Glorious Epochs*, p. 16.
7 *Srimad Bhagavata Purana, Book 10*, trans. Edwin Bryant (2003), p. 113.
8 Arrian, *Campaigns of Alexander*, trans., Aubrey de Sélincourt (1971), p. 256.
9 The page is reproduced in Alice Albinia's book *Empires of the Indus – The Story of a River* (2008).
10 Savarkar, *Six Glorious Epochs*, p. 40.
11 Hemachandra Raychaudhuri, *Political History of Ancient India* (1996), p. 586.
12 Savarkar, *Six Glorious Epochs*, p. 41.
13 Thomas Trautmann, *Kautilya and the Athashastra – A Statistical Investigation of the Authorship and Evolution of the Text* (1971), p. 14, 22.
14 Savarkar, *Six Glorious Epochs*, p. 45.
15 Ibid., p. 44.
16 Ibid., p. 34.
17 Savarkar, *Six Glorious Epochs*, p. 10.
18 Auriel Stein, *On Alexander's Track to the Indus – Personal Narrative of Explorations on the North-west Frontier of India* (London: MacMillan and Co., 1929), pp. 44–5.
19 Plates with articles excavated at Sirkap can be found in John Marshall's *A Guide to Taxila* (1918).
20 John Marshall, *Taxila – An Illustrated Account of Archaeological Excavations carried out under the orders of the Government of India between the years 1913 and 1934* (1951), p. 43.
21 Marshall, op. cit., p. 43.
22 Vinayak Damodar Savarkar, *The Maratha Movement (Hindu Pad Padashahi)* –

216 Notes

   Story of the Maratha Struggle to Re-establish Sovereign Hindu Power (2003), p. 20.
23 Savarkar, *Six Glorious Epochs*, p. 1.
24 Ibid., p. 17.
25 Savarkar, *The Maratha Movement*, p. iii.
26 Savarkar, *Six Glorious Epochs*, p. 4.
27 Hayden White, *Metahistory – The Historical Imagination in Nineteenth-century Europe* (1975), p. 38.
28 Hobsbawm, *Nations and Nationalism*, p. 124.
29 Jawaharlal Nehru, *The Discovery of India* (1946), p. 465.
30 Partha Chatterjee, *Nationalist Thought and the Colonial World – A Derivative Discourse* (1993), p. 145.
31 Friedrich Engels, 'Socialism: Utopian and Scientific', *The Marx and Engels Reader*, ed. Robert Tucker (1978), p. 685.
32 Ernest Gellner, *Encounters with Nationalism* (1995), p. 17.
33 Chatterjee, *Nationalist Thought*, p. 159.
34 Jawaharlal Nehru, *Glimpses of World History* (2004), pp. 355–6.
35 Friedrich Nietzsche, 'On the Uses and Disadvantages of History for Life', *Untimely Meditations*, trans. R. J. Hollingdale (2003), p. 68, emphasis in original.
36 Nehru, *Discovery of India*, pp. 224–5.
37 Nehru, *Glimpses of World History*, p. 60.
38 Nehru quoted by Bikhu Parekh, *Crisis and Change in Contemporary India*, eds, Upendra Baxi and Bhiku Parekh (1995), p. 48.
39 White, *Metahistory*, p. 25.
40 Nehru, *Glimpses of World History*, p. 57.
41 Ibid., p. 54.
42 Nehru, *Glimpses of World History*, pp. 209–10.
43 Jules Michelet, *History of the French Revolution*, trans. George Cocks (1967), p. 450.
44 Nehru, *Glimpses of World History*, p. 210.
45 Nehru, *Glimpses of World History*, p. 210.
46 Chatterjee, *Nationalist Thought*, p. 147.
47 Ibid.
48 Savarkar, *The Maratha Movement*, p. 22.
49 Ranajit Guha, *Dominance without Hegemony – History and Power in Colonial India* (1997), p. 101.
50 Ibid., p. 103. Emphasis is mine.
51 *The History of the Trial of Warren Hastings*, vol. 6 (1796), p. 350.
52 Sara Suleri, *The Rhetoric of English India* (1992), p. 51.
53 Bernard S. Cohn, *Colonialism and Its Forms of Knowledge – The British in India* (1996), p. 74.
54 Ibid., p. 68.
55 Romila Thapar, *The Penguin History of Early India – From the Origins to AD 1300* (2002), p. 204.
56 Michel Foucault, 'Governmentality', in *The Foucault Effect: Studies in Governmentality*, eds G. Burchell, *et al.* (1991), p. 91.
57 Thapar, *Early India*, p. 194.
58 Ranajit Guha, '*Dominance without Hegemony* and its Historiography', *Subaltern Studies 6 – Writings on South Asian History and Society*, ed. Ranajit Guha (1999), p. 239.
59 Wolpert, *A New History*, p. 188.
60 B. Chaudhuri, *The Cambridge Economic History of India*, vol. 2: *c.* 1757 – 1970, ed. Dharma Kumar, p. 298.
61 Statistics in B. Chaudhuri, *Cambridge Economic History*, p. 299. Wolpert, *A New History of India*, p. 188.

Notes   217

62 Bankim Chandra Chatterjee, *Anandamath*, trans. Basanta Roy (1992), p. 43.
63 Nicos Poulantzas, *State, Power, Socialism*, trans. Patrick Camiller (2000), p. 77. Emphasis is in original.
64 Rudyard Kipling, *Kim* (1987) p. 52.
65 Edward Said, *Culture and Imperialism* (1993), p. 178.
66 Stanley Wolpert, *A New History of India* (2004), p. 233. Emphasis is mine.
67 Chatterjee, *Nationalist Thought*, p. 73.
68 Letter quoted by C. A. Bayly, *Indian Society and the Making of the British Empire* (1997), p. 50.
69 Partha Chatterjee, 'A Religion of Urban Domesticity: Sri Ramakrishna and the Calcutta Middle Class', *Subaltern Studies 7 – Writings on South Asian History and Society*, eds., Partha Chatterjee and Gyanendra Pandey (1999), p. 41.
70 Ranajit Guha, *A Rule of Property for Bengal – An Essay on the Idea of Permanent Settlement* (1996), p. 160.
71 Ibid., p. 54.
72 Chaudhuri, *The Cambridge Economic History of India*, vol. 2, p. 301.
73 Pamphlet reproduced in *Archives of Empire, Volume 1 – From the East India Company to the Suez Canal*, eds, Barbara Harlow and Mia Carter (2003), p. 28. Emphasis is mine.
74 Bankim Chandra Chatterjee, *Anandamath*, trans. Basanta Roy (1992), p. 91.
75 Chatterjee, *Nationalist Thought*, p. 63.
76 Ibid., p. 77.
77 Gellner, *Encounters with Nationalism*, p. 179.
78 Gellner, op. cit., p. 179.
79 Gellner, *Encounters with Nationalism*, pp. 178–9.
80 Ernest Gellner, *Nations and Nationalism* (2007), p. 74.
81 Ibid.
82 Ibid., p. 77.
83 Elie Kedourie, *Nationalism* (2004), p. 1.
84 Gellner, *Nations and Nationalism*, p. 69, 76.
85 Sunil Khilnani, *The Idea of India* (1998), p. 39.
86 Chatterjee, *Nationalist Thought*, p. 10.
87 Michael Hardt and Antonio Negri, *Multitude – War and Democracy in the Age of Empire* (2005), p. 128.
88 Gargi Bhattacharya, 'South Asian Cultural Studies – Lessons from Back Home?' *South Asian Popular Culture*, 1: 1, 2003, pp. 3–11.
89 Chatterjee, *Nationalist Thought*, p. 168.
90 White, *Metahistory*, p. 171, emphasis in original.
91 Gyanendra Pandey, 'In Defense of the Fragment: Writing about Hindu–Muslim Riots in India Today', *Representations* 37: 2, 1992, p. 28.
92 Arvind Sharma, 'On Hindu, Hindustan, Hinduism and Hindutva', *Numen*, 49, 2002, p. 30.
93 V. T. Shetty, foreword to B. R. Ambedkar's *Why Go for Conversion?* (1981), p. 1.
94 Satish Kolluri, 'Minority Existence and the Subject of (Religious) Conversion', *Cultural Dynamics*, 14: 2002, p. 83.
95 Ibid. p. 83.
96 Dibyesh Anand, 'Anxious Sexualities: Masculinity, Nationalism and Violence', *The British Journal of Politics and International Relations*, Political Studies Association, 9: 2007.
97 Poulantzas describes the sudden awareness of violence descending on theorists suffering from Eurocentric light-mindedness when it comes to regimes in the East: Nicos Poulantzas, *State, Power, Socialism*, trans. Patrick Camiller (2000), p. 80.
98 Partha Chatterjee, *Nationalist Thought*, pp. 136–7. Peter Heehs, 'Shades of Orientalism: Paradoxes and Problems in Indian Historiography', *History and Theory*, 42, 2003, p. 172.

218 Notes

99. Thapar, *Early India*, p. 16.
100. G. Aloysius, in his account *Nationalism without a Nation in India* (2005), also neglects to mention V. D. Savarkar's ideas of Hindutva.
101. Khilnani, *The Idea of India*, p. 83.
102. Thapar, *Early India*, p. 19.
103. Dipesh Chakrabarty, 'Postcoloniality and the Artifice of History: Who Speaks for "Indian" Pasts?', *Representations*, Special Issue: Imperial Fantasies and Postcolonial Histories', 37, 1992, p. 1.
104. Ibid., p. 8.
105. Chakrabarty, 'Postcoloniality and the Artifice of History', p. 11. Keith Jenkins, *Re-thinking History* (2003), p. 81.
106. Partha Chatterjee, *The Nation and Its Fragments – Colonial and Postcolonial Histories* (1993), p. 36.
107. Sudeshna Guha, 'Negotiating Evidence: History, Archaeology and the Indus Civilisation', *Modern Asian Studies* 39, 2, 2005, p. 400.
108. Jenkins, *Re-thinking History*, p. 81.
109. I am simplifying the complex methodological permutations in American anthropology that Chakrabarty's analysis owes much of its force to. In Guha's characterisation of the leading proponent of the 'historical' method for anthropological categories, Bernard Cohn, we might say that Chakrabarty, too, is involved in examining 'social and cultural phenomena within processes of long-term secular change'. Bernard S. Cohn, *An Anthropologist among the Historians and Other Essays*, ed. Ranajit Guha (2006), pp. ix–x.
110. Dipesh Chakrabarty, 'The Difference-Deferral of a Colonial Modernity: Public Debates on Domesticity in British Bengal', *Subaltern Studies 8 – Essays in Honour of Ranajit Guha*, eds David Arnold and David Hardiman (1999), p. 77.
111. Claude Lévi-Strauss, *Structural Anthropology 2*, trans. Monique Layton (1994), p. 273.
112. Ibid., p, 274.
113. David Hardiman, 'The Indian "Faction": A Political Theory Examined' and Ranajit Guha's manifesto statement 'On Some Aspects of the Historiography of Colonial India', in *Subaltern Studies 1 – Writings on South Asian History and Society*, p. 223, 8, emphasis is mine.
114. B. R. Ambedkar, *What Gandhi and Congress Have Done to the Untouchables* (1945), p. 44. Gandhi came from a merchant caste family in Gujerat. *Bania* is a pejorative term roughly equivalent to the Napoleonic characterisation of the avaricious 'shopkeeper'.
115. Tilak quoted by Guha, *Dominance without Hegemony*, p. 104.
116. Michel Foucault, 'Nietzsche, Genealogy, History', *Language, Counter-memory, Practice – Selected Essays and Interviews by Michel Foucault*, trans. Donald Bouchard and Sherry Simon (1980), p. 147.
117. Guha describes the Subaltern project in terms of investigating the colonial archives for lacunae in which the historian may be able to discern moments of an 'historic failure of the nation to come to its own'. Ranajit Guha, 'On Some Aspects of the Historiography of Colonial India', p. 7, emphasis in original.
118. Chatterjee, *Nationalist Thought*, p. 132.
119. Jenkins, *Re-thinking History*, p. 75.
120. Sudipta Kaviraj, 'A Critique of the Passive Revolution', *State and Politics in India*, ed. Partha Chatterjee (1998), p. 52, emphasis is mine.
121. Chakrabarty, 'Postcoloniality and the Artifice of History', p. 16.
122. Partha Chatterjee, 'More on Modes of Power and the Peasantry', *Subaltern Studies 2 – Writings on South Asian History and Society*, ed. Ranajit Guha (1999), p. 322.
123. Gayatri Spivak, 'Subaltern Studies: Deconstructing Historiography', *Subaltern Studies 4 – Writings on South Asian History and Society*, ed. Ranajit Guha (1999), p. 357.

124 Thapar, *Early India*, p. 20.
125 Gyanendra Pandey, 'The Appeal of Hindu History', *The Oxford India Hinduism Reader*, eds Vasudha Dalmia and Heinrich von Stietencorn (2007), p. 354. See the following brilliant essays: 'Encounters and Calamities': The History of a North Indian Qasba in the Nineteenth Century', *Subaltern Studies 3 – Writings on South Asian History and Society*, ed. Ranajit Guha (1999), 'The Colonial Construction of 'Communalism': British Writings on Banaras in the Nineteenth Century, *Subaltern Studies 6*, ed. Ranajit Guha (1999).
126 Partha Chatterjee, *A Possible India – Essays in Political Criticism* (1998), p. 230. Emphasis is mine.
127 Reproduced in Donald Bloxham, *The Great Game of Genocide – Imperialism, Nationalism, and the Destruction of the Ottoman Armenians* (2007), Pl. 2.
128 See Ranajit Guha, *A Rule of Property for Bengal – An Essay on the Idea of Permanent Settlement* (1996).
129 Kaviraj, *State and Politics in India*, p. 52.
130 Vinayak Savarkar, *Hindutva – Who is a Hindu?* (1989), p. 18.
131 Tilak quoted in *Modern Hindu Thought – The Essential Texts*, ed. Arvind Sharma (2002), p. 206.
132 Swatantrya Veer Savarkar, *Hindu Sanghatan – Its Ideology and Immediate Programme (A Collection of His Three Presidential Speeches at Karnavati (Ahmadabad), Nagpur and Calcutta)* (1940), p. 3.
133 Gandhi asserts: 'It was not that we did not know how to invent machinery, but our forefathers knew that, if we set our hearts after such things, we would become slaves and lose moral fibre. They therefore, after due deliberation, decided that we should only do what we could with our hands and our feet.' M. K. Gandhi, *Hind Swaraj and Other Writings* (1997), pp. 68–9.
134 Quoted by Chatterjee, *The Nation and Its Fragments*, p. 61, italics signify words in English.
135 Ashis Nandy, *The Intimate Enemy – Loss and Recovery of Self under Colonialism* (1999), p. x.
136 Savarkar, *Hindutva*, p. 141.
137 Savarkar, *Hindu Sanghatan*, pp. 22–3.
138 Ibid., p. 85.
139 Savarkar, *Hindu Sanghatan*, p. 36.
140 Savarkar, *Hindutva*, p. 86.
141 Célestine Bouglé, *Essays on the Caste System by Célestine Bouglé*, trans. D. Pocock (1971), pp. 78–9.
142 Gandhi, *Hind Swaraj*, p. 68.
143 Radhakrishnan, *The Hindu View of Life – The Famous Upton Lectures of 1926* (1964), p. 70.
144 Ibid., p. 69.
145 Savarkar, *Hindutva*, p. 19.
146 Radhakrishnan, *The Hindu View of Life*, p. 42.
147 Gayatri Spivak, *Outside in the Teaching Machine* (1993). Savarkar, *Hindu Sanghatan*, p. 17.
148 Savarkar, *Hindutva*, p. 135.
149 Ibid., p. 100.
150 Ibid., p. 114.
151 Maria Misra, *Vishnu's Crowded Temple – India since the Great Rebellion* (2007), p. 170.
152 Savarkar, *War of Independence*, p. ix.
153 Ibid., p. 285.
154 Ibid., p. 456.
155 Savarkar, *Hindu Sanghatan*, p. 21.

220 *Notes*

156 Benedict Anderson adopts Walter Benjamin's distinction between calendrical 'empty' time and a Messianic temporality to describe nationalist history as community in *Imagined Communities – Reflections on the Origin and Spread of Nationalism* (1991), p. 24.
157 Quoted by Pandey, 'The Appeal of Hindu History', p. 356.
158 Ibid., p. 362.
159 Pandey, 'The Appeal of Hindu History', p. 363.
160 Savarkar, *Hindutva*, p. 4.
161 Ibid., p. 9.
162 Savarkar, *Hindutva*, p. 136.
163 Savarkar, *Hindu Sanghatan*, p. 20.
164 Ibid. p. 2.
165 Wolpert, *A New History of India*, pp. 35–6.
166 Savarkar, *Hindutva*, p. 122.
167 Savarkar, *War of Independence*, p. 144.
168 Savarkar, *Hindutva*, p. 11.
169 Ibid., p. 94, 12.
170 Ibid., p. 15.
171 Pandey, 'The Appeal of Hindu History', p. 354.
172 Savarkar, *Hindutva*, p. 70.
173 Savarkar, *Hindu Sanghatan*, p. 77.
174 Ibid., p. 80.
175 Sujata Bose and Ayesha Jalal, *Modern South Asia – History, Culture, Political Economy* (1998), p. 23.
176 Savarkar, *Six Glorious Epochs*, p. 267.
177 Chatterjee, *Nation and Its Fragments*, p. 82.
178 Yoginder Sikand, *Muslims in India since 1947 – Islamic Perspectives on Inter-faith Relations* (2004), p. 135.
179 Catherine Asher and Cynthia Talbot, *India before Europe* (2006), p. 27.
180 Savarkar, *Hindutva*, p. 46.
181 Martin Heidegger, *Being and Time*, trans., John Macquarrie and Edward Robinson (2005), p. 43.
182 Savarkar, *Hindutva*, pp. 42–3.
183 Abul Fazl, *The Akbar Nama of Abu-l-Fazl*, vol. 1, trans. H. Beveridge (1998), p. 150.
184 Abul Fazl, *Akbar Nama*, vol. 2, p. 68.
185 Ibid., p. 67.
186 Ibid.
187 Ibid., p. 44.
188 Savarkar, *Hindutva*, pp. 21–2.
189 Ibid., p. 30.
190 Savarkar, *Hindutva*, p. 49.
191 Savarkar, *Hindu Sanghatan*, p. 61.
192 *Hindutva*, p. 36.
193 Chatterjee, *The Nation and Its Fragments*, p. 88.
194 Quoted in Chatterjee, *The Nation and Its Fragments*, p. 81.
195 Ibid., p. 81.
196 Chatterjee, *The Nation and Its Fragments*, p. 80.
197 Ibid, p. 81.
198 Savarkar, *Hindutva*, p. 94, 123.
199 Savarkar, *Six Glorious Epochs*, p. 268.
200 Ibid., p. 275.
201 Sigmund Freud, *The Interpretation of Dreams* (1991), p. 285.
202 Radhakrishnan, *The Hindu View of Life*, p. 31, 37, 39.

4 B. R. Ambedkar and the Hindu past

1. B. R. Ambedkar, *Who Were the Shudras? – How They Came to be the Fourth Varna in the Indo-Aryan Society* (1970), p. xxi.
2. Elie Kedourie, *Nationalism* (2004), p. 104.
3. Friedrich Nietzsche, *The Will to Power*, trans. R. J. Hollingdale and Walter Kaufmann (1968), p. 71.
4. Ambedkar, *Who Were the Shudras?* p. xxi, and B. R. Ambedkar, *The Untouchables – Who Were They and Why They Became Untouchables?* (1948), p. vii.
5. Ambedkar, *The Untouchables*, p. viii.
6. Edward Gibbon, *The Decline and Fall of the Roman Empire* (1998), p. 27.
7. Ambedkar, *The Untouchables*, p. 119.
8. Max Weber, *The Religion of India – The Sociology of Hinduism and Buddhism*, trans. Hans Gerth and Don Martindale (1960), p. 36.
9. Ibid., p. 37.
10. Ibid, p. 60.
11. Ibid., p. 93, 96.
12. Ambedkar, *The Untouchables*, p. 36.
13. Ibid., p. 40.
14. Ibid., p. 117.
15. Vinayak Damodar Savarkar, *Six Glorious Epochs of Indian History*, trans. S. T. Godbole (1971), pp. 84–6.
16. Ibid., p. 101.
17. Romila Thapar, *The Penguin History of Early India – From the Origins to AD 1300* (2002), p. 19.
18. Oliver Mendelsohn and Marika Vicziany, *The Untouchables – Subordination, Poverty and the State in Modern India* (1998), pp. 116–17.
19. Thapar, *Early India*, p. 201.
20. Jawaharlal Nehru, *The Discovery of India* (1946), p. 487.
21. Mendelsohn and Vicziany, *The Untouchables*, p. 112.
22. T. S. Wilkinson, *Ambedkar and the Neo-Buddhist Movement*, eds T. S. Wilkinson and M. M. Thomas (1972), p. vii.
23. Mendelsohn and Vicziany, *The Untouchables*, p. 79.
24. Ibid., p. 79.
25. B. R. Ambedkar, *Why Go For Conversion?* trans. Vasant Moon (1981), p. 11.
26. Ambedkar, *The Untouchables*, p. i.
27. Ambedkar, *Who Were the Shudras?*
28. Friedrich Nietzsche, *Twilight of the Idols and The Anti-Christ*, trans. R. J. Hollingdale (2003), p. 69.
29. Nietzsche, *The Will to Power*, p. 71.
30. M. K. Gandhi, *Hind Swaraj and Other Writings* (1997), p. 71.
31. Louis Dumont, *Homo Hierarchicus – The Caste System and Its Implications*, trans. Mark Sainsbury, *et al.* (1980), p. 233.
32. Gandhi, *Hind Swaraj*, p. 52.
33. Ibid., p. 90.
34. Ibid., p. 61.
35. Ibid., p. 188.
36. Ambedkar, *Who Were the Shudras?*, p. 69.
37. M. S. Golwalkar, *Bunch of Thoughts* (1988), p. 109.
38. M. S. Golwalkar, *We, or Our Nation Defined* (1947), p. 13.
39. Stanley Wolpert, *A New History of India* (2004), p. 187.
40. Immanuel Kant, 'An Answer to the Question: What Is Enlightenment?', *Kant's Political Writings*, trans. H. B. Nisbet, ed. Hans Reiss (1970), p. 59. Emphasis in original.

222 Notes

41 B. R. Ambedkar, *What Congress and Gandhi Have Done to the Untouchables* (1945), p. 34.
42 Ibid., p. 256.
43 Ibid., p. 163.
44 Ibid., p. 166.
45 Maria Misra, *Vishnu's Crowded Temple – India since the Great Rebellion* (2007), p. 160.
46 Ambedkar, *What Congress and Gandhi Have Done*, p. 243.
47 Ibid., p. 247.
48 Ranajit Guha, *Dominance without Hegemony – History and Power in Colonial India* (1997), p. 119.
49 Célestine Bouglé, *Essays on the Caste System by Célestine Bouglé*, trans. D. Pocock (1971).p. 65.
50 Ambedkar, *What Congress and Gandhi Have Done*, p. 44.
51 Ibid., p. 170.
52 Letter to Ramsay MacDonald quoted in Ambedkar, *What Congress and Gandhi Have Done*, p. 87.
53 Ibid., p. 74.
54 Upendra Baxi, 'Emancipation as Justice: Babasaheb Ambedkar's Legacy and Vision', *Crisis and Change in Contemporary India*, eds, Baxi and Parekh (1995), p. 124.
55 Weber, *Religion of India*, p. 9.
56 Susan Bayly gets this detail wrong in *Caste, Society and Politics in India from the Eighteenth Century to the Modern Age* (2001), p. 257.
57 Baxi and Parekh, *Crisis and Change*, p. 141, 143.
58 Ibid., p. 123;Friedrich Nietzsche, *Untimely Meditations*, trans. R. J. Hollingdale (2003), p. 76.
59 Vinayak Damodar Savarkar, *Hindutva – Who Is a Hindu?* (1989), p. 27.
60 Ambedkar, *Who Were the Shudras?*, pp. 38–9.
61 Ibid., p. 33.
62 Ambedkar, *What Congress and Gandhi Have Done*, p. 206.
63 Ibid., pp. 205–206.
64 Savarkar, *Hindutva*, p. 86.
65 Gandhi, *Hind Swaraj*, p. 70.
66 Ambedkar, *Who Were the Shudras?*, p. 41.
67 Savarkar, *Hindutva*, p. 27.
68 Bouglé, *Essays on the Caste System*, p. 25.
69 Ambedkar, *Who Were the Shudras?*, p. 46.
70 Ambedkar, *What Congress and Gandhi Have Done*, p. 190.
71 Mandelsohn and Vicziany, *The Untouchables*, p. 101.
72 Dumont, *Homo Hierarchicus*, p. 223.
73 Bouglé, *Essays on the Caste System*, p. 100.
74 Ambedkar, *Who Were the Shudras?*, p. 82.
75 Ibid., p. 81.
76 Ibid., p. 76.
77 Ibid., p. 103.
78 Bouglé, *Essays on the Caste System*, p. 54.
79 Ambedkar, *Who Were the Shudras?*, p. 107.
80 Ibid., pp. 118–19.
81 Ibid., p. 137.
82 Ibid., p. 141.
83 Ibid., 152.
84 Ibid., p. 154.
85 Ibid., p. 169.
86 Ibid., p. 220.

87 Ibid., p. 221.
88 Ibid., p. 226.
89 Ibid., p. 196.
90 Ibid., p. 197.
91 Ibid., p. 187.
92 Vinayak Damodar Savarkar, *Indian War of Independence – 1857* (1947), p. 540.
93 Gandhi, *Hind Swaraj*, p. 39.
94 Savarkar, *War of Independence*, p. 210.
95 Savarkar, *Hindutva*, p. 51.
96 Ibid., p. 58.
97 Ibid., p. 62.
98 Stewart Gordon, *The Marathas, 1600–1818* (1993), p. 47.
99 Savarkar, *Hindutva*, p. 64.
100 Ibid., p. 70.
101 Gordon, *The Marathas*, p. 19.
102 Ibid., p. 63.
103 Quoted by Andrew Ward, *Our Bones Are Scattered – The Cawnpore Massacres and the Indian Mutiny of 1857* (2004), p. 29.
104 Ibid., p. 29.
105 Gordon, *The Marathas*, p. 66.
106 Ambedkar, *Who Were the Shudras?*, p. 201.
107 Ibid., p. 209.
108 Ibid., p. 210.
109 Guha, *Dominance without Hegemony*, p. 47, emphasis added.
110 Ibid., p. 42.

5 V. S. Naipaul's 'India'

1 Friedrich Nietzsche, *Untimely Meditations*, trans. R. J. Hollingdale (2003). p. 62.
2 Ranajit Guha, 'Dominance without Hegemony and its Historiography', *Subaltern Studies 6 – Writings on South Asian History and Society*, ed. Ranajit Guha (1989), p. 309.
3 Ibid., emphasis added.
4 Romila Thapar, 'Politics and the Re-writing of History in India', *Critical Quarterly* 47, 1–2 (2005), p. 196.
5 Ibid., p. 201, 195.
6 Vinayak Damodar Savarkar, *Six Glorious Epochs of Indian History*, trans. S. T. Godbole (1971), pp. i, ii.
7 Vinayak Damodar Savarkar, *The Maratha Movement (Hindu Pad Padashahi) – Story of the Maratha Struggle to Re-establish Sovereign Hindu Power* (2003), p. 8.
8 Ibid.
9 Savarkar, *The Maratha Movement*, p. 9.
10 Savarkar, *Six Glorious Epochs*, p. ii.
11 Ibid., p. iii.
12 Michael Hardt and Antonio Negri, *Multitude – War and Democracy in the Age of Empire* (2005), p. 128.
13 Edward Said, *Culture and Imperialism* (1993), p. 20.
14 Fawzia Fustafa, *V. S. Naipaul* (1995), p. 137.
15 Rob Nixon, *London Calling – V. S. Naipaul, Postcolonial Mandarin* (1992), p. 6.
16 Edward Said, *The World, the Text and the Critic* (1991).
17 See <http://nobelprize.org/literature/laureates/2001/naipaul-lecture-e.html>, 2.
18 Gayatri Spivak, 'Subaltern Studies – Deconstructing Historiography', in Ranajit Guha, ed., *Subaltern Studies 4* (1985), pp. 332–3, emphasis added.

19 Said, *Culture and Imperialism*, p. 27.
20 See William Dalrymple's article, 'Trapped in the Ruins', *Review*, *The Guardian* (London: 20 March 2004), pp. 4–6.
21 Jean-Paul Sartre, *Critique of Dialectical Reason*, vol. 1, trans. Alan Sheriden-Smith, (2004), p. 69.
22 Benedict Anderson, *Imagined Communities – Reflections on the Origin and Spread of Nationalism* (1991), p. 24.
23 Frantz Fanon, *The Wretched of the Earth*, trans. Constance Farrington (1990), p. 9.
24 Ibid., p. 123.
25 Said, *Culture and Imperialism*, p. 58.
26 Partha Chatterjee, *Nationalist Thought and the Colonial World – A Derivative Discourse* (1993), p. 10.
27 Fanon, *Wretched of the Earth*, p. 28, 31.
28 Maurice Merleau-Monty, *Adventures of the Dialectic*, trans. Joseph Bien (1973), pp. 97–8.
29 Judie Newman, *The Ballistic Bard – Postcolonial Fictions* (1995), p. 119.
30 See extracts from early texts cited by Patrick French in 'It Was As If He Had Seen a Ghost', *The Sunday Times' Culture* magazine (London: 18 January 2004), pp. 44–5.
31 *The Vintage Book of Indian Writing, 1947–1997*, Salman Rushdie and Elizabeth West, eds (1997), pp. xix.
32 Immanuel Kant, *Critique of Pure Reason*, trans. Paul Guyer and Allen Wood (1998), p. 251.
33 The metaphor is Naipaul's own and opens his *India – A Million Mutinies Now* (1990), p. 6.
34 See <http://nobelprize.org/literature/laureates/2001/naipaul-lecture-e.html>, 2.
35 Said, *Culture and Imperialism*, p. 263.
36 Gargi Bhattacharya, 'South Asian Cultural Studies – Lessons from Back Home?', *South Asian Popular Culture*, 1 (2000), pp. 3–11.
37 Paul Brass, *The Politics of India Since Independence* (1997), p. 229.
38 V. S. Naipaul, *India – A Wounded Civilization* (1977), p. 117.
39 Brass, *The Politics of India Since Independence*, p. 229.
40 Raymond Williams, 'Culture is Ordinary', *Convictions*, ed. Norman MacKenzie (1958), p. 78.
41 Elias Canetti, *Crowds and Power*, trans. Carol Stewart (1984), p. 32, 33.
42 Naipaul, *India – A Wounded Civilization*, p. 58.
43 Ibid., pp. 119–25.
44 Dipesh Chakrabarty, 'Postcoloniality and the Artifice of History: Who Speaks for "Indian" Pasts?', *Representations* 37: 1992, p. 11.
45 Naipaul, *India – A Wounded Civilization*, p. 13.
46 V. S. Naipaul, *Beyond Belief – Islamic Excursions Among the Converted Peoples* (1998), p. 2.
47 Naipaul, *India – A Million Mutinies Now*, p. 6.
48 Oliver Mendelsohn and Marika Vicziany, *The Untouchables*, p. 101.
49 Naipaul, *India, A Million Mutinies Now*, p. 3.
50 Ibid., p. 95–6, 106, emphasis added.
51 Naipaul, *India – A Million Mutinies Now*, p. 97.
52 Mendelsohn and Vicziany, *The Untouchables – Subordination, Poverty and the State in Modern India* (1998), p. 214.
53 Naipaul, *India – A Million Mutinies Now*, p. 99.
54 Ibid., p. 102.
55 Naipaul, *India – A Million Mutinies Now*, p. 104, emphasis added.
56 Ashis Nandy, *The Intimate Enemy – Loss and Recovery of Self under Colonialism* (1999), pp. 84–5.
57 Ibid., p. 83.

58 Chakrabarty, 'Postcoloniality and the Artifice of History', p. 17; Fanon, *The Wretched of the Earth*, p. 197; Nixon, *London Calling*, p. 137.
59 Nandy, *The Intimate Enemy*, p. 80.
60 V. S. Naipaul, *The Mimic Men* (1969), p. 18, emphases added.
61 V. S. Naipaul, *The Overcrowded Barracoon* (1976), p. 13.
62 Nietzsche, *Untimely Meditations*, p. 73.
63 Naipaul, *India – A Wounded Civilization*, p. 117.
64 V. S. Naipaul, *An Area of Darkness* (1964), p. 70.
65 Sugata Bose and Ayesha Jalal, *Modern South Asia – History, Culture, Political Economy* (1998), pp. 36–7.
66 Naipaul, *India – A Wounded Civilization*, p. 117.
67 Homi Bhabha, *The Location of Culture* (1995), p. 142.
68 Ibid., p. 88.
69 Chakrabarty, 'Postcoloniality and the Artifice of History', p. 9.
70 Bhabha, *The Location of Culture*, p. 88.
71 Naipaul, *An Area of Darkness*, p. 74.
72 Naipaul, *India – A Million Mutinies Now*, p. 142.
73 Naipaul, *India – A Wounded Civilization*, p. 13.
74 Ibid.
75 Bose and Jalal, *Modern South Asia*, p. 28.
76 Canetti, *Crowds and Power*, pp. 497–8.
77 Nietzsche, *Untimely Meditations*, p. 68.
78 Ernest Gellner, 'The Coming of Nationalism and Its Interpretation – The Myths of Nation and Class', *Mapping the Nation*, ed. Gopal Balakrishnan, p. 98.
79 Ibid., p. 102.
80 Ibid., p. 99.
81 Ibid., p. 101.
82 Naipaul, *India – A Wounded Civilization*, p. 18.
83 M. K. Gandhi, *Hind Swaraj and Other Writings* (1997), p. 30.
84 Naipaul, *India – A Wounded Civilization*, p. 18.
85 Partha Chatterjee's historical sense ingeniously works these terms in *The Nation and Its Fragments – Colonial and Postcolonial Histories* (1993), p. 173.
86 Karl Marx, 'The British Rule in India', *The Marx and Engels Reader*, p. 653.
87 Gellner, *Mapping the Nation*, pp. 102–3, emphasis added.
88 Bose and Jalal, *Modern South Asia*, p. 48.
89 Chatterjee, *The Nation and Its Fragments*, p. 181.
90 Ibid, p. 181.
91 Chatterjee, *The Nation and Its Fragments*, pp. 183–4.
92 Naipaul, *Beyond Belief*, p. 71, emphasis added.
93 Chatterjee, *The Nation and Its Fragments*, p. 88.
94 Ibid., p. 94.
95 Naipaul, *Beyond Belief*, p. 59.
96 Chatterjee, *The Nation and Its Fragments*, p. 97.
97 Earl Lovelace, *Salt* (1996), pp. 218–19.
98 Naipaul, *Beyond Belief*, p. 59.

6 Salman Rushdie and the *agon* of the past

1 Salman Rushdie, *Imaginary Homelands – Essays and Criticism, 1981–1991* (1991), p. 25.
2 Friedrich Nietzsche, *Twilight of the Idols and The Anti-Christ*, trans. R. J. Hollingdale (2003), p. 45.
3 Ranajit Guha, *Dominance without Hegemony – History and Power in Colonial India* (1997), p. 47; Hayden White, *Metahistory – The Historical Imagination in Nineteenth-century Europe* (1975), p. 37.

4 D. C. R. A. Goonetilleke, *Salman Rushdie* (1998), p. 2; Rushdie, *Imaginary Homelands*, p. 377.
5 Rushdie, *Imaginary Homelands*, p. 377.
6 White, *Metahistory*, p. 37.
7 Rushdie, *Imaginary Homelands*, p. 387.
8 Salman Rushdie, *Shame* (1984), p. 28, emphases in original.
9 Salman Rushdie, *Midnight's Children* (1982), p. 295.
10 Rushdie, *Imaginary Homelands*, p. 385.
11 Ibid., p. 14, emphasis added.
12 Nietzsche, *Twilight of the Idols and The Anti-Christ*, p. 161.
13 Edward Said, *The World, the Text and the Critic* (1991), p. 202, emphasis added.
14 Salman Rushdie, 'Why I Have Embraced Islam', *The New York Times*, 28 December 1990.
15 Sara Suleri, *The Rhetoric of English India* (1992), p. 102.
16 Michel de Certeau, *The Writing of History*, trans. Tom Conley (1988), p. 8, emphasis in original.
17 Salman Rushdie, *The Enchantress of Florence* (2008), p. 83.
18 Certeau, *The Writing of History*, p. 22.
19 Emile Durkheim, *The Division of Labour in Society*, trans. W. D. Halls (1997), p. 71.
20 Rushdie, *Imaginary Homelands*, p. 385.
21 Ibid., p. 379.
22 Claude Lévi-Strauss, *Structural Anthropology 1*, p. 24.
23 Rushdie, *Imaginary Homelands*, pp. 381–2.
24 Rushdie, *Shame*, p. 251.
25 Ibid., p. 240.
26 Thomas Carlyle, *The French Revolution – A History* (2002), p. xviii; Rushdie, *Shame*, pp. 241–2.
27 Friedrich Nietzsche, *Untimely Meditations*, trans. R. J. Hollingdale (2003), p. 65.
28 Ibid., p. 67.
29 Rushdie, *Imaginary Homelands*, p. 378, emphases in original.
30 Michel Foucault, *Power/Knowledge Knowledge – Selected Interviews and Other Writings 1972–1977 by Michel Foucault*, ed. Colin Gordon, p. 81, emphasis in original.
31 Aijaz Ahmad, *In Theory – Classes, Nations, Literatures* (1994), p. 108.
32 Ibid., p. 130.
33 Nietzsche, *Untimely Meditations*, p. 78.
34 Ibid., p. 79.
35 Ahmad, *In Theory*, p. 134.
36 Nietzsche, *Untimely Meditations*, p. 70; Homi Bhabha, *Location of Culture* (1995), p. 139.
37 Rushdie, *Imaginary Homelands*, p. 12.
38 Frederic Jameson, *Marxism and Form – Twentieth Century Dialectical Theories of Literature* (1974), p. 71.
39 Walter Benjamin, *Schriften*, vol. 1, eds Theodor Adorno and Gretel Adorno (1955), p. 487.
40 Salman Rushdie, *The Moor's Last Sigh* (1996), p. 173.
41 Ibid., p. 302.
42 Ibid., p. 80.
43 Ibid., p. 227.
44 Ibid., p. 84, emphasis in original.
45 Amitav Ghosh, *The Shadow Lines* (1988), p. 221. See also Amitav Ghosh, *In an Antique Land* (1992), pp. 236–7; 'The Slave of MS. H.6', Amitav Ghosh, *Subaltern*

Studies 7 – Writings on South Asian History and Society, eds Partha Chatterjee and Gyanendra Pandey (1999).
46 Rushdie, *Moor's Last Sigh*, p. 173, 220.
47 Salman Rushdie, *The Satanic Verses* (1988), p. 111, 335.
48 Immanuel Kant, *Critique of Pure Reason*, trans. Paul Guyer and Allen Wood (2000), p. 179.
49 Walter Benjamin, *Illuminations*, trans. Harry Zohn (1992), p. 171.
50 Friedrich Nietzsche, *The Birth of Tragedy out of the Spirit of Music*, trans. Shaun Whiteside (2003), p. 39, 85.
51 Gerald Hawting, *The Idea of Idolatry and the Emergence of Islam: From Polemic to History* (1999), p. 134.
52 Quoted in Hawting, *The Idea of Idolatry*, p. 131.
53 For a strong refutation of the pseudonymous Christoph Luxenberg's thesis in *Die syro-aramäische Lesart des Koran. Ein Beitrag zur Entschlüsselung der Koransprache* (Berlin: Das Arabische Buch, 2000), see François de Blois in *Journal of Qur'anic Studies* 5: 1, 2003.
54 Benjamin, *Illuminations*, pp. 215–16.
55 Rushdie, *Imaginary Homelands*, p. 394.
56 Benjamin, *Illuminations*, p. 254.
57 Rushdie, *The Satanic Verses*, p. 320.
58 Peter Ackroyd, *London – The Biography* (2001), p. 95, 2.
59 Rushdie, *Midnight's Children*, p. 368.
60 T. S. Eliot, *Collected Poems 1909–1962* (1963), p. 40.
61 Rushdie, *Shame*, p. 89, 124; Rushdie, *Midnight's Children*, p. 10.
62 Benjamin, *Illuminations*, p. 245.
63 Ibid., p. 249.
64 Gilles Deleuze and Félix Guattari, *Anti-Oedipus – Capitalism and Schizophrenia*, trans. Robert Hurley, *et al.* (1984), p. 85.
65 Suleri, *Rhetoric of English India*, p. 193.
66 Edward Said, *Culture and Imperialism* (1993), p. 373.
67 Edward Said, 'Figures, Configurations, Transfigurations', *Race and Class* 32: 1, 1990.
68 Edward Said, *Orientalism – Western Conceptions of the Orient* (1991), p. 21.
69 Said, *Culture and Imperialism*, p. 373, emphasis added.
70 Said, 'Figures, Configurations, Transfigurations', p. 9.
71 Ahmad, *In Theory*, p. 34.
72 Said, *Culture and Imperialism*, p. 370, 371.
73 Edward Said, *Covering Islam – How the Media and the Experts Determine How We See the Rest of the World* (1981).
74 Edward Said, foreword to *Selected Subaltern Studies*, eds Ranajit Guha and Gayatri Spivak (1988), p. ix.
75 Faiz Ahmed Faiz, *The Rebel's Silhouette – Selected Poems*, trans. Agha Shahid Ali (1995), p. xvi.
76 Rushdie, *The Satanic Verses*, pp. 334–5.
77 Faiz, *Rebel's Silhouette*, pp, 77, 5.
78 Inderpal Grewal, 'Salman Rushdie: Marginality, Women and Shame', *Genders* 3: 1988, p. 42.
79 Assia Djebar, *Far from Medina*, trans. Dorothy Blair (1994), pp. xv, 75.
80 Srinavas Aravamudan, '"Being God's Postman Is No Fun Yaar"', *Diacritics* 19: 2, 1989, p. 12.
81 Djebar, *Far from Medina*, p. 76.
82 Akbar Ahmed, 'Death in Islam: The Hawkes Bay Case', *Pakistan Society – Islam, Ethnicity and Leadership in South Asia*, ed., Aijaz Ahmad (1986), p. 57.
83 Certeau, *Writing of History*, p. 118.

84 Suleri, *Rhetoric of English India*, p. 205.
85 Dante, *The Comedy of Dante Alighieri the Florentine – Cantica 1 – L'Inferno*, trans. Dorothy L. Sayers (1988), p. 247.
86 Gustave Doré, *The Doré Illustrations for Dante's Divine Comedy* (1976), p. 56.
87 Ghosh, *The Shadow Lines*, p. 102.
88 Salman Rushdie, *East, West* (1995), p. 44.
89 Certeau, *Writing of History*, p. 154, emphasis in original.
90 James Buchan, 'Kashmir', *Granta* 57: 'India – The Golden Jubilee', pp. 64–5.
91 Roland Barthes, 'Historical Discourse', *Structuralism – A Reader*, ed. Michael Lane (1970), p. 148.
92 Certeau, *Writing of History*, p. 151, 118, emphases in original.
93 Ghosh, *The Shadow Lines*, p. 221.
94 Ibid., p. 227.
95 Ibid., p. 228.
96 Ibid., p. 226.
97 Ghosh, *In an Antique Land*, p. 210.
98 Ghosh, *The Shadow Lines*, p. 213; Ghosh, *In an Antique Land*, p. 208.
99 Ghosh, *In an Antique Land*, pp. 209–10, emphasis in original.
100 Buchan, 'Kashmir', pp. 66–7.

Conclusion

1 Georg Wilhelm Friedrich Hegel, *Lectures on the Philosophy of World History*, Introduction: Reason in History, trans. H. B. Nisbet (1993), p. 61.
2 Rabindranath Tagore, *Nationalism* (1917), pp. 106–107.
3 Partha Chatterjee, *Nationalist Thought and the Colonial World – A Derivative Discourse* (1993), p. 168.
4 Ibid., p. 170.
5 Ibid., p. 51.
6 Hegel, *Lectures on the Philosophy of World History*, p. 53, 61, 62.
7 Ibid., p. 59.
8 Chatterjee, *Nationalist Thought*, p. 153.
9 Ibid, p. 153.
10 Extract from the *Pioneer*, 1921, quoted by Shahid Amin, 'Gandhi as Mahatma: Gorakhpur District, Eastern UP, 1921–1922', *Subaltern Studies 3 – Writings on South Asian History and Society*, ed., Ranajit Guha (1999), p. 5.
11 Lenin, 'Left-wing Communism, an Infantile Disorder' quoted by G. A. Cohen, *Karl Marx's Theory of History* (2004), p. ix.
12 Chatterjee, *Nationalist Thought*, p. 53.
13 Nicos Poulantzas, *State, Power, Socialism*, trans. Patrick Camiller (2000), p. 43. Emphasis in original.
14 Hayden White, *Tropics of Discourse – Essays in Cultural Criticism* (1985), p. 105.
15 Amin, 'Gandhi as Mahatma', p. 4.
16 Chatterjee, *Nationalist Thought*, p. 6, emphasis in original.
17 Gellner, *Mapping the Nation*, ed. Gopal Balakrishnan (1996), p. 103.
18 Tagore, *Nationalism*, p. 13.
19 Sarvepalli Gopal, *Jawaharlal Nehru – A Biography* (1995), p. 27.
20 Chatterjee, *Nationalist Thought*, p. 100.
21 Ibid., p. 147.
22 A. J. P. Taylor, *The Course of German History – A Survey of the Development of German History since 1815* (2006), p. 105.
23 Chatterjee, *Nationalist Thought*, p. 132.
24 Taylor, *Course of German History*, p. 94.
25 Elie Kedourie, *Nationalism* (2004), p. 23, 21.

26 Ibid., p. 33. Hegel is the honourable exception. His formulations about statecraft were, Kedourie tells us, anti-nationalist.
27 Ibid., p. 35.
28 Jawaharlal Nehru, *The Discovery of India* (1946), p. 431.

References

Abrams, M. H., *Natural Supernaturalism – Tradition and Revolution in Romantic Literature* (New York: Norton, 1973).
Ackroyd, Peter, *London – The Biography* (London: Vintage, 2001).
Adorno, Theodor and Max Horkheimer, *Dialectic of Enlightenment*, trans. John Cumming (London: Verso, 1999).
Ahmad, Aijaz, *In Theory – Classes, Nations, Literatures* (London: Verso, 1994).
—— *Pakistan Society – Islam, Ethnicity and Leadership in South Asia* (Karachi: Oxford University Press, 1986).
Ahmed, Akbar, 'Death in Islam: The Hawkes Bay Case,' *Pakistan Society – Islam, Ethnicity and Leadership in South Asia*, ed. Aijaz Ahmad (1986).
Akmeşe, Handan Nezir, *The Birth of Modern Turkey – The Ottoman Military and the March to World War I* (New York: I. B. Tauris, 2005).
Albinia, Alice, *Empires of the Indus – The Story of a River* (London: John Murray, 2008).
Aloysius, G., *Nationalism without a Nation in India* (Delhi: Oxford University Press, 2005).
Althusser, Louis, *Lenin and Philosophy and Other Essays*, trans. Ben Brewster (New York: Monthly Review Press, 2001).
—— *The Humanist Controversy and Other Writings*, trans. G. M. Goshgarian, ed. François Matheron (London: Verso, 2003).
Althusser, Louis and Étienne Balibar, *Reading Capital*, trans. Ben Brewster (London: Verso, 2004).
Ambedkar, B. R., *What Gandhi and Congress Have Done to the Untouchables* (Bombay: Thacker and Co., 1945).
—— *The Untouchables – Who Were They and Why They Became Untouchables?* (Delhi: Amrit Book Co., 1948).
—— *Who Were the Shudras? – How They Came To Be the Fourth Varna in the Indo-Aryan Society* (Bombay: Thacker, 1970).
—— *Why Go for Conversion?* trans. Vasant Moon (Bangalore: Dalit Sahitya Akademy, 1981).
Amin, Shahid, 'Gandhi as Mahatma: Gorakhpur District, Eastern UP, 1921–1922', *Subaltern Studies 3 – Writings on South Asian History and Society*, ed. Ranajit Guha (Delhi: Oxford University Press, 1999).
Anand, Dibyesh, 'Anxious Sexualities: Masculinity, Nationalism and Violence', *The British Journal of Politics and International Relations*, Political Studies Association, 9: 2007, pp. 257–69.

Anderson, Benedict, *Imagined Communities – Reflections on the Origin and Spread of Nationalism* (London: Verso, 1991).
Anderson, Perry, *Passages from Antiquity to Feudalism* (London: Verso, 2006).
Aravamudan, Srinavas, '"Being God's Postman Is No Fun Yaar": Salman Rushdie's The Satanic Verses', *Diacritics* 19: 2, (1989), pp. 3–20.
Arendt, Hannah, *Eichmann in Jerusalem – A Report on the Banality of Evil* (London: Penguin, 2006).
Arrian, *The Campaigns of Alexander*, trans. Aubrey de Sélincourt (London: Penguin, 1971).
Asher, Catherine and Cynthia Talbot, *India before Europe* (Cambridge: Cambridge University Press, 2006).
Auden, W. H., *Selected Poems*, ed. Edward Mendelson (London: Faber, 1979).
Auerbach, Erich, *Mimesis – The Representation of Reality in Western Literature*, trans. Willard Trask (Princeton: Princeton University Press, 2003).
Barthes, Roland, *Structuralism – A Reader*, ed. Michael Lane (London: Jonathan Cape, 1970).
Baudrillard, Jean, *Simulacra and Simulation*, trans. Sheila Glaser (Ann Arbor: University of Michigan, 1994).
Baxi, Upendra and Bhiku Parekh Parekh, eds, *Crisis and Change in Contemporary India*, (New Delhi: Sage and Thousand Oaks, 1995).
Bayly, C. A., *Indian Society and the Making of the British Empire* (Cambridge: Cambridge University Press, 1997).
Bayly, Susan, *Caste, Society and Politics in India from the Eighteenth Century to the Modern Age* (Cambridge: Cambridge University Press, 2001).
Benjamin, Walter, *Illuminations*, trans. Harry Zohn (London: Fontana, 1992).
―― *The Correspondence of Walter Benjamin and Gershom Scholem, 1932–1940*, ed. Gershom Scholem, trans. Gary Smith and André Lefevere (Massachusetts: Harvard University Press, 1992).
―― *Schriften*, vol. 1, eds Theodor Adorno and Gretel Adorno (Frankfurt: Suhrkamp Verlag, 1955).
Berman, Marshall, *All That Is Solid Melts into Air* (London: Verso, 1983).
Bhabha, Homi, *The Location of Culture* (London: Routledge, 1995).
Bhattacharya, Gargi, 'South Asian Cultural Studies – Lessons from Back Home?', *South Asian Popular Culture*, 1:1 (2003), pp. 3–11.
Bloch, Ernst, Georg Lukacs, Bertolt Brecht, Walter Benjamin and Theodor Adorno, *Aesthetics and Politics* (London: Verso, 1992).
Blois, François de, *Journal of Qur'anic Studies* 5: 1 (2003), pp. 92–7.
Bloom, Harold, *The Western Canon – The Books and School of the Ages* (London: Papermac, 1996).
Bloxham, Donald, *The Great Game of Genocide – Imperialism, Nationalism, and the Destruction of the Ottoman Armenians* (Oxford: Oxford University Press, 2007).
Bose, Sujata and Ayesha Jalal, *Modern South Asia – History, Culture, Political Economy* (London: Routledge, 1998).
Bouglé, Célestine, *Essays on the Caste System by Célestine Bouglé*, trans. D. Pocock (Cambridge: Cambridge University Press, 1971).
Bourdieu, Pierre, *Distinction – A Social Critique of the Judgement of Taste*, trans. Richard Nice (London: Penguin, 2003).
Brass, Paul, *The Politics of India Since Independence* (Cambridge: Cambridge University Press, 1997).

Braudel, Fernand, *The Mediterranean and the Mediterranean World in the Age of Philip II*, vol. 1, trans. Siân Reynolds (California: California University Press, 1995).
Buchan, James, 'Kashmir', *Granta* 57: 'India – The Golden Jubilee' (1997), pp. 59–83.
Burchell, G., C. Gordon and P. Miller, eds, *The Foucault Effect: Studies in Governmentality* (Chicago: University of Chicago Press, 1991).
Burkhardt, Jacob, *Force and Freedom: An Interpretation of History*, ed. James Nichols (New York: Meridian Books, 1955).
—— *Judgements on History and Historians*, trans. Harry Zohn (Boston: Beacon Press, 1958).
Burke, Edmund, *Burke, Paine, Godwin and the Revolution Controversy*, ed. Marilyn Butler (Cambridge: Cambridge University Press, 1993).
Burrows, Guy, *The Land of the Pigmies* (London: C. A. Pearson, 1898).
Burton, Antoinette, 'Who Needs the Nation? Interrogating 'British' History', *Journal of Historical Sociology*, 10:3 (1997), pp. 227–48.
Bury, J. B. 'The Science of History', *The Varieties of History: From Voltaire to the Present*, ed. Fritz Stern (New York: Vintage Books, 1973).
Butler, Judith, *The Psychic Life of Power – Theories in Subjection* (California: Stanford University Press, 1997).
Callinicos, Alex, *Making History – Agency, Structure and Change in Social Theory* (Cambridge: Polity, 1987).
—— *Theory and Narratives – Reflections on the Philosophy of History* (Cambridge: Polity, 1997).
—— *Against Postmodernism – A Marxist Critique* (Cambridge: Polity Press, 2002).
Canetti, Elias, *Crowds and Power*, trans. Carol Stewart (London: Penguin, 1984).
Carlyle, Thomas, *A Carlyle Reader – Selections from the Writings of Thomas Carlyle*, ed. G. B. Tennyson (New York: Modern Library, 1969).
—— *The French Revolution – A History* (New York: The Modern Library, 2002).
Certeau, Michel de, *The Writing of History*, trans. Tom Conley (New York: Columbia University Press, 1988).
Césaire, Aimé, *Discourse on Colonialism*, trans. Joan Pinkham (New York: Monthly Review Press, 1972).
Chakrabarty, Dipesh, 'Postcoloniality and the Artifice of History: Who Speaks for "Indian" Pasts?', *Representations* 37: 1992, pp. 1–26.
—— *Subaltern Studies 8 – Essays in Honour of Ranajit Guha*, eds David Arnold and David Hardiman (Delhi: Oxford University Press, 1999).
Chatterjee, Bankim Chandra, *Anandamath*, trans. Basanta Roy (Delhi: Orient Paperbacks, 1992).
Chatterjee, Partha, *The Nation and Its Fragments – Colonial and Postcolonial Histories* (New Jersey: Princeton University Press, 1993).
—— *Nationalist Thought and the Colonial World – A Derivative Discourse* (London: Zed Books, 1993).
—— *A Possible India – Essays in Political Criticism* (Delhi: Oxford University Press, 1998).
—— *Subaltern Studies 2 – Writings on South Asian History and Society*, ed. Ranajit Guha (Delhi: Oxford University Press, 1999).
—— *Subaltern Studies 7 – Writings on South Asian History and Society*, eds Partha Chatterjee and Gyanendra Pandey (Delhi: Oxford University Press, 1999).
Chaudhuri, B., *The Cambridge Economic History of India*, vol. 2: *c.* 1757–1970, ed. Dharma Kumar (Cambridge: Cambridge University Press).

Cohen, G. A., *Karl Marx's Theory of History – A Defence* (Oxford: Oxford University Press, 2004).
Cohn, Bernard, *Colonialism and Its Forms of Knowledge – The British in India* (New Jersey: Princeton University Press, 1996).
—— *An Anthropologist amongst the Historians and Other Essays*, ed. Ranajit Guha (New Delhi: Oxford University Press, 2006).
Collingwood, R. G., *The Idea of History* (Oxford: Oxford University Press, 1994).
Condillac, Étienne Bonnot de, *Essay on the Origin of Human Knowledge*, trans. Hans Aaarsleff (Cambridge: Cambridge University Press, 2001).
Condorcet, Jean-Antoine-Nicholas de Caritat, marquis de, *Sketch for a Historical Picture of the Progress of the Human Mind*, trans. June Barraclough (London: Weidenfeld and Nicholson, 1955).
Conrad, Joseph, *Heart of Darkness* (New York: Norton, 1988).
Dalrymple, William, Review, *The Guardian* (London: 20 March 2004), pp. 4–6.
Dante, *The Comedy of Dante Alighieri the Florentine – Cantica 1 – L'Inferno*, trans. Dorothy L. Sayers (London: Penguin, 1988).
Deleuze, Gilles and Félix Guattari, *Anti-Oedipus – Capitalism and Schizophrenia*, trans. Robert Hurley, Mark Seem and Helen Lane (London: Athlone, 1984).
Derrida, Jacques, *Of Grammatology*, trans. Gayatri Spivak (Baltimore: Johns Hopkins, 1976).
—— *Monolingualism of the Other: Or, the Prosthesis of Origin*, trans. Patrick Mensah (California: Stanford University Press, 1998).
Djebar, Assia, *Far from Medina*, trans. Dorothy Blair (London: Quartet Books, 1994).
Doré, Gustave, *The Doré Illustrations for Dante's Divine Comedy* (New York: Dover, 1976).
Dumont, Louis, *La Civilisation indienne et nous* (Paris: Colin, Coll. Cahiers des Annales, 1964).
—— *Homo Hierarchicus – The Caste System and Its Implications*, trans. Mark Sainsbury, Louis Dumont and Basia Gulati (Chicago: Chicago University Press, 1980).
Durkheim, Emile, *The Division of Labour in Society*, trans. W. D. Halls (New York: The Free Press, 1997).
—— *Suicide – A Study in Sociology*, trans. John Spaulding and George Simpson (London: Routledge, 2002).
Durkheim, Émile and Marcel Mauss, *Primitive Classification*, trans. Rodney Needham (Chicago: University of Chicago Press, 1963).
Eagleton, Robert and Susan Pitt, 'The Good of History: Ethics, Post-structuralism and the Representation of the Past', *Rethinking History* 2: 3, 1998, pp. 359–69.
Eliot, T. S., 'The Wasteland', *Selected Poems* (London: Faber, 1961).
—— *Collected Poems 1909–1962* (London: Faber, 1963).
—— *Selected Prose*, ed. Frank Kermode (London: Faber, 1975).
—— *On Poetry and Poets* (London: Faber, 1990).
Ellmann, Richard, *Yeats – The Man and the Masks* (London, Penguin, 1987).
Evans, Richard, *In Defence of History* (London: Granta, 2000).
Faiz, Faiz Ahmed *The Rebel's Silhouette – Selected Poems*, trans. Agha Shahid Ali (Amherst: University of Massachusetts, 1995).
Fanon, Frantz, *The Wretched of the Earth*, trans. Constance Farrington (London: Penguin, 1990).
al-Fazl, Abu, *The Akbar-Nama*, trans. Henry Beveridge (Delhi: Asiatic Society of Bengal, 1972).

―― *The Akbar Nama of Abu-l-Fazl*, vol. 1, trans. H. Beveridge (Delhi: Low Price Publications, 1998).
Foucault, Michel, *Language, Counter-memory, Practice – Selected Essays and Interviews by Michel Foucault*, trans. Donald Bouchard and Sherry Simon (Ithaca: Cornell University Press, 1980).
―― *Power/Knowledge – Selected Interviews and Other Writings 1972–1977 by Michel Foucault*, ed. Colin Gordon (London: Harvester Wheatsheaf, 1980).
―― *The History of Sexuality, An Introduction*, trans. Robert Hurley (London: Penguin, 1990).
―― 'Governmentality', in G. Burchell, C. Gordon and P. Miller, eds *The Foucault Effect: Studies in Governmentality*, (Chicago: University of Chicago Press, 1991).
―― *The Archaeology of Knowledge*, trans. Alan Sheridan (London: Routledge, 1995).
―― *The Order of Things – An Archaeology of the Human Sciences* (London: Routledge, 2003).
French, Patrick, *The Sunday Times' Culture* magazine (London: 18 January 2004), pp. 44–5.
Freud, Sigmund, *The Interpretation of Dreams* (London, Penguin: 1991).
Frye, Northrop, *Anatomy of Criticism – Four Essays* (London: Penguin, 1990).
Fukuyama, Francis, *The End of History and the Last Man* (London: Penguin, 1992).
Fustafa, Fawzia, *V. S. Naipaul* (Cambridge: Cambridge University Press, 1995).
Gandhi, M. K., *Hind Swaraj and Other Writings* (Cambridge: Cambridge University Press, 1997).
Gellner, Ernest, *Encounters with Nationalism* (Oxford: Blackwell, 1995).
―― *Mapping the Nation*, ed. Gopal Balakrishnan (London: Verso, 1996).
―― *Nations and Nationalism* (Oxford: Blackwell, 2007).
Ghosh, Amitav, *The Shadow Lines* (London: Bloomsbury, 1988).
―― *In an Antique Land* (London: Granta, 1992).
―― *Subaltern Studies 7 – Writings on South Asian History and Society*, eds Partha Chatterjee and Gyanendra Pandey (Delhi: Oxford University Press, 1999).
Gibbon, Edward, *The Decline and Fall of the Roman Empire* (Hertfordshire: Wordsworth Editions, 1998).
Gilgamesh, The Epic of trans. Andrew George (London: Penguin, 2003).
Golwalkar, M. S., *We, or Our Nation Defined* (Nagpur, 1947).
―― *Bunch of Thoughts* (Bangalore: Jagarana Prakashana, 1988, first published 1966).
Goody, Jack, *The Theft of History* (Cambridge: Cambridge University Press, 2006).
Goonetilleke, D. C. R. A., *Salman Rushdie* (London: Macmillan, 1998).
Gopal, Sarvepalli, *Jawaharlal Nehru – A Biography* (Delhi: Oxford University Press, 1995).
Gordon, Stewart, *The Marathas, 1600–1818* (Cambridge: Cambridge University Press, 1993).
Grafton, Anthony, *What Was History? The Art of History in Early Modern Europe* (Cambridge: Cambridge University Press, 2007).
Grewal, Inderpal, 'Salman Rushdie: Marginality, Women and Shame', *Genders* 3: (1988), pp. 24–42.
Guha, Ranajit, *A Rule of Property for Bengal – An Essay on the Idea of Permanent Settlement* (Durham: Duke University Press, 1996).
―― *Dominance without Hegemony – History and Power in Colonial India* (Massachusetts: Harvard University Press, 1997).
―― *Subaltern Studies 1 – Writings on South Asian History and Society*, ed. Ranajit Guha (Delhi: Oxford University Press, 1999).

—— *Subaltern Studies 6 – Writings on South Asian History and Society*, ed. Ranajit Guha (Delhi: Oxford University Press, 1999).
Guha, Ranajit and Gayatri Spivak, eds, *Selected Subaltern Studies* (New York: Oxford University Press, 1988).
Guha, Sudeshna, 'Negotiating Evidence: History, Archaeology and the Indus Civilisation', *Modern Asian Studies* 39, 2, 2005, pp. 399–426.
Hardiman, David, 'The Indian "Faction": A Political Theory Examined', *Subaltern Studies 1 – Writings on South Asian History and Society*, ed. Ranajit Guha (Delhi: Oxford University Press, 1999).
Hardt, Michael and Antonio Negri, *Multitude – War and Democracy in the Age of Empire* (London: Hamish Hamilton, 2005).
Harlow, Barbara and Mia Carter, eds, *Archives of Empire, Volume 1 – From the East India Company to the Suez Canal* (Duke University Press: Durham, 2003).
[Hastings, Warren] The History of the Trial of Warren Hastings, vol. 6 (London: J. Debrett, 1796).
Hawting, Gerald, *The Idea of Idolatry and the Emergence of Islam: From Polemic to History* (Cambridge: Cambridge University Press, 1999).
Heehs, Peter, 'Shades of Orientalism: Paradoxes and Problems in Indian Historiography', *History and Theory*, 42, 2003, pp. 169–95.
Hegel, Georg Wilhelm Friedrich, *Hegel, The Philosophy of History*, trans. J. Sibree (New York: Dover Publications, 1956).
—— *Lectures on the Philosophy of World History*, Introduction: Reason in History, trans. H. B. Nisbet (Cambridge: Cambridge University Press, 1993).
—— *Phenomenology of Spirit*, trans. A. V. Miller (Oxford: Oxford University Press, 1977).
Heidegger, Martin, *Nietzsche – The Will to Power as Art; The Eternal Recurrence of the Same*, trans. David Krell (San Francisco: Harper Collins, 1991).
—— *Being and Time*, trans. John Macquarrie and Edward Robinson (Oxford: Blackwell, 2005).
Herder, Johann Gottfried, *Philosophy of the History of Man*, trans. T. Churchill (London: J. Johnson, 1800).
Herodotus, *The Histories*, trans. Aubrey de Sélincourt (London: Penguin, 2003).
Hill, Christopher, *The Century of Revolution, 1603–1714* (London: Routledge, 2002).
Hobsbawm, E. J., *Nation and Nationalism since 1780 – Programme, Myth, Reality* (Cambridge: Cambridge University Press, 2005).
Homer, *The Iliad*, trans. Robert Fagles (London: Penguin, 1991).
Huntingdon, Samuel, *The Clash of Civilisations and the Remaking of the World Order* (London: The Free Press, 2002).
Hyam, Ronald, *Britain's Declining Empire – The Road to Decolonisation, 1918–1968* (Cambridge: Cambridge University Press, 2006).
Jalal, Ayesha, *Democracy and Authoritarianism in South Asia – A Comparative and Historical Perspective* (Cambridge: Cambridge University Press, 1998).
James, C. L. R., *The Black Jacobins – Toussaint L'Ouverture and the San Domingo Revolution* (London: Penguin, 2001).
Jameson, Frederic, *Marxism and Form – Twentieth Century Dialectical Theories of Literature* (New Jersey: Princeton University Press, 1974).
—— 'Third World Literature in the Era of Multinational Capital', *Social Text* 15, 1986, pp. 65–88.
—— *Postmodernism, or, the Cultural Logic of Late Capitalism* (London: Verso, 1996).
Jenkins, Keith, *Re-thinking History* (London: Routledge, 2003).

Kant, Immanuel, *Kant's Political Writings*, trans. H. B. Nisbet, ed. Hans Reiss (Cambridge: Cambridge University Press, 1970).

—— *Critique of Pure Reason*, trans. Paul Guyer and Allen Wood (Cambridge: Cambridge University Press, 2000).

—— *Toward Perpetual Peace and Other Writings on Politics, Peace, and History*, ed. Pauline Kleingeld, trans. David Colclasure (New Haven: Yale University Press, 2006).

Kaviraj, Sudipta, *State and Politics in India*, ed. Partha Chatterjee (Delhi: Oxford University Press, 1998).

Kedourie, Elie, *Nationalism* (Oxford: Blackwell, 2004).

Kennedy, Emmet, *A Philosophe in the Age of Revolution – Destutt de Tracy and the Origins of 'Ideology'* (Philadelphia: The American Philosophical Society, 1978).

Khalidi, Rashid, *The Iron Cage – The Story of Palestinian Struggle for Statehood* (Oxford: Oneworld, 2006).

Khilnani, Sunil, *The Idea of India* (London: Penguin, 1998).

Kierkegaard, Soren, *Fear and Trembling*, trans. Alastair Hannay (London: Penguin, 2003).

Kipling, Rudyard, *Kim* (Oxford: Oxford University Press, 1987).

Kolluri, Satish, 'Minority Existence and the Subject of (Religious) Conversion', *Cultural Dynamics*, 14: 2002, pp. 81–95.

Lefebvre, Georges, *The French Revolution*, trans. Elizabeth Evanson (London: Routledge, 2005).

Lemprière, John, *Lemprière's Classical Dictionary* (London: Routledge, 1987).

Lenin, V. I., *Revolution at the Gates – A Selection of Writings from February to October 1917*, ed. Slavoj Žižek (London: Verso, 2002).

Lévi-Strauss, Claude, *Structural Anthropology 1*, trans. Claire Jacobson and Brooke Schoepf (London: Penguin, 1993).

—— *Structural Anthropology 2*, trans. Monique Layton (London: Penguin, 1994).

Locke, John, *An Essay Concerning Human Understanding*, ed. Kenneth Winkler (Indiana: Hackett, 1996), p. 148.

Lovelace, Earl, *Salt* (London: Faber and Faber, 1996).

Lyotard, Jean-François, *The Differend – Phrases in Dispute*, trans. Georges Van Den Abbeele (Minneapolis: University of Minnesota Press, 1988).

—— *The Postmodern Condition – A Report on Knowledge*, trans. Geoff Bennington and Brian Massumi (Manchester: Manchester University Press, 1997).

Machiavelli, Niccolò, *The Prince*, trans. George Bull (London: Penguin, 2003).

MacIntyre, Alasdair, *After Virtue* (London: Duckworth, 1981).

Marshall, John, *A Guide to Taxila* (Calcutta: Superintendent Government Printing, 1918).

—— *Taxila – An Illustrated Account of Archaeological Excavations carried out under the orders of the Government of India between the years 1913 and 1934* (Cambridge: Cambridge University Press, 1951).

Marx, Karl, *Grundrisse*, trans. Martin Nicolaus (London: Penguin, 1993).

Marx, Karl and Friedrich Engels, *The Marx and Engels Reader*, ed. Robert Tucker (New York: Norton, 1978).

—— *The Communist Manifesto* (London: Penguin, 1985).

—— *The German Ideology*, ed. C. J. Arthur (London: Lawrence and Wishart, 1999).

Mendelsohn, Oliver and Marika Vicziany, *The Untouchables – Subordination, Poverty and the State in Modern India* (Cambridge: Cambridge University Press, 1998).

Merleau-Ponty, Maurice, *Adventures of the Dialectic*, trans. Joseph Bien (Evanston: Northwestern University Press, 1973).

Metcalf, Thomas, *Ideologies of the Raj* (Cambridge: Cambridge University Press, 1998).
Michelet, Jules, *History of the French Revolution*, trans. George Cocks (Chicago: University of Chicago Press, 1967).
Misra, Maria, *Vishnu's Crowded Temple – India since the Great Rebellion* (London: Penguin Allan Lane, 2007).
Montesquieu, Charles-Louis de Secondat, Baron de la Brède et de, *The Persian Letters* (1758 edition), trans. George Healey (Indianapolis: Hackett, 1999).
Mustafa, Fawzia, *V. S. Naipaul* (Cambridge: Cambridge University Press, 1995).
Naipaul, V. S., *An Area of Darkness* (London: Penguin, 1964).
—— *The Mimic Men* (London: Penguin, 1969).
—— *The Overcrowded Barracoon* (London: Penguin, 1976).
—— *India – A Wounded Civilization* (London: Penguin, 1977).
—— *India – A Million Mutinies Now* (London: Minerva, 1990).
—— *Beyond Belief – Islamic Excursions Among the Converted Peoples* (London: Abacus, 1998).
Namboodripad, E. M. S., *Marxism and Indology*, ed. Debiprasad Chattopadhyaya (Calcutta: K. P. Bagchi, 1981).
Nandy, Ashis, *The Intimate Enemy – Loss and Recovery of Self under Colonialism* (Delhi: Oxford University Press, 1999).
Narain, A. K., 'Alexander and India', *Greece and Rome*, 12: 2, 1965, pp. 155–65.
Narayan, R. K., *The Mahabharata – A Shortened Modern Prose Version* (London: Penguin, 2001).
Nehru, Jawaharlal, *The Discovery of India* (London: Meridian, 1946).
—— *Glimpses of World History* (New Delhi: Penguin, 2004).
Newman, Judie, *The Ballistic Bard – Postcolonial Fictions* (London: Arnold, 1995).
Nietzsche, Friedrich, *The Will to Power*, trans. R. J. Hollingdale and Walter Kaufmann (New York: Vintage, 1968).
—— *Twilight of the Idols and The Anti-Christ*, trans. R. J. Hollingdale (London: Penguin, 2003).
—— *The Birth of Tragedy Out of the Spirit of Music*, trans. Shaun Whiteside (London: Penguin, 2003).
—— *Thus Spoke Zarathustra – A Book for Everyone and No One*, trans. R. J. Hollingdale (London: Penguin, 2003).
—— *Untimely Meditations*, trans. R. J. Hollingdale (Cambridge: Cambridge University Press, 2003).
—— *The Pre-Platonic Philosophers*, trans. Greg Whitlock (Chicago: University of Illinois Press, 2006).
Nixon, Rob, *London Calling – V. S. Naipaul, Postcolonial Mandarin* (Oxford: Oxford University Press, 1992).
Nkrumah, Kwame, *Class Struggle in Africa* (London: Panaf, 1970).
Novick, Peter, *That Noble Dream – The 'Objectivity Question' and the American Historical Profession* (Cambridge: Cambridge University Press, 1999).
Pandey, Gyanendra, 'In Defense of the Fragment: Writing about Hindu–Muslim Riots in India Today', *Representations* 37: 2 (1992), pp. 27–55.
—— *Subaltern Studies 3 – Writings on South Asian History and Society*, ed. Ranajit Guha (Delhi: Oxford University Press, 1999).
—— *Subaltern Studies 6*, ed. Ranajit Guha (Delhi: Oxford University Press, 1999).
—— *The Oxford India Hinduism Reader*, eds Vasudha Dalmia and Heinrich von Stietencorn (New Delhi: Oxford University Press, 2007).

Pappe, Ilan, *The Ethnic Cleansing of Palestine* (Oxford: Oneworld, 2007).
Plutarch, *The Age of Alexander – Nine Greek Lives by Plutarch*, trans. Ian Scott-Kilvert (London: Penguin, 1973).
Poulantzas, Nicos, *State, Power, Socialism*, trans. Patrick Camiller (London: Verso, 2000).
Radhakrishnan, *The Hindu View of Life – The Famous Upton Lectures of 1926* (London: Allen and Unwin, 1964).
Raychaudhuri, Hemachandra, *Political History of Ancient India* (Delhi: Oxford University Press, 1996).
Rigby, S. H., *Marxism and History – A Critical Introduction* (Manchester: Manchester University Press, 1998).
Risley, H. H., *The People of India* (London: W. Thacker, 1915).
Rushdie, Salman, *Midnight's Children* (London: Picador, 1982).
—— *Shame* (London: Picador, 1984).
—— *The Satanic Verses* (London: Viking Press, 1988).
—— *The New York Times*, 28 December 1990.
—— *Imaginary Homelands – Essays and Criticism, 1981–1991* (Granta: London, 1991).
—— *East, West* (London: Vintage, 1995).
—— *The Moor's Last Sigh* (London: Vintage, 1996).
—— *The Enchantress of Florence* (London: Jonathan Cape, 2008).
Rushdie, Salman and Elizabeth West, eds, *The Vintage Book of Indian Writing, 1947–1997* (London: Vintage, 1997).
Said, Edward, *Covering Islam – How the Media and the Experts Determine How We See the Rest of the World* (New York: Pantheon, 1981).
—— *Selected Subaltern Studies*, eds Ranajit Guha and Gayatri Spivak (New York: Oxford University Press, 1988).
—— 'Figures, Configurations, Transfigurations', *Race and Class* 32: 1 (1990), pp. 1–16.
—— *Orientalism – Western Conceptions of the Orient* (London: Penguin, 1991).
—— *The World, the Text and the Critic* (London: Vintage, 1991).
—— *Culture and Imperialism* (London: Chatto and Windus, 1993).
Sartre, Jean-Paul, *Critique of Dialectical Reason*, vol. 1, trans. Alan Sheriden-Smith (London: Verso, 2004).
Savarkar, Vinayak Damodar, *Hindu Sanghatan – Its Ideology and Immediate Programme (A Collection of his Three Presidential Speeches at Karnavati (Ahmadabad), Nagpur and Calcutta)* (Bombay: N. V Damle, 1940).
—— *Indian War of Independence – 1857* (Bombay: Phoenix, 1947).
—— *Six Glorious Epochs of Indian History*, trans. S. T. Godbole (Bombay: Bal Savarkar, 1971).
—— *Hindutva – Who Is a Hindu?* (Bombay: S. S. Savarkar, 1989).
—— *The Maratha Movement (Hindu Pad Padashahi) – Story of the Maratha Struggle to Re-establish Sovereign Hindu Power* (Delhi: Hindi Sahitya Sadan, 2003).
Sen, Amartya, *The Argumentative Indian – Writings on Indian History, Culture and Identity* (London: Allen Lane, 2005).
Sharma, Arvind, 'On Hindu, Hindustan, Hinduism and Hindutva', *Numen*, 49, 2002, pp. 1–36.
Shetty, V. T., *B. R. Ambedkar's Why Go For Conversion?* (Bangalore, Dalit Sahitya Akademy, 1981).
Sikand, Yoginder, *Muslims in India since 1947 – Islamic Perspectives on Inter-faith Relations* (London: Routledge-Curzon, 2004).

Smith, Adam, *The Wealth of Nations, Books 1 to 3* (London: Penguin, 1999).
Spivak, Gayatri, *Outside in the Teaching Machine* (London: Routledge, 1993).
—— *A Critique of Postcolonial Reason – Toward a History of the Vanishing Present* (Massachusetts: Harvard University Press, 1999).
—— *Subaltern Studies 4 – Writings on South Asian History and Society*, ed. Ranajit Guha (Delhi: Oxford University Press, 1999).
Srimad Bhagavata Purana, Book 10, trans. Edwin Bryant (London: Penguin, 2003).
Stein, Auriel, *On Alexander's Track to the Indus – Personal Narrative of Explorations on the North-west Frontier of India* (London: MacMillan and Co., 1929).
Stone, Lawrence, 'The Revival of Narrative', *Past and Present*, 85 (1979), pp. 3–24.
Suleri, Sara, *The Rhetoric of English India* (Chicago: The University of Chicago Press, 1992).
Tagore, Rabindranath, *Nationalism* (London: Macmillan, 1917).
Taylor, A. J. P., *The Origins of the Second World War* (London: Penguin, 1991).
—— *The Course of German History – A Survey of the Development of German History since 1815* (London: Routledge, 2006).
Thapar, Romila, 'Epic and History', *Past and Present*, 125 (1989), pp. 3–26.
—— *The Penguin History of Early India – From the Origins to AD 1300* (London: Penguin, 2002).
—— 'Politics and the Re-writing of History in India', *Critical Quarterly* 47, 1–2 (2005), pp. 195–203.
Tilak, Bal Gangadhar, *Modern Hindu Thought – The Essential Texts*, ed. Arvind Sharma (Delhi: Oxford University Press, 2002).
Trautmann, Thomas, *Kautilya and the Athashastra – A Statistical Investigation of the Authorship and Evolution of the Text* (Leiden: E. J. Brill, 1971).
—— *Time – Histories and Ethnologies*, eds Diane Hughs and Thomas Trautmann (Ann Arbor: The University of Michigan Press, 1998).
Vico, Giambattista, *New Science – Principles of the New Science Concerning the Common Nature of Nations*, trans. David Marsh (London: Penguin, 2001).
Virgil, *The Aeneid*, trans. David West (London: Penguin, 1991).
Voltaire, François-Marie Aroet, *Candide and Other Stories*, trans. Roger Pearson (Oxford: Oxford University Press, 1998).
Ward, Andrew, *Our Bones Are Scattered – The Cawnpore Massacres and the Indian Mutiny of 1857* (London: John Murray, 2004).
Weber, Max, *The Religion of India – The Sociology of Hinduism and Buddhism*, trans. Hans Gerth and Don Martindale (Illinois: The Free Press, 1960).
—— *The Protestant Ethic and the Spirit of Capitalism*, trans. Talcott Parsons (London: Routledge, 2004).
Wheatcroft, Andrew, *Infidels – A History of the Conflict between Christendom and Islam* (London: Penguin, 2004).
White, Hayden, *Metahistory – The Historical Imagination in Nineteenth-century Europe* (Baltimore: The Johns Hopkins University Press, 1975).
—— *Tropics of Discourse – Essays in Cultural Criticism* (Maryland: The Johns Hopkins University Press, 1985).
—— *The Content of the Form – Narrative Discourse and Historical Representation* (Baltimore: Johns Hopkins University Press, 1987).
—— *Probing the Limit of Representation – Nazism and the 'Final Solution'*, ed. Saul Friedlander (Massachusetts: Harvard University Press, 1996).
Wilkinson, T. S., *Ambedkar and the Neo-Buddhist Movement*, eds T. S. Wilkinson and

M. M. Thomas (Madras: The Christian Institute for the Study of Religion and Society, 1972).
Williams, Raymond, 'Culture is Ordinary', *Convictions*, ed. Norman MacKenzie (London: MacGibbon and Kee, 1958).
—— *Marxism and Literature* (Oxford: Oxford University Press, 1977).
Wolpert, Stanley, *A New History of India* (New York: Oxford University Press, 2004).
Yates, Frances, *The Rosicrucian Enlightenment* (London: Routledge, 2004).
Yeats, W. B., *Yeats's Poems*, ed. A. Norman Jeffares (London: Papermac, 1991).
Žižek, Slavoj, *Violence* (London: Profile Books, 2008).

Index

Abrams, M. H. 31
Ackroyd, Peter 191
Adorno, Theodor and Max Horkheimer 20, 80–2
Ahmad, Aijaz 193
Ahmed, Akbar 195
Akmeşe, Handan Nezir 25
Albinia, Alice 86
Aloysius, G. 38
Althusser, Louis 7, 16, 28, 43, 44, 68
Althusser, Louis and Étienne Balibar 69
Ambedkar, B. R.: pure history 134; origins of *chaturvarnya* 135, 147–50; *Swadeshi* campaign and Gandhi 141–43; Shivaji 150–55
Amin, Shahid 202
Anand, Dibyesh 108
Anderson, Benedict 164, 220n156
Anderson, Perry 82
Aravamudan, Srinavas 194
Arendt, Hannah 7
Arrian 53, 85, 87–88
Asher, Catherine and Cynthia Talbot 126
Auden, W. H., *The Shield of Achilles* 69, 82
Auerbach, Erich 3, 35, 36, 40, 75–7, 79–80, 82, 89, 187

Barthes, Roland 35, 198
Baudrillard, Jean 10–11, 14, 16, 83, 191
Baxi, Upendra and Bhiku Parekh Parekh 109–10, 144
Bayly, C. A. 101
Bayly, Susan 222n56
Benjamin, Walter 7–8, 10–11, 47, 49, 50, 51, 52, 67, 164, 181, 189, 190, 191, 192, 196
Berman, Marshall 21
Bhabha, Homi 22, 25, 26, 27, 171–72

Bhattacharya, Gargi 106, 165
Blois, François de xi, 190
Bloom, Harold 78, 80
Bloxham, Donald 25
Bose, Sujata and Ayesha Jalal 174, 176
Bouglé, Célestine 119, 147, 148
Bourdieu, Pierre 71
Brass, Paul 165, 166
Braudel, Fernand 24, 25, 29, 30, 70, 71
Buchan, James 200
Burkhardt, Jacob 30
Burrows, Guy 56
Burton, Antoinette 72–3
Bury, J. B. 68
Butler, Judith 6

Callinicos, Alex 13, 14, 16, 19, 20, 35
Canetti, Elias 166, 174
Carlyle, Thomas 3, 5, 184
Certeau, Michel de 183, 197, 200
Césaire, Aimé 56, 57, 58, 62, 111
Chakrabarty, Dipesh 44, 109, 110–11, 112, 113, 114, 115, 117, 166, 170, 172, 218n109
Chatterjee, Bankim Chandra 99–103
Chatterjee, Partha 19, 31, 100, 103, 115, 129, 148, 164, 172, 176
Chaudhuri, B. 98, 101–2
Cohen, G. A. 202
Cohn, Bernard 15–16, 38, 44, 218n109
Collingwood, R. G. 51, 52
Condillac, Étienne Bonnot de 66–7, 72
Condorcet, Jean-Antoine-Nicholas de Caritat, marquis de 64, 67
Conrad, Joseph 58, 163

Dalrymple, William 163, 174
Dante Aligheri 196
Deleuze, Gilles and Félix Guattari 192

242 Index

Derrida, Jacques 27, 56, 62, 202
Djebar, Assia 194
Doré, Gustave 196
Dumont, Louis 12, 140, 147
Durkheim, Émile 56, 60

Eagleton, Robert and Susan Pitt 3, 4–5
Eliot, T. S. 8, 13–14, 21, 22, 70–4, 76, 80, 171, 196
Ellmann, Richard 14
Engels, Friedrich, *Socialism: Utopian and Scientific* 91; see also Marx, Karl
Evans, Richard 7

Faiz, Faiz Ahmed 192, 193–4
Fanon, Frantz 8, 26, 58, 164, 167, 170
al-Fazl, Abu 16, 17, 127
Foucault, Michel 5, 7, 9, 16, 29, 32, 39, 40, 41, 60, 61–2, 63, 64, 68, 97, 202
French, Patrick 164
Freud, Sigmund x, 71, 131
Frye, Northrop 4
Fukuyama, Francis 19, 78
Fustafa, Fawzia 162

Gandhi, M. K. 18, 19, 31, 37, 44, 45, 47, 48, 78, 84, 90, 94, 95, 98, 99, 105, 112, 113, 116, 117, 119, 120, 121, 137, 138, 139, 145, 146, 148, 151, 155, 162, 167, 172, 201, 202, 203, 205, 219n133, see also Ambedkar, B. R
Gellner, Ernest 22, 23–30, 32, 39, 42, 91, 103–04, 115, 164, 175–6, 177, 203–4
Ghosh, Amitav 189, 197, 198–200
Gibbon, Edward 134,
Gilgamesh, The Epic of 75
Golwalkar, M. S. 121, 141
Goody, Jack 26
Goonetilleke, D. C. R. A. 180
Gopal, Sarvepalli 205
Gordon, Stewart 152
Grafton, Anthony 76
Grewal, Inderpal 194
Guha, Ranajit x, 36–7, 38, 39, 40, 42, 47, 64, 95, 96, 98, 110, 142, 143, 148, 155, 159, 160, 167
Guha, Sudeshna 110

Hardiman, David 112
Hardt, Michael and Antonio Negri 106, 162
Harlow, Barbara and Mia Carter 102
Hawting, Gerald 190

Heehs, Peter 108
Hegel, Georg Wilhelm Friedrich 5, 6, 7, 8, 9, 11, 19, 21, 31, 44, 65, 194, 201, 202, 203
Heidegger, Martin 80, 127
Herder, Johann Gottfried 18, 51–7, 64, 65, 66, 76, 84, 85, 92, 119, 133, 134, 138, 140, 202
Herodotus 51, 53, 74, 75, 80, 82, 83, 87
Hill, Christopher 32
historiography: art and science 4, 51; Benjamin's ironic comprehension 7; colonialism 111–12, 159, 160; danger of distraction for Fernand Braudel 29; determined by appeal to Reason ix; Foucault's discursive trope 9, 16, 113; foundations of nationalist historiography in Puranic lore 89, 103, 108–9, 115, 127, 128–9; holocausts 35–6, 50; identity 114; impact of nationalism 14, 15, 23, 37, 117, 141, 178; Indian historiography 30, 37–8; intuitive structure of feeling 14; Lyotard and history's legitimising function 41–2; Marxism and Enlightenment *philosophes* 36, 63, 64–8; modernity and critical uses of historiography 109–11, 144, 148, 178; narrative and myth 70, 72–3, 77, 79–80; narrative plot 8, 33–4; postcolonial and subaltern 38; post-structuralism and the problem of representation 3, 6, 18, 48, 63, 69; realist form 33; science of signs or semiological practice 61–3; *sui generis* ideology 3, 16, 19, 49; Vico's poetic or anthropological formulation 57; vital for social order 40–1, 178; worldview and inescapable ideological component 18, 38, 170, 198, 203
Hobsbawm, E. J. 84, 90
Homer 72, 73, 81, 187
Huntingdon, Samuel 20
Hyam, Ronald 76

Jalal, Ayesha 31
James, C. L. R. 63
Jameson, Frederic 13, 20–2, 23, 31–2, 34, 38, 40, 43, 47, 48, 56, 70, 71, 78, 109, 114, 186
Jenkins, Keith 50, 63, 64, 110, 113

Kant, Immanuel 11, 34, 141, 165, 206
Kaviraj, Sudipta 115, 116
Kedourie, Elie 133, 206

Index

Kennedy, Emmet 68
Khalidi, Rashid 76
Khilnani, Sunil 104–5
Kierkegaard, Soren 76, 79
Kipling, Rudyard 87, 99, 100
Kolluri, Satish 107

Lefebvre, Georges 62, 66, 77
Lemprière, John 83
Lenin, V. I. 71, 90
Lévi-Strauss, Claude 111, 118, 141, 183, 188
Locke, John 64, 65, 66, 67
Lovelace, Earl 178
Lyotard, Jean-François 12, 13, 14, 16, 39, 41, 42, 49, 50, 56, 72

Machiavelli, Niccolò 50
MacIntyre, Alasdair 39, 71, 72
Marshall, John 87, 88, 89
Marx, Karl 6, 8, 10, 20, 21, 43, 44, 46, 47, 52, 64, 65, 66, 68, 69, 73, 91, 175, 208n18
Marx, Karl and Friedrich Engels 21, 34, 45, 205
Mauss, Marcel 60
Mendelsohn, Oliver and Marika Vicziany 137, 167
Merleau-Ponty, Maurice 164
Metcalf, Thomas 55
Michelet, Jules 94
Misra, Maria 120
Montesquieu, Charles-Louis de Secondat, Baron de la Brède et de 27
Mustafa, Fawzia 162

Naipaul, V. S.: Gandhi 172; Islam's iconoclasm and cultural memory 177–9; objectivity 160, 162–5, 169, 170; Pax Britannica 159, 165, 167; subalternity 165–9; violent cult of Islam 120, 174
Namboodripad, E. M. S. 45–6, 47
Nandy, Ashis 117, 169, 170, 172, 173, 176
Narain, A. K. 53
Narayan, R. K. ix
nationalism: anti-colonial resistance 56–8, 76, 96, 112, 141, 143, 164, 165, 172, 193; determined by emotion and faith ix, 53; eclectic vision of the past 8; étatisme 90–1, 101, 104–5, 106, 113, 118, 184, 201, 203–6; Gellner's cultural explanation 23, 28, 39, 105, 175, 203–4;

Hindu nationalism and communalism 84, 107–9, 113 –15, 119, 140, 142, 147, 161, 162, 165; imagined community 164; irredentism 16, 20, 23–8, 92, 193, 201; nation as an indeterminate epistemological category 38; Nehru's ideal 90–2; proto-nationalism 85–90, 153, 154; secularism 15; self-sameness 7; subaltern politics 36–7, 143, 150, 151, 155, 160; supersession by capitalist market 45–7, 193
Nehru, Jawaharlal 15, 31, 47, 48, 75, 76, 77, 89, 90–5, 104–5, 106, 107, 108, 120, 137, 139, 144, 160, 184, 186, 196, 200, 202, 204–6
Newman, Judie 164
Nietzsche, Friedrich 6, 11, 21, 59, 60, 61, 68, 75, 76, 80, 92, 93, 133, 139, 159, 163, 170, 171, 173, 177, 178, 180, 186, 187, 189, 191
Nixon, Rob 162, 169, 170
Nkrumah, Kwame 25
Novick, Peter 63

Pandey, Gyanendra 107, 108, 112, 115, 120, 125, 128
Pappe, Ilan 78
Plutarch 19, 60, 86
Poulantzas, Nicos 108, 217n97, 202

Radhakrishnan 119, 120, 131
Raychaudhuri, Hemachandra 86, 123
Rigby, S. H. 69
Risley, H. H. 84, 147
Rushdie, Salman 164; ironic comprehension of the past 180–2, 185, 187; Islam and temporality 183–6; modernism 187–9; *see also* Benjamin, Walter
Rushdie, Salman and Elizabeth West 165

Said, Edward 8, 47, 72, 100, 162, 163, 164, 165, 182, 192, 193
Sartre, Jean-Paul 163, 164
Savarkar, Vinayak Damodar: Alexander's attempted conquest of India 85–7; Islam and Muslims 28, 126–8, 131; Puranic lore and Hindu proto-nationalism 57, 95, 116, 118–20, 123–5, 128, 129, 131
Sen, Amartya 12
Sharma, Arvind 107
Shetty, V. T. 107
Sikand, Yoginder 126
Smith, Adam 32

Spivak, Gayatri 114, 120, 163, 208n18
Srimad Bhagavata Purana 85
Stein, Auriel 87–8
Stone, Lawrence 69, 70, 72
Suleri, Sara 96, 182

Tagore, Rabindranath 6, 201
Taylor, A. J. P. 4, 5, 7, 205
Thapar, Romila ix, x, 70, 72, 108–9, 111, 114, 115, 116, 117, 120, 136, 137, 161, 162, 201
Tilak, Bal Gangadhar 112, 113, 116, 118, 141
Trautmann, Thomas 19, 87

Vico, Giambattista 51, 52, 57, 58, 59, 60, 62, 64, 67, 72
Virgil 81

Voltaire, François-Marie Aroet 59, 138, 183, 185, 186

Ward, Andrew 153
Weber, Max 44, 78, 135, 210n103
Wheatcroft, Andrew 26, 27
White, Hayden 6, 7, 8, 9, 16, 18, 20, 33–7, 38, 39, 40–2, 43, 78, 80, 82, 90, 106, 110, 181, 195, 203, 204
Wilkinson, T. S. 137
Williams, Raymond 14, 15, 16, 19, 20, 22, 51, 55, 71, 166
Wolpert, Stanley 98, 100, 124, 141

Yates, Frances 17
Yeats, W. B. 10, 14, 15, 23

Žižek, Slavoj 6

For Product Safety Concerns and Information please contact our EU
representative GPSR@taylorandfrancis.com
Taylor & Francis Verlag GmbH, Kaufingerstraße 24, 80331 München, Germany

www.ingramcontent.com/pod-product-compliance
Lightning Source LLC
Chambersburg PA
CBHW062134300426
44115CB00012BA/1921